APPROACHES TO LUCRETIUS

Both in antiquity and ever since the Renaissance Lucretius' *De Rerum Natura* has been admired – and condemned – for its startling poetry, its evangelical faith in materialist causation, and its seductive advocacy of the Epicurean good life. *Approaches to Lucretius* assembles an international team of classicists and philosophers to take stock of a range of critical approaches to which this influential poem has given rise and which in turn have shaped its interpretation, including textual criticism, the text's strategies for engaging the reader with its author and his message, the 'atomology' that posits a correlation of the letters of the poem with the atoms of the universe, the literary and philosophical intertexts that mediate the poem, and the political and ideological questions that it raises. Thirteen essays take up a variety of positions within these traditions of interpretation, innovating within them and advancing beyond them in new directions.

DONNCHA O'ROURKE is Lecturer in Classics at the University of Edinburgh. He is author of *Propertius and the Virgilian Sensibility* (Cambridge, forthcoming) and co-editor of *Didactic Poetry of Greece, Rome and Beyond: Knowledge, Power, Tradition* (Swansea, 2019).

APPROACHES TO LUCRETIUS

Traditions and Innovations in Reading
the De Rerum Natura

EDITED BY

DONNCHA O'ROURKE

University of Edinburgh

CAMBRIDGE
UNIVERSITY PRESS

CAMBRIDGE
UNIVERSITY PRESS

University Printing House, Cambridge CB2 8BS, United Kingdom

One Liberty Plaza, 20th Floor, New York, NY 10006, USA

477 Williamstown Road, Port Melbourne, VIC 3207, Australia

314–321, 3rd Floor, Plot 3, Splendor Forum, Jasola District Centre, New Delhi – 110025, India

79 Anson Road, #06–04/06, Singapore 079906

Cambridge University Press is part of the University of Cambridge.

It furthers the University's mission by disseminating knowledge in the pursuit of education, learning, and research at the highest international levels of excellence.

www.cambridge.org
Information on this title: www.cambridge.org/9781108421966
DOI: 10.1017/9781108379854

First published 2020

A catalogue record for this publication is available from the British Library.

Library of Congress Cataloging-in-Publication Data
NAMES: O'Rourke, Donncha, editor.
TITLE: Approaches to Lucretius : Traditions and innovations in reading the de rerum natura / edited by Donncha O'Rourke.
DESCRIPTION: New York : Cambridge University Press, 2020. | Includes bibliographical references and index.
IDENTIFIERS: LCCN 2019060030 (print) | LCCN 2019060031 (ebook) | ISBN 9781108421966 (hardback) | ISBN 9781108433105 (paperback) | ISBN 9781108379854 (ebook)
SUBJECTS: LCSH: Lucretius Carus, Titus. De rerum natura.
CLASSIFICATION: LCC PA6484 .A67 2020 (print) | LCC PA6484 (ebook) | DDC 187–DC23
LC record available at https://lccn.loc.gov/2019060030
LC ebook record available at https://lccn.loc.gov/2019060031

ISBN 978-1-108-42196-6 Hardback

Contents

Figures

Notes on Contributors

ELIZABETH ASMIS, Professor of Classics at the University of Chicago, is author of *Epicurus' Scientific Method* (Ithaca, 1984). She has written extensively on ancient Greek and Roman philosophy and aesthetics, with special attention to developments after Aristotle. She is currently working on Epicurean social philosophy and the reception of Greek philosophy in the Roman period and later.

DAVID BUTTERFIELD is Senior Lecturer in Classics at the University of Cambridge and Fellow and Director of Studies in Classics at Queens' College. He is the author of *The Early Textual History of Lucretius'* De Rerum Natura (Cambridge, 2013) and the editor of *A. E. Housman: Classical Scholar* (London, 2009) and *Varro Varius: The Polymath of the Roman World* (Cambridge, 2015). He has published numerous articles, mainly on textual criticism, codicology and the history of scholarship, and is currently preparing a new Oxford Classical Text of Lucretius.

JOSEPH FARRELL is Professor of Classical Studies and M. Mark and Esther K. Watkins Professor in the Humanities at the University of Pennsylvania. His books include *Vergil's* Georgics *and the Traditions of Ancient Epic* (Oxford, 1991), *Latin Language and Latin Culture* (Cambridge, 2001) and *Juno's* Aeneid*: Narrative, Metapoetics, Dissent* (Princeton, forthcoming).

EMMA GEE was educated at the Universities of Sydney and Cambridge, and has worked at the Universities of Exeter, Sydney and St Andrews. She is currently an independent scholar in the Classics, academic tutor, and student and teacher of Ashtanga yoga. Her research interests include ancient astronomy and its reception, and the ancient afterlife. Her latest book, *Mapping the Afterlife from Homer to Dante*, is forthcoming (Oxford, 2020).

viii

NORA GOLDSCHMIDT is Associate Professor of Classics and Ancient History at Durham University. Her publications include *Shaggy Crowns: Ennius' Annales and Virgil's Aeneid* (Oxford, 2013), *Afterlives of the Roman Poets: Biofiction and the Reception of Latin Poetry* (Cambridge, 2019) and (with Barbara Graziosi) *Tombs of the Ancient Poets: Between Literary Reception and Material Culture* (Oxford, 2018).

DUNCAN F. KENNEDY is Emeritus Professor of Latin Literature and the Theory of Criticism at the University of Bristol. He is the author of *The Arts of Love: Five Studies in the Discourse of Roman Love Elegy* (Cambridge, 1992), *Rethinking Reality: Lucretius and the Textualization of Nature* (Ann Arbor, 2002) and *Antiquity and the Meanings of Time: A Philosophy of Ancient and Modern Literature* (London, 2013), as well as numerous articles that explore the interpretation of classical literature. He is currently writing a series of essays on the emergence of metaphysical thinking.

A. D. MORRISON is Professor of Greek at the University of Manchester, where he has taught since 2001. His books include *The Narrator in Archaic Greek and Hellenistic Poetry* (Cambridge, 2007), *Apollonius Rhodius, Herodotus and Historiography* (Cambridge, 2020) and (as co-editor) *Lucretius: Poetry, Philosophy, Science* (Oxford, 2013). He edited *Classical Quarterly* between 2013 and 2018. Current projects include a commentary on Callimachus for the Cambridge Greek and Latin Classics series, a *G&R* New Survey on Hellenistic poetry and co-directing the AHRC project on Ancient Letter Collections (2016–21).

JASON NETHERCUT is Assistant Professor of Classics at the University of South Florida. His publications and ongoing research focus on Lucretius and his position in literary history, and on the relationship between poetry and philosophy in the *De Rerum Natura*. His book, Ennius Noster*: Lucretius and the* Annales, is forthcoming with Oxford University Press.

TIM O'KEEFE is Associate Professor of Philosophy at Georgia State University. He has published extensively on Epicureanism, including two books – *Epicurus on Freedom* (Cambridge, 2005) and *Epicureanism* (London, 2009) – and articles on topics such as the Epicureans on the mind–body relation, freedom of action, sensible qualities, friendship, justice and death. His interests range broadly, and he has also published on the Pyrrhonian sceptics, the Cyrenaics and Aristotle's cosmology.

DONNCHA O'ROURKE is Lecturer in Classics at the University of Edinburgh. His doctoral career at Trinity College Dublin was followed by a British Academy Postdoctoral Fellowship at Corpus Christi College, Oxford. He is the author of *Propertius and the Virgilian Sensibility* (Cambridge, forthcoming) and of articles on various aspects of Augustan poetry, especially elegy. His other editorial projects include (with Lilah Grace Canevaro) *Didactic Poetry of Greece, Rome and Beyond: Knowledge, Power, Tradition* (Swansea, 2019) and (with Isabelle Torrance) *Classics and Irish Politics, 1916–2016* (Oxford, 2020).

WILSON H. SHEARIN is Associate Professor of Classics at the University of Miami. He is author of *The Language of Atoms* (Oxford, 2015) and co-editor of *Dynamic Reading* (Oxford, 2012). Currently, he is writing on Lucretius and Lucan and completing editorial work on *The Oxford Handbook of Roman Philosophy*.

BARNABY TAYLOR is Fellow and Tutor in Classics at Exeter College, Oxford, and Associate Professor of Classics at the University of Oxford. His interests include Lucretius, Cicero and Varro.

FABIO TUTRONE is a Research and Teaching Fellow in Latin literature at the University of Palermo. His research focuses on the history of Roman literature, science and philosophy, with special regard to Lucretius, Seneca and the Latin reception of Greek thought. He has particular interest in literary topics of cognitive and anthropological relevance. His publications include *Filosofi e animali in Roma antica: Modelli di animalità e umanità in Lucrezio e Seneca* (Pisa, 2012).

Preface

This volume has its origin – albeit now somewhat remotely – in a conference on 'Lucretius in Theory' held at the University of Edinburgh in late 2013. That event, of which *Approaches to Lucretius* is the end-product, took place in connection with the editor's tenure of a British Academy Postdoctoral Fellowship, and was made possible by generous funding from that source. Also to be gratefully acknowledged is the additional support towards the material costs of the conference received from the School of History, Classics and Archaeology at the University of Edinburgh, the Classical Association and the Institute of Classical Studies.

A number of individuals are to be warmly thanked for their contributions to that initial endeavour or for their input since: Gordon Campbell; Monica Gale; Fiachra Mac Góráin; Damien Nelis; Alessandro Schiesaro; Simon Trépanier; Pamela Zinn. Two anonymous readers appointed by the Press provided valuable expertise at a formative stage and again on presentation of a full set of chapters. Michael Sharp and his team at Cambridge University Press have been responsive and understanding guides; Yassar Arafat, Lesley Hay and Bethany Johnson saw the volume through production with meticulous care. Finally and emphatically, the contributors have given generously of their time over the life-cycle of this project, and have been Epicureans in their forbearance during its long gestation.

Abbreviations

Abbreviations for ancient authors and texts generally follow the conventions of the fourth edition of the *Oxford Classical Dictionary* (eds. S. Hornblower, A. Spawforth and E. Eidinow; Oxford, 2012). Journal titles are abbreviated according to the conventions of *L'Année Philologique*. The following standard abbreviations are also used:

Arrighetti	Arrighetti, G. (1973) *Epicuro: Opere.* Turin.
CW I	Marx, K., and Engels, F. (1975) *Collected Works Vol. I: Karl Marx: 1835–43.* New York.
DK	Diels, H., and Kranz, W. (eds.) (1951) *Die Fragmente der Vorsokratiker* (4 vols.). Berlin.
KD	Epicurus, *Kuriai Doxai* (= Diogenes Laertius 10.139–54).
MEGA	Marx, K., and Engels, F. (1975) *Karl Marx, Friedrich Engels Gesamtausgabe.* Berlin.
MEW	Marx, K., and Engels, F. (1968) *Werke. Ergänzungsband Part I: Schriften, Manuskripte, Briefe bis 1844.* Berlin.
MRR	Broughton, T. R. S. (1951–2) *The Magistrates of the Roman Republic* (2 vols.). Cleveland; (1986) Vol. 3. Supplement. Atlanta.
RAC	Klauser, T., et al. (eds.) (1941–2000) *Reallexikon für Antike und Christentum: Sachwörterbuch zur Auseinandersetzung des Christentums mit der antiken Welt.* 23 vols. Stuttgart.
RE	Pauly, A., Wissowa, G., et al. (eds.) (1839–1980) *Paulys Real-Encyclopädie der classischen Altertumswissenschaft.* 24 vols., 19 vols., and supplement (15 vols.). Stuttgart.
Roscher	Roscher, W. H. (1884–1937) *Ausführliches Lexikon der griechischen und römischen Mythologie.* 6 vols. and supplement. Leipzig.
Usener	Usener, H. (1887) *Epicurea.* Leipzig. (Reprinted with Italian translation and notes by I. Ramelli: Milan, 2002.)

Introduction
Approaching Lucretius
Donncha O'Rourke

The period in which this collection of essays came into being has witnessed what it would describe as a 'trending' of Lucretius and Epicureanism (for their destinies are intertwined) in classical studies and beyond. *In primis*, in the category of general nonfiction, Stephen Greenblatt's bestselling *The Swerve: How the World Became Modern* (published in the UK as *The Swerve: How the Renaissance Began*) won the 2012 Pulitzer Prize for its vivid narrative of the rediscovery of Lucretius' *De Rerum Natura* in 1417;[1] on the specialist market, too, a recent monograph could hail 'another renaissance of Lucretius in contemporary scholarship', footnoting an extensive bibliography to prove the point;[2] and in the mass media, *The Guardian* newspaper sustained an eight-part series on Lucretius in 2013.[3] Lucretius is not an author that our times have to rehabilitate.

To lay claim to a particular Epicurean *kairos*, however, would be to downplay the track record of the *DRN* always to find contemporary urgency:[4] the collective achievement of recent scholarship has in fact been to demonstrate the powerful force, both centripetal and centrifugal, exerted by Lucretius (and Epicurus) in different traditions of all the major cultural and historical movements of the European West since the 'rediscovery' of the text in 1417 – and well before.[5] The historically embedded approaches on which these studies in classical reception focus are all the more invested, or reactionary, given the radical worldview that the *DRN* propounds in its evangelical, startling and voluptuous (or, at times,

---

[1] Greenblatt 2011. See www.pulitzer.org/winners/stephen-greenblatt (last accessed 26 July 2018). *The Swerve* also won the 2011 National Book Award for Nonfiction (www.nationalbook.org/nba2011_nf_greenblatt.html#.W10JPC8ZNEI: last accessed 26 July 2018).
[2] Passannante 2011: 4 with n. 9. See also Holmes and Shearin 2012: 20 with n. 46.
[3] Woolerton 2013.
[4] On the perennial modernity of Lucretius across different disciplines see the essays collected in Lezra and Blake 2016.
[5] For an overview of ancient and later reception see the essays collected in Gillespie and Hardie 2007.

bludgeoning) Latin. With a relentless flow of scientific argumentation, Lucretius insists that all experience, be it mundane or marvellous, trivial or terrifying, is demonstrably the outcome of two irreducible constituents of reality: atoms and void. This materialism replaces divine providence with a fully rational, anti-creationist and non-teleological account of nature. It maintains that our world is neither privileged nor unique, but rather is decaying and transient. The individual, too, is subject to the same laws: there can be no afterlife of any kind when the atoms of the soul are dispersed upon death; love is a mechanism, not a mystery, and like other passions can and should be avoided; ambition and the pursuit of wealth are similarly deleterious. Holding to this stark view of nature and our place in it, the *DRN* includes searing denunciations of traditional religious belief, scathing critiques of conventional values based on status and power, and biting satire of those who adhere to irrational conceptions of reality. At the same time, it holds out the promise of true happiness based on the pleasure of easily attainable contentment in mind and body.[6]

The *DRN* knows it will be alluring and rebarbative in equal measure, and models its own reception in the addressee's willingness or unwillingness to imbibe its healing message (1.102–3, 1.936–50, 4.11–25).[7] The tradition of interpreting Lucretius begins within the text, then, and has flourished ever since. Such was the sympathy and antipathy that the *DRN* stirred among its readers in the next generations through to late antiquity that, even after the text disappeared from circulation in the late Middle Ages, it continued to exert its influence through secondary reference and citation in the indirect tradition, flying sometimes above and sometimes below the radar of conscious engagement.[8] When the text resurfaced in the direct tradition, Renaissance readers continued this pattern of response to its seductive charms and – as they then were – dangerous heresies, whether openly or in silence, in opposition or assent, albeit assent from behind a veil of feigned disinterest that has been termed 'the dissimulatory code'.[9] Reactions to Epicurean materialism, ethics and social theory continued in this mixed vein through the Early Modern period and beyond: Lucretius

[6] For a concise and lucid introduction to the poem see Gale 2001a.

[7] For a reading of Lucretius' 'honeyed cup' as programmatic for a wider strategy of alluring 'provisional argumentation' see Nethercut 2019.

[8] Lucretius' ancient reception (on which see, e.g., Gale 2000; Hardie 2009; Dykes 2011; Earnshaw 2013) and with it his transmission through the indirect tradition (on which see Passannante 2011; Butterfield 2013: 46–135), though recognized by Greenblatt 2011: 23–4, 51–3, is one of the grounds on which a strong narrative of 'rediscovery' has been challenged: for this and other critiques see Pugh et al. 2013.

[9] Prosperi 2007. See also Haskell 2007: 185–95, 201; Brown 2010; Palmer 2014.

found unlikely translators among puritans and libertines alike;[10] corpus-
cular theory and theology both collided and, to a point, were reconciled
during the Scientific Revolution;[11] by extension Lucretius and Epicureanism became a battleground also in Enlightenment political theory.[12] To
one strand of Romanticism Lucretius' uncompromising rationalism was
anathema, but for another his celebration of nature and evocation of the
sublime made him a kindred spirit.[13] To be witnessed throughout the
history of the *DRN*'s reception, then, are the declinations or swerves of
'misprision', those wilful rewritings that Harold Bloom has aptly theorized
from Lucretius' account of the atomic *clinamen*.[14]

Many of the debates behind these swerves and collisions continue to be
current, even if they no longer relate to Lucretius in quite the same way. In
his foreword to Hermann Diels' 1924 translation of the *DRN*, Albert
Einstein admired Lucretius' confidence in the 'kausalen Zusammenhang'
of the world, though not without a certain distance and, perhaps, wry
irony ('For anyone who does not quite dwell in the spirit of our time, but
occasionally feels like a spectator of his environment and, especially, of the
mental attitude of his contemporaries, the work of Lucretius will exercise
its magic … Where is the modern nation that holds and expresses such
noble sentiments towards a contemporary?').[15] Atomic physics has moved
on, but the philosophy of science, especially in the French tradition, has
found continuing relevance in Lucretius' account of nature.[16] Gilles
Deleuze revisited the *DRN* throughout his career in theorizing his pluralist
and de-Platonizing intervention in materialist philosophy;[17] this line of
thinking is taken up by Michel Serres in his 1977 book *La naissance de la
physique dans le texte de Lucrèce: fleuves et turbulences*,[18] which reasserts the
place of the swerve in contemporary physics as a kind of 'chaos theory'

---

[10] Johnson 2000: 79–102; Barbour 2007: 158–61; Hopkins 2007; Goldberg 2009.

[11] Johnson and Wilson 2007; Haskell 2007:195–201; Baker 2007.

[12] Barbour 2007; Wilson 2008.

[13] See conveniently Priestman 2007. See also Timpanaro 1988; Bloom 2011: 133–71.

[14] First at Bloom 1973: 14, 19–45 (esp. 42–5); see now Bloom 2011: 133–71.

[15] The first and last sentences of Einstein's foreword (1924: via-b): 'Auf jeden, der nicht ganz im
Geiste unserer Zeit aufgeht, sondern seiner Mitwelt und speziell der geistigen Einstellung der
Zeitgenossen gegenüber sich gelegentlich als Zuschauer fühlt, wird das Werk von Lukrez seinen
Zauber ausüben … Wo ist die moderne Nation, die solch noble Gesinnung gegenüber einer
Zeitgenossin hegt und ausspricht?'

[16] For an overview of engagement with Lucretian materialism in twentieth-century thought see
Goldberg 2009: 31–62. For literary perspectives see also Gillespie and Mackenzie 2007. See also
Johnson 2000, esp. 127–55.

[17] See Johnson 2017. See also Holmes 2012; Montag 2016.

[18] Translated into English in Serres 2000. For discussion see Holmes 2016.

avant la lettre; Lucretius' perspective on natural process relativizes humans as part of this fluid environment in a way that encourages more enlightened ecological thinking.[19] Lucretius' representation of nature in the *DRN* thus continues to remind its readers that prevailing accounts of reality entail unscrutinized assumptions that might be reconstructed in alternative scientific approaches that, though they may be no closer to 'reality', may be more benign.[20]

Lucretius has always been enjoying his *kairos*, then, and has engaged different readers in different ways at different times. As the citations accompanying the foregoing survey indicate, instances of this engagement have become a principal focus of Lucretian studies in recent years.[21] It hardly needs to be emphasized that the dynamics of reception structure every approach to Lucretius as well as being in themselves the focus of an approach. As the present collection of essays turns its attention 'back' to the *DRN* itself, then, it does so with a heightened awareness of how every interpretation is mediated by, and a product of, its tradition. In some chapters that awareness comes more directly to the fore (e.g., in discussing the approaches to Lucretius adopted by Jerome, Saussure and Marx, or the approaches adopted by Lucretius to the Homeric Hymns, Plato and Cicero), but it is present throughout (e.g., in drawing attention to the ideologies that guided earlier interventions in textual criticism, in breaking free from the constraints of Cartesian dualism, or in comparing and contrasting the approaches taken by philosophical and literary source-hunters). The thirteen chapters are grouped in five categories of critical approach covering textual criticism, author and reader (a kind of cognitive narratology), 'atomology' (pursuing Lucretius' analogy of atoms and letters), allusion and intertextuality, and politics broadly defined. While taking stock of these established traditions of Lucretian scholarship, the collection as a whole aims to show that there is scope also for innovation and fresh insight, both in the extension of established methodologies and in their intersection with new developments.[22]

The sole chapter in Part I on 'The Text' ('Critical Responses to the Most Difficult Textual Problem in Lucretius') stands as a reminder at the head of this volume that all encounters with Lucretius are mediated at

---

[19] See Bennett 2010, esp. x–xi, 17–19, 118–19.

[20] Kennedy 2002 shines a Lucretian spotlight on 'realist' and 'constructivist' approaches to nature.

[21] For earlier studies in this vein see Hadzsits 1963; Alfonsi 1978. See also Gordon 1962: 13–24, introducing a history of editions and translations to 1961.

[22] Gale 2007a: 1–17 presents a comprehensive Lucretian 'Kritikgeschichte'. See also Campbell 2011; Kennedy 2015.

the level of the text itself by the hazards of transmission and the particulars of editorial decision. It is a sobering fact that all surviving manuscripts of the *DRN* descend from a single lost archetype that was copied about 800 years after Lucretius' death. The role of textual criticism is to reconstruct scientifically the stemma of the tradition back to the archetype and from there to conjecture how the text stood when it left the author's hands and first went into circulation. In the evolution of this philological science Lucretius has played a prominent role: in his edition of 1850, Lachmann used stemmatic criticism to brilliant effect, as Richard Tarrant has put it, 'to conjure up, as if by magic, not just the existence but also the physical appearance of the archetype, a manuscript that had been lost for more than a thousand years'.[23]

In this important first chapter, David Butterfield alights on a six-line passage in the proem to Book 1 (44–9, repeated at 2.646–51) that, for its logical and syntactical incongruity with the surrounding text, has attracted a host of responses in the traditions of both textual and literary criticism. In cases such as this the stakes are high, since the passage under analysis would amount *in situ* to nothing less than a philosophical volte-face, declaring as it does that, contrary to the opening invocation of Venus as bringer of peace, the gods are in fact sublimely detached from our world like model Epicureans (its introductory *enim* therefore makes little sense connectively, and no preparation is made for the switch of addressee to Memmius from line 50). In the heated debate as to whether Lucretius thought the gods exist really or only symbolically,[24] this textual crux has considerable import. In this chapter the merits and demerits of earlier responses to this problem are tested in a way that asks literary and philosophical scholars to consider the extent to which their readings may be bound up in decisions (or assumptions) about the constitution of the text. While the inverse may also be true, close scrutiny of the text and its transmission may in some instances shift the burden of proof: for example, if the indirect tradition proves beyond reasonable doubt that there can have been no vocative to Memmius in line 50, then the absence of same before that point requires the conclusion that some lines have been lost. Butterfield deduces that the six lines were copied from their original and correct location in Book 2 as a marginal cross-reference that later infiltrated the text proper. In the absence of a more convincing explanation to the

---

[23] Tarrant 2016: 17. On Lachmann's method see Timpanaro 2005: 102–14.
[24] See Konstan 2011 (esp. 63–4) and Sedley 2011 for the 'realist' and 'idealist' positions, respectively.

contrary, the crux must itself be seen as in origin a critical response that generated its own critical offshoot. In such ways as these, editorial solutions to textual cruces unwind the interventions and errors that in some cases inaugurated traditions of reader response, and in others were already embedded in those traditions.

Textual criticism instantiates the most direct encounter possible between the author of the *DRN* and its reader insofar as its endeavour, at root, is to restore the text to the condition in which it was bequeathed to posterity by Lucretius (whether he finished the poem or not). As a didactic poem, the *DRN* remodels this encounter in multiple permutations by foregrounding a pedagogical *mise en scène* in which the first-person voice of the poet-teacher endeavours to impart new knowledge to a named but unspeaking (which is not necessarily to say unresponsive) addressee who functions, inter alia, as a comparand for the reader in his or her own engagement with the text. Much profit has been brought to the study of the *DRN* through scrutiny both of this didactic scenario as presented within the text (the 'teacher-student constellation', as it has been called)[25] and of its relation to contexts of reception beyond the text, both as projected by the text in its heavily implied reader or 'reader-addressee' (the 'you'),[26] and in the actual or empirical reader (you) who may or may not identify with the readers named or implied within the text, and who will have a personal conception of the 'ideal reader' that the text hopes to find.[27] This last distinction is not always made, but that oversight, if such it is, is a reminder that another layer of reading might always be added in potentially infinite cumulation outwards from the Lucretius–Memmius nucleus.[28] To take the example of one landmark approach, we might say that Philip Mitsis' analysis of how Lucretius' implied readers will distance themselves from the addressee patronized in the text is a reading that itself separates Mitsis off as the 'ideal reader' according to his view of the *DRN*;[29] Mitsis' reading is in this way enabled by the reader-addressee dynamics of the text, and can be observed as such from a viewpoint at a further remove again. Far from a theory-driven regress into interpretative nihilism, this 'meta-cognitive' approach might itself be seen as an effective learning strategy,[30] and the

---

[25] See Volk 2002: 73–83.

[26] With differences in the degree of separation between named and implied readers see Townend 1978; Clay 1983: 212–66; Keen 1985; Mitsis 1993; Sharrock 1994: 5–17, esp. 12–13, 15–17.

[27] See Conte 1994: xvii–xxii, 1–34 (on the ideal reader) and xx, 133 (for the distinction between 'ideal' and 'empirical' readers).

[28] See Sharrock 1994: 8; compare the remarks of Lowrie 1995.   [29] Mitsis 1993.

[30] See Canevaro 2019 for this idea applied to Hesiod.

sense of detachment to which it gives rise would be especially germane to the Epicurean agenda.

The chapters in Part II ('Lucretius and his Readers') take up these lines of analysis with emphasis on considerations that have received little or no attention to date in the study of the *DRN*. Back from the dead in all three of them is a figure that the critical shift towards the reader so decidedly – and, given the fallacious biographical circularity of previous times, so usefully – eclipsed: the author. The suicidal madman of Jerome's biographical note, and of many later elaborations, is rehabilitated in Nora Goldschmidt's chapter on 'Reading the "Implied Author" in Lucretius' *De Rerum Natura*' – not, however, as the biological entity that wrote the poem, but as a mode of reception encoded in the text and brought to life on every reading of it. This chapter, then, is an approach to *Lucretius* himself, now understood as the author constructed by the text; indeed, the condition of that text as witnessed in Butterfield's chapter becomes, in Goldschmidt's analysis, not the consequence of Lucretius' psychological state, but the cause of it. Similarly, on this view, the splintering of the author into 'Lucretius' and 'anti-Lucretius' can be seen as an aspect of the text's biofiction. Approaching Lucretius from this perspective takes the biographical fallacy not as a trap but as a creative strategy that accounts for the sensibility of the text (or our sense thereof) and allows us, after all, to read with the author in view – an instinctive way of reading that ancient writing anticipates and accommodates.[31]

The author as perceived by the reader plays a role also in Barnaby Taylor's chapter ('Common Ground in Lucretius' *De Rerum Natura*') on the first-person plural pronouns and verbs used by the didactic *praeceptor* to co-opt the addressee in a shared enterprise, and categorized by actual readers as they negotiate their own inclusion in – or exclusion from – the Epicurean Garden over the course of reading and rereading the poem. The counterpart of the assured Epicurean, whose first-person plurals a given reader may already share or later come to share, is the flawed anti-Lucretius whose crises of conviction will then be reassuring or alienating according to the individual reader's commitment to Epicureanism. As Taylor points out, the ambivalence as to who may be included in Lucretius' first-person plurals – which, with Goldschmidt, we can see as implying the poem's author – enables each reader to write the didactic plot of their own experience of the *DRN*.

---

[31] Compare Peirano 2012 on the strategies of Latin pseudepigrapha. See also Goldschmidt 2019.

A different aspect of the common ground between the author and reader comes into focus in the final chapter of this section by Fabio Tutrone ('Coming to Know Epicurus' Truth: Distributed Cognition in Lucretius' *De Rerum Natura*'). The 'common ground' shown by Taylor to be a strategy of Lucretius' co-option of his reader is, for Tutrone, established by a process of 'distributed cognition' or 'extended mind'. This phenomenon, already inherent in language and text as instruments of communication, is pertinent to a poetic genre that foregrounds an interactive framework. It is especially pertinent in the case of an Epicurean didactic poem that, as such, holds to a materialist view of cognition according to which ideas are formed and communicated quite literally by the redistribution of atoms to the mind via senses that, though they may be deceived, cannot lie. Tutrone thus strips away Cartesian dualism to reveal a *DRN* that finds the key to cognition in the external world and that accordingly mobilizes itself as a distributed artefact of cognition in that world, equating itself with the nature of things right down to a correspondence between the letters and atoms of which it and the world are composed. Attuned in this way to the embodied mind, the *DRN* aims at nothing less than to reproduce its author in the person of the reader.

The chapters in Part III ('The Word and the World') take up the analogy with which the previous part concludes in extending the text of the *DRN* ontologically into the material world in which the reader is situated. Lucretius' frequent comparison of the letters (*elementa*) of which the *DRN* is composed to the atoms (*elementa*) of which the world is constituted (1.196–8, 823–9, 907–14; 2.688–99, 1013–22) takes up what is, at face value, an analogy that seems to have been posited by the Greek atomists Leucippus and Democritus,[32] and pursues it to suggest a degree of equivalence between letters and atoms that arguably goes some way beyond mere analogy. This line of analysis came to prominence in Paul Friedländer's seminal study of Lucretian 'atomology', which argued that different kinds of wordplay in the *DRN* can be shown to instantiate the natural connection between signifier and signified, as posited in the linguistic theory outlined at 5.1028–90 and, by extension, in the analogy of atomic and lexical *elementa*: thus, for example, *ignis* (fire) and *lignum* (wood) are naturally similar both in their linguistic and atomic composition; by the same principle, *amor* (love) is no less and no more than the

---

[32] The principal sources are Arist. *Metaph.* 1.4, 985b12–19; *Gen. corr.* 1.2, 315b6–15. For discussion in connection with Lucretius see Snyder 1980: 31–51; Dionigi 1988: 11–38; Armstrong 1995.

umor (fluid) that drives it.[33] While Friedländer's (and perhaps any) interpretation of Epicurean linguistic theory is open to challenge,[34] the con-
tention that in his wordplay '[t]he poet was never more serious' proved
enormously influential,[35] and has since been developed in explorations of
how different aspects of the text reflect the nature of the universe as its
imago mundi,[36] or even of the instantiation of the universe in the *DRN*
itself as its atomic *simulacrum*.[37] Not all scholars are comfortable with the
extension of the analogy to the ontological level, but even on the level of
structural similitude this line of analysis has been remarkably productive.[38]
In a materialist creation, however, all metaphor must be metonymy: the
Lucretian wor(l)d urges readers to pursue the synecdochic relation of
textual *simulacra* to *simulacra* of the cosmos.

The limits of 'atomology' are, in a very particular way, the focus of the
first chapter in this section ('Infinity, Enclosure and False Closure in
Lucretius' *De Rerum Natura*'). Here Donncha O'Rourke explores how
Lucretius' poem seeks to represent an infinite *rerum natura* within the
bounds of a text that of necessity must come to an end, limited as it is by
the material confines of its book-roll. An infinite universe of unlimited
atoms and void is an essential plank of Epicurean philosophy, but also one
that is notoriously difficult to comprehend intellectually. Failure of Lucretius' universal text to embrace infinity would see the whole Epicurean
system come crashing down: since that endeavour seems doomed to failure
in the finite space of text, Lucretius' success in enacting infinity through
strategies of false closure, serial repetition and evocation of the sublime is
nothing short of a triumph.

The coordination of the literary text with the material universe of which
it is a part is an operating principle also in the intertextual composition of
the poem, as Jason Nethercut shows in Chapter 6 ('Lucretian Echoes:
Sound as Metaphor for Literary Allusion in *De Rerum Natura* 4.549–94').
In this case Lucretius' explanation of the phenomenon of echo is self-
reflexively backed up in the reconfiguration of source texts into the literary
echoes of the *DRN*: the literary reconstitution – which is also to say in the
atomic 'metathesis' – of this pre-Epicurean source material (for poems are
material) produces a new Epicurean text with a worldview that is, likewise,
radically reconfigured. In this way, as Nethercut argues, the *DRN*

[33] Friedländer 1941 (quoted in the next sentence at 17, n. 3).   [34] West 1982; Dalzell 1987.
[35] Snyder 1980; Dionigi 1988 [2005].
[36] Armstrong 1995; D. Fowler 1995; P. Fowler 1997; Kennedy 2000; Gale 2004.
[37] Thury 1987; Schiesaro 1994.   [38] See the overview in Volk 2002: 100–5.

contributes to a later Epicurean 'poetics', witnessed chiefly in Philodemus, that upholds the orthodoxy of the coordination of form and content.

A later reconfiguration of Lucretian atomology is the subject of Wilson Shearin's chapter ('Saussure's *cahiers* and Lucretius' *elementa*: A Reconsideration of the Letters–Atoms Analogy'). At the conclusion of this part of the volume, Shearin's discussion amply demonstrates the rightful role of Swiss linguist and semiotician Ferdinand de Saussure as precursor of atomological Lucretiana in the scholarship of the later twentieth century and beyond. Saussure's co-called 'anagrams' of Lucretius' text may be hair-raising, but Shearin argues that their emphasis on non-auditory configuration and on potentiality attends to aspects of Lucretian atomology that have received less attention than is their due. If Saussure here controversially abandons his adherence to structuralism, one might say he effects a 'swerve' from the usual trajectory of his linguistic system: just as Epicurus introduced the swerve to accommodate Democritean atomism to the spontaneity of nature, so Saussure introduces a declination to relax his own linguistic determinism. Epicurus' attraction for Saussure, then, lies precisely in the paradox of his commitment to a system that yet is free of aprioristic teleology.

The chapters in Part IV of the volume ('Literary and Philosophical Sources') focus on one of the principal questions brought to bear on the *DRN* – that of other texts against which it may be compared and which mediate its interpretation. This subfield has witnessed a considerable evolution and proliferation of approaches, from the *Quellenforschung* that seeks to identify the Epicurean or other philosophical texts on which the *DRN* may have been modelled,[39] to the study of allusion and intertextuality, which pursue author-centred and reader-driven perspectives, respectively, on the diverse literary texts that the *DRN* in one way or another brings to mind, reworks and potentially disrupts.[40] While in the study of Latin literature scholarly practice at large has shifted decidedly away from *Quellenforschung*, which is chiefly associated with the scholarly interests of the nineteenth and early twentieth centuries, to intertextuality, which since the 1980s has come to be one of the dominant methodologies practised by Latinists,[41] Lucretius has to some extent bucked the trend

---

[39] For some recent approaches in this vein see Sedley 1998; Piazzi 2005; Warren 2007; Montarese 2012.

[40] Brown 1982; Gale 2007b; Garani 2007; Nethercut 2014. Lucretius' appropriation of Thucydides' account of the Athenian plague (Thuc. 2.47–54) at 6.1138–286 is a key case-study: see Commager 1957; Bright 1971; Foster 2009, 2011.

[41] For an overview see O'Rourke and Pelttari forthcoming.

in regard to the question of his adherence to Epicurus' *On Nature* –
whether the lost *magnum opus* in thirty books, a large epitome thereof,
or the synoptic letters preserved by Diogenes Laertius. If anything, discussion of this question has remained vital even as the study of Lucretian
allusion and intertextuality has grown. As the responses in this volume
indicate, a landmark work of scholarship in this area has been David
Sedley's 1998 monograph, *Lucretius and the Transformation of Greek
Wisdom*, which advances a strong thesis to the effect that the *DRN* as we
have it represents an unfinished project to deliver an orthodox metaphrasis
of Epicurus' original thirty-seven-book treatise in a six-book didactic epic.
Strong theses will court controversy, but *Quellenforschung* may be said duly
to retain its relevance in the case of a text that professes such fidelity to its
source as the *DRN* does in respect of Epicurus. Similarly, while scholarship
is less inclined than it once was to polarize literary and philosophical
approaches (not least given philosophy's interest in poetry, and poetry's
reciprocal interest in philosophy), the *DRN* is a text that attracts that
dichotomy in acknowledging the tension of its versification of a philosophy noted for its misgivings about poetry – a point already highlighted by
Goldschmidt in Chapter 2.

In Chapter 8 ('Arguing over Text(s): Master-Texts vs. Intertexts in the
Criticism of Lucretius'), Andrew Morrison resists the consensus that
would reconcile the philosophical content with the poetic form of the
DRN, drawing attention instead to the reading practices visited on the
poem, comparing those that tend to correlate the *DRN* with philosophical
'master-texts' (be these specific texts extant or lost, e.g., Epicurus' *On
Nature*, or a philosophical system more generally, e.g., Epicureanism) to
those that tune into and interpret its dialogue with other literary intertexts
(which, in Conte's terms, could similarly be 'exemplary models', such as
Ennius' *Annales*, or non-specific 'code models', such as the epic genre).[42]
The more strongly one reads against a master-text, argues Morrison, the
more rebellious the heterogeneous *DRN* should seem to us to be, both as
poem and intertextual entity. With Taylor, then, we may say that both
interpretative approaches offer 'common ground' to the text's different
readers, such that the urge to synthesize an intertextual poem with a
philosophical master-text will be a function of different readers' constructions of their implied author's strategies for the promotion of *ataraxia*.

Tim O'Keefe proposes a different way of looking at Lucretius' literary
and philosophical sources in Chapter 9 ('Lucretius and the Philosophical

---

[42] See Conte 1986: 31.

Use of Literary Persuasion'). Highlighting the difficulties and limitations of arriving at a definitive understanding of Lucretius' originality based on his adherence or otherwise to philosophical tradition (the 'master-texts' of the previous chapter), O'Keefe looks instead to what is philosophically innovative in the manner of Lucretius' exposition – in particular, the psychology of philosophical persuasion in tactics such as appealing to the emotions, challenging cultural conditioning, and embedding non-rational modes of persuasion, such as ridicule, within logical argumentation. Insofar as the question of philosophical sources continues to press, the theorization of some of these tactics in the fragments of Philodemus again makes for instructive comparison, as in Chapters 6 and 11.

A third approach to literary and philosophical models in the *DRN* is on display in Chapter 10 ('The Rising and Setting Soul in Lucretius, *De Rerum Natura* 3'). Here, Emma Gee showcases Lucretius' polemical engagement with Cleanthes' *Hymn to Zeus* and Cicero's *Aratea* – poems that, in their reception if not also in origin, are no less philosophical than the *DRN*, albeit of a different (Stoicizing) persuasion. Gee takes as her case-study Lucretius' argument for the mortality of the soul, which by a process of 'intertextual metaphor' is subtly but systematically compared to the stars in Cicero's *Aratea* – a comparison of some pertinence in that souls and stars are for both Lucretius and Cicero made up of the same stuff and subject to the same laws of nature, but fundamentally contrasting insofar as for Lucretius those laws enforce an atomic physics that requires the eventual destruction of souls and stars alike. In view of the analogy of letters as atoms and text as universe discussed earlier in the volume, Lucretius' reconstitution of Cicero's poem in the service of his own becomes a kind of intertextual palingenesis in which the *Aratea* is reconfigured as the *DRN*, similar and sometimes even identical in verbal form, but radically reborn in terms of philosophical content. In Harold Bloom's terminology, but also Lucretius', we see the 'swerve' of the Epicurean's 'misprision', or wilful taking amiss, of his Stoic model in order himself to become an author (and authority) as strong as Cicero.

The collision of ideologies witnessed in Part IV of the volume comes to the fore in Part V on 'Worldviews'. Ranging across history, political theory and the history of theory, the broad chronological and conceptual coverage of this section aims to show some of the different ways in which the *DRN* and Epicureanism ignite heated interpretation, as well as the processes involved in such interpretation, and what is at stake intellectually and ideologically in these processes. Scholarship in this domain has often focused on the engagement of the *DRN* with the social and cultural discourses of the late republic,[43] for example, in evaluating the poem's political leanings, be they Caesarian, republican, or even proto-imperial,[44] and in examining its redeployment of political and military imagery in its discussions of atomic physics and Epicurean ethics – and indeed in its description of Epicurus himself.[45]

Contributing to this strand of scholarship, Joseph Farrell in Chapter 11 of this volume ('Was Memmius a Good King?') scopes out new possibilities for a 'Memmian' reading of the *DRN* through careful excavation of historical detail that connects some of the stand-out sections of the poem – for example, the Hymn to Venus, the diatribe against erotic infatuation in Book 4, and the contrasting descriptions of Athens that frame Book 6 – to the C. Memmius disgraced in the consular elections of 53 BC (by far the most likely historical candidate for the addressee of the poem). Inter alia, these connections are consistent with Gregory Hutchinson's proposed re-dating of the poem to the period of Memmius' exile to Athens and the impending civil war at Rome,[46] although those who prefer an earlier date might credit the *DRN* with remarkable prescience given its intensifying relevance to events as they unfolded.[47] Contributing also to scholarly advances in the understanding of Roman Epicurean political theory, Farrell brings his reading of the *DRN* into sharp relief through comparison with Philodemus' more deferential approach to his addressee, L. Calpurnius Piso Caesoninus, in *On the Good King According to Homer*. In effect, then, the *DRN* puts into practice what is merely theorized in Philodemus' *On Flattery* and *On Frank Criticism*.

The potential of the *DRN* to mobilize political theory has often been witnessed in its reception, as amply demonstrated in recent scholarship. In Chapter 12 ('A Tribute to a Hero: Marx's Interpretation of Epicurus in his Dissertation'), Elizabeth Asmis contributes to the study of the reception history of Epicureanism with an assessment of Karl Marx's own approach to Epicurus in his doctoral dissertation – an approach largely mediated by Lucretius given the centrality it accords to the atom's 'swerve' (for which the primary Epicurean source is *DRN* 2.216–93). Because of its

---

[43] See generally Nichols 1976; Minyard 1985; Grimal 1978. For more incisive studies of Lucretian political thought see Fowler 1989a; Schrijvers 1996; Hutchinson 2001; Schiesaro 2007a, 2007b; Pope 2017. On gender politics see Nugent 1994; Fowler 1996; Kennedy 2008; Sharrock 2008; Gordon 2012; Pope 2018.

[44] See Farrington 1939; Momigliano 1941; Kennedy 2013; Valachova 2018: 164–8.

[45] Sykes Davies 1931–2: 32–8; Buchheit 1971; Cabisius 1985; Fowler 1989a; Asmis 2008a; Shearin 2015: 61–97.

[46] Hutchinson 2001.

[47] For arguments in support of the traditional (earlier) date see Volk 2010; Krebs 2013.

minimal deviation from otherwise linear downward movement, the atom –
and, with it, Epicurean philosophy – liberates itself from the determinism
of its Democritean precursor, just as the human individual avoids stress
and pain in opting for *ataraxia* and *aponia*. For this reason, Marx celebrated the swerve as a principle of autonomous action and a first form of
self-consciousness – a reading of some significance in view of Marx's later
analysis of class consciousness.[48] While Marx's reconstruction of Epicurus
was surely influenced by his own historical situation and outlook, Asmis'
chapter shows that, despite (or because of) the differences of context and
interpretation, Marx's dissertation offers a number of valuable insights
from a philosophical point of view. In particular, it highlights the problem
of whether priority should be assigned to universal law or human freedom:
does the mind exercise control or should causal power be assigned to the
atoms? Whether or not Epicurus himself recognized and resolved this
difficulty, Marx's Epicurus avoids the problem *tout court* by making the
swerve – and, ultimately, abstract individual freedom – itself the dominant
principle, in effect inscribing an ethical mandate at the core of the
Epicurean system. It might be remarked that Marx's own swerve away
from Epicurus' argument is what demonstrates his theory, yet the scope for
a proto-Marxist reading of the *DRN* is thought-provoking – not least in
highlighting the political power of the swerve as the cause of human
freedom.[49] On this reading, the *DRN* contains within itself the origin of
a theory of praxis, and it makes a powerful statement that Marx reserved
for the conclusion of his dissertation Lucretius' presentation of Epicurus as
a Promethean freedom fighter (*DRN* 1.62–79), rebelling against traditional belief in the gods and freeing humankind from oppression.

Lucretius' description of Epicurus' victory over superstition provides a
focal point also for Chapter 13 by Duncan Kennedy ('Plato and Lucretius
on the Theoretical Subject'), which concludes the volume with a salutary
meditation on the nature of theory itself as a processual and, therefore,
provisional and contextual phenomenon – and one that, as the chapters in
this section show, tends to retain the political dimension of its original
civic function (the *theoros* being mandated by his city to be a 'spectator' at
a Panhellenic festival and to report back afterwards). Kennedy argues that
Lucretius' celebration of Epicurean triumph and enlightenment overwrites

---

[48] Cf. Norbrook 2015: 26 on the Lucretian significance behind Marx's phrase 'new forces of
production and relations of production do not develop out of nothing, nor drop from the sky'
(cf. *DRN* 1.150 and 5.793).

[49] Farrington 1939 presents a Marxist's reading of Epicureanism and Lucretius.

the allegory of the cave in Plato's *Republic* to present a worldview that, for all its differences to what we might call Platonic metaphysics, also deals with a level of reality beyond the realm of the senses and accessed through processes of thinking in which the 'theoretical subject' is engaged. Relativized in this way, Plato and Lucretius can be seen to constitute their differing theories of reality through what Bruno Latour would term different 'modes of veridiction' – the tools of the trade that, being context-specific and ever liable to be updated, are ultimately transient rather than legitimating. Theories, however, are wont to be forcefully articulated.[50] No less than the political dispensation theorized in Plato's *Republic*, Lucretius' 'freedom fighter' perpetrates his own kind of violence in positing a worldview to lord it over all others. This final chapter, then, zooms out from *Approaches to Lucretius* to consider readings, theories and approaches themselves as processes of reception that readers of Lucretius' electrifying poem, present and future, might see not so much as 'reporting back' on the text as conditioning what we as *theoroi* see in it.

While the various approaches to Lucretius surveyed in this volume represent some of the principal ways of reading the *DRN* at present, they make no claim to being definitive or exhaustive. For example, there are no sections specifically devoted to matters of language and style, to debates about Lucretian theology or linguistic theory, or indeed to reception *per se*. Yet it is hoped that these approaches, too, have not gone unobserved in the course of the volume, just as those that are explicitly surveyed resurface in chapters beyond their own sections. Readers might therefore wish to imagine (or use the Index to guide) their own bespoke ways of assembling *Approaches to Lucretius*. To give what may be a pertinent example, one of the strands that tethers the various chapters together in ways less obviously signalled is that of 'atomology', which runs throughout the volume beyond the confines of Part III. In respect of textual criticism, Gerard Passannante has suggested that the first editors of the *DRN* found themselves enacting Lucretius' analogy between the letters of his poem and the atoms of the universe in their very act of reconstituting the newly recovered text and restoring through it a lost understanding of the material world: 'The Renaissance humanist read the poem, one could say, as the poem read the humanist.'[51] Intertextuality with the *DRN* is also a kind of metathesis that reconstitutes Lucretian ideas with varying degrees of swerve. In this way, all acts of reception – including our own – are expressions of its

---

[50] See, for example, Tarrant 2016: 30–48 on the rhetoric of textual criticism.
[51] Passannante 2011: 13.

Figure 1 *The Basic Material is Not the Word But the Letter*, Nathan Coley (2018).
University of Edinburgh Art Collections, © Studio Nathan Coley. Reproduced with the
permission of the University of Edinburgh Art Collections

materialist philosophy. A thought-provoking instance of this may be witnessed in the main concourse of Edinburgh University Library (Figure 1),
where since 2018 readers have been greeted by Scottish artist Nathan
Coley's enigmatic 'textwork', a large-scale installation of light bulbs spelling
out the phrase 'THE BASIC MATERIAL IS NOT THE WORD BUT THE
LETTER' – a sentence the artist derived from the archive of his compatriot
and colleague Ian Hamilton Finlay (1925–2006) housed in the same
building. For readers of the *DRN*, the installation stands as a material
expression of Lucretian atomism, reconstituted through the unseen intertextual channels that course through all our libraries and lives.

PART I

The Text

Critical Responses to the Most Difficult Textual Problem in Lucretius

David Butterfield

The text of Lucretius' *De Rerum Natura* (*DRN*) has suffered various indignities in the past two millennia: it failed to be brought to completion by its author,[1] became a rare text by the fourth century[2] and survived the fall of Rome in perhaps only two or three copies.[3] The version that survives in our earliest extant manuscripts (of the ninth century AD) had already been annotated with hundreds of shorter notes by a couple of ancient readers, perhaps when still written on papyrus rolls.[4] Over the course of several transcriptions, the poem suffered many accidental omissions and transpositions, along with well over a thousand verbal corruptions; in the manuscript from which our text descends – a book perhaps made in the eighth century – one leaf came loose and was returned to the book the wrong way round, and a significant corner of another leaf was somehow lost. Although we can recreate the format of this book (the archetype of the tradition)[5] with minute precision, it has long since disappeared from the world. Nevertheless, three of its close descendants survive to us, each made in the scriptoria of the Carolingian Empire: a direct copy, the Oblongus (O, c. 800), a copy made some fifty years later from a sibling of O, the Quadratus (Q, c. 850), and a sibling of Q that only survives in three defective sets of leaves, which contain about 45 per cent of the work (S, late ninth century). The next oldest manuscript of Lucretius that survives dates to the 1430s: both it and the fifty-four other manuscripts that survive from the Renaissance ultimately derive from the two and a half extant Carolingian manuscripts, a fact that deprives them of independent value for reconstructing the poem's text.

---

[1] I have set out the case for this at Butterfield 2014: 20–5.
[2] See the evidence gathered at Butterfield 2013: 56–101.
[3] For a brief sketch of the 'prehistory' of Lucretius' direct transmission see Butterfield 2013: 268–72.
[4] I will return to these *capitula* at the close of this chapter.
[5] Butterfield 2013: 299–304 (cf. 17).

Therefore, although Lucretius has been dealt a better hand than many
an ancient author, it remains a fact that the manuscripts from which the
poem must be constructed were all copied from a single version of the
poem written some 800 years after his death. It is thus unsurprising that
the *DRN*, after centuries of corruption, has seen a considerable amount of
debate and dispute about how to reconstitute its text. Some scholars have
sought to transpose sections of the poem at dozens of places in the text;[6]
some have rejected a considerable portion of the text as un-Lucretian,
resulting from posthumous additions;[7] some have inclined towards
extreme conservatism;[8] some have veered into trigger-happy emendation.[9]
These competing attitudes have been prompted not only by significant
differences between the areas of expertise of editors – whether philological,
philosophical or literary – but also by the prevailing methodologies of the
era, whether it be the zenith of conjectural activity in the late nineteenth
century or of textual conservatism in the late twentieth. In this chapter, the
merits and demerits of these conflicting text-critical approaches will be
considered hand in hand.

Notwithstanding the centuries of scholarly toil and trouble, there
remain several *loci conclamati* in the poem where we are faced with scores
of emendations but still have no confidence about what Lucretius wrote.[10]
The majority of these are awkward problems at the verbal or syntactical
level but do little to obscure or pervert our understanding of Lucretius'
poem or philosophical system as a whole. Even with problems on a larger
scale, such as whether the near-identical passages 1.926–50 and 4.1–25
should stand in both locations (as transmitted), a certain solution to the
crux would not radically change how we read and interpret the poem.[11]

Instead, for the most difficult textual problem thrown up by the work
we must turn to its very beginning. Much the most notorious oddity of
Lucretius' Epicurean manifesto is its grandiose opening 'hymn' to Venus.
The poem begins with the high-flown vocative *Aeneadum genetrix*, which
in the second line is explicitly revealed to be a divine addressee, *alma
Venus*. Thereafter, this enthused and apparently heartfelt prayer to Venus

[6] Most notably Brieger 1894 and Bockemüller 1873–4.
[7] Most notably Müller 1975 and Deufert 1996, a conviction still evident in Deufert 2019.
[8] For example Bailey 1947; Leonard and Smith 1942.
[9] Most notably Lachmann 1850; Munro (especially in his first edition of 1864); Orth 1961; García
Calvo 1997.
[10] Particularly striking examples are 2.42–3, 3.658, 3.962, 4.545, 5.312 and 5.1442. The last was
described by Bailey 1947: III.1546 ad loc. as 'perhaps the most desperate textual crux in Lucretius'.
[11] One such solution to the crux of 1.926–50 and 4.1–25 is suggested by O'Rourke in this volume
(p. 120).

as the omnipotent goddess of nature continues for over forty lines (1.1–43), drawing upon all of the formulaic features of divine invocation: the expansion of the vocative address with appositive phrases and relative clauses (1–4), polyptotic repetition of the second-person pronoun (6–8, 12–13), sweeping reference to the realms of the sky, earth and sea (2–20), delay of the main second-person verb (*gubernas*, 21), emphasis of the deity's individual power (21–3, 31–2), a call for personal poetic assistance (24–5, 28), followed by a prayer seeking peace for the world (29–30) – and more specifically for the addresser's immediate environs (i.e. Rome, 40). Incorporated into the prayer are the conventional mythic images of Venus as the seductive goddess and illicit lover of Mars *armipotens*, whom she should induce with her amorous charms to secure the desired cessation of warfare.

No Roman reader would bat an eyelid at such a prœmium to a late-Republican poem cast in archaizing Latin hexameters. However, the content of this opening would have utterly stumped any paid-up Epicurean. Not only was it a central tenet of that philosophical school that the Greco-Roman institutions of prayer and religion were misconceived, since they wrongly supposed that deities could and would intervene in human affairs, but Lucretius himself states expressly in the poem that the gods are unmoved by human concerns.[12] It is therefore baffling that the *DRN*, a careful summary of Epicurean doctrine from first principles upwards, opens with a traditional and direct prayer to Venus, beseeching her not just to aid its composition but also to grant peace to war-torn Rome.

The purpose of this chapter is not to rake over the many complex explanations that have been offered since the fifteenth century for this astounding decision of Lucretius, whether artistic or philosophical.[13] It is instead to analyse a second striking problem that confronts every reader of the text within a few minutes of starting the work. This problem arises in a short passage that, in the text as transmitted, stands in remarkably difficult relation to the proem, and calls for a critical solution of a different order. This crux has provoked myriad different responses but, for all that fervid activity, there remains no consensus as to what should be done. I will argue that this impasse results from insufficient attention being given to a wide range of philological, and indeed logical, matters, combined with a conservative impulse to explain away oddities on the shaky ground that what

---

[12] On 'idealist' v. 'realist' interpretation of Epicurus' gods see Tutrone in this volume (pp. 89–93). For my reconstruction of Lucretius' understanding see Butterfield 2018.

[13] See further O'Keefe in Chapter 9 of this volume.

an unknown scribe wrote some nine centuries after Lucretius' death is probably sound.

The close of Lucretius' 'hymn' to Venus runs as follows (38–43):

> hunc tu, diua, tuo recubantem corpore sancto
> circumfusa super, suauis ex ore loquellas
> funde petens placidam Romanis, incluta, pacem;
> nam neque nos agere hoc patriai tempore iniquo
> possumus aequo animo nec Memmi clara propago
> talibus in rebus communi desse saluti.

Bending round him from above, goddess, as he lies on your sacred body, pour from your lips sweet utterances, as you seek quiet peace for your Romans, illustrious one. For in this unjust time for our country neither can we act with untroubled mind, nor can the noble family of Memmius let down the commonwealth in such circumstances.[14]

The prayer is then immediately followed by these six lines (44–9):

> omnis enim per se diuom natura necessest
> immortali aeuo summa cum pace fruatur
> semota ab nostris rebus seiunctaque longe;
> nam priuata dolore omni, priuata periclis,
> ipsa suis pollens opibus, nihil indiga nostri,
> nec bene promeritis capitur nec tangitur ira.

For the whole nature of the gods must of itself necessarily enjoy immortal life amidst the utmost peace, far removed and separated from our affairs; for devoid of pain, devoid of danger, itself powerful by its own resources, and not needing us at all, it is neither appeased with services nor touched by wrath.

The text then takes a quite different turn once more (50–3):

> quod superest, uacuas auris <animumque sagacem>
> semotum a curis adhibe ueram ad rationem,
> ne mea dona tibi studio disposta fideli,
> intellecta prius quam sint, contempta relinquas.

For the rest, apply to true philosophy unpreoccupied ears <and a keen intelligence> free from cares, lest you spurn and discard my gifts, set out for you with faithful zeal, before they have been apprehended.

Lucretius then turns to outline the contents of the poem (54–61), before lavishly praising Epicurus' achievements (62–79) and passionately condemning the destructive powers of religion (80–101). Although this development involves some rough-and-ready transitions, the content is

---

[14] The Latin text and translation throughout this chapter are my own, unless otherwise stated.

unobjectionably sound. By contrast, in the preceding run of lines 38–53 two particularly striking issues emerge. The first is that the passionate request to Venus for aid is immediately explained by an account (44–9, introduced by *enim*) of how and why the gods, Venus included, are not affected by or concerned with human events (let alone able to govern the workings of all nature on earth!). The second is that this incongruous explanation is directly followed by an imperative (51 *adhibe*) which can no longer refer to Venus, who alone is addressed up to line 43, but must refer instead to Memmius, who – though the addressee of the poem – has not yet been addressed at all.[15] We thus have two transitions (43 to 44, and 49 to 50) that are manifestly unsatisfactory in their transmitted form. As Courtney (2001: 25) has put it straightforwardly: verses 44–9 'make perfect nonsense of this passage'.[16] But the solution to the problems they pose is hard to seek: Bailey (1947: II.585) even called the matter 'a minor 'Homeric question''.[17] In order to make any progress, it will be necessary to discuss each of these problems of transition separately before arguing for how they are intimately connected.

The six verses 1.44–9 are particularly famous, and not primarily for their problematic presence in this location. For they are an approximate versification of the first – and arguably most important – of Epicurus' *Kuriai Doxai*: τὸ μακάριον καὶ ἄφθαρτον οὔτε αὐτὸ πράγματα ἔχει οὔτε ἄλλῳ παρέχει, ὥστε οὔτε ὀργαῖς οὔτε χάρισι συνέχεται· ἐν ἀσθενεῖ γὰρ τὸ πᾶν τὸ τοιοῦτον ('The blessed and imperishable neither suffers trouble nor creates it in another, so that it is not constrained by wrath or favour, for all such things exist in the weak.') The pairing ζῷον ἄφθαρτον καὶ μακάριον is also used explicitly of god by Epicurus at *Ep. Men.* 123. The versified doctrine is thus eminently Epicurean.

Can we be sure, however, that these Epicurean lines are Lucretian? Yes, for the self-same verses occur in Book 2. At 598–643 Lucretius recounts the cult of Cybele, the Magna Mater, and provides an explanation of the allegorical meaning of the various elements of her worship. This strikingly animated account closes with the self-conscious remark at 644–5: *quae* [i.e. these explanations of her worship] *bene et eximie quamuis disposta ferantur,* | *longe sunt tamen a uera ratione repulsa* ('however well and outstandingly

---

[15] See Farrell in Chapter 11 of this volume for discussion of Lucretius' address to Memmius.

[16] Gale 1994: 215 is less forceful but no less clear: 'The only claim which can be made here with any degree of confidence is that the text probably cannot stand as transmitted.'

[17] In a similar vein Sedley 1989a: 280 has called this 'the most hotly and inconclusively debated passage in Lucretius'.

presented these verses are, they are nevertheless far removed from true reason'). There then follow six verses (646–51) that are entirely identical to 1.44–9. Yet in this location the lines explain (likewise introduced by *enim* at 646) how it is incorrect to conceive of the Earth as the sentient Mother Goddess, for the gods have no physical interaction with, or spiritual concern for, the human world. This is stated plainly in the immediately following verses (652–4): *terra quidem uero caret omni tempore sensu,* | *et quia multarum potitur primordia rerum,* | *multa modis multis effert in lumina solis* ('Indeed the earth lacks sensation at all times, and because it contains the first-beginnings of many things it brings forth many things in many ways into the light of the sun'). Verses 646–54 therefore provide the crucial explanation for the polemical assertion of 644–5: the allegorical reading of the worship of Cybele must be rejected because neither she nor any god has interaction with the human world, and the earth is accordingly devoid of any divine feeling.

There can be no doubt, then, that the six lines under dispute are Lucretian. The question is instead whether they are Lucretian in their current location at 1.44–9: did the poet really choose to place them at so strikingly dissonant and early a position in the work? More specifically, should they immediately follow and immediately precede verses 43 and 50?

The stark incongruence of the verses – evident to anyone, at least on their first reading – has been ridiculed since the Renaissance. The annotator (s.XV$^{4/4}$) of the Renaissance manuscript Vat. Ottob. Lat. 2834 wrote the following alongside the lines (1^r): *Si in deo non est nec gratia nec ira, cur invocas ad Venerem, quae tua sententia surda est? hoc non tibi sed iis convenit qui deos moveri praecibus mortalium aiunt.*[18] Such concerns were felt more broadly: in the first Aldine edition of 1500, the editor Hieronymus Avancius transposed the six verses, placing them after 61, despite the fact that they do not cohere in that location with the preceding verses. In his preface, however, rather than defending this particular transposition he recommended the expunction of the lines.[19]

---

[18] 'If there is neither grace nor anger in god, why do you call upon Venus, who in your opinion is deaf? This befits not you but those who say the gods are moved by mortal prayers.' For a full transcription of the annotation see Reeve 2005: 148 n. 95. Half a century later, Piero Vettori (Victorius) gave a detailed account of the problem in a letter to Giovanni Della Casa of 1553 (Vettori 1586: 61–2). In a more antagonistic vein, Cardinal Melchior de Polignac observed in his *Anti-Lucretius* (1747) *vocet demens, quos tendat perdere, divos,* | *immemor ipse sui* (5.35–6).

[19] 'unum affirmare ausim, *Omnis enim per se divum natura necesse est,* cum quinque sequentibus ex prologo, cum abundent, demendos esse, hos aptius legas, cum de magna matre agit.'

Soon after, in the Juntine edition (Candidus 1512), the verses were actually deleted from the text – and without any signal of their removal. The source of the initial suggestion to remove the lines has been attributed to two celebrated fifteenth-century Lucretians, Giovanni Pontano (Pontanus) and Michael Marullus. In fact, the first suggestion that they are un-Lucretian probably precedes both scholars: an annotation stemming from the work of Francisco Vidal de Noya (Noianus), who worked on Lucretius in the third quarter of the fifteenth century, appears in the margin of the Cambridge manuscript of the poem (CUL Nn II 40, c. 1460): *hi sex versus ex secundo libro in hunc locum translati sunt non poet<a>e opera sed scriptorum ignorantia.*[20]

Despite this general fifteenth-century scepticism about the six verses, and their actual deletion in the Juntine edition, they remained present in the proem throughout the sixteenth, seventeenth and eighteenth centuries. Editions throughout this period – including those of Lambinus (1563, 1570³), Gifanius (1565, 1595²), Creech (1695), Havercamp (1725), Wakefield (1796–7) and Forbiger (1828) – followed the Aldine in placing the lines after 1.61, although they were often bracketed in the early nineteenth century.[21] It was not until the seminal edition of Karl Lachmann (1850) that the verses were once more removed entirely from the poem, a decision that was followed by almost all editions of the subsequent hundred years.[22] However, Josef Martin (1934) thought fit to reintroduce them in his Teubner text of 1934, where they still stand in his final edition (1963⁵).[23] He was not alone in resurrecting faith in the paradosis, but no generalization can be made about critical attitudes in his wake. To judge from texts published in the last seventy years, scholars' opinions on the verses are in a state of chaos: some retain them, with or

---

[20] 'These six lines were transferred here from the second book thanks not to the poet but to scribal ignorance.'

[21] They were retained in their transmitted position in the text of Alter (1787) because his edition was based as closely as possible upon the Viennese manuscript (ÖNB Vind. 170, s.XV).

[22] See, for instance, Bockemüller 1873–4; Kelsey 1884; Warburton Lee 1884; Bailey 1900, 1922²; Merrill 1907; Ernout 1920; Duff 1923. Although Bernays 1852, Munro 1864 etc., Merrill 1917 and Diels 1923–4 all printed the lines between brackets, none supposed that Lucretius placed them there in the text.

[23] From his second edition (1953) onwards, Martin transposes 50–61 to after 135. Other over-ingenious attempts to retain the lines by transposition elsewhere in the proem were offered by Giuffrida 1940–50: II.68 n. 27 (1–43, 50–61, 44–9, 62–148); Gimpel 1981 (1–43, 80–101, 62–79, 44–9, 102–26, 50–61, 127–48). Based upon the ordering of Lucretian citations in Lactantius' *De Ira Dei* Canfora 1973 suggested the ordering 1–43, 62–79, 44–61, 136–45, 80–135, 146–8; the flimsy arguments for this elaborate reconstruction were well rebutted by Giancotti 1980.

without comment,[24] some bracket them, with or without explanation,[25] and some omit them entirely.[26]

In order to unearth the core features of the debate, let us approach the transmitted text with an open mind. If Lucretius did place verses 1.44–9 in their transmitted location, and the text is free of lacunae, explanation must be given of the following issues:

(i)   Since *enim* stands in 44, what is the explanatory connection of lines 44–9 with what precedes?[27] How can an assertion of the gods' isolated state and disinterest in worldly affairs be offered as the explanation for Lucretius' prayer to Venus for her personal intervention in a human crisis? If the lines are meant to somehow 'correct' the opening hymn, would we not expect an adversative particle (~ 'and yet')? If the connection is – as would be most natural – to the immediately preceding lines (41–3), *enim* is nonsensical: the remoteness of the gods cannot explain either why Lucretius lacks mental peace or why Memmius and his family in particular[28] must serve the state in its time of crisis.[29] Even if – as some critics have tried to claim[30] – *enim* instead refers farther back to 38–40, where Venus is asked to induce Mars with sweet talk to bring peace to Rome, or even to the whole prayer for peace of 29–40, that provides no relief. Instead, three fresh problems arise:

---

[24] Cochez 1954; Paratore and Pizzani 1960; Orth 1961; Gigon 1971; M. F. Smith in Rouse and Smith 1975, 1992³; Dionigi in Dionigi and Canali 1990; Giancotti 1994; García Calvo 1997; Flores 2002–9; Schrijvers 2008; Piazzi 2011.

[25] Valentí 1961; Büchner 1966; Müller 1975; Deufert 2019 (citing Noianus, as p. 25 above).

[26] Brown 1984. These verses cannot be found in the current Oxford and Budé texts, Bailey 1922 and Ernout 1920.

[27] It disguises the problem to talk of 'the slight oddity of *enim*' (O'Hara 2007: 58 n. 7). Bailey gives passing references to two instances of *enim* (Bailey 1947: II.602): 5.407, where it explains the assertion of 5.405–6, that the myth of Phaethon is a poetic fiction; and 2.645 (an error for 646), where (introducing the same six lines) it explains the assertion of 2.644–5, that the Cybele myth is untrue. There is no similar assertion to which *enim* at 1.44 could refer.

[28] The absurd suggestion of Gimpel 1981: 12–13 to read *Memmi clara propago* (42) as a vocative can be dismissed; but, even it were correct and Lucretius himself were to attend to Rome's *communis salus*, the problem of connection is in no way mitigated.

[29] Giancotti 1978: 218–21 sought to relate the force of *enim* to the close of 1.43, i.e. that Memmius cannot *tempore iniquo* fail the *communis salus*. The supposed explanation would be that Memmius must help out Rome because the gods cannot, since their isolation in divine *ataraxia* leaves them disinterested in human affairs. This curious idea only heightens the nonsense of Lucretius' having spent his poem's dramatic opening asking Venus for peace, and the perversity of the imperative left hanging at verse 40 (*funde*). More absurd are the claims of Alfieri 1929: 84 that *enim* serves as an adversative demonstrative particle, and of Schrijvers 1970: 190–1, followed independently by Segura Ramos 1982, that *enim* explains *tu* (Venus) in 38, since she alone – though a goddess – can offer help when all other gods are indifferent to human affairs!

[30] See p. 30 below.

(ii)   it is odd, as well as inelegant, for an *enim* clause to explain some-
        thing that has already been directly explained by the *nam* clause of
        41–3 – that Venus should seek peace from Mars because Rome
        desperately needs it.

(iii)   *omnis diuom natura* (44) demonstrates that the explanation afforded
        by verses 44–9 applies to the totality of the gods: the proem's
        connection with Venus in particular is therefore weakened, and the
        assertion of Lucretius at 31 as to her unique ability to bring peace
        (*tu sola potes tranquilla pace iuuare | mortalis*) loses its specific force.

(iv)   the relevance of line 49 (*nec bene promeritis capitur nec tangitur ira*)
        remains obscure: how could the gods' being immune to favour or
        anger possibly explain Venus' role as a peace-giver to humans; or
        how could Mars stir up war if he is not so moved as a god?

Before progressing further with these difficulties of connection, we must
turn to the line that follows these strange verses. For 1.50 is fundamentally
defective in our authoritative manuscripts (OQS), where we read *quod
superest ut uacuas auris*. The close of the line was presumably lost late in the
poem's transmission, owing to damage to the corner of 2^r of the archetype,
which page the verse ended.[31] An early correction in O, apparently made
by the Anglo-Saxon or Irish scholar Dungal in the early ninth century,
deleted the otiose and unmetrical *ut* to restore the opening *quod super est
uacuas auris*. This is doubtless correct, but how should we complete the
line, introducing a term that can be modified by *semotum* in the following
line? Since only Venus has been addressed prior to this point, and since
1.50–61 must refer to the didactic addressee of the poem (who cannot of
course be Venus *in statu pupillari*), it has often been supposed that
Memmius must have been mentioned in the lost portion of 1.50.[32] To
remedy this loss, his name has been introduced by emendation since the
Quattrocento. In a number of (unauthoritative) Renaissance manuscripts
(most notably LF), and consequently in the earliest printed editions, we
find the line *quod super est uacuas aures mihi Memmius et te*. Although *te* is
unobjectionable with *semotum* (51), the use of nominative *Memmius* as a
vocative – a licence unattested in Lucretius – is vanishingly unlikely. The
same problem applies to the conjecture found in other Renaissance manuscripts (AB), *quod super est quaeso uacuas mihi Memmius auris*, and that of
the Juntine edition (1512), *quod super est uacuas mihi quaeso Memmius*

---

[31] Butterfield 2013: 300.

[32] As Lachmann 1850 stated ad loc.: 'ut poeta a Venere orationem ad Memmium ne nomine quidem
      appellatum deflecteret fieri nullo modo potuit.'

aures, both of which also require the emendation of *semotum* to *semotus*.[33] In fact, we do not find the introduction of the expected vocative *Memmi* (as used nine times elsewhere in the poem) until the mid-nineteenth century, when Lachmann suggested *quod super est uacaus auris animumque age, Memmi*. Imperatival *age*, however, is without parallel outside the first foot of Lucretius' hexameters – and forms part of the collocation *nunc age* in all fifteen instances. More probable was the suggestion of Hermann Sauppe, *quod superest, Memmi, uacuas auris animumque*, although the conjecture still requires an explanation of how *Memmi* became corrupted into *ut* in the manuscript tradition.

The breakthrough in solving this crux came with the observation of Jacob Bernays that the *Scholia Veronensia* on Virgil provide a Lucretian citation at *G.* 3.3 (*cetera quae uacuas tenuissent carmina mentes*): uacuas mentes *scribentum intellegendum: sic Lucretius* uacuas aures animumque sagacem. accipitur et uacuas otiosas.[34] Although no such verse ending is preserved in our manuscripts of the *DRN*, the lines form both a metrically and logically sound conclusion to the defective verse 1.50: *quod super est uacuas auris animumque sagacem*. Elsewhere in the poem, Lucretius speaks positively of an *animus sagax* (1.402, 2.840, 4.912),[35] which would be a crucial attribute for Memmius when digesting the Epicurean curriculum.[36] Some critics have suggested that the *Scholia Veronensia* here instead mis-report a different Lucretian verse, 4.912: *tu mihi da tenuis auris animumque sagacem*. However, the fact that the Virgilian scholia cite the Lucretian verse specifically for the word *uacuas*, which is subsequently glossed as *otiosas*, renders it as good as certain that the quotation originally contained such an adjective;[37] it would be poor method indeed to suppose that Lucretius originally wrote *uacuas* for *tenuis* at 4.912. The credentials of the *Scholia* are good: they cite Lucretius on four occasions and their transmitted text is generally accurate.[38] If, as is supposed, they are a fourth-

---

[33] There is nothing to commend in Lambinus' introduction of a more exotic vocative: *quod super est uacuas aures mihi Memmiada et te.*

[34] '(*other songs that would have captivated unpreoccupied minds*): i.e. the *unpreoccupied minds* of writers: thus Lucretius writes *unpreoccupied ears and a keen intelligence. Unpreoccupied* means "at rest."'

[35] At 1.402–3, in particular, Lucretius states that he need give only a few examples to support his case because Memmius' (or the general reader's) *animus sagax* will allow them to do the rest of the intellectual work. Deufert (1996: 38–9) after Vahlen (1877: 479–80) thinks *sagacem* inappropriate with *uacuas auris*.

[36] *semotum* therefore has full participial force in 51.

[37] Lucretius also uses *uacuus* in a similar sense at 2.46 (*uacuum pectus*).

[38] See further Butterfield 2013: 72–3. In support of the possibility of direct access to the poem, it is worth noting that the *Scholia Veronensia* are able to cite verse 1.92 *ad Aen.* 12.718, which does not appear elsewhere in the indirect tradition.

or fifth-century compilation that drew upon the Virgilian scholarship of Aemilius Asper (first or second century AD), there is no reason to doubt that they had access to an appreciably superior text than what is preserved in the direct transmission of the *DRN*. The particularly prominent position of this quoted line – effectively the first words of the Epicurean lesson proper – would have made it especially accessible to the scholiastic community. We therefore have this late Virgilian compilation to thank for providing the largest supplement (i.e. of two and a half feet) to the text of Lucretius from an indirect source.[39]

It emerges, then, that Memmius was not mentioned in the original form of 1.50. But since a wholly unmarked transfer from Venus to Memmius remains impossible, it follows that he must have been addressed at some point beforehand. Further support for this conclusion is provided by the formula *quod superest* (50).[40] Lucretius uses this phrase twenty-two times in the poem, in a manner that is relatively clear-cut: when it does not mean literally 'what remains' (1.921, 2.183, 3.905, 4.195, 5.206) or 'what is more' (2.546), its role is either to resume a sentence after a subordinate clause,[41] or to continue a broader argument by introducing a new sentence on the same theme;[42] in two cases (both in Book 6: 91, 906), it introduces a new topic. While it is therefore not impossible that *quod superest* at 1.50 begins a new sentence and ushers in a new subject, it seems inconceivable that this casual formula could fudge the *non sequitur* of invoking Memmius' keen mental application after Venus' godly detachment. Much more probable is that *quod superest* continues a longer sentence, in whose prior half (now lost) Memmius was first addressed as pupil.

* * *

Faced with the problems presented by both 44–9 and 50, it is impossible to conclude that the text as transmitted is what Lucretius intended. In fact, between the late fifteenth and the early twentieth century, almost no one sought to preserve the text in this fashion. Nevertheless, in the 1930s Otto

---

[39] Emendations made subsequently to Bernays' discovery can therefore be disregarded: Goebel: *quod super est uacuas auris nobis animumque*; Munro: *quod super est uacuas auris corque, inclute Memmi*; Plasberg: *quod super est et tu uacuas aures animumque*; Diels: *quod super est, Gai, uacuas auris animumque*; Schadewaldt: *quod super est tu da uacuas auris animumque*; Bitterlich-Willmann: *quod superest nobis uacuas auris animumque*; Orth: *quod superest, rebus uacuas auris animumque*; Canfora: *quod superest et tu uacuas auris animumque*; García Calvo: *quod super est tu te in uacuas, mi Memmiada, auris*; Flores: *quod super est, Memmi, uacuas aures mihi teque.*

[40] The analysis of Woltjer 1896 remains the most detailed contribution on this point.

[41] 2.39, after *quoniam*; 2.491 and 6.1000 after *ubi*; 5.64 after a parenthetic explanation.

[42] 3.350, 4.595, 768, 1283, 5.261, 772, 1241, 6.219, 423.

Regenbogen (1932: 69–77) suggested a compromise position, namely that
Lucretius, after composing the opening hymn of his poem (1–43), wished
to give an alternative and true account of the gods, of which 1.44–9 would
form a part.[43] However, he argues, Lucretius was prevented by death from
reworking the poem's opening so as to make the lines fit. The resulting
conclusion is that the poet wrote neither more nor less than what survives –
even if it does not reflect his ultimate desires. While this is not entirely
impossible, the suggestion is unappealing: Lucretius would have had to
incorporate a great deal of additional material to bridge the gap in a
satisfactory manner, and all such doctrinal clarification would have
deprived the proem of its force and postponed unsatisfactorily the introduction of Memmius and Epicurus.

In the same year 1932, a more remarkable defence of the verses in their
transmitted location was made by Paul Friedländer, who argued that 44–9
were so congruent with the surrounding lines that no lacuna could be
suspected.[44] Given this remarkable claim, it is unsurprising that on closer
inspection his argument – both in this initial article and in its later, fuller
account (Friedländer 1939) – is woefully inadequate. Rather vaguely,
Friedländer claims that the logical role of *enim* is tied to 38–40 – 'and
ultimately even to 29–32' (1939: 372, n. 9a – evidently a late addition).
Astoundingly, he argues that there is no opposition between 1.44–9 and
what precedes, for which he only offers the observation that *pace* of 45 may
echo *pacem* of 40. But this is to overlook the crucial distinction in the
species of peace under consideration: Lucretius prays to Venus to allow
peace in the Republic and suppress civil strife; the peace of the gods is a
state of divine *ataraxia*, unconnected to any temporal or transient affairs
outside the *intermundia*. The difference is not just one of scale but of
nature.[45] Friedländer also must suppose that 1.50 (for which he does not
offer a text) follows on seamlessly from 44–9. Despite the rhetorical
bluster, no cogent argument is offered to support his claim that verses

[43] A brief announcement of this theory was reported in *Humanistische Gymnasium* 41 (1930): 100.
A similar idea had been floated by Giussani 1896–8 ad loc. – who wondered whether the verses
were 'un richiamo marginale' – but was rejected on the ground that 'il contrasto colla precedente
invocazione è così vivo, che non pare possa esser casuale'. The same idea was later suggested as a
possible alternative by Bignone 1919: 433, and subsequently supported by M. F. Smith in the
revised Loeb (Rouse and Smith 1975), who stated ad loc.: 'In view of this manifest lack of revision,
it seems unnecessary and unwise to assume a lacuna either before or after the lines.' Nevertheless,
the facing English translation precedes the lines with '[I pray for peace,]'.
[44] Friedländer 1932: 43: 'vv. 44–49 suo loco et uno tenore cum ceteris a Lucretio positos esse, ita ut
neque antea neque postea ullum lacunae indicium iure deprehendatur.'
[45] This objection was first made by Büchner 1936: 105.

1.44–9 'are the systematic culmination of the whole prooemium which without them would miss not alone [*sic*] its poetic unity but also its purpose as a piece of Epicurean doctrine' (1939: 370). For this we get no argument beyond the claim that *enim* (44) 'is the symbol of his conviction that this harmonizing of what after all is discrepant had succeeded κατὰ τὸ δυνατὸν ποιητῇ' (ibid.: 372).

Despite the weakness of this defence, retention of the lines without further alteration found a partial – if remarkably varied – following. In the immediate aftermath of Friedländer's first article Martin supported the choice in his Teubner (1934);[46] among later editors only Orth (1961), Gigon (1971) and Piazzi (2011) have likewise made no change to the standard text; García Calvo (1997) and Flores (2002) retain the lines but introduce the improbable *Memmi* into 1.50. Among scholars not charged with producing a text, a number in the past three decades have sought to defend the lines as transmitted.[47] Several of these efforts were doomed to failure by their lamentable disregard of the actual problems that need to be tackled: Clay (1983: 94–5)[48] and Minyard (1985: 36–7)[49] offer nothing of substance;[50] O'Hara (2007: 62), after clearly outlining some of the problems the lines cause, nevertheless embraces the inconsistency with the undefended claim that 'lines 44–9 do work well in their context'. In fact, his supposed 'third way' of reading the lines (62–4) merely frustrates by appealing to a current critical tolerance for textual inconsistency and a supposed pattern of misdirection at the outset of epic poems. The most recent statement in favour of the lines, by Fratantuono (2015: 20), is opaque.[51]

More productive has been the philosophical attempt to read the proem not as a true prayer made in good faith but as an elaborate exercise in

---

[46] However, in his four subsequent editions he transposed the lines that follow: see n. 23.

[47] Prior to this period, sporadic scholarly support had been given to the lines – mostly without treating the problems head-on – by Barra 1952: 18–21, 1984; Elder 1954: 98–100; Arnaldi 1957: 182; Grimal 1957; Kleve 1966: 91–3; Pasoli 1970: 374; Bollack 1978: 32–5; Marchetta 1989.

[48] '[Lucretius] introduced a foreign conception of divinity which destroys the very motivation for prayer ... We are present here at the collision of two worlds.'

[49] 'Lucretius affords a brief vision of his goal [to create 'a different meaning for the opening of the poem'] in verses 44–9, designed to shock the reader into a confusion about the coherence of this assertion with the preceding hymn.'

[50] Yet more perversely, Minadeo 1968: 241–3 sought to dispel the problem by arguing that 1.44–9 are 'not a formal theological statement' and need not be taken as doctrine. However, when the verses reappear at 2.646–51, he regarded them as 'unmistakably a direct statement of Epicurean theology'. The same approach, which involves the special pleading that *semota* and *seiuncta* need to be read temporally ('when removed and far disjoined'), was repeated in Minadeo 1969: 117–18.

[51] 'We might consider that these lines are genuine and intended for this place in the opening movements of the poets [*sic*], and that they are deliberate in their shocking import in context.'

allegory. Lest a reader fail to understand the foregoing hymn and its misleading imagery, it has been supposed that verses 44–9 represent a purposefully placed 'Lucretian palinode' or 'Epicurean corrective'. Sedley (1989a; 1998, Chapter 1) argued that Lucretius' desire to emulate Empedocles in the proem of 1–43 was so strong as to lead him into territory that required an instant and clear correction:[52] 'The connexion of thought could no doubt have been made clearer; but I would be reluctant to rob Lucretius of this important Epicurean modification of Empedoclean theology.'[53] For all its awkwardness, Sedley finds cause to leave the text unchanged: '[t]he sudden reversal is too characteristic of Lucretius to be lightly dismissed' (1998: 27).[54] If this really was the intended aim of Lucretius, the result is an outstanding failure.

If any of these arguments for retaining the text without change were convincing, the poem's proem would not be just a disconcerting and illogical opening to a work that proclaims the clarity of its reason and argument, but also an astoundingly awkward start to a graduated didactic poem. It would surely be bizarre for the reader to be wrong-footed at so early a stage, especially if they (Memmius or another) are not expected to be already versed in Epicureanism. To quote O'Hara (albeit against his case): 'How can we have a didactic poem whose prologue can be understood only by those in the know, those who do not need teaching?' (2007: 60). Quite so: we must not accept the blasé indifference of many scholars to the absurd progression of the text – not least in so early and prominent a position of the poem.

It follows that the text cannot stand as transmitted. To remedy the problems outlined above, there are five possible responses to the text. These are set out below, with a brief summary of scholarly support:

(i)   The verses are Lucretian but there is a lacuna before 1.44 alone:
      Romanes (1935: 7) suggested that only one verse had been lost at this point, and offered *at quoniam, Memmi, me nec dea nec deus audit* as an example of 'some such bald recantation of 1–43'. This view – albeit with no suggestion of the content and size of the

---

[52] The idea of Lucretius losing his head in a poetic fervour before regaining control was advanced in brief by Perelli 1969: 169.

[53] Sedley 1998: 27. In the original version of this chapter Sedley wrote 'very reluctant' (1989a: 291).

[54] Courtney 2001: 205 has argued, rather mischievously, that the lines are retained because of philosophers' natural proclivity to complex arguments: 'such scholars are in many cases professional students of philosophy … and they like to devise ingenious solutions to philosophical problems'.

lacuna – was also adopted by Leonard and Smith (1942) and Cochez (1954) without argument.[55]

(ii)   The verses are Lucretian but there is a lacuna after 1.49 alone:

Bailey, despite deleting the verses in both editions of his Oxford Text (1900, 1922²), eventually reached the conclusion in his commentary (1947) that the lines should be retained, but that a lacuna was required after 1.49. His defence (1940: 288) was that verses 1.44–9 appear to be a 'suspension of thought' from 40, interrupted by the tangential remark at 41–3. A similar solution was also proposed by Giancotti (1978: 157–234, at 217–25; see also his edition of 1994).[56]

(iii)   The verses are Lucretian but there are lacunae both before 1.44 and after 1.49:

This view was first advanced by Bignone (1919: 430–1). Rejecting the idea that the verses were an interpolation, he instead supposed that they formed part of an explanation of how the gods' peace could bring similar peace to Memmius. In his more mature summary of his theory, he was explicit (1945: II.429, 441–2) that a lacuna must stand before 1.44; he implicitly supported a lacuna before 1.50. This view has only since been followed in the selective text and commentary of Paratore and Pizzani (1960).

(iv)   The verses were not written here by Lucretius, and 1.50 should follow 1.43:

This view, although implied by editors since the mid-nineteenth century who have bracketed the verses, has not been explicitly supported in argument. Given the impossibility of Memmius' being addressed without clear statement of the change of addressee, this alteration is only possible if a different text is read in 1.50.[57] This was the decision of Diels (1923–4), Valentí (1961), Müller (1975), Brown (1984) and Deufert (1996: 32–40, 2019), who all restored *Memmi* to that verse. Büchner (1966) differed in following

---

[55] At the close of a tortuous footnote considering various possibilities, Salemme 1980: 66–7 n. 24 suggests without further clarification that this may be the least improbable solution.

[56] A strange compromise was reached by Cole 1998: 11–12. While granting that the lines were 'obviously composed for [2.646–51]', he argues that if verses 46 and 48 are deleted, the remaining four lines 44–5, 47, 49 can stand without any preceding lacuna. He also suggests that 31–40 and 44–9 are authorial doublets, attributing peace either to Venus alone or to all divinities respectively. No argument is given for how the transmitted text came into being.

[57] Mussehl 1912: 52–7 argues that Bernays' supplement to 1.50 can stand without a preceding lacuna by supposing that the proem was written in two quite distinct phases (1–43, 50–135) that were not satisfactorily unified.

Bitterlich-Willmann's emendation (*quod superest nobis uacuas auris animumque*), thus avoiding direct mention of *Memmi* on the rather perverse ground that actually signalling the change in addressee would be superfluous ('satis esse videtur Memmium poetae – cf. 26 et 42 – semper ante oculos versari').[58]

(v)   The verses were not written here by Lucretius, and a lacuna must be posited between 1.43 and 1.50:[59]

This is instead the common view of those who have rejected the verses since Lachmann (1850), who declared that a 'lector frustra curiosus'[60] had transferred them here from their proper position in Book 2. This solution was followed among editors by Bernays (1852), Bockemüller (1873–4), Munro (1864, 1886[4]), Bailey (1900, 1922[2]), Van der Valk (1903), Merrill (1907), Ernout (1924) and Rouse (1924);[61] Brieger (1894, 1899[2]) posited a lacuna too but supposed that verses 50–61 were out of place. Among scholars this view has been adopted by Schmid (1938: 346), Deichgräber (1940: 56–7), Schilling (1954: 347–8), Müller (1959: 121 and 124), Pizzani (1959: 72–5),[62] Asmis (1982: 470), Courtney (1987: 11; 2001: 201–6), Gale (1994: 215–17)[63] and Hutchinson (2001: 150 n. 2); Volk (2010: 129 n. 10) leaves the question open.

The argument thus far can steer our choice between these options. Given the effectively certain restoration of line 50 from the *Scholia Veronensia*, options (ii) and (iv) are impossible, as Memmius must have been addressed prior to that line. The inconcinnity of verses 44–9, and the utter illogicality of *enim* (44), render the prospect of no transitional verses, i.e. option (i), impossible. As for option (iii), it would be a singular and remarkable feature of transmission that a lacuna has chanced to occur both before 1.44 and after 1.49, in each case removing an amount of text

[58] A small number of modern scholars have agreed that 1.44–9 were not written here by Lucretius but have reverted to the solution of transposition: Ritschl (and Barwick): 1–43, 136–45, 50–148; Bockemüller: 1–43, 62–101, 136–45, 155, 50–61, 104–35; Brieger: 1–43, 62–79, [lacuna], 136–45, 80–101, 102–35; Giussani: 1–43, 62–79, [lacuna], 136–45, 50–61, 80–135.

[59] The argument of Friedländer 1939: 372 that '[i]f the six verses are dropped, the sense of the address to the addressee becomes very superficial' seems to ignore the possibility of positing a lacuna.

[60] I take this characteristically laconic expression to mean a reader who was interested enough to juxtapose Lucretius' doctrines with his opening lines but who was acting in vain if he thought it was restoring a better text.

[61] Rouse's note ad loc. states that the lines 'have taken the place of verses in which L. passed from Venus to Memmius'.

[62] Pizzani 1959: 171 also conceded the possibility that Lucretius added the verses in his text at this point with the aim (left unfulfilled) of developing them later.

[63] Gale nevertheless leaves open solution (iii) as a possibility.

(of presumably multiple lines) that happened to be self-contained sentences or clauses, and leaving behind the self-contained passage of verses 44–9. Such a collocation of chance errors, occurring so early in the work, seems vanishingly unlikely.[64] An alternative version of (iii), namely that Lucretius intended to add text before and after 1.44–9 but failed to do so because of his premature death, cannot be ruled out. However, although it seems beyond reasonable doubt that the poem is incomplete, it is striking that there is no example of such clear incongruence as this in the work, and remarkable that such a manifestly problematic fragment was left unaltered by either Lucretius himself or some conscientious admirer who revised the poem for posthumous publication.

The only option that remains is (v), i.e. to regard 1.44–9 as verses that Lucretius did not write there, and which have somehow ousted material that he did.[65] If this conclusion is indeed correct, how could such verses appear in the text? Suggestions of active interpolation – i.e. of a subsequent figure's inserting lines into the poem as Lucretius' own – are improbable and without a convincing parallel in the poem.[66] Most attempts to explain the transference have tended to see it as an informal attempt to undermine or ridicule the poet, rather than some freak accident. Apparently the first suggestion of this kind was made by Isaac Vossius, who (in the 1660s or 1670s) wrote alongside 1.44–9 in his copy of Faber (1662: Trin. Coll. Cam. Adv. b 13 3): *non nemo eos* [=2.646–51] *huc transtulerit, ut ostenderet Lucretium sibi adversari, qui cum deos mortalia non curare affirmet, Venerem tamen invocet.*[67] Indeed, given the physical separation from the middle of Book 2, the conclusion does seem unavoidable that these lines were moved here by another hand.[68]

---

[64] We may note that the first widely accepted lacuna in modern editions of the poem occurs after 1.860.

[65] This is the explanation given by Courtney 1987: 11–12.

[66] For a more detailed discussion see the arguments of Butterfield 2014 against Müller 1975 and Deufert 1996.

[67] 'Some individual transferred them here in order to show Lucretius in conflict with himself, since he states that the gods do not care about mortal affairs, yet he invokes Venus.'

[68] In a similar vein, Lachmann 1850 claimed ad loc.: 'quos versus ... lector frustra curiosus in hunc locum transtulisse videretur'; Harder 1882, in his *index* to Lachmann's commentary, describes this figure as an 'interpolator irrisor qui poetam reprehendens versus adscripsit' (also including 3.412, 743 and 5.1344–6, which are generally accepted as genuine by modern editors), in contrast to the separate work of the supposed 'interpolator philosophus'; Diels 1923–4 says that they arose 'ex antiqui interpretis commentario interposita ut contradictio poetae argueretur'; Fischer 1924: 69–70 supposed that the verses were copied by a 'vir stoicu[s] vel christianu[s]' in the second century AD 'ut demonstretur ad oculos omnium hos sex versus non modo convenire atque congruere cum illis prooemii versibus, sed potius contrarios esse'; finally, Büchner 1966 supposes that they arose 'ex annotatione cuiusdam malevoli et contraria percontantis'. This interpolation was supported

It is highly probable that the verses arise from the marginal copying by an ancient reader of 2.646–51, Lucretius' most direct account of the nature of Epicurean gods in the poem. Whether this was prompted by a desire to gloss the ideal version of Epicurean *pax* (e.g., *pacem* in 1.40), or *semotum a curis* (1.51), or the *summa caeli ratio deumque* (1.54), or rather to contrast Lucretius' remarkable opening to the poem with his subsequent and pellucid assertion of Epicurean doctrine, we cannot know. Whatever the circumstances of this personal annotation, these marginal verses were later (between the third and seventh centuries) taken to be mistakenly omitted verses of Lucretius, and were inserted into the text, perhaps being wrongly taken as a replacement of the (now lost) verses they flanked. There are thus not two lacunae – itself improbable – but only one to be posited, produced not by chance omission on the scribe's part but by the incorrect belief that a marginal annotation was designed to correct and replace the text alongside which it stood.

To close this survey, we should inspect two further fields for evidence, the indirect tradition and the *capitula* transmitted in the Lucretian tradition. First, then: can any insight be drawn from those authors who cite Lucretius and thereby preserve his verses by distinct lines of transmission? Given their poignancy and beauty, it is unsurprising that verses 1.44–9 = 2.646–51 are cited, in full or in part, by several authors of late antiquity: Lactantius *De Ira Dei* 8.1 cites all six verses; 1.44–7 = 2.646–9 are cited by 'Lactantius Placidus' *ad* Stat. *Theb.* 3.659; 1.48 = 2.650 is cited by Servius *ad Aen.* 12.794; finally, 1.49 = 2.651 is cited by ps.-Acro *ad Hor. Sat.* 1.5.101 and Servius *ad Buc.* 8.17 and *ad Aen.* 6.376. Frustratingly, however, all of these citations lack any reference to a given book of the poem, leaving open whether they came from Book 2 or their duplicated location in Book 1. However, the verse 1.49 = 2.651 is also cited twice by Nonius (c. 400 AD). Although no book is quoted for its appearance at 657L, a reference is given at 382L: for a crux as ill-starred as this, it is perhaps inevitable that each branch of the Nonian stemma gives a different reading: *lib. I* is read by Lindsay's a but *lib. II* by L (the most reliable manuscript). Faced with this, we must conclude either that in one

by G. P. Goold, albeit in his marginalia: in his copy of Bailey 1922 he glosses 1.44–9 with the comment 'plana interpolatio'. In his major work on Lucretian interpolation, Deufert 1996: 40 regards the verses as a 'Randglosse' prompted by *summa caeli ratio deumque* at verse 54: a subsequent scribe took the marginal verses to be an accidental omission and incorporated them into the only place that seemed possible. This interpolation is duly classed under his 'category D', 'Ergänzung, Erweiterung, Erklärung eines philosophischen Lesers'.

branch *I* is a corruption of *II* (a common enough error of haplography), or that in the other branch *II* is a dittographical corruption of *I*, and that Nonius, working nearly half a millennium after Lucretius, could already find a text where these verses were inserted in Book 1. Since the evidence suggests that Nonius' Lucretian source was independent of the line of transmission that spawned OQS,[69] the former option squares much more neatly with the sum total of evidence available.

Turning to the second field, we find one final clue about what has happened in the *capitulum* that appears in the text before 1.44 (Figure 2). One hundred and seventy-two casual subject headings or *capitula* intersperse the manuscripts of the poem, which typically summarize the contents of the verses that immediately follow.[70] These were added marginally by (probably two) readers in late antiquity and later became incorporated into the text transmitted by our Carolingian manuscripts. The first author, evidently familiar with mainstream Epicurean texts, recorded a number of quotations in Greek, including the beginning of *KD* 1 before 2.646–51: τὸ μακάριον καὶ ἄφθαρτον.[71] This summary presumably stood in the margin alongside these verses at the time someone chose to copy them into the margin of Book 1 alongside 1.43 ... 50.[72] But whoever added 1.44–9 marginally (perhaps the second marginal annotator) was not sufficiently familiar with Greek to reproduce its script, and instead converted it into Latin letters. Either he or subsequent scribes corrupted the text further (compare Figures 2 and 3): *toma carion caeapitraton*.[73] If the verses were placed by Lucretius in Book 1, it is near impossible to explain why the first *capitulum* for these lines would be in Latin script and defective (Figure 2), but the second *capitulum* for their appearance in Book 2 – some 1,700 lines later – would be in accurate Greek letters (Figure 3). Much more probable is that the Greek *capitulum*, competently entered at Book 2, was indeed copied and banalized into its new marginal location in Book 1 by a later hand. If so, we must conclude that, later in transmission, both it and the verses beneath it were incorporated into the body text of the poem's

---

[69] See Butterfield 2013: 61–7.   [70] This summarizes chapter 3 of Butterfield 2013.

[71] This Greek appears correctly in majuscules, save for the corruption of the first two alphas into deltas. This same error also occurs in S, who writes the third and fourth alphas as lambdas; Q omitted the title for the rubricator who never came.

[72] Whatever conclusion one reaches about 1.44–9, it is impossible, as suggested by Friedländer 1939: 372, that this preceding *capitulum* was authored by Lucretius.

[73] The same corruptions are preserved by S; as usual, the *capitulum* was not entered by the rubricator in Q.

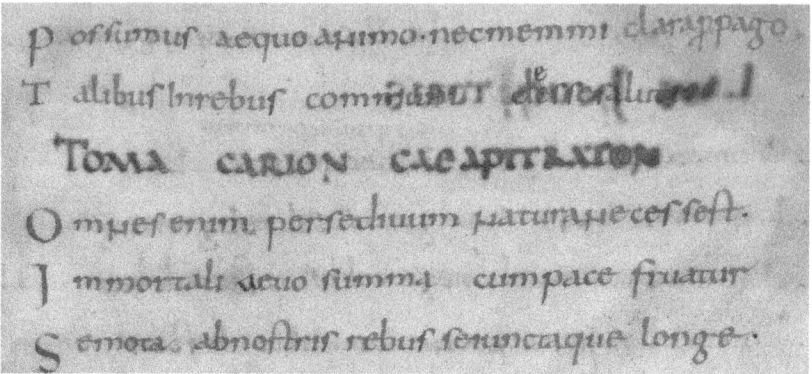

Figure 2   Leiden University Libraries, Voss. Lat. F 30 (Codex Oblongus): 2ʳ
(detail showing *DRN* 1.42–6).
Reproduced with the permission of Leiden University Libraries

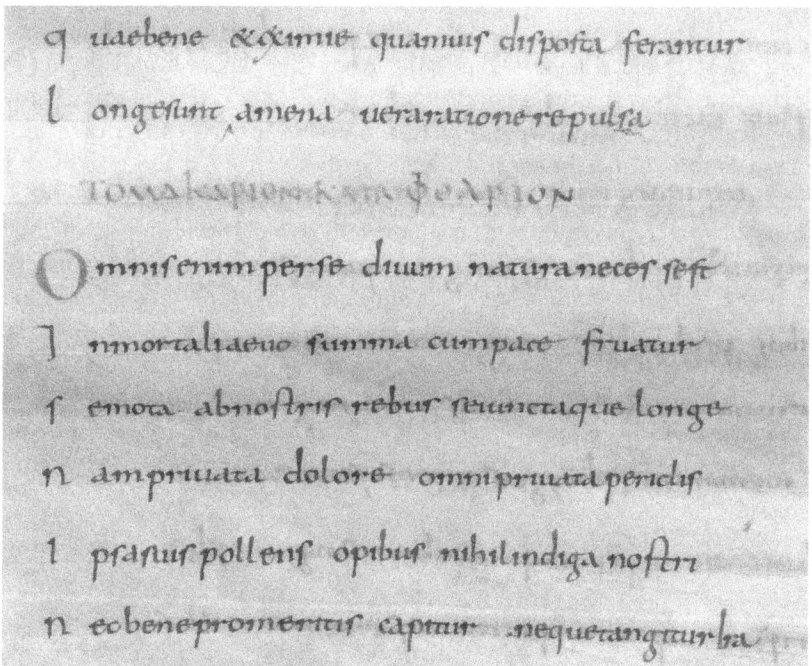

Figure 3   Leiden University Libraries, Voss. Lat. F 30 (Codex Oblongus): 45ᵛ
(detail showing *DRN* 2.644–51).
Reproduced with the permission of Leiden University Libraries

proem, like most, or perhaps even all other, marginal annotations in the work.[74]

*   *   *

This problem is located deep within tricky territory where it is very difficult to reach any firm conclusion. Nevertheless, although certainty is impossible, the evidence available, when scrutinized in its totality, points conclusively against the transmitted text (especially once 1.50 has been restored from the *Scholia Veronensia*) being correct. Either (v) some (half a dozen?) lines have been lost in transmission, ousted by the unwarranted inclusion of 1.44–9, or – much less probably – (iii) Lucretius did not live to write the (perhaps very many) transitionary verses that he intended for this crucial phase of the proem. If, as I have argued, (v) reflects the truth of the matter, some questions will always remain unanswerable. How many verses have been lost? How does *quod superest* develop what was stated? How was Memmius first directly addressed? At what point did Lucretius intend for the conventional theology of the proem first to be revealed as false to his readers? Thankfully, an editor of the poem is at liberty to leave these interesting but irresoluble speculations at the feet of his readers.

---

[74] By the time of the archetype, two *capitula* had been mistakenly written as if Lucretian verses (1.41, 705); contrariwise, seven Lucretian verses were written as *capitula* (2.42–3, 3.672a, 759, 805, 905, 949); O seemingly extended this error, by mistaking thirteen further Lucretian verses as *capitula* (1.11, 411, 2.95, 502, 508, 608, 809, 887, 909, 962, 1012, 1023, 1112), a mistake that Q made only once (1.565).

PART II

Lucretius and his Readers

CHAPTER 2

Reading the 'Implied Author' in Lucretius' De Rerum Natura

Nora Goldschmidt

In his *Chronicle* for the year 94 BC, Jerome provides the following short notice about the author of the *De Rerum Natura* (*DRN*):[1]

> Titus Lucretius poeta nascitur: qui postea amatorio poculo in furorem versus, cum aliquot libros per intervalla insaniae conscripsisset, quos postea Cicero emendavit, propria se manu interfecit anno aetatis XLIIII.
>
> The poet Titus Lucretius was born. In later life he was sent mad by a love-potion; having composed a number of books in the intervals of his madness, later edited by Cicero, he died by his own hand at the age of 43.

Jerome's miniature biography – the only biographical document about Lucretius that survives from antiquity – has long haunted the reception of Lucretius' poem.[2] Supplemented by an expanded fake *Life* originally believed to have been based on ancient sources known as the *Vita Borgiana*, which added, among other details, a 'wicked woman' (*femina improba*) behind the *poculum amatorium*, Jerome's terse *Life* swelled into a full-blown biographical tradition:[3] Lucretius' wife, 'Lucilia', piqued at the lack of attention she received from her husband (she 'found her master cold', as Tennyson put it), secretly administered a love potion which drove the poet mad and led to his eventual suicide.[4] This story has, as Martha

---

I am very grateful to the European Research Council for their generous funding of *Living Poets: A New Approach to Ancient Poetry* at Durham University, which helped to support the research for this chapter.

[1] Jerome, *Chronicon* ad Ol. 171.1–3 (96–94 BC): text Rostagni 1944, 58–9.

[2] Donatus, Jerome's teacher, also states briefly in his *Vita Vergilii* (6) that Virgil assumed the *toga virilis* on the day Lucretius died.

[3] On the *Vita Borgiana*, discovered at the end of the nineteenth century, see Fabbri 1984; Solaro 2000; Palmer 2014: 101–2.

[4] Tennyson, 'Lucretius' (1868), l.2. The name 'Lucilia' (which also appears in Chaucer's prologue to 'The Wife of Bath's Tale') seems to appear first in Walter Map's twelfth-century *De nugis curialium* (*On Courtly Fripperies*), IV.3: Solaro 2000: 14–16. On the thriving tradition of lives of Lucretius in the Renaissance see further Palmer 2014: 140–91; on the nineteenth-century biofictional reception of the *DRN* see Goldschmidt 2019: 130–55. An alternative version of Lucretius' biography, which takes its ultimate cue from a misread medieval scholion on Ovid's *Ibis*, features Lucretius' homosexual lover, Asterion: Solaro 1993: 60–3; Palmer 2014: 133.

Nussbaum aptly puts it, 'served for centuries as an informal blueprint for interpretation' of Lucretius' poem.[5] From early modern forgeries to Victorian poetry, from twentieth-century fiction to contemporary film, Lucretius' text has consistently been construed through the tale of its author's 'discomposed brain'.[6]

The image of the melancholy and suicidal author of the *DRN* has exercised a similar influence on scholarship on the poem. Textual problems suggest that Lucretius' poem was abruptly aborted, which has led several readers to seek biographical explanations for the state of the text. But the habit of psychologizing the author extends far beyond textual issues to fundamentally colour interpretations of the poem's content. In his canonical three-volume commentary, Cyril Bailey, for example, discerns an 'unnatural preoccupation' with suicide in the poem, which gives credit to the story of the poet's self-murder, finding the *DRN* itself 'not without confirmation' of 'the kind of pessimistic depression, which from time to time might lead to a "breakdown"' or psychopathological 'hallucination'.[7] Among historians, T. P. Wiseman similarly gives credence to Jerome's story, going several steps further to find in Lucretius' text other biographical tales to tell; since the imagery of the *DRN* evinces an intimate familiarity with herbs and potions, we might infer that Lucretius was probably a medic, or, since the poem is strikingly observant about the details of the sound of the saw, he may have been a carpenter.[8] At its most extreme, failing to engage with the poem in a way that is free from the bias of biography, this approach to the *DRN* could easily be dismissed, in Holford-Strevens' memorable words, as the 'failure of Lucretian biography'.[9] In a perpetual feedback loop, the story of Lucretius' life, and especially the state of his mind, originally inferred from the text itself,

---

[5] Nussbaum 1994: 141.
[6] For Lucretius' 'discomposed brain' see Matthew Arnold, 'On the modern element in literature', in Super 1960–77: 1.33. For fictional prose lives see, notably, Marcel Schwob's short story, 'Lucrèce', in *Vies imaginaires* (1896), and Luca Canali's novel, *Nei pleniluni sereni. Autobiografia immaginaria di Tito Lucrezio Caro* (1995). G. Maccioni's short film, *Cose Naturali* (2010), dramatizes a modern version of Lucretius' biography on screen. For the reception of Lucretius see, e.g., Reeve 2007; Priestman 2007; Passannante 2011; Greenblatt 2011; Palmer 2014; Norbrook, Harrison and Hardie 2015; Goldschmidt 2019: 130–55. See also the Introduction to this volume.
[7] Bailey 1947: 1.11: 'it is not difficult to imagine Lucretius suffering from a recurrent depression, which even had its influence on the "lucid intervals" in which his work was done'.
[8] Wiseman 1974: 40–3; 21–5. For Wiseman, '[t]here is no usable external evidence, only the picture we can get out of the poem itself. But with Lucretius that should be enough' (1974: 13). For defence of the factuality of Jerome's account see also, esp., Stampini 1896 with Bailey 1947: 1.8–9. On the tendency to read the *DRN* 'as a work betraying anxiety, melancholy, and even mental instability on the part of its author' see Gale 2007a: 3 n. 11.
[9] Holford-Strevens 2002: 23.

has – consciously or unconsciously – been applied in interpreting the poem, and, for Holford-Strevens and others, scholarship would do well to purge all remnants of this fallacious reading practice from the rightful analysis of the text.[10]

Yet rather than an abject 'failure' of biographical fact-finding, the biographical and psychological bias that has so marked the artistic and scholarly reception of the *DRN* for so long can, instead, be welcomed as a valid and fruitful strategy of reading. Though we might like to think that we can access a 'pure' version of the *DRN* free from the perceived psychological or biographical presence of the author, the text of the *DRN* itself fundamentally undercuts that aim, calling for just such a 'biased' reading. Written in a culture in which texts were regularly mined for evidence of the life of the poet, where biography was an established mode not only of reading texts but of writing them, there is an important sense in which the *DRN* itself is partially responsible for how we have tended to read the author in the text.[11] Rather than dismissing biographical and cognate readings of the poem, therefore, or, conversely, finding apparent 'facts' to defend them, this chapter explores the terms of that partial responsibility. Drawing on Wayne Booth's concept of the 'implied author' and its later developments, it examines the textually constructed author in the *DRN* – a construct which partly overlaps with, but also goes significantly beyond, the didactic *persona* – to explain the pervasive presence of the author that readers have so often found, and continue to find, in the dynamics of Lucretius' text.

The Textualization of the Author

In his seminal article on the *DRN*, Gian Biagio Conte crucially brought to the fore the presence in the poem of an 'implied reader'.[12] Drawing on the work of Wolfgang Iser, who defined the *impliziter Leser* not as an extra-textual figure existing in reality, but as a role constructed and defined implicitly in the text itself ('an expression of the role offered by the text

---

[10] Holford-Strevens 2002; Kenney 2014: 5, with Cherniss 1943 for the 'biographical fallacy' in the reading of classical texts.

[11] For biofictional receptions of Latin poetry in antiquity see Goldschmidt 2019: 10–21.

[12] 'Instructions for a Sublime Reader: Form of the Text and Form of the Addressee in Lucretius' *De rerum natura*' = Conte 1994: 1–34. Conte's essay was originally published in Italian as an introductory essay to Luca Canali's translation of Lucretius (= Conte 1990); some of the main ideas were foreshadowed earlier in Conte 1966.

[which] is in no way an abstraction derived from a real reader'),[13] Conte argued that 'the form of the text' and 'the form of the reader' in the *DRN* are one and the same. Independent of the poem's named addressee, Memmius, who is mentioned a mere eleven times in the poem, the reader of the *DRN* is constructed and defined by the text itself, regardless of any historical or biographical reality:

> Th[e] reader-addressee is a form of the text; it is the figure of the recipient as anticipated by the text. To this prefiguration of the reader all future, virtual readers must adapt themselves ... In short, the text's form and intentionality determine the reader's form.[14]

Formulated in the wake of a theoretical turn away from authors towards texts and readers, Conte's essay emerges from a critical milieu that sought to leave behind the fruitless search for the author's putative 'intention', emphasizing textuality over reality and readers over authors.[15] As Roland Barthes famously put it, 'the birth of the reader must be at the cost of the death of the Author',[16] and, for Conte, the textually constructed reader in the *DRN* is the fundamental driving force behind how we ought to interpret the poem, so much so that the figure of the author himself disappears: the poem's 'addressees are not only other people (who must be taught) but also the poet himself (who has already learned and now becomes a missionary)'.[17]

   Yet the co-option of the author as reader has its drawbacks. Dispensing with the author, 'that somewhat decrepit deity of the old criticism',[18] has done much to push textual interpretation away from the tenacious 'intentional fallacy' that has continued often detrimentally to haunt classical scholarship in particular, and which Conte, among others, has been instrumental in dissipating.[19] But once released from the concept of a knowable author 'out there', the critical pendulum can also swing the other way. As Seán Burke eloquently formulated it, 'the concept of the author is never more alive than when pronounced dead'.[20] The idea of the 'author' fulfils a primary desire, even a necessity, for the reader. As Roland Barthes himself conceded:

[13] Iser 1978: 36.
[14] Conte 1994: xx. For similar readings of the constructed 'implied reader' as 'a creation of the poem itself' see, e.g., Clay 1983: 212 (212–25); Volk 2002: 74.
[15] For Conte's broader theoretical position during roughly the same period see Conte 1986.
[16] Barthes 1995: 130.   [17] Conte 1994: 8.   [18] Barthes 1974: 211.   [19] Feeney 1989: 206.
[20] Burke 1992: 7.

It is not that the Author may not 'come back' in the Text, in his text, but he then does so as a 'guest' ... [H]is life is no longer the origin of his fictions but a fiction contributing to his work; there is a reversion of the work on to the life (and no longer the contrary) [il y a réversion de l'œuvre sur la vie (et non plus le contraire)].[21]

Especially given the absence of external biographical sources for a text like the *DRN*, we cannot historicize the 'real' author, with the result that, more than in most texts, the 'reversion of the text on to the life' is complete. As the reception history of the poem energetically attests, we yield to our desire for the presence of the author by finding him, like Conte's reader, in the text itself, a construct independent of objective biographical reality.

It is in this context that the concept of the textually constructed 'implied author' can be particularly useful in interpreting the *DRN*. The term is primarily associated with Wayne Booth's 1961 study of the novel form, *The Rhetoric of Fiction*.[22] As Booth saw it, it is irrelevant whether the 'implied author' corresponds with the real author 'out there': what matters is essentially the textual presence of the author, which – like Conte's (or Iser's) reader – is constructed by the text. As Booth explains: the 'implied author is always distinct from the "real man" – whatever we may take him to be – who creates ... a "second self", as he creates his work'.[23] Moreover, more than simply a guest appearance in the text, Booth's main aim is to account for our sense of a sensibility behind the text as a whole. Not simply the 'narrator', or *persona* or the 'I' of the novel or poem, the 'implied author' is the sense that we extrapolate from the totality of the text:

> 'Persona', 'mask', and 'narrator' are sometimes used, but they more commonly refer to the speaker in the work who is after all only one of the elements created by the implied author and who may be separated from him ... Our sense of the implied author includes not only the extractable meanings but also the moral and emotional content ... It includes, in short, the intuitive apprehension of a completed artistic whole ... that which is expressed by the total form.[24]

Booth was heavily criticized in the 1980s and 1990s, when the postmodern deconstruction of authorship was at its peak, for not being radical enough: the implied author, his critics argued, was no less exclusionary a concept

---

[21] Barthes 1971: 161.
[22] Booth 1961. The concept is defended and expanded to poetry in Booth 2005. For a comprehensive history of the concept and its later reception see Kindt and Müller 2008 and Schmid 2009, and for a summary of and contribution to recent debates, see Richardson 2011: 1–10.
[23] Booth 1961: 151.   [24] Booth 1961: 73–4.

than the notion of the 'Author', perpetuating the illusion of a world *hors texte* peopled by human beings as whole entities with clear boundaries. Moreover, there is, Booth's critics argued, a contradiction in his thinking: how can a textual construct made up of norms of the text as a whole also be the sender in a communicative model of sending and receiving a message?[25] Yet the 'implied author' need not be seen as an ontological fact embedded in the text for all time, but rather as a mode of reception encoded in the text.[26] It is primarily in this adapted form that Booth's concept continues to have currency in modern critical theory. A 'construct inferred and assembled by the reader from all the components of the text', Booth's 'implied author' can be crucial to understanding how it is that literary texts function in reception.[27] The concept continues to generate controversy, particularly in regards to how the implied author might be accounted for in narratological terms, and also in respect of the precise role played by the reader in its construction, but it remains powerfully attractive to many, partly because the search for the author in the text – for all its potential contradictions – seems instinctively to reflect how most readers read.[28]

Lucretius' readers, in particular, have for centuries discovered a version of the author in the text, and though each reading might be skewed by individual bias, there is, with Lucretius perhaps more than any other poet, a critical mass of reception history starting in antiquity itself which has found the author in the 'moral and emotional content' of the *DRN*. It is as the idea of the author fashioned by readers but 'grounded in the indexes of the text' that the implied author can be most useful to understanding what it is about the *DRN* that has led to its long and rich biographical reception history.[29]

---

[25] As David Bordwell put it in *Narration in the Fiction Film* (published in 1985), Booth's concept mistakenly (for Bordwell) imposes 'the classic communication diagram: a message is passed from sender to receiver', whereas narrative should in fact be seen as an impersonal communication system: Bordwell 1985: 62. Booth's use of the language of agency (the extract above refers, for example, to the ways in which 'the author *creates* a "second self"') may have exacerbated such criticism from proponents of radical textuality.

[26] *Pace* Kindt and Mueller 2008: 'Exit IA, 3.1', 152–5, who resist the 'reception' version of the implied author concept on the grounds of lack of empirical studies.

[27] Rimmon-Kenan 2002: 88; cf. Chatman 1990: 74–89.

[28] Among key narratologists, Bal 1985 has been a particularly vocal critic of the implied author; Genette 1983 includes a chapter on the concept in *Narrative Discourse Revisited*, in which he acknowledges the importance of the implied author as 'everything the text lets us know about the author' (148), but sees it as having no role as an identifiable narrative agent. The debate continues: see esp. the special issue of *Style* (Richardson 2011) as well as Booth's own defence of the concept in Booth 2005. For useful summaries of the controversy see esp. Kindt and Mueller 2008 and Schmid 2009: 165–7.

[29] For this particular formulation of the implied author see Schmid 2009: 161.

The Author in the *De Rerum Natura*

Responding to Alfred Lord Tennyson's poem 'Lucretius', a powerful psychological re-imagination of Lucretius' final hours supersaturated with echoes of the *DRN*, Richard Jebb declared with the conviction of a nineteenth-century reader that he found confirmation of Tennyson's biographical endeavour in the 'real Lucretius' as read from the poem itself:

> The *De Rerum Natura* leaves with any one who reads it attentively a distinct impression of the personality of Lucretius; for he has no conventional literary reserve, no hesitation about speaking of himself when it is natural to do so. He has the concentrated earnestness of a prophet, who feels only that he has a message, and must speak it.[30]

Jebb's confident declaration that the *DRN* gives a 'distinct impression of the personality of Lucretius' might at first sight seem puzzling. In contrast to comparable Latin texts, the *DRN* tells us strikingly little in explicit terms about its author. There are no details about his place of birth, his upbringing or family, or the trajectory of his literary and philosophical career. Yet despite the dearth of concrete information, the poem nevertheless seems to make the almost mesmerizing impression on 'anyone who reads it' that we *know* its author.

One way in which that illusion of intimate knowledge is conveyed is through the *DRN*'s use of first-person verbs, not only in the singular *I*-from in which Lucretius seems to 'reveal himself',[31] but also in the frequent use of plural *we*-verbs. The *DRN* uses these forms far more frequently than other Latin scientific texts, and since the Latin 'we' can often also be read as modulating simply to mean 'I', Lucretius, as he 'puts his arm around the reader's shoulder' to observe the world, seems to be speaking directly from personal experience 'without hesitation', as Jebb put it.[32] Even when couched in the third person, the narrative voice can seem so emotive as to be speaking from first-hand experience. We seem to be able to sense the author's psyche behind such fervidly compelling passages as the gripping description of sexual frustration 'as madness grows day by day' (4.1069 *in . . . dies gliscit furor*), or the discussion of suicide (3.79–84), mirroring,

---

[30] Jebb 1868: 98 ('the Lucretius whom it describes has a close resemblance to the real Lucretius . . . the picture is not merely a picture, but happens to be a portrait also', p. 97).

[31] Clay 1983: 213 on *studeo* (1.24).

[32] For Lucretius' verbal embrace see Lehoux 2013: 137, who counts 228 'we' verbs and 237 pronouns referring to 'we/us/our' in the poem, excluding the obvious 'royal we' and formulaic phrases. Cf. Volk 2002: 77. See further Taylor in Chapter 3 of this volume.

perhaps, the author's own 'unnatural preoccupation';[33] we think we can see
Lucretius revealing himself in the account – famously identified by Jebb's
contemporary Matthew Arnold as a compelling 'picture of *ennui*' – of
benighted individuals going about their frenzied daily lives as 'each man
tries to flee from himself' (3.1068 *hoc se quisque modo fugit*), or even the
bizarre imaginings of wild beasts (5.1308–49), the result, perhaps of
'hallucination' or 'a madman's dream'.[34] Such passages seem to lend
themselves to the kinds of readings witnessed in the biographical tradition
which see the text as a gateway into the consciousness of its author.

All this is broadly consonant with what is often identified as the narrator
or '*persona*' of the *DRN*, 'the "I" or part of the "we" of the poem', as Diskin
Clay puts it, which can seem to constitute the mask through which 'Titus
Lucretius Carus speaks'.[35] But our sense of 'Titus Lucretius Carus', the
textualized author in the *DRN*, is more complex than the concept of the
speaking *persona* alone can account for. The sense of the author in the text
goes significantly beyond – and sometimes directly undercuts – the narrative voice itself to include other aspects of the poem's 'total form'.[36] In
order to illustrate this, the remainder of this chapter focuses on three
passages of explicit authorial self-construction in the voice of the "I" or
part of the "we" of the poem. Written in the first person, each of these
makes a crucial contribution to the Lucretian *persona* as conventionally
understood, but, fundamentally, each passage also invites readers very
clearly to make the connection (and sometimes the disjunction) between
the first-person *persona* and the implied author constructed from all the
components of the text.

Words and the Poet

Part way through the prologue to Book 1 of the *DRN*, the 'I' of the poem
pauses to reflect on the poet's task (*DRN* 1.136–45):[37]

> Nec me animi fallit Graiorum obscura reperta
> difficile inlustrare Latinis versibus esse,
> multa novis verbis praesertim cum sit agendum

---

[33] Bailey 1947: 1.12.
[34] 'hallucination': Bailey 1947: I.7; 'madman's dream': Postgate (in Leonard and Smith 1942: 13). For Arnold see 'On the modern element in literature' in Super 1960–77: I.33.
[35] Clay 1983: 213.
[36] See Booth 1961: 158 *et passim* on the distance between the narrator, who may be unreliable, and the implied author.
[37] Text: Bailey 1922. Translations are my own.

propter egestatem linguae et rerum novitatem;
sed tua me virtus tamen et sperata voluptas   140
suavis amicitiae quemvis efferre laborem
suadet et inducit noctes vigilare serenas
quaerentem dictis quibus et quo carmine demum
clara tuae possim praepandere lumina menti,
res quibus occultas penitus convisere possis.   145

And it does not escape me that it is difficult to cast light on the dark discoveries of
the Greeks in Latin verse, especially since many things must be treated in new
words because of the poverty of the language and the novelty of the material; but
your excellence and the pleasure of the sweet friendship I hope for persuade me to
endure any labour and lead me to stay awake through the tranquil nights, seeking
by what words and what poetry I may at last be able to open to your mind the
clear light by which you may look into the hidden heart of things.

The passage features one of the very few concrete details the poem seems
to give about its author's life.[38] We learn about Lucretius' lucubrations as
he sits awake through the dark, calm nights (142 *noctes vigilare serenas*) to
reach the kind of thrilling inner light he wants to pass on, willing to endure
any labour (141 *quemvis efferre laborem*) to fulfil that task.[39] The effect is to
create the illusion that we have been given a strikingly direct insight into
the poetic psyche, a sort of voyeuristic glimpse, as Bailey implies, into
Lucretius' study.[40] It is the kind of detail that helped to engender
Tennyson's insomniac Lucretius, listening to inner storms and expound-
ing the workings of his rapidly unravelling mind in the darkness of the
lonely night. Though there is, perhaps, a nagging sense of contradiction in
the background in what the speaker tells us and hence about his ultimate
reliability – he writes in an Epicurean calm (142 *serenas*) that is paradoxically fraught with *labor* (141) – all this could well be attributed to the old
construction of poetic *persona*.[41]

Crucially, however, one of the most explicit apparent snapshots of the
poet's mind comes yoked together with the famous statement, often
taken in isolation, about the difficulty of poetic language.[42] Like the
night outside, the dark discoveries of the Greeks (*Graiorum obscura
reperta*) require illumination, but the Latin language, so the poet feels,
is not up to the task (136–9). Since the politics of linguistic and cultural
translatability that Lucretius here signals (136–7 *Graiorum . . . Latinis*)

---

[38] Canali 1995 takes the title of his fictional biography from the *noctes . . . serenas* of 142.
[39] For Lucretian *labor* cf. *DRN* 2.730; 3.419.   [40] Bailey 1947 ad 1.142.
[41] For an attempt to reconcile the apparent paradoxes of Lucretian *labor* see Gale 2000: 152–3.
[42] Cf. also 1.832; 3.260 on the 'poverty of the Latin language', *patrii sermonis egestas*.

cannot have been on Epicurus' horizon, the point here is also one about the relationship between *lingua* (language *tout court*) and *res* (the material universe), suggesting in the chiastic arrangement of line 139 a kind of hendiadys in the collocation *linguae et rerum*.[43] Recent scholarship has been concerned to point out that language itself is an active agent in the philosophical poetics of the *DRN*. Words are intimately linked to the poem's philosophical purpose: as Wilson Shearin puts it, they *do* things to the poem's readers.[44] But even as they function as agents in the poem's Epicurean message, words in the *DRN* also play an active part in the construction of the reader's sense of the author in the text. The famous slipperiness and shiftiness of language in the poem enacts the relationship between the poem and the universe, atoms and words, or the possible disjunction between Latin poetry and Greek philosophy, but as we read it, it also enacts the mental state, as we construe it, of the text's implied author. In a poem in which the difficulty of finding the 'right' word is regularly dramatized in the text itself, where meaning slips and shifts from one instance to the next, the author's own struggle, expressed aloud in this passage, seems to inhere in poetic language itself. In other words, the author's own troubles, mental and poetic (his *labor*), so the poem encourages us to infer, are directly reflected in the language of the *DRN*. In Booth's terms, our sense of the implied author extends to the work's 'total form', and in this famous moment of poetic self-construction, the language of the poem is made to encode the struggle within the poet's psyche. From here on in, reading the words on the page, we are encouraged to think, is partly a road to reading the mind of the poet.

Instructions for a Sublime Author

Later in Book 1, in what is effectively the 'second prooemium' to the poem, the speaker pauses once again to reflect on the poet's task in the first-person voice (*DRN* 1.922–34):[45]

---

[43] On the relationship between 'word' and 'world' see also the chapters by Tutrone, O'Rourke, Nethercut and Shearin in this volume.

[44] Shearin 2015: vii on the poem as 'centrally concerned with doing things to its readers' from the perspective of speech act theory (associated with J. L. Austin's *How to Do Things with Words*). On aspects of the different linguistic strategies of the *DRN* see also the chapters by Taylor, Tutrone and Shearin in this volume.

[45] For this passage in Book 1 as a 'second prooemium' see Bailey 1947: II.756. Lines 926–50 are repeated with minor changes as the proem to Book 4: see Bailey 1947 ad loc.

sed acri
percussit thyrso laudis spes magna meum cor
et simul incussit suavem mi in pectus amorem
musarum, quo nunc instinctus mente vigenti   925
avia Pieridum peragro loca nullius ante
trita solo. iuvat integros accedere fontis
atque haurire, iuvatque novos decerpere flores
insignemque meo capiti petere inde coronam
unde prius nulli velarint tempora musae;   930
primum quod magnis doceo de rebus et artis
religionum animum nodis exsolvere pergo,
deinde quod obscura de re tam lucida pango
carmina, musaeo contingens cuncta lepore.

But a great hope has struck my heart with a sharp spur of fame and at the same time has thrust the sweet love of the Muses into my breast; inspired by it now, with a strong mind, I wander through the pathless places of the Muses trodden by no foot before mine. I love to approach the untouched springs and to drink there; I love to pluck new flowers and to seek a glorious crown for my head from places where the Muses have crowned no-one's brows before: first because I teach great things, and I proceed to unloose the mind from the tight knots of superstition; then because the subject is so dark and the lines I write so full of light, as I touch all with the Muses' charm.

In his essay on the implied reader in the *DRN*, Conte identified this passage (922–6) in particular as part of an encoded set of 'instructions for a sublime reader' set out in the poem. For Conte, the sublime in the *DRN* – moments of the flight of the mind, as author and reader stand in awe of the grandeur and terror of the universe, struck with the sheer exhilaration of scientific truth – is associated fundamentally with its effects on the reader.[46] As Conte puts it, the sublime 'offers a model of spiritual attitudes and moral conduct ... that exalts the reader and makes him capable of spiritual greatness', and this includes the author himself who is co-opted as an implicit addressee of his own poem.[47]

Yet, although the reader-in-the-text might well be steered to learn the truth of Epicureanism through the experience of the sublime as conveyed in the *DRN*, that experience of reading can also be retrojected onto another textual construct: the implied author. This passage, in particular,

---

[46] Citing Ps. Longinus 1.4 and 7.2, Conte notes that even Pseudo-Longinus 'implies that the sublime's true locus is in the reader's mind': Conte 1994: 19. For the sublime in the *DRN* see esp. Porter 2007; Hardie 2009: 67–228; Most 2012; Porter 2016: 445–54; O'Rourke in this volume (pp. 116–17).

[47] Conte 1994: 21, 19.

cries out to be read as one such moment of authorial construction.[48] As Conte rightly notes, *mente vigenti* in line 925 points to the popular Varronian etymology for the inspired *vates* (*a vi mentis*), which can further be associated with the Greek *mantis* and the divine frenzy, *mania*, that goes with it.[49] Inspired with a Bacchic *thyrsus* (923), as presented here, the poet as *vates* might be leading by example in setting a pattern for the kind of readerly qualities the text demands; but he might also be setting out instructions for how to imagine the author as constructed by the text, struck with the thrill of divine inspiration – gripped by 'a godlike pleasure and a thrill of awe' (*divina voluptas* | ... *atque horror*, 3.28–9) as he responds to the sublime – and perhaps even on the cusp of another kind of *furor*.[50]

This author-centred reading of the sublime is borne out by the poem's reception history. While ancient readers may have been called to action by the Lucretian sublime in 'an exchange between the spectacle and the spectator',[51] it is notable that it is through the sublime, too, that they remembered the poet: *docti furor arduus Lucreti* ('the sublime *furor* of learned Lucretius', as Statius put it at *Silvae* 2.7.76).[52] It may even be that ancient readers took Lucretian *furor* further to full-blown biographical proportions by taking up the link between Empedocles and Lucretius, already latent in the text of the *DRN*, to project the well-known suicide of the Greek philosopher – who jumped into Mount Etna leaving only a bronze sandal behind him[53] – onto their conceptualization of the implied author of the *DRN*, thus anticipating Jerome by several centuries.[54] Whatever the extent of ancient extrapolations of the author's insanity,

---

[48] Bailey identified this passage as '[b]y far the most illuminating' in understanding the poet's 'Character, Mind, and Temperament' (1947: 1.13).

[49] Conte 1994: 11. For Varro's twin etymologies for the word *vates* (*a versibus viendis*, from plaiting verses, and *a vi mentis*, from the forcible mental impulse associated with poetic inspiration) see *Serv. Dan.* on *Aen.* 3.443; Isid. *Orig.* 8.7.3.

[50] Meaning the frenzy of inspiration, *furor* can also shade into 'madness': *OLD* s.v. On poetic inspiration in antiquity as a kind of madness see Hardie 2009: 217.

[51] Conte 1994: 22.

[52] For the crucial importance of the sublime in the ancient reception of Lucretius more generally see esp. Hardie 2009: 67–228; Porter 2007; Porter 2016: 445–73. Newlands 2011: 241–2 suggests that a literal interpretation of the word *furor* in Statius 'contribute[d] to the legend of Lucretius' madness found in ... Jerome'; cf. Bailey 1947: I.8–12.

[53] Diogenes Laertius 8.69.

[54] See Canfora 1993: 99–105; Hardie 2009: 212–3 on the mad poet at the end of Horace's *Ars poetica*, who is both *sublimis* (*Ars P.* 457) and *vesanus* (*Ars P.* 455), and specifically the image of the suicidal Empedocles leaping into Etna as a stand-in for Lucretius. For Lucretius 'taking possession' of Empedocles' *persona* see Conte 1994: 11.

the link between the Lucretian sublime and Lucretian madness has been made by generations of readers since. As Matthew Arnold eloquently put it, the *DRN*'s sublime presentation of the secrets of the universe seems to give us a vivid sense not just of how the Epicurean should behave, but of the mind of the author implicit in the poem:

> With stern effort, with gloomy despair, he seems to rivet his eyes on the elementary reality, the naked framework of the world, because the world in its fullness and movement is too exciting a spectacle for his discomposed brain. He seems to feel the spectacle of it at once terrifying and alluring; and to deliver himself from it he has to keep perpetually repeating his formula of disenchantment and annihilation.[55]

The poem's ability to 'feel the spectacle at once terrifying and alluring' of the nature of the universe clearly has an impact on its readers, real or textually constructed. But in the end, those very readers have persistently linked that quality in the text not so much with Epicurean truth as with the 'gloomy despair' of the 'discomposed brain' of its imagined author.

L'anti-Lucrèce chez Lucrèce

Hard on the heels of the description of the poet's sublime inspiration, the 'second prooemium' continues with one of the most well-known similes in the *DRN*, functioning as virtual short-hand for the poem itself (*DRN* 1.936–47):[56]

> sed veluti pueris absinthia taetra medentes
> cum dare conantur, prius oras pocula circum
> contingunt mellis dulci flavoque liquore,
> ut puerorum aetas improvida ludificetur
> labrorum tenus, interea perpotet amarum   940
> absinthi laticem deceptaque non capiatur,
> sed potius tali pacto recreata valescat,
> sic ego nunc, quoniam haec ratio plerumque videtur
> tristior esse quibus non est tractata, retroque
> vulgus abhorret ab hac, volui tibi suaviloquenti   945
> carmine Pierio rationem exponere nostram
> et quasi musaeo dulci contingere melle.

---

[55] 'On the modern element in literature', in Super 1960–77: I.33.
[56] The lines are repeated almost verbatim at 4.11–22.

But just as doctors, when they try to administer foul-tasting wormwood to children, first smear the edges of the cups with the sweet, yellow syrup of honey, so that the guileless age of childhood may be deluded as far as the lips and drink up the bitter juice of wormwood, and though taken in be not taken ill, but rather, revived by it, they may grow well, so I now do: since this doctrine commonly seems quite harsh to those who have not dealt with it, and since people shrink back from it, I have chosen to set forth my doctrine to you in sweet-speaking Pierian song, and, as it were, to smear it with the Muses' delicious honey.

There is a famous paradox here. Epicureanism perceived poetry as ineffectual at best and pernicious at worst, so that, on the surface of things, there is an unresolvable problem: Lucretius' medium seems to undermine his message.[57] That paradox may be argued away by various methods. Lucretius, for example, as well as Latinizing a philosophy that did not have Roman cultural concerns on its horizon, might be seen inversely as bringing back his chosen medium of poetry into the philosophical fold by 'Epicureanizing' it in various ways.[58] Interpretive strategies have shifted from emphasizing the apparent dichotomy between irreconcilable media to attempting to reconcile them, and back again to embracing inconsistency as a creative mode of operation.[59] But, as Monica Gale puts it, it is precisely in this simile that the poem itself is 'in part responsible' for that perceived dichotomy.[60] Poetry, 'the sweet honey of the Muses' (1.947 *musaeo dulci ... melle*), is presented as the contrasting medium that will lead the poem's readers to the medicine of Epicurean philosophy, *decepta ... non capiatur* (941). Yet, as we read the poem – from the problematic Hymn to Venus at its beginning to the plague at its end – things don't cohere quite as the speaker would like us to think.

The sense of a fundamental fissure in the text between the medium and the message has historically led readers to author-based readings. From Cardinal Melchior de Polignac's *Anti-Lucretius* in the eighteenth century to M. Patin's 'L'anti-Lucrèce chez Lucrèce' in the nineteenth, it is precisely an overriding sense of an 'implied author' in the *DRN*, inherent not simply in the first-person passages but in the text as a whole, that lies behind the long tradition of deliberately seeking out contradictions in the text by

---

[57] Volk 2002: 94 and 86 n. 48; Asmis 1995; Gale 1994: 14–18.
[58] See, e.g., Gale 1994, esp. 138–55; Schrijvers 1970, who links the psychagogic function of poetry here to Epicurean theories of perception; Volk 2002: 95, taking line 935 to mean that 'the speaker's act is not against Epicurean reason specifically'.
[59] Lehoux, Morrison and Sharrock 2013: 6–7. On inconsistency see esp. O'Hara 2007.
[60] Gale 1994: 1–2.

looking for the 'anti-Lucretius in Lucretius'.[61] Like Jerome, Polignac and Patin may have been fundamentally driven by an anxiety about a philosophy inimical to Christianity, seeking to 'declaw . . . and defang' a doctrine felt to be close to atheism or worse by calling into question the mental state of the poem's author.[62] Yet one of the reasons the 'anti-Lucretian' mode of reading has been so compelling, continuing to haunt, in one way or another, much of the subsequent work on the poem, is precisely because it conforms to the notion of authorial presence that seems to be evoked in the textual universe of the poem. Read as an extrapolation from the text's 'total form', the author can be seen, in Patin's words, as, 'so to speak, the first anti-Lucretius'.[63] In bringing to the fore the dichotomy between poetry and philosophy in the first person, the honeyed cup simile plays an important role in justifying that mode of reading by encouraging us to link the 'author' attempting to reconcile his poetic medium and philosophical message with the apparent contradictions in the text as a whole. In Booth's terms, the narrative 'I' of the poem (who can be fallible or unreliable) is not the *same* as the implied author (who is extrapolated from all the components of the text), but it is passages like these that ask us to read the implied author as a pervasive presence – beyond the poetic *persona* – in the *DRN*.

Conclusion: Authors and Readers

Critical shifts in discussions of Latin poetry towards readers and away from authors have done much to liberate interpretation by swinging the critical pendulum away from the ultimately futile reconstruction of authorial intention or the questionable production of positivistic biography to focus on the texts themselves. Yet turning back to the text can also allow us to swing the critical pendulum back again from the reader to the author, this time conceived as a construct extrapolated by readers from the text. As Roland Barthes, the most readerly of twentieth-century readers, put it, 'in the text, in a way, I *desire* the author, I need his figure'.[64] Understood in Booth's terms as a construct encoded in the text and picked up in

---

[61] Though Polignac's *Anti-Lucretius* is a general attack against materialism, he, too, often reads a divided mind in the *DRN*: *Deinde vocet demens quos tentat perdere Divos,| immemor ipse sui* (5.35–6): Polignac 1747: 184.

[62] On nineteenth-century readings: Johnson 2000: 127; on Jerome: Holford-Strevens 2002.

[63] Patin 1868: 1.118; Johnson 2000: 124. On Patin see further esp. Johnson 2000: 123–4, 127.

[64] Barthes 1975: 27. Cf. Burke 1992.

reception by readers, the author can and should still have a central role in how we interpret texts like the *DRN*.

One of the reasons the implied author concept has come in for criticism is that the precise role of the reader in constructing it is difficult to pin down. Is the implied author a fixed entity in the text that needs to be accounted for in narratological or ontological terms? Or is it wholly reader-generated, and therefore open to 'misreading', re-reading, and revision depending on the proclivities of individual readers? Or is it something in between?[65] Seen as a product primarily of interpretation rather than narration, the passages picked out in this chapter could potentially generate different pictures of the author than the ones put forward here – ones less divided, less contradictory, less subject to the putative psychological pressures which Lucretius' Epicurean poem seems to entail. At the same time, what is striking about the case of the *DRN* is that the poem comes to us with the burden of several centuries of author-centred reception associated with the biographical legend of the madness of Lucretius. Generations of readers have put the author of the poem front and centre of their interpretations, and, more often than not, found in the *DRN* the document of a divided mind. Ultimately, the cumulative desire among the poem's readers to find the author in the text highlights important interpretive possibilities, suggesting that the author should play as active a part in approaches to Lucretius as the long-established implied reader. Far from simply holding 'a certain nuisance value',[66] the insights of reception are worth taking seriously. More than most texts, as its reception history attests, Lucretius' poem demands to be read in an author-centred way, and the implied author offers a crucial avenue to that mode of reading. We cannot ultimately know the 'real' inner or outer 'world of Titus Lucretius',[67] but the implied author, set up in the fabric of the *DRN* and picked up in reception by its readers, goes some way towards allowing us to accommodate that desire.

---

[65] Schmid 2009; cf. Richardson 2011.   [66] Kenney 2014: 5.
[67] Cf. Wiseman 1974 for the search for the 'two worlds' of Lucretius.

CHAPTER 3

Common Ground in Lucretius' De Rerum Natura

Barnaby Taylor

Introduction

This chapter is about ambiguity and readerly experience in *De Rerum Natura* (*DRN*). In his poem, Lucretius addresses a singular reader who, on eleven occasions, is named as Memmius. Each reader who is not Memmius is free to choose whether or not also to consider him- or herself as an addressee of the poem; whether or not to self-identify as an additional target of the high number of second person singular addresses the poem contains. Some readers may do so; others may conceive of themselves as third-party witnesses to a personal communication between Lucretius and Memmius,[1] nor need we expect each reader to be consistent in this regard. In this chapter I will for the most part be anticipating readers who do, on at least some occasions, consider themselves also to be addressees of the poem. That said, it will, I hope, become clear that many of my arguments will also apply, *mutatis mutandis*, to those readers who adopt a more distanced stance.

My particular focus will be Lucretius' use of first person plurals (whether verbs, pronouns, or possessive adjectives), of which *DRN* contains a strikingly high number. By my count, one such form occurs on average once every 12.5 lines of the poem (586 forms in a 7,380-line poem). That this is indeed a high rate may be demonstrated with a brief comparison to other Latin didactic poets: in Virgil's *Georgics* a first person plural form is encountered on average once every fifty-three lines; in Manilius' *Astronomica*, once every sixty-three lines. The regular use of first person plurals has been recognized as one way in which Lucretius seeks to

For helpful discussion of the ideas expressed in this chapter I am indebted to audiences at the Edinburgh Lucretius conference, the Oxford Philological Society, and the Cambridge B Club, as well as to Solmeng-Jonas Hirschi, Donncha O'Rourke, Matthew Leigh and the anonymous reviewers for Cambridge University Press. Remaining errors are my own.
[1] For an example of such an interpretation see the influential analysis of Mitsis 1993.

explore common ground – in the form of shared experiences, knowledge, even emotions – between poet and reader.[2] Any attempt to map the contours of this common ground, however, will soon hit upon a significant complicating factor, namely the various ambiguities of the Latin first person plural, a grammatical form which can have a variety of different meanings. While sometimes the meaning of a given form is made clear by context, often it is not, and the resultant ambiguity, I suggest, is likely to produce different interpretations from different readers, or indeed from the same reader at different stages of his or her Epicurean education.[3] Before moving on to my analysis of the poem, I will briefly outline a few distinct shades of meaning in the first person plural, which I will be drawing on in my discussion of common ground. First, the distinction between the genuine plural and the plural-for-singular (or *pluralis auctoris*):

6.26–7   exposuitque bonum summum, quo tendimus omnes
                       quid foret

and he set forth what is the greatest good, at which we all aim.[4]

1.429   id quod iam supera tibi paulo ostendimus ante.[5]

that which I have already demonstrated to you above, just a moment ago.

6.26-7 describes Epicurus' demonstration that all creatures pursue pleasure. The scope of *tendimus* in that line extends to include all human beings. *Tendimus*, then, is a genuine plural. *Ostendimus* at 1.429 is a clear instance of *pluralis auctoris*, that is, the use of a first person plural form to refer to a singular speaker or author.[6] Despite its plural form, *ostendimus* has a singular subject, namely the poet himself, who here refers the reader back to his exposition earlier in the poem.

For an example of ambiguity between the genuine plural and the *pluralis auctoris*, consider the following passage from Book 1 (498–502):

---

[2] Important accounts of the Lucretian first person plural are provided by Clay 1983: 212–66, Volk 2002: 73–83, Gale 2005: 179–81, and Lehoux 2013: 136–9. Many of the arguments in this chapter build, in some way or other, on the observations of these scholars.

[3] For this reason I do not think it possible to assign a secure individual semantic value to each and every first person plural in the poem; for a different approach see the tabulations of Fanti 2017: 74 n. 48. For the importance of allowing room in our analyses of *DRN* for various different readerly responses see the illuminating comments of O'Hara 2007: 68–9 and Gale 2018: 84–6.

[4] I use the text of Rouse and Smith 1992. Translations in this chapter, unless otherwise indicated, are my own.

[5] Cf. 1.531; 4.672.

[6] See Pinkster 2015: 1119–20; Hofmann and Szantyr 1965: 19–20; Kühner and Stegmann 1955: 1.87–9.

> sed quia vera tamen ratio naturaque rerum
> cogit, ades, paucis dum versibus expediamus
> esse ea quae solido atque aeterno corpore constent,
> semina quae rerum primordiaque esse docemus,
> unde omnis rerum nunc constet summa creata.

But because true reasoning and the nature of things nevertheless constrain, pay attention, until in a few verses I explain that there are those things which consist of body solid and eternal, which we teach to be the seeds of things and their first-beginnings, from which the entire sum of things has now been created.

How should we describe *docemus* at 501? This could be read as another instance of *pluralis auctoris* (cf. *expediamus* at 499, which surely is).[7] Alternatively, *docemus* could be interpreted as a genuine plural, with both Lucretius and Epicurus (and, perhaps, further *Epicurei*) included among its subjects.[8] How the verb is interpreted is likely to vary from reader to reader, perhaps in accordance with each reader's preconceptions of Lucretius as an Epicurean teacher (is he conceived as a solitary agent, or as a member of a wider community of Epicurean teachers?).

The second distinction I am interested in (and the one on which I will spend the most time) is that between inclusive and exclusive first person plurals.[9] An inclusive first person plural includes among its subjects the addressee of the act of speaking; an exclusive first person plural does not. *Tendimus* at 6.26, then, is inclusive, including among its subjects, as it must, the didactic addressee. *Docemus* at 1.501, which does not include the didactic addressee among its subjects, is exclusive. We may note here that plural-for-singular usages like *ostendimus* at 1.429 and *expediamus* at 1.499 will always be exclusive, while genuine plurals may be either inclusive or exclusive. The inclusive/exclusive distinction often gives rise to ambiguities of its own, consideration of some examples of which will form a central part of the analysis of this chapter.

Thirdly, I will devote some time to discussing a certain type of generic first person plural.[10] While first person plural expressions may often be substituted with first person singular expressions and remain true, this is

---

[7] It does not follow from the proximity of plural-for-singular *expediamus* that *docemus* should also be interpreted as plural-for-singular: compare, for example, 4.881–2, where we find unambiguous examples of plural-for-singular and genuine plural in close proximity to one another: *dico animo nostro primum simulacra meandi | accidere atque animum pulsare, ut diximus ante* ('I say that, first, images of moving fall upon our mind, and strike the mind, as I have said earlier').

[8] Compare, e.g., διδάσκομεν at Demetrius Laco, *On Poems* I, *PHerc.* 188 col. 10.5–6 McOsker (= col. 8 Romeo).

[9] For brief discussion of this distinction in Lucretius see Clay 1983: 219, 222.

[10] For the generic first person plural see Pinkster 2015: 743.

not always the case. Consider the English sentence 'we put a man on the moon', used inclusively: neither speaker nor addressee needs to have been involved in the space programme for this sentence to make sense when spoken between them. It describes an achievement to which they can both lay claim by dint of group membership, but which is a feature of the personal experience of neither. I will call this a 'collective' use of the generic first person plural: speaker and addressee consider themselves part of a group, some of whose members carried out the act referred to with the first person plural verb. In this case, the property of having put a man on the moon is thus transferred to both speaker and addressee via a process of part–whole metonymy. I will suggest that readers of *DRN* will, depending on the range of their personal experiences, regularly encounter inclusive first person plurals which invite 'collective' interpretation along these lines. I will go on to consider the implications of this for Lucretius' empiricism.

Common Ground and the Didactic Plot

Lucretius' use of first person plurals, and (just as importantly) the reader's interpretation of their ambiguities, play an important role in the poem's didactic plot.[11] A clear example of this is provided by his use of first person plurals in metalinguistic contexts. One thing that Lucretius assumes himself to share with his reader is knowledge of the Latin language, and this ubiquitous feature of the common ground is occasionally given explicit voice via the use of inclusive first person plurals in passages of metalinguistic reflection:

quo pacto verba quoque ipsa
inter se paulo mutatis sunt elementis,
1.912–4   cum ligna atque ignes distincta voce notemus.

Just as the very words, too, are made of up letters changed just a little, when we use distinct names to refer to wood and fires.

nam nil esse potest aliud nisi lumine cassus
4.368–9   aër id quod nos umbram perhibere suëmus.

For that which we are accustomed to name shadow can be nothing other than air devoid of light.

quam cum perscidit, extemplo cadit igneus ille
6.297–8   vertex quem patrio vocitamus nomine fulmen.

---

[11] On which see esp. Fowler 2000c. See also Gale 2004; Trépanier 2007.

when it has burst the cloud apart, at once that fiery eddy falls, which in the tongue of our fathers we call the thunderbolt.

> in summo sunt vertice enim crateres, ut ipsi
> nominitant, nos quod fauces perhibemus et ora.   6.701–2

For at the highest summit are craters, as they call them, which we call throats, or mouths.

Notemus, perhibere suëmus, vocitamus and *perhibemus* are (for speakers of Latin) inclusive: each of these passages highlights a feature not of specialized Epicurean language but rather of the ordinary, everyday language used by all Latin speakers: non-technical terms like 'wood', 'fire', 'shadow', 'thunderbolt', together with mildly technical expressions like '[volcano] mouth'.[12] The 'we' of these passages is not 'we Epicureans', nor indeed 'we human beings' (compare, e.g., *quo tendimus omnes* at 6.26), but rather 'we Romans' (cf. *patrio nomine* at 6.298 and the comparison with Greek speakers [the subjects of *nominitant*] at 6.701–2). A Roman reader, then, would consider him- or herself to be included in these first person plural expressions.

Not all examples of metalinguistic reflection in the first person plural in *DRN*, however, concern such everyday language. Consider the following examples:

> quae nos materiem et genitalia corpora rebus
> reddunda in ratione vocare et semina rerum
> appellare suëmus et haec eadem usurpare
> corpora prima, quod ex illis sunt omnia primis.[13]   1.58–61

Which, in giving our account, we are accustomed to call matter, and bodies generative of things, and seeds of things, and to name these same things first bodies, since all things have their being from them as primary elements.

> est igitur nimirum id quod ratione sagaci
> quaerimus admixtum rebus, quod inane vocamus.[14]   1.368–9

Beyond doubt, therefore, there exists, mingled in with things, that which we seek with keen reasoning, which we call void.

---

[12] For comparable expressions in the texts of Epicurus himself see, e.g., the discussion of time at *Ep. Hdt.* 72–3: καθ' ὃ τὸν πολὺν ἢ ὀλίγον χρόνον ἀναφωνοῦμεν (72 'in virtue of which we articulate the words 'long time' and 'short time''); καθ' ὃ χρόνον ὀνομάζομεν (73 'in virtue of which we use the word 'time''). In these cases the implicit subjects of each verb are 'we Greek speakers'. (Translations: Long and Sedley 1987: 1.34.)

[13] On this passage see, in this regard, the helpful comments of Clay 1983: 334 n. 126.

[14] The phrase *quod inane vocamus* recurs at 1.426, 439, 507 and 1074.

servitium contra paupertas divitiaeque,
libertas bellum concordia, cetera quorum
adventu manet incolumis natura abituque,
1.455–8   haec soliti sumus, ut par est, eventa vocare.

On the other hand, slavery, poverty, wealth, freedom, war, harmony and the other things by whose arrival and departure the nature of things remains untouched, these we are accustomed, as is right, to call accidents.

nunc agere incipiam tibi, quod vementer ad has res
4.29–30   attinet, esse ea quae rerum simulacra vocamus.

Now I will begin to tell you something highly pertinent to these matters – that there are what we call images of things.

While each of the terms under discussion in these examples is quite ordinary, the specific use to which it is being put is not: the terms *corpus*, *inane*, *eventa* and *simulacra* do not usually bear the specialized meanings they are given here; nor would these meanings be known to a neophyte reader on first picking up the poem. The first person plural expressions in these passages, therefore, are not inclusive but (at least initially) exclusive, whether they are to be interpreted as *plurales auctoris* or as genuine plurals (with *nos Romani Epicurei* understood as the implied subject).[15]

First person plural metalinguistic expressions in *DRN*, then, point to the existence of two distinct linguistic communities: on the one hand, Roman readers with an ordinary knowledge of the Latin language; on the other, a narrow subset of the first: users of a specialized Epicurean vocabulary (and this latter group may, at the outset of the poem, include no more than one member, viz. Lucretius himself).

While we can say with some confidence that most readers, on their first reading of the poem, will be unfamiliar with these specialized Epicurean usages, and will accordingly interpret such terms as *appellare suëmus* at 1.60

---

[15] Clay (1983: 334 n. 126) adopts the latter reading, without mention of the former. Lucretius' use of metalinguistic first person plurals when discussing technical terms is closely matched by Epicurus himself, in whose texts we find such expressions as: *Ep. Hdt.* 40 τόπος δὲ εἰ μὴ ἦν ὃ κενὸν καὶ χώραν καὶ ἀναφῆ φύσιν ὀνομάζομεν ('and if place, which we call "void", "space", and "intangible nature" did not exist'; closely imitated by Lucretius at 1.426–7: *tum porro locus ac spatium, quod inane vocamus, | si nullum foret . . .*); *Ep. Hdt.* 46 τούτους δὲ τοὺς τύπους εἴδωλα προσαγορεύομεν ('we call these images "idols"', with which compare *DRN* 4.30, quoted above: *ea quae rerum simulacra vocamus*); *Ep. Pyth.* 89 καὶ ἐν κόσμῳ καὶ μετακοσμίῳ ὃ λέγομεν μεταξὺ κόσμων διάστημα ('both in a world and in an inter-world, as we call the space between worlds'; on the Epicurean *metakosmion* see Tutrone in this volume, p. 92). While some such expressions in Epicurus may be interpreted as plural-for-singular, the context in which Epicurus was writing (as the leader of a philosophical school with multiple members, some of whom he addresses in his letters) makes it plausible that these expressions of Epicurus are genuine inclusive first person plurals, indicating specialized usages current within the Epicurean community.

and *vocamus* 1.369 as exclusive first person plurals, we need not assume that this state of affairs will continue for long. In the rhetoric of the poem, Epicurean group membership is by no means closed off to the reader. Indeed, that Lucretius expects his readership not only to come around to Epicurean doctrine but also to adopt his own forms of linguistic expression is made explicit at 1.481, at the conclusion to Lucretius' discussion of essential and inessential properties (*eventa* and *coniuncta*) at 1.478–82:

> perspicere ut possis res gestas funditus omnis
> non ita uti corpus per se constare neque esse,
> nec ratione cluere eadem qua constet inane,
> sed magis ut merito possis eventa vocare
> corporis atque loci, res in quo quaeque gerantur.

So that you may clearly see that no events at all abide or exist *per se* (unlike body), nor are they reputed to exist in the same way as does void,[16] but rather so that you may justly call them accidents of body, and of the place in which each event occurred.

The reader is here encouraged to adopt the same form of expression (the use of the term *eventa*) as was previously described using (what would have first been read as) an exclusive first person plural form (1.458 *haec soliti sumus, ut par est, eventa vocare*). As readers' Epicurean education progresses, they are thus envisaged as adopting the specialized language of Roman Epicureans like Lucretius.[17]

This sequence demonstrates how the ambiguity between inclusive and exclusive first person plurals may function within the didactic plot. The plot of *DRN* is not just the story of the reader being taught Epicurean doctrine, but is also a story about linguistic change, as the reader progressively assimilates the particular technical usages he or she encounters in the text. A reader who, on first coming to the poem, reads *vocamus* in the phrase *quod inane vocamus* as an exclusive first person plural, speaking to the existence of a linguistic community of which he or she is not a member, may, as the first book of the poem progresses, come to see later iterations of the same phrase as potentially inclusive forms. The meaning of this repeated phrase, then, might vary depending on when, in the progress of

---

[16] This use of *cluere* to refer to a specialized philosophical usage is striking: the closest example elsewhere in *DRN* is perhaps 4.53, on the *simulacra*: *cuiuscumque cluet de corpore fusa vagari*; contrast the universal scope of *quaecumque cluent* at 1.449.

[17] See also 2.658–9 (*concedamus ut hic terrarum dictitet orbem | esse deum Matrem*), where we find an inclusive (note the jussive force of the subjunctive, which suggests joint action of speaker and addressee: Pinkster 2015: 497) first person plural in the context of a discussion of the acceptability of a certain metaphorical expression.

his or her Epicurean education, each reader encounters it. This effect of the plot will of course vary depending on each reader's temperament and level of engagement with the doctrine (there may be as many didactic plots as there are readers), and the ambiguity between inclusive and exclusive readings of a form like *vocamus* means that there is no one plot set down for readers to follow; they may interpret such forms as they choose, either eventually assenting to an inclusive reading, or resisting Lucretius' attempts at inclusion and continuing to read them exclusively. The built-in ambiguity, then, between inclusive and exclusive first person plural forms leaves sufficient room for both assent and resistance: the reader may interpret them freely, in accordance with the degree of common ground they perceive themselves to share with the poet at any given time.

Common Ground and the Characterization of Poet and Reader

Any account of the didactic plot of *DRN*, then, must be alive to the distinction between inclusive and exclusive readings of first person plurals and the power this ambiguity grants the reader to shape their own relationship with the text. I turn now to a related question: Lucretius' use of first person plural expressions to characterize the relationship between poet and reader. Lucretius sometimes uses first person plurals to refer to the act of philosophical inquiry. Here are three examples from Book 1:

1.368–9
> est igitur nimirum id quod ratione sagaci
> quaerimus admixtum rebus, quod inane vocamus.

Beyond doubt, therefore, there exists, mingled in with things, that which we seek with keen reasoning, which we call void.

1.423–5
> cui nisi prima fides fundata valebit,
> haud erit occultis de rebus quo referentes
> confirmare animi quicquam ratione queamus.

unless faith in sensation is first firmly grounded, there will be nothing by which, making an appeal concerning things hidden, we may confirm anything by the reasoning of the mind.

1.699–700
> quo referemus enim? quid nobis certius ipsis
> sensibus esse potest, qui vera ac falsa notemus?

For to what shall we appeal? What can be more certain for us than the senses themselves, that we may distinguish between true things and false?

Elsewhere in *DRN*, Lucretius characterizes his reader not simply as a passive recipient of philosophical doctrine, but as someone who is actively engaged in philosophical inquiry: at 1.402–9 Lucretius encourages Memmius to use the proofs for the existence of void he has encountered so far in the poem to discover new ones for himself; a similar, albeit more general, message is conveyed to the reader at 1.1114–17; at 4.572–4 Lucretius even envisages his reader going on to teach others the science of acoustics.[18] As such, the engaged reader will have reason to interpret the first person plural forms listed above inclusively, as characterizing Epicurean inquiry (and, in particular, the inquiry undertaken in *DRN*) as something in which reader and poet are, together, actively engaged.[19] Lucretius' practice here cleaves very close to that of Epicurus, who not only uses inclusive first person plurals to describe the act of philosophical inquiry,[20] but twice uses first person plural forms of ἀνάγω in much the same way as Lucretius uses the calques *referemus* at 1.699 and *referentes* at 1.424.[21]

Lucretius makes it quite clear that his intended reader is a newcomer to Epicurean philosophy. Occasionally, however, he nevertheless uses first person plural forms to refer to explicitly Epicurean attitudes and philosophical principles. Consider the following example (2.284–7):

> Quare in seminibus quoque idem fateare necessest,
> esse aliam praeter plagas et pondera causam
> motibus, unde haec est nobis innata potestas,
> de nilo quoniam fieri nil posse videmus.

Wherefore you must confess that, likewise, in seeds too, there is, besides weights and impacts, another cause of motion, whence this ability is born in us, since we see that nothing may come to be from nothing.

Read inclusively, such forms as *videmus* at 287 go further than to cast the reader as Lucretius' fellow-traveller in philosophical inquiry: they attribute to the reader Epicurean beliefs and attitudes. Here Lucretius uses the principle that nothing comes from nothing (demonstrated at *DRN* 1.149–214) as a premiss in his argument on the swerve.[22] The first person plural *videmus* asserts that both Lucretius and his reader are aware of the truth of this principle; that this is intended to be read as an inclusive use of

---

[18] On these and other related passages see Clay 1983: 225; Volk 2002: 81–2; Gale 2005: 177–8; Schiesaro 2007b: 66–8. For similar engagement with the reader in Epicurus himself see *Ep. Hdt.* 83 with Clay 1983: 175.

[19] This point is well illustrated by Volk (2002: 77–8), who speaks of philosophical inquiry in *DRN* as a 'joint enterprise' between teacher and student; see also Gale 2004: 56; Gale 2005: 176.

[20] E.g., *Ep. Hdt.* 35, 37, 38, 49, 56, 58, 72, 79, 81, 82.

[21] *Ep. Hdt.* 38 and *KD* 22, with Usener 1977, 50; see also *Ep. Hdt.* 37, 72.

[22] For the role of the 'nothing comes from nothing' principle in this argument see Fowler 2002: 362–4 ad *DRN* 2.287.

the first person plural is made highly likely by the second person singular *fateare* at 284: the reader is being asked to recognize a new truth (*fateare*) on the basis of something he or she already knows – *videmus*. Here, then, Lucretius uses *videmus* to characterize the reader's response to the arguments of Book 1;[23] the reader, Lucretius asserts, has imbibed the doctrine of the first book and, together with Lucretius, applies that doctrinal knowledge to the argumentation of Book 2. This inclusive first person plural, then, constitutes an explicit assertion of readerly progress by Lucretius.[24] We can identify a similar pattern in Epicurus: the letter to Menoeceus, which has been interpreted as being aimed at a less specialized readership than the letters to Herodotus and Pythocles,[25] nonetheless occasionally invites the reader to include him- or herself among the subjects of first person plural expressions of belief in Epicurean doctrine.[26]

Lucretius' attempts to attribute to his reader, via inclusive first person plurals, the beliefs and attitudes associated with Epicurean inquiry is only one half of the story here. As has been convincingly demonstrated by Gale, joint engagement in and commitment to Epicurean inquiry is not the only kind of intimacy Lucretius seeks to establish with his reader:[27] elsewhere, Lucretius uses first person plurals to cast himself as a subject of the experiences of the unenlightened reader – experiences which we would not expect an enlightened Epicurean to have had. We may call this 'didactic empathy': cases in which Lucretius uses an assertion of common ground in order to represent himself as sharing in the reader's emotional pains and difficulties.[28]

---

[23] This response is anticipated at 1.155–6 *ubi viderimus nil posse creari | de nilo* ('when we will have become aware that nothing can be created from nothing').

[24] Contrast the claim of Keen (1985: 2) that the text does not contain suggestions of progress on the part of the reader: 'What we have in Lucretius is the description and exposition of a philosophical system over the course of which the perceptions and understanding of the reader do not change, at least insofar as that is reflected in the poet's addresses to him.' Clearly I disagree. For important positive accounts of the representation of readerly progress in *DRN* see Clay 1983: 216–20; Gale 2004; 2005. For more on Keen see n. 42 below.

[25] See Bailey 1926: 327; for mixed readership in the letter to Herodotus see Clay 1983: 60–5.

[26] See, for example, *Ep. Men.* 129–30.

[27] See Gale 2005: 180 for variations in Lucretius' idealized relationship with his reader: 'The speaker sometimes groups himself with the pupil as a member of the Epicurean community in contrast with the unenlightened, sometimes with the pupil as one of the unenlightened in contrast with the transcendent greatness of Epicurus himself; at other times, the speaker distances himself from the pupil, as one who has already found the path to true reason, and is therefore qualified to induct the pupil in turn.'; see also Gale 2018: 72–5. Here we may also bear in mind Fowler's (2000b) stress on the variety of ways in which Lucretius characterizes his own didaxis.

[28] See Clay (1983: 222–3), who explains, in his discussion of 1.132–3 (*quae res nobis vigilantibus obvia mentes | terrificet*), how 'to reach his reader, Lucretius must put himself in his place'; see also Cox 1971: 14; Segal 1990: 49–50, 57 and 46–73 *passim*. This tendency on the part of the poet is closely

On three separate occasions in the poem we find adults' unfounded fears compared to young boys' fear of darkness (2.55–8 = 3.87–90 = 6.35–8):

> nam veluti pueri trepidant atque omnia caecis
> in tenebris metuunt, sic nos in luce timemus
> interdum nilo quae sunt metuenda magis quam
> quae pueri in tenebris pavitant finguntque futura.

For just as children tremble and are afraid of all things in the blind dark, thus we, sometimes, fear in the light things which should no more be feared than what children dread and imagine will happen in the dark.

Mitsis identifies this passage as one of 'a relatively stable set of textual indications that the poet treats his readers as children'.[29] This is quite correct: *timemus* is surely inclusive in scope. As Gale points out, however, the first person plural verb necessarily includes Lucretius himself among its subjects.[30] This may be thought to distinguish this passage quite sharply from the honey and wormwood analogy, which sets up a clear asymmetry between Lucretius (the enlightened therapist) and the reader (compared there to a sick child): here both poet and reader are represented, analogically, as children. It is hard, then, to identify in these passages the same sort of 'aggressive' condescension between poet and reader that Mitsis correctly identifies in the paediatric analogy. While self-inclusion via first person plurals can of course be a feature of medical condescension ('and how are we today?'), I find it difficult to identify condescension even of that weaker type here: doctors do not routinely ascribe patients' symptoms to themselves, even if only to put said patients at their ease. Here, then, we find a poet/reader dynamic that seems quite different from that laid out in the paediatric analogy. Here, instead of condescending to the reader, Lucretius adopts the reader's own perspective, suggesting empathetically that occasional (*interdum*) possession of unfounded fears, of which he as a therapist has set out to cure the reader, is in fact just one more feature of their shared experience.

Lucretius' willingness to include himself among those who suffer from unfounded fears is further demonstrated in the diatribe against the fear of death that ends Book 3. First, consider the framing of the first speech of

related to his 'ability to enter imaginatively into the minds of his opponents' (Martindale 2005: 194).

[29] Mitsis 1993: 115.

[30] Gale 2005: 181; Gale contrasts this 'sympathetic identification' of pupil and teacher at 2.56–8 with the former 'idealistic identification' of pupil and teacher in the Proem to Book 2.

nature at 3.931–51. The speech is a reproach, put into the mouth of
nature herself, levelled at one who experiences emotional disturbance at
the thought of death. The recipient of the reproach, however, is characterized by Lucretius as *alicui nostrum* – one of us (932). The poet is, at least
potentially, included among those who may be subject to such a
reproach.[31] Likewise, when the speech is over, Lucretius asks his reader
not 'how will you respond?' but rather *quid respondemus?* (950).[32] Similar
self-characterization can be identified closer to the end of the book, at
3.1076–84:[33]

> Denique tanto opere in dubiis trepidare periclis
> quae mala nos subigit vitai tanta cupido?
> certa quidem finis vitae mortalibus adstat,
> nec devitari letum pote quin obeamus.
> praeterea versamur ibidem atque insumus usque,
> nec nova vivendo procuditur ulla voluptas;
> sed dum abest quod avemus, id exsuperare videtur
> cetera; post aliud, cum contigit illud, avemus,
> et sitis aequa tenet vitai semper hiantis.

1080

Again, what terrible craving for life compels us to live so anxiously amid doubts
and dangers? Indeed, a fixed end of life awaits mortals, nor can death be avoided,
but we must go to meet it. Moreover, we move and live our life always in the same
place, nor by living is any new pleasure forged; but while that which we desire is
absent, it seems to surpass all other things; later, when we have it, we desire
something else, and a constant thirst for life always holds us, open-mouthed.

If, as he claims to have done, Lucretius has accepted the truth of Epicurean
doctrine, then he should not be subject to lust (*cupido*), craving (*avemus*)
or thirst (*sitis*) for life – emotions incompatible with an ataraxic state of
being. Once again, we find here evidence of Lucretius utilizing first person
plural forms to cast himself among the ethically and emotionally
unenlightened.

Such examples are not limited to Book 3: at 4.1089–90 a first person
plural form (*habemus*) is used to include the poet among those who suffer
insatiable erotic desire; at 5.1204–10, we find first person plurals (*suspici-
mus, nobis*) used to describe human fear at the prospect of gods who
control the cosmos;[34] at 6.246–55 a first person plural (*reamur*) is used
to describe fear that a black, cloud-filled sky is filled with the darkness of

---

[31] Kenney 2014 ad loc.: 'L. tactfully includes himself among the rebuked.'
[32] On the indicative see Heinze 1897 ad loc.; Kenney 2014 ad loc. See also Wallach 1976: 62–3.
[33] On which passage in this regard see Segal 1990: 71–2.
[34] See also 5.1218–21, with Clay 1983: 223–4.

Acheron. Nor is this phenomenon limited to the description of negative emotional states: at 4.814–17 we find Lucretius including himself among those who are prone to fall into cognitive error through faulty reasoning:

> cur igitur mirumst, animus si cetera perdit
> praeterquam quibus est in rebus deditus ipse?
> deinde adopinamur de signis maxima parvis
> ac nos in fraudem induimus frustraminis ipsi.

Why, then, should one be surprised if the mind loses all things except those to which it is itself surrendered? Moreover, we form significant additional opinions on the basis of small signs,[35] and lead ourselves into the delusion of self-deception.[36]

These examples of didactic empathy, I suggest, are instances of what I called above the 'collective' first person plural.[37] Lucretius is a member of a group (human beings), some, or perhaps most, of whom, including many of his readers, suffer emotional disturbance and cognitive error of the sorts in question here. As such, he uses universalizing first person plural expressions even though the kinds of experience in question are not strictly universal: Lucretius, the reader assumes, does not suffer from regular mental anguish concerning death or the gods, nor does he regularly fall into cognitive error of the sort outlined at 4.814–7. This collective usage enables him to include himself, empathetically, in the negative experiences and emotions of his readers. In passages such as these, the conceptual distance between teacher and student is minimized; this serves to elide the space between ignorance and enlightenment, and in so doing humanizes and familiarizes the teacher in the eyes of the student.[38] The didactic

---

[35] See also 4.465 on the (false) *opinatus animi quos addimus ipsi*.

[36] See Bailey 1947: III.1278 for the role of 816–17 in the argument here. To those passages whose first person plurals directly ascribe fear and error to Lucretius we may add those where the phrase *ne . . . reamur* is used to express a risk of shared fear or error: see 4.37–8 *ne forte animas Acherunte reamur | effugere aut umbras inter vivos volitare* ('lest by chance we think that souls escape Acheron, or that shades fly about among the living'); 5.78–81 *ne forte haec inter caelum terramque reamur | libera sponte sua cursus lustrare perennis, | morigera ad fruges augendas atque animantis, | neve aliqua divom volvi ratione putemus* ('lest by chance we think that these, free and of their own will, complete their perpetual courses between earth and sky, obliging to help the growth of crops and animals, or in case we think that they turn by any design of the gods'); 6.762–4 *ianua ne pote eis Orci regionibus esse | credatur, post hinc animas Acheruntis in oras | ducere forte deos manis inferne reamur* ('in case it should be believed that there could be a gate to Orcus in those regions, and in case by chance we should then think that the gods of the underworld lead souls from there down to the regions of Acheron').

[37] See above, pp. 61–2.

[38] Philodemus in *On Frank Criticism* (fr. 9) describes a teaching strategy according to which the teacher 'may ascribe errors . . . even to himself as a heuristic device' (translation: Konstan, Clay, Glad, Thom and Ware 1998; I am grateful to James Warren for drawing my attention to the

model, in these passages, is less one of simple information exchange between teacher and student, and more one of the joint exploration of common emotional and experiential ground.[39]

We find, then, in *DRN*, first person plurals being used to characterize the poet–reader relationship in two quite different ways: sometimes they encourage inclusion of the reader in Lucretius' Epicurean project; on other occasions they include the poet himself in the reader's own emotional difficulties. How should we expect readers to respond to such variety? We could take this combination of partial Epicurean enlightenment alongside occasional (n.b. *interdum* at 2.57 = 3.89 = 6.37) and understandable lapses into emotional turmoil as a kind of model for what the average reader may hope to achieve. Then again, we need not impose a single ideal readerly response to what is in fact a multiplicity of readerly representations: the ambiguities of the first person plural, and in particular the ambiguity between its inclusive and exclusive interpretations, leave room for multiple responses, each of which may, again, be expected to differ in accordance with the level of progress each individual reader has reached, and with the level of engagement they bring to the text. A neophyte reader, for example, encountering *id quod ratione sagaci | quaerimus* (1.368–9, translated above at p. 66) for the first time, may have reason to interpret it exclusively, lacking as yet the confidence to include him- or herself in Lucretius' quest; a sceptical reader may respond similarly to *de nilo quoniam fieri nil posse videmus* at 2.287. How, we might ask, would an ataraxic reader, or a reader who has progressed far along the path to tranquillity, interpret the assertion that *veluti pueri . . . sic nos in luce timemus | interdum* (2.55–7 = 3.87–9 = 6.35–7)? If we assume that Lucretius' poem has at least the potential to convert its readers, it is important for us to consider how, during or after

potential relevance of this text). It is clear from the context, however, that Philodemus has in mind *past* errors, not habitual ones of the sort we find Lucretius ascribing to himself via such phrases as *in fraudem induimus* (4.817). To Epicurus himself is attributed the view that the wise man, once he has become wise, will neither resume the opposite state *nor intentionally feign to do so* (Diog. Laert. 10.117 μηδὲ πλάττειν ἑκόντα). Such a stricture may seem at odds with Lucretian practice as it is described here; see, however, the next note.

[39] We find some traces of this kind of empathetic self-inclusion in Epicurus himself. In particular (see Clay 1983: 223), Lucretius' empathetic first person plurals at 5.1204–10, where emotional disturbance is connected to the need for scientific understanding, match the language of *KD* 11 (Diog. Laert. 10.142): Εἰ μηθὲν ἡμᾶς αἱ τῶν μετεώρων ὑποψίαι ἠνώχλουν καὶ αἱ περὶ θανάτου, μήποτε πρὸς ἡμᾶς ᾖ τι, ἔτι τε τὸ μὴ κατανοεῖν τοὺς ὅρους τῶν ἀλγηδόνων καὶ τῶν ἐπιθυμιῶν, οὐκ ἂν προσεδεόμεθα φυσιολογίας ('Were we not upset by the worries that celestial phenomena and death might matter to us, and also by failure to appreciate the limits of pains and desires, we would have no need for natural philosophy'; translation: Long and Sedley 1987: 1.155). The counterfactual conditional implies that we (including the speaker, Epicurus) are indeed troubled by such suspicions.

the process of conversion, their experience of the text – and the didactic relationship at its heart – is likely to change, including on re-reading.[40] Readers of this sort – readers for whom the poem has been a success – may, on reaching this final stage, find themselves alienated not only from the familiar world they once knew, but also from the poet himself, being unable to interpret *timemus* and similar empathetic gestures inclusively. Empathy with the beginner, then, may come at the cost of estrangement from the more advanced student.[41]

Common Ground and Empirical Experience

One of the most common functions of first person plural forms in *DRN* is to point to the various forms of empirical experience upon which Lucretius' arguments are based. Epicureans hold sensory experience to be the foundation of all philosophical inquiry, as Lucretius states quite plainly on several occasions (1.423–5, 699–700; 4.482–3). In line with this central principle, Lucretius' arguments regularly involve appeals to empirical evidence provided by the senses, either to provide premises from which conclusions may be inferred, or to serve as sources for analogical thought about the unseen world.[42] Unfamiliar, potentially alienating conclusions are thus shown to flow from perfectly familiar features of experience. Sometimes these appeals to empirical experience use second person singular forms; sometimes empirical evidence is simply stated as fact without recourse to mention of its perception; on two occasions we find empirical experience invoked via a first person singular form (*vidi*).[43] Very regularly, however, we find an expression with a first person plural form used to

---

[40] For the importance of re-reading to the plot of a didactic poem see esp. Fowler 2000c: 211; Trépanier 2007.

[41] Alternatively, it might be suggested that empathetic interventions of this kind would lead successful readers to a more forgiving stance vis-à-vis the possibility of occasional (*interdum*) failure, on their part or others', to maintain tranquillity. This would be at odds, however, with the vision of the perfect tranquil life that Epicurus promises to those who accept his doctrines (see, e.g., *Ep. Pyth.* 116, Diog. Laert. 10.117, *Ep. Men.* 135).

[42] See further Tutrone in Chapter 4 of this volume. The importance of sensory experience to Lucretius' philosophical methodology may help to explain the preponderance of perception verbs in *DRN* (for which see, e.g., Keen 1985; Lehoux 2013). It is important to note, however, that a large proportion of perception verbs in *DRN* do not refer to states of affairs involving actual perception: *video*, for example, is regularly used to refer to higher, non-perceptual cognitive functions (see, for example, *videmus* at 2.287, discussed above at pp. 67–8). This makes it difficult to draw firm conclusions about the role of sense-perception in *DRN* based solely on a count of perception verbs (*pace* Keen 1985; Lehoux 2013).

[43] 4.577–9 (on the echo) and 6.1044–7 (on the 'Samothracian stone'). See also 4.969–70 on Lucretius' own dreams, with Sedley 1998: 53 n. 60.

introduce empirical evidence into Lucretian arguments. Often the verb in question is a perception verb; on other occasions it may be a verb that refers to an activity that grants us sensory experience.[44]

The reader is given good reason to interpret these 'empirical' first person plural forms as inclusive.[45] They often point to common experiences that a reader is highly likely to have had; it is natural, in such instances, for readers to include themselves among the verb's subjects. So, we find first person plural forms used to refer to such universal experiences as the perception of seasonal changes (1.175 *videmus*), and of propagation and growth in flora (2.709, 713 *videmus*); of letters on a page (1.197 *videmus*); of moving objects (1.342 *cernimus*); of reflections in water (1.1060 *videmus*); of the dawn (2.149 *videmus*); of things seen at a distance (2.315 *possimus cernere*); of the sea (2.768 *videmus*); the experience of visual glare (3.363 *cernere . . . nequimus*); the feel of objects touched in the dark (2.747 *tangimus*); of a stone knocked with a toe (4.265 *tundimus*); the suffering of an injury that draws blood (4.1050 *icimur ictu*).

First person plurals expressing empirical experience sometimes indicate more culturally or geographically specific contexts, with which we may nonetheless assume many Roman readers would have been familiar: the sight of worn down pavements (1.316 *conspicimus*); of wine going through a sieve (2.391 *videmus*); dreams of smoking altars (3.431 *cernimus*); the taste of the air near the sea (4.223 *cum mare versamur propter*); the experience of medicine working on the body (3.511 *cernimus . . . videmus*). In one famous instance (2.532–40), a first person plural perception verb (*videmus*) is used to point not to a particular empirical experience as much as to the lack of such experience (in this case, of elephants in Italy), which is itself to be considered probative.

For many of Lucretius' readers, we may assume that experiences of the sort listed above would have been sufficiently familiar (or, in the case of the elephants, sufficiently unusual) as to invite an inclusive reading of the first person plural expressions which describe them.[46] In none of these cases would it be reasonable to assume that Lucretius is referring either to his

---

[44] On first person plural perception verbs in *DRN* see esp. Lehoux 2013: 137–8. For the widespread role of appeals to collective experience in scientific arguments more generally see Lehoux 2012: 133–54.

[45] See also Lehoux 2013: 137–8.

[46] We may note here the possibility that the range of experiences on which the reader can draw may increase during the process of reading. A reader sitting in a sunlit room, reading through 2.112–24, may pay greater attention than usual to the dust motes moving in the air; and has there ever been a reader who, on first encountering 4.447–52, did not at once press a finger beneath one eye?

own personal experience or to the private experience of a group of which he, and not the reader, is a member.

Such instances allow us to construct a model of Lucretian communication as the mutual exploration of common empirical ground between poet and reader, teacher and student. Rather than a dyadic model of Lucretian didaxis, with information being simply passed from teacher to student, we may construct a triadic model, featuring the generation, via inclusive first person plurals encompassing teacher and student, of shared focus on a third element drawn from common experience, the student's understanding of which is then transformed via the rational techniques of Epicurean therapy. The regular use of inclusive first person plural expressions enables Lucretius to orientate his lessons around the publicly accessible world of which both he and his reader have direct empirical experience. By drawing in this way on the reader's perceptual experience, Lucretius encourages the reader to interpret the world in accordance with Epicurean principles: starting with perception, and working from there.

But perhaps so regular an anticipation of empirical common ground with the reader is too optimistic. There may never have been a reader who could honestly assent to his or her own inclusion in every 'empirical' first person plural in *DRN* (and there certainly is no such reader today). The more culturally or geographically specific the empirical experience invoked in an argument, the higher the likelihood that a reader will be unfamiliar with it, especially once the text has travelled beyond the confines of Lucretius' own milieu, and, indeed, one doesn't have to look far to identify first person plural expressions referring to experiences which, despite Lucretius' occasional rhetorical insistence on their regularity (see *saepe* at 3.526 and 4.61), can hardly have been universal even for Lucretius' earliest readers: the operation of an iron forge (6.149 *demersimus*); the appearance of snakeskins caught on brambles (4.61 *saepe videmus*), of an irrigation wheel (5.516 *videmus*), of a human body dying by slow degrees (3.526 *saepe ... cernimus*), or of a tangram puzzle (2.780 *cernimus*); the taste of the air when wormwood is mixed in one's presence (4.224 *tuimur*).

For readers without these specific experiences, I suggest, apparently 'empirical' first person plural expressions like these are obvious candidates for what I referred to above as 'collective' interpretation: as instances of an inclusive 'we' referring to things which, while strictly outside the experience of the reader, are within the experience of members of a group – whether defined as human beings, Romans, or more narrowly still – of which the reader also considers him- or herself to be a member.[47] When, at 6.148–9, Lucretius describes how white-hot iron 'hisses when we have dipped it into cold water nearby', how should we expect the reader inexperienced in the work of the forge to respond? Surely by interpreting *demersimus* as inclusive nonetheless – as a verb of which they can consider themselves subject by dint of their membership of a group some of whose members often engage in or witness the activity in question; the operation of the forge, understood in this way, is a feature of collective human experience, even if the reader has never actually had experience of it. A lack of personal experience on the part of the reader, then, need not rule out inclusive interpretation of 'empirical' first person plurals; depending on the experience of each reader, such collective interpretation may indeed be a regular feature of readerly engagement with the evidence presented in *DRN*.

The result is that some of Lucretius' arguments will be understood by readers as relying not on their own personal empirical experiences, but rather on what they have heard about the experiences of others, which is to say, on testimony – things they have heard reported, or read about, and trust sufficiently as to consider them a normal feature of collective human experience.[48] So, for a reader who, for example, does not know the smell of wormwood, the lines *dilutaque contra | cum tuimur misceri absinthia, tangit amaror* (4.223–4 'on the other hand, when we watch as wormwood is diluted and mixed, a bitter sensation arises') may be of a quite distinct evidentiary order than, say, *vites autumno fundi suadente videmus* (1.175 'we see vines putting forth fruit under the influence of autumn'), provided that said reader's experience of viticulture is more extensive than his or her experience of the apothecary. The latter use of *videmus*, for such a reader, describes perceptual experience, which, on the Epicurean model, will provide the foundation for reasoning about the world; the former example, from the reader's perspective, is based not on direct experience, but rather on the testimony of others.

For some of Lucretius' arguments to be based on testimony rather than the reader's own experience is not in itself a problem: sometimes in *DRN* Lucretius appeals to the testimony of others as reliable evidence for what happens in the world, especially in far-flung places likely to be unfamiliar to readers.[49] To take just one example, his use of the term *fama*:

---

[47] See above, pp. 61–2.

[48] On the interplay of cultural memory and embodied experience in *DRN*, also as re-remembered and re-experienced through the text of *DRN*, see also Tutrone in Chapter 4 of this volume.

[49] To which examples may be added the two first person singular expressions listed at n. 43.

namque Ceres fertur fruges Liberque liquoris
vitigeni laticem mortalibus instituisse;
cum tamen his posset sine rebus vita manere,
ut fama est aliquas etiam nunc vivere gentis.   5.14–17

For Ceres is said to have established the growing of crops for mortals, and Liber the liquid of vine-born fluid; and yet life could have remained without these things, as it is said that some tribes live even now.[50]

quod genus Idaeis fama est e montibus altis
dispersos ignis orienti lumine cerni,
inde coire globum quasi in unum et conficere orbem.   5.663–5

Just as it is said that from the high mountains of Ida scattered fires are seen as the sun rises, and then they come together as it were into one ball, and make an orb.

In each of these cases we find direct appeal not to the evidence of the senses, but rather to other people's reports of their own empirical experience (see esp. *cerni* at 5.664). So, relying on testimony to construct one's arguments is not in itself a bad thing. We should note, however, that, whereas one's own empirical experience, for Epicureans, will always be reliable, the same cannot, of course, be said for the testimony of others. Elsewhere in *DRN*, for example, Lucretius speaks of the harmful falsehoods propagated by *fama*: the *fama deum* at 1.68, for example, or the mythologized tale of Tantalus at 3.981 (*ut famast*). Unlike in the case of empirical experience, then, the inquirer cannot simply take the evidence of testimony on trust: selective judgement has to be applied, making testimony a less reliable source of evidence than perception.

When a reader interprets one of Lucretius' first person plural perception verbs collectively, reading it as a reference not to his or her own experience (which is lacking) but rather to generic human experience, the line between empirical evidence and mere testimony becomes blurred, and the certainty which, for Epicureans, normally accompanies the individual subject's perceptions is lent, catachrestically, to the less reliable world of testimony and collectivity. This blurring of lines is of course itself a feature of Lucretius' didactic technique, encouraging readers to treat pieces of evidence of different evidentiary value (experience vs testimony) in the same way, as equally deserving of credence. I do not seek here to suggest that we, as critics, may reliably distinguish between 'real' and 'collective' inclusive first person plurals in the poem (except insofar as they pertain to our own experiences as individuals); rather, where this distinction is to be

---

[50] On which Bailey cites Caes., *B Gall.* 6.22.

drawn will vary from reader to reader – and, again, this is a function of the ambiguity of the first person plural. The point is that the prevalence of 'empirical' first person plural expressions in *DRN* will, for some readers, mask a reliance on testimony in place of actual experience; sometimes, a Lucretian invitation to look and see will in fact have to be read as a request to rely on what one has heard from others, and to take it on trust.

Conclusion

I have tried in this essay to draw attention to some ambiguities regularly encountered in Lucretian first person plurals, and to the variety of ways in which readers may respond to them. While some of my attention has been directed towards the consideration of Lucretius' didactic intentions with respect to common ground, I have tried not to limit myself to such an approach, preferring to lay stress on the power of such ambiguities to shape the poem's meaning at the point of reception. Such an approach may bear fruit even in the case of the most important first person plural in the poem, at 3.830 – the triumphant climax (*igitur*) of the long train of arguments for the mortality of the soul that runs through the heart of the third book:

> nil igitur mors est ad nos neque pertinet hilum.

> Death therefore is nothing to us, and matters not at all.

To whom may *nos* refer here? The argumentative context suggests that it is meant universally (and therefore inclusively): death is nothing to *all of us*.[51] On this reading, we are faced with a binary choice of assent or dissent: those readers who have accepted the arguments of the book will accept the claim; those readers who have not yet been brought around will not. For those who are still struggling, however, an alternative is possible: the reader who has not yet been freed from fear, but who yet desires and feels the attraction of an ataraxic life, may be tempted to read this not as a universal claim, but rather as an (as yet exclusive) expression of the promise of Epicureanism – as the particular slogan (taken into Latin directly from the Greek of *Kuria Doxa* 2; see also *Ep. Men.* 124–5) of a school whose leader was famous for, among other things, facing his own death with tranquillity and calm. Death, then, is nothing to *us*; follow us, and it can be nothing to you, too.

---

[51] See also 3.926, which clearly indicates an inclusive meaning: *multo igitur mortem minus ad nos esse putandumst* ('therefore one must think that death is much less important to us'). For possible reconstructions of Epicurus' argument see the excellent Warren 2004a, especially Chapters 2 and 3.

Every such ambiguity in the Lucretian first person plural introduces a new fork in the road for the reader, a new direction in which the didactic plot may or may not progress. Even where Lucretius may seek to lay out a certain interpretative path for the reader, we remain free to adopt alternative readings, exploiting the ambiguities of Lucretian language to adopt a form of resistant reading that is nonetheless permitted by the text. The result is a text that can speak differently both to different readers and to the same reader on different readings, or at different stages in his or her Epicurean education.

CHAPTER 4

Coming to Know Epicurus' Truth: Distributed Cognition in Lucretius' De Rerum Natura

Fabio Tutrone

Introduction: from Descartes to Epicurus

During the past few days I have accustomed myself to leading my mind away from the senses; and I have taken careful note of the fact that there is very little about corporeal things that is truly perceived, whereas much more is known about the human mind, and still more about God ... And indeed the idea I have of the human mind, in so far as it is a thinking thing, which is not extended in length, breadth or height and has no other bodily characteristics (*res cogitans, non extensa in longum, latum et profundum, nec aliud quid a corpore habens*), is much more distinct than the idea of any corporeal thing.[1]

The fourth of René Descartes' *Meditations on First Philosophy* (1641) reports the results of a decidedly unEpicurean exercise in abstraction which would have left Lucretius in dismay. A careful reader of the *De Rerum Natura* (*DRN*), Descartes is willing to present his notion of corporeal substance – the so-called *res extensa* – in terms which are reminiscent of Lucretian physics.[2] But when it comes to the boundary between mind and body, self and world, Cartesian dualism plays its trump card, reinforcing the traditional metaphysical discourse by means of arguments that have been exceptionally influential in the history of Western thought. The malicious may say that, nearly ten years after the appearance of the *Meditations*, the bitterly cold Swedish winter took Lucretius' revenge, for a few days before dying from pneumonia at the court of Queen Christina, Descartes wrote to a friend that 'during the winter men's thoughts freeze like the water'.[3]

---

[1] Descartes 1996: 37.

[2] For a quick sketch of the relationship between Cartesian and Lucretian cosmology see Johnson and Wilson 2007: 136. A detailed treatment of Descartes' peculiar corpuscularianism is offered by Garber 1992: 117–55.

[3] Descartes 1903: 467 ('il me semble que les pensées des hommes se gelent icy pendant l'hyuer aussy bien que les eaux'), a letter to Brégy written in Stockholm on 15 January 1650. Descartes died on 11 February 1650.

Lucretius' readers know that psychic life is, so to speak, a matter of matter – and that too much cold air in the soul makes the individual weak.[4]

Until recently, Descartes' idea that the human mind is, by definition, a non-extended entity (*res cogitans, non extensa*), enclosed in the body but constitutionally different from common bodily and worldly realities, found wide acceptance among students of cognitive sciences. Cartesian internalism, though variously modified, was long the norm, and the mind was reputed to pursue its quiet life within 'the ancient fortress of skin and skull'.[5] Only in the past few decades have the barriers between outer and inner worlds begun to blur, projecting the process of cognition as a complex *distributed* phenomenon. The case of Lucretius and Epicurean philosophy discussed in this essay aims to show that the narrow fortress of the knowing self is not as ancient as some present-day theorists are inclined to think, and that the very concept of distributed cognition, broadly construed, has a history of its own with deep roots in Greco-Roman physiology. Lucretius' poem provides especially compelling evidence that, on the one hand, Epicurean epistemology conceives of cognition as a material process extended (or *distributed*) across the borders of atomic bodies, and that, on the other hand, true knowledge can be achieved only through cooperative didactic techniques. However, before approaching the *DRN*, it is necessary to explain briefly why contemporary cognitive scientists are ready to claim that 'the Cartesian tradition is mistaken in supposing that the mind is an inner entity of any kind, whether mind-stuff, brain states, or whatever'.[6] Over the past twenty-five years, not only has the body–mind division been radically questioned, but also brain-based materialist theories (such as functionalism)[7] have been increasingly superseded by a situated understanding of knowledge and knowing agents.

As Philip Robbins and Murat Aydede observe, the newly emerging tendency to see cognition as *embodied, enactive, distributed, embedded* or *extended* points to three central ideas, all united by their focus on the situatedness of the mental: 'First, cognition depends not just on the brain

---

[4] Cf. *DRN* 3.290–1; 299–301. On the distance between Descartes' model of intellectual investigation and the ancient philosophical tradition see Konstan 2009.

[5] To borrow the words of a prominent opponent of traditional internalism: Clark 2003: 5.

[6] Van Gelder 1995: 380. Emblematic is the exclamatory title of Bruno Latour's review (Latour 1995) of Hutchins 1995a: *cogito ergo sumus!*

[7] On the theoretical bases of functionalism see Block 1980: 171–306. Most typically, functionalists argue that mental states and operations rely on physical processes but add the crucial point that different material conditions can result in the same psychic functions. Interestingly, according to Nussbaum and Rorty 1992, the conceptual origins of functionalism should be traced back to Aristotle.

but also on the body (the embodiment thesis). Second, cognitive activity routinely exploits structure in the natural and social environment (the embedding thesis). Third, the boundaries of cognition extend beyond the boundaries of individual organisms (the extension thesis)'.[8] Admittedly, a deep breach in the bastion of the computational mind was opened by Edwin Hutchins' ethnographic study of Western and Micronesian sailing practices. According to Hutchins, 'the thinker in this world is a very special medium that can provide coordination among many structured media – some internal, some external, some embodied in artefacts, some in ideas, and some in social relationships'.[9]

An even more decided step away from traditional internalism was marked by the so-called extended mind (EM) hypothesis, first proposed by Andy Clark and David Chalmers.[10] According to Clark and Chalmers, not only does the environment play an active role in driving cognitive processes (*active externalism*), but the boundaries of the mind extend into the world at large, insofar as '*beliefs* can be constituted partly by features of the environment'.[11] This radical thesis is famously illustrated through the example of an Alzheimer's patient (Otto) routinely retrieving information from his notebook in the very same way a cognitively standard agent (Inga) retrieves information from her memory. However, it should be noted that the extended mind theory puts greater emphasis on the *complementarity* between outer and inner resources rather than on their parity.[12] Far from arguing that the mind has been recently transformed into a cyborg device due to the replacement of normal cognitive faculties with sophisticated, post-humanizing technologies, EM supporters believe that human beings tend by nature to offload cognition onto external cognitive technology. In their view, humans are, as Clark nicely puts it, 'natural-born cyborgs',[13] and the beginning of cognitive technology is *language* – which, as two other scholars notice, 'extends cognizers' individual and joint performance powers, distributing the load through interactive and collaborative cognition'.[14]

---

[8] Robbins and Aydede 2009b: 3.
[9] Hutchins 1995a: 316. Hutchins 1995b investigated the interactions between pilots, tools and representational media within an airline cockpit. One should also mention at least the path-breaking surveys of Norman 1991, and Zhang and Norman 1994, and the methodological points of Kirsh 2006.
[10] Clark and Chalmers 1998. See, more recently, Clark 2003 and Wilson 2004.
[11] Clark and Chalmers 1998: 12 (authors' italics).
[12] See, e.g., Clark and Chalmers 1998: 17, and now Sutton 2010: 204–8.
[13] Clark 2003. See also Latour 1993 for an effective revision of the (not very ancient) dichotomy between natural skills and cultural tools.
[14] Dror and Harnad 2008: 1. According to Clark and Chalmers 1998: 18, 'without language, we might be much more akin to discrete Cartesian "inner" minds'.

By describing human discourse *sensu lato* as an intrinsically interactive and collaborative undertaking,[15] heavily dependent on 'the general paraphernalia of language, books, diagrams, and culture',[16] cognitive scientists have opened up a stimulating new perspective for literary and historical research. As the most symbolically powerful elaboration of language for the sake of communicative interaction, literature acquires the traits of a quintessentially human experience. And such traits are even more evident in the case of literary genres constitutively aimed at knowledge exchange such as ancient didactic poetry. Moreover, it seems imperative for present-day scholars in the humanities to devise interdisciplinary approaches to what John Sutton calls 'historical cognitive science'.[17] According to Sutton, this very promising field of inquiry should basically work between two projects: on the one hand, 'the analysis of other and older theories of mind, of how they relate to and differ from current approaches, and of what forgotten or neglected explananda they bring into focus'; on the other hand, the investigation of 'cognitive practices' (as opposed to purely theoretical constructs) reflecting culturally embedded views about self and mind as well as 'different historical forms of mental activity'.[18]

In the present chapter, I shall be considering both an older theory of mind (Epicurus' epistemology, with its physical, psychological and ethical implications) and a set of historical cognitive practices (the instruments of didactic persuasion employed by Lucretius as a poet-speaker guiding his addressee in the gradual discovery of a bravely new Epicurean world). As for Epicurus' account of cognition and the mental, I will argue that its characteristic emphasis on the interaction between mind and world, things and senses – between different but ontologically cognate atomic bodies – presents the reader with a distinctively ancient idea of extended mind. I will then show how the Epicurean faith in the veracity of sense-perceptions and the reliability of analogical inductions lays the foundations of Lucretius' didactic method. Standing at the crossroads between poetry and philosophy, this method tries to involve the addressee (both intellectually and emotionally) in the cooperative construction of an

---

[15] Cf., e.g., Dror and Harnad 2008: 20.   [16] Clark and Chalmers 1998: 8.

[17] See Sutton 1998: 10–15.

[18] Sutton 2000: 117. As Sutton 2008: 52 notes, interdisciplinary cooperation should allow history to 'take its place alongside ethnography and developmental psychology as a key testing-ground for the whole framework' of the distributed cognition hypothesis. It is noteworthy that, as we shall see, Lucretius situates every form of human thinking – including Epicurus' thought – as the product of the history of civilization.

internalized cognitive artefact: the image of the atomic cosmos, faithfully reflected in the text.

Research in historical cognitive science has already produced significant results in conceptual areas related to our topic.[19] Also in the domain of classical studies, an awareness has emerged that 'just as humans have always relied on bodily and external resources, we have always developed theories, models and metaphors to make sense of the ways in which how we think is dependent on being in the world'.[20] At present, however, the scholarly literature devoted to such issues is only nascent. It is very significant that in his search for the 'philosophical antecedents' of the notion of situated cognition, Shaun Gallagher barely touches upon classical antiquity, citing only the Aristotelian value of *phronēsis* and the Stoics' situation-based moral reasoning. Gallagher's rather pessimistic conclusion is that 'nothing like a fully developed concept of situated cognition is to be found prior to the twentieth century'.[21] It is up to classical scholars to show that long before the winter of the Cartesian self there flourished a profusion of alternative, non-internalist paradigms of cognition – and among them Lucretius' Epicurean mind stands out for its sharpness.

Atoms Within: Epicurus' Extended Mind

Lucius Manlius Torquatus, the Epicurean spokesman in Cicero's *De finibus*, boldly restates Epicurus' repudiation of dialectic, the branch of logic which, according to the Stoics, includes epistemology and makes a first fundamental contribution to the attainment of truth.[22] Epicurus,

[19] Sutton 1998 has offered a thorough survey of the 'moral physiology' of the modern age, pointing out several 'surprisingly clear resonances' of twentieth-century connectivism (XIII). Sutton 2000 has interpreted the medieval and Renaissance memory arts (which are profoundly indebted to the tradition of ancient mnemotechnique) as sciences of self based on the integration of inner and outer resources (see also Sutton 2010: 208–13). Tribble 2005 has used Hutchins' model of distributed cognition to explain how actors and companies in Shakespearean England managed to rehearse and perform a strikingly large number of plays in a very short time (see, most recently, Tribble 2011).

[20] I quote from the on-line presentation of the project *A History of Distributed Cognition*, based at the University of Edinburgh (www.hdc.ed.ac.uk/welcome-hdc, accessed 8 February 2017).

[21] Gallagher 2009: 35–6. Similarly, in his survey of the 'scientific antecedents' of situated cognition, Clancey 2009 never refers to any ancient author. One should perhaps avoid using terms like 'antecedent' or 'anticipation' which (more or less consciously) adumbrate a teleological outlook: since humans are natural-born cyborgs tending to offload their cognitive tasks onto the environment, it is anything but surprising that theoretical models of distributed cognition have been put forth over the centuries – without any consistent order or plan.

[22] Cic. *Fin.* 1.63–4 (all translations from ancient texts are mine). On the paramount importance of logic, traditionally divided into rhetoric and dialectic, for the Stoic system see Diog. Laert. 7.42. Sext. Emp. *Math.* 7.22 sharply distinguishes between the Stoic and the Epicurean approaches to the problem of knowledge. Cf. Long 1996.

Torquatus says, 'has attached the greatest importance to physics (*in physicis plurimum posuit*)', for 'it is by this science that the meaning of words, the nature of language, and the criterion (*ratio*) of consistency and contradiction can be examined'. It is essential to have 'solid knowledge of natural things (*stabilem scientiam rerum*)' and keep to Epicurus' canon (*regula*) – a gift fallen from heaven to guide human cognition (*cognitionem omnium*) and verify the judgement of the senses (*sensuum iudicia*). Epicurus' treatise *On the Criterion* is no longer extant,[23] but we have sufficient evidence to understand what Torquatus is referring to. Differently from the Stoics, Epicurus replaces logic with canonic (κανονική) and joins this part of philosophy to physics 'as both preliminary and subordinate to it'.[24] According to Epicurus, inasmuch as human perceptions (αἰσθήσεις), pre-conceptions (προλήψεις) and feelings (πάθη) are not charged with beliefs, but simply register physical experiences, they can (and should) serve as criteria of truth (κριτήρια τῆς ἀληθείας) – as 'straight edges' of the cognitive field.[25] It is in this sense that, as Torquatus argues, natural science allows understanding of the laws of language, knowledge, and reasoning. Classical logic is totally useless since, as Diogenes Laertius makes clear, 'those who study nature should be content to make progress in accordance with the very voice of things (κατὰ τοὺς τῶν πραγμάτων φθόγγους)'.[26]

The claim that the key to human cognition lies in the objectively knowable reality of the external world may perhaps sound bizarre to many modern, post-Cartesian ears. But it is perfectly reasonable in light of Epicurus' physical system and Lucretius' penetrating exposition. To better understand this, one first needs to look at Epicurus' own account of cognition in the *Letter to Herodotus* (46–53) – an abridged version of the detailed treatment given in *On Nature*, Books 2–4.[27] After explaining that the infinity of changing material worlds is made up of atoms and void, Epicurus teaches that all bodies emit a stream of 'impressions' (τύποι), also

---

[23] Cf. Diog. Laert. 10.27. The relevant evidence about Epicurus' *On the Criterion*, also known as *Canon*, is gathered in Usener, frr. 34–6.

[24] Asmis 1999: 261. An extensive treatment of Epicurean canonic and its value as a method of scientific research is offered in Asmis 1984.

[25] See Diog. Laert. 10.31–4. Epicurus, *KD* 24, warns that if one does not adhere to such criteria, confusion arises and true knowledge is not attained. On the Epicurean faith in the veracity of sense-perceptions and its Aristotelian background see now Hahmann 2015. See also Everson 1990 on Epicurus' understanding of perception as a cognitive fact 'produced by an external object and . . . entirely determined by that object' (172).

[26] Diog. Laert. 10.31.

[27] See the reconstruction of Epicurus' fragmentary physics treatise in Sedley 1998: 114–16.

called 'emanations' (ἀποστάσεις), 'effluences' (ἀπόρροιαι) and, more frequently, 'images' (εἴδωλα), impinging on sentient beings.[28] The thin
particles emitted reproduce the shape and colour of the body from which
they quickly and continuously flow, as they maintain a 'sympathy' (συμ-
πάθεια) with the pulsation of atoms within the body.[29] At the same time,
the size of the images is also suitable (ἐναρμόττον) for the sight (ὄψις) and
thought (διάνοια) of perceiving organisms, which are themselves atomic
compounds engaging in an interactive response to the incoming stream
(what Epicurus defines as the subject's 'application' or ἐπιβολή).[30] One
can already see that Epicurus gets rid of the historically influential '*pre-
supposition that the mental must be different in kind – categorically
different – from anything bodily or worldly*' – to quote a sensible
twentieth-century supporter of the so-called embodiment and embeddedness thesis.[31] Indeed, not only is the Epicurean mind of an entirely bodily
nature – as Lucretius forcefully argues in Book 3 of his poem – but it also
acts in the very same way as the five senses, developing perceptions,
applications, and representations (φαντασίαι). As Elizabeth Asmis
observes, 'the dependence of the mind on newly arriving images is a
peculiarity of Epicurean psychology that provoked much criticism in
antiquity. It conflicts with the well-entrenched position that, unlike the
five senses, the mind has objects of its own, which it can call up whenever
it likes, regardless of what happens to it from outside'.[32]

In Epicurean gnoseology, perception and thought exist solely as the
effect of an interaction between inner and outer particles: we see (and
think of) coloured three-dimensional solids even if, on a deeper

---

[28] *Ep. Hdt.* 46. Lucretius (4.26–109) famously translates εἴδωλα with *simulacra*, but his occasional use
of other terms (such as *membranae* and *cortex*) is reminiscent of Epicurus' variations on the theme.
See Dalzell 1974.

[29] *Ep. Hdt.* 48–50. The impressions have the same shape as the original solids (46 ὁμοιοσχήμονες τοῖς
στερεμνίοις), because a 'commensurate impact' (σύμμετρος ἐπερεισμός) arises from the vibration
(πάλσις) deep within the body (50). The 'sympathy' between things and images is repeatedly
highlighted also with respect to the specific dynamics of hearing (52–3). See now Verde 2010:
116–45, with further bibliography.

[30] I cannot agree with Annas 1992: 162, that Epicurus' 'physical account of perception is a totally
receptive one; no room seems to be made for aspects like awareness'. Among other things, epistemic
processes like 'application' (ἐπιβολή, a function performed by both the mind and the senses: *Ep.
Hdt.* 50) and 'apperception' (ἐπαίσθησις, the cognitive decoding of sounds and their content
following the first general perception: Bailey 1926: 200 and Keen 1981: 61) – attest to a truly
participative view of cognition.

[31] Haugeland 1998: 228 (author's italics).

[32] Asmis 1999: 271. Roman readers like Cicero were clearly impressed by the fact the Epicureans
interpreted *both* sight *and* thought as a material response to flowing images: see, e.g., *Fin.* 1.21; *Nat.
D.* 1.107–8.

ontological level, human minds, external bodies and cognitive artefacts are parts of a network of atoms separated by void and having no other qualities than size, shape, weight and movement.[33] Significantly, Epicurus asserts that 'the generation of images is simultaneous with human thought (ἄμα νοήματι συμβαίνει)', so that 'we see the shapes of things and think of them (διανοεῖσθαι) when something from the external objects enters into our minds'.[34] This clarification explains why we have an immediate and uninterrupted perception of solids in spite of the progressive and discontinuous nature of their eidolic streams, but it also mirrors Epicurus' belief in the ontological connection between mind and world. As Lucretius points out in Book 4 of the *DRN* (746–8), 'any one whatsoever of such fine images can easily bestir our mind (*animum*) through a single impression, for the mind itself (*mens ipsa*) is thin (*tenuis*) and incredibly easy to move (*mire mobilis*)'. In the psychological discussion of Book 3, Lucretius has already shown that the human mind is made up of very subtle atoms and moves more quickly than any other entity. It is this similarity in their constitutions that makes the encounter between mind and images cognitively productive.[35]

For Epicurus and his followers, sense-perception and mental life are aspects of cognition distributed across body, soul and environment – the first two elements being wholly material components of a temporary aggregate. Notably, when explaining the reasons why different kinds of food produce different sensory effects, Lucretius refers to both the shape of the incoming atoms and the recipient's response. Already in Book 2, it is made clear that atomic particles have various shapes resulting in different macroscopic bodies as well as in largely diverging perceptive experiences (2.333–477). In the gnoseological treatment of Book 4, Lucretius focuses more specifically on the sense of taste and remarks on its distributed

---

[33] That atomic particles have no other qualities than these is extensively shown by Lucretius (2.730–885).

[34] *Ep. Hdt.* 48–9. The same point is made by Epicurus in Book 2 of *On Nature*, frr. 24.50–1 Arrighetti (*PHerc* 1149/993 4 IV): see Arrighetti 1973: 217–18. A close relationship between atomic motion and human thought is established also in the (notably different) context of kinetic theory: see *Ep. Hdt.* 61, with the thorough remarks of Konstan 1979: 413–14.

[35] Cf. *DRN* 3.182–5; 374–97. The treatment in the *DRN* recalls, with a few minor variations, the teachings of Epicurus, *Ep. Hdt.* 63–6 (see Gottschalk 1996). In Book 3, Lucretius distinguishes between the rational, leading part of the soul – the *mens* or *animus* placed in the chest – and the irrational, sensorial part (*anima*) distributed across the body. Yet the poet is very careful in noting (3.136–9) that this is a merely functional distinction: for even if the *animus* experiences internal states concerning the sphere of knowledge and emotions (3.145–6), *animus* and *anima* are strictly connected parts of a unitary material organism. See Mehl 1999 and Konstan 2008: 8–11.

character (4.615–72).[36] According to the poet, not only does every substance contain a special class of atomic shapes – so that smooth atoms (659 *levissima corpora*) produce sweet taste, in contrast with rough and hooked ones (662 *aspera . . . hamataque*) – but various types of atomic *figurae* also coexist in the very same substances. Such different *figurae* are selected at a later stage on the basis of the recipient's condition. Since, like the external atoms, the pores in the mouth of living beings (*intervalla, viae* or *foramina*) have different shapes, they tend to admit into the body those atoms which conform with them.[37] This explains why some animals enjoy hellebore, which humans reject as poisonous. But it also explains why honey tastes sweet to the healthy and bitter to the sick.[38] For Lucretius, 'both kinds of atoms (i.e. the smooth and the rough/hooked ones) are mixed up in the flavour of honey' (671): it is the atomic dispositions in the recipient's body (667 *positurae principiorum*), depending on health and other physical variables, which ultimately influence the choice of one or another class of external atoms.

Clearly, in Epicurean theory, different perceptive possibilities are inherent in the material constituents of things, but the task of actualizing them is entrusted to sentient atomic beings. No radical separation between objects and senses can be established because, as Lucretius argues at length in Book 2 (865–990), all perceiving organisms (*sensilia*) arise from atoms, which are principles devoid of feeling (*insensilia*). Plutarch informs us that Epicurus applied such a distributed model of sensation 'to everything called and held to be bitter, sweet, purgative, soporific, or shining, for nothing has an independent quality and power (αὐτοτελῆ ποιότητα καὶ δύναμιν), or is more active than passive when entering bodies, but gives rise to different dispositions and blendings in different bodies'.[39] In the case of sight and thought, atomic images can be significantly modified during their journey to the sense organs. According to Lucretius, for

---

[36] See Rosenmeyer 1996.

[37] For Epicurus, both the sense organs and the mind are endowed with pores which allow access to the eidolic streams: see *Ep. Hdt.* 47 and the evidence from *On Nature* discussed by Leone 2002a: 126–8 and 2002b. See also Diogenes of Oenoanda, fr. 9 col. 3.6–4.2, with the comments of Smith 1993: 446–9. At the moment of death, the same pores which allow sensation let the swift soul atoms come out: see *DRN* 3.558–91 and Philodemus *On Death* 4 col. 8.6–24.

[38] The 'real' taste of honey is an *exemplum classicum* of ancient epistemology, famously used by the Sceptics. Sext. Emp. *Pyr.* 2.63 attests that the controversy dates back at least to Democritus and Heraclitus. See Perin 2010.

[39] Plut. *Adv. Col.* 1110b–c. Plutarch quotes verbatim from Epicurus' lost *Symposium* (cf. 1109f) and *Against Theophrastus* (frr. 29–30; 58–60 Usener), where the effects of wine and the perception of colours were discussed (cf. also *DRN* 4.324–52). *Pace* Usener, the passage just cited (fr. 30) comes from the *Symposium*.

instance, optical illusions are typically produced outside the human mind. If seen from far away, square towers may appear round because the friction of the air blunts the corners of the travelling *simulacra* before they reach the eye (*DRN* 4.353–63).[40] Of course, when it comes to the 'sixth sense' known as mind, external phenomena can have especially far-reaching consequences for the sphere of individual and social beliefs. In an attempt to show 'whence come those things that come to mind' (4.722–3 *unde | quae veniunt veniant in mentem*), Lucretius discusses the exemplary case of mythological figures like Centaurs. Humans conceive of such non-existent (albeit culturally and psychologically relevant) creatures because the thin images that stir the mind – which are even thinner than those provoking vision – occasionally combine with each other in the air.[41] 'When the image of a horse and that of a man happen to meet', Lucretius says, 'they easily and promptly adhere' (4.741–2), transmitting to the mind a perceptive appearance which may be falsely interpreted as proving the existence of a human–animal hybrid – the mythical Centaur. Again, in the Epicurean view, sense-perception is reliable. But it is also the product of an *extended* and *distributed* phenomenon, later processed by consciousness.[42]

A further (perhaps the most striking) example of Epicurus' cognitive externalism is his theory about the origins of the idea of god. Lucretius provides valuable evidence about this theory in Book 5 of his poem, when describing the historical stage at which mankind started to worship the gods and have religious awe. According to the poet, the minds of early humans were impressed by the images of outstanding beings looking physically strong, beautiful, incorruptible, peaceful, and blessed.[43] Such images occurred in waking life (5.1170 *animo . . . vigilante*), but even more

---

[40] For the Epicureans, perception is true in this case as well, for atomic images have actually taken a round shape (cf. Sext. Emp. *Math.* 7.208–9). Error occurs when we superimpose our own beliefs onto the facts reported by the senses (Epicurus *Ep. Hdt.* 50; *DRN* 4.379–468). And that's why we should always verify whether a perception waiting confirmation (προσμένον) is supported by evidence (ἐπιμαρτυρηθήσεσθαι). See Annas 1992: 159–61 and Asmis 1999: 283–5.

[41] 4.722–44. Epicurus, *Ep. Hdt.* 48, synthetically refers to the emergence of 'sharp aggregates in the environment' (συστάσεις ἐν τῷ περιέχοντι ὀξεῖαι). Lucretius (4.735–8) specifies that the *simulacra* may both emanate from solids and arise spontaneously in the air before blending with each other. On Lucretius' 'theory of myth as a misinterpretation of sense-data' and its cultural background see Gale 1994: 91–3.

[42] According to Epicurus, *Ep. Hdt.* 50, false beliefs such as those of traditional mythology arise at the crucial stage of opinion formation (ἐν τῷ προσδοξαζομένῳ), when atomic films are rationally interpreted. At 5.878–924, Lucretius forcefully warns against the mythological belief in hybrids (see Campbell 2003: 140–61).

[43] *DRN* 5.1169–82. Like all processes of Epicurean cultural history, the conceptual elaboration of the gods' images is entirely non-teleological and necessarily goes through a series of trials and errors. See Schiesaro 1990: 140–68.

in sleep (1171 *magis in somnis*), for, as Lucretius has shown in Book 4
(757–822; 907–1029), in the dream state the mind is impinged on by
simulacra which are not scrutinized by reason and the senses.[44] Since the
nineteenth century there has been much controversy among scholars over
the actual sources of the images which, according to the Epicureans,
provide humans with the preconception (πρόληψις) of gods.[45] Taking
literally the assertion in the *Letter to Menoeceus* that 'there are gods' (θεοὶ
μὲν γάρ εἰσίν), some interpreters – the so-called 'realists' – have argued that
Epicurus believed in the existence of immortal and blessed beings emitting
their extremely fine images from interstellar space.[46] On the contrary,
others – the so-called 'idealists' – have claimed that the Epicurean gods
are mere 'psychological processes' or 'thought-constructs'[47] resulting from
an 'innate predisposition of the human subject'.[48] As a rule, Epicurean
'predispositions', or 'preconceptions' (προλήψεις), are not innate at all, for
they are general conceptual patterns routinely activated by language and
formed out of repeated sensory impressions.[49] Yet idealists maintain that
the preconception of gods is unique precisely insofar as it is inborn. The
main evidence adduced to support such a claim comes from Book 1 of
Cicero's *De natura deorum*, where Velleius, the Epicurean spokesman,
contends that 'we have implanted, or rather inborn, knowledge (*insitas
vel potius innatas cognitiones*) of the gods', explicitly qualifying this kind of
knowledge as a preconception shared across cultures.[50]

   However, as David Konstan has shown, neither of the participial
adjectives employed by Cicero – *insitus* and *innatus* – imply the modern

[44] Cf. also Diogenes of Oenoanda, fr. 3 col. 3.6–6.3, and the notes of Clay 1980.
[45] Especially controversial has proved the reading of Epicurus *Ep. Men.* 123–4.
[46] It should be recognized that most of the students of Epicurean theology have committed to a realist
   view: see, e.g., Mansfeld 1993; Giannantoni 1996; Santoro 2000; Wigodsky 2004; Konstan 2011.
[47] Both definitions are used in Long and Sedley 1987: 1.144–9, whose theory has precedents in the
   studies of Lange 1866 and Scott 1883. Contemporary idealists include Bollack 1975: 225–38 and
   Obbink 1989, 1996, 2002.
[48] Sedley 2011: 48, an especially forceful defence of Epicurus' 'theological innatism'.
[49] Diog. Laert. 10.33 defines preconceptions as 'a kind of apprehension (κατάληψις), or correct
   opinion (δόξα ὀρθή), or notion (ἔννοια), or a general stored concept (καθολικὴ νόησις
   ἐναποκειμένη), that is, memory (μνήμη), of what has often appeared from outside' (I agree with
   Sedley 2011: 40 n. 28, that the final genitive should be attached to all the preceding accusatives).
   According to Diogenes, for instance, 'as soon as the word "human being" is spoken, the impression
   (τύπος) of a human being is also conceived by the mind in accordance with the preconception
   (κατὰ πρόληψιν) and on the basis of previous sense perceptions'. See Asmis 1984: 63–80 and
   Glidden 1985.
[50] Cic. *Nat. D.* 1.43–5. The Greek term πρόληψις is repeatedly mentioned and alternatively translated
   as *anticipatio* or *praenotio*. Velleius goes on to claim that 'the same nature that gave us the
   impression (*informatio*, Cicero's translation of τύπος) of gods as such, has also engraved in our
   minds (*insculpsit in mentibus*) the idea that they are eternal and blessed'.

idea of innateness according to which a concept is fully present in the mind from the very moment of birth.[51] Plautus, Terence, and Cicero himself typically use *innatus* in the sense of 'developed' or 'grown upon', a sense directly connected with the parent verb *innascor* and substantially identical with that of *insitus*.[52] As participle of *insero*, *insitus* recalls the Roman agricultural practice of grafting, thus suggesting that, in Epicurus' view, the preconception of gods is implanted into the human mind like a slowly growing twig originally taken from elsewhere. Indeed, in the introduction to his account of the origins of religious awe, Lucretius sets as his task to explain 'whence even now the dread implanted in human beings comes' (5.1165 *unde etiam nunc est mortalibus insitus horror*). What he describes immediately thereafter is a gradual cognitive process by which the repeated experience of external phenomena – first of all, of the gods' *simulacra* – shapes the mind.[53] Already in the first section of Book 5 (181–6), when rejecting the belief that the gods created mankind, the poet rhetorically asks 'where the very preconception of humans implanted in the gods came from (*ipsa notities hominum divis unde insita primum est*)', if there existed yet no external model. *Insita notities* is another translation for πρόληψις. And by definition, all Epicurean preconceptions – including those in the minds of the gods – derive from the embodied and embedded experience of the world.[54]

Consistent support for a realist (and, so to speak, externalist) interpretation of Epicurean theology also comes from the Herculaneum papyri. A fragmentary treatise attributed to Demetrius Laco (*PHerc.* 1055) strongly upholds the view that god has human shape, a rarefied atomic structure making him immortal, and, above all, 'real existence along with rationality' (σὺν | λογ[ι]σμῷ τὴν ὑπόστα|σιν ἔχη<ι>). The human mind can grasp the shape of god by way of inference (διὰ ἐπ[ι]σπασμούς), as the fine composition of the mind allows it to have direct apprehension of the constitutionally similar god images (ὁμ[ο]ίων ἔχει | κατάληψιν).[55] Likewise, in his work *On the Gods* (Περὶ θεῶν), of which only fragments of Books 1 (*PHerc.* 26) and 3 (*PHerc.* 152/157)

<hr/>

[51] Konstan 2011: 66–8. [52] See, e.g., Plaut. *Mil.* 1063; Ter. *Hec.* 543; Cic. *Top.* 69; *Tusc.* 3.2.
[53] See esp. 5.1175 (*semper*) and 1181 (*multa et mira videbant*), for the idea of different, recurring experiences.
[54] Cf. Asmis 1984: 69.
[55] See col. 14–22 in the edition of Santoro 2000: 96–9; 141–77. Note that κατάληψις is the same term employed by Diog. Laert. 10.33 to elucidate the Epicurean concept of πρόληψις. It is certainly no accident that the author of *PHerc.* 1055 devotes an important section of his theological discussion (col. 9–13) to show how memories of previous perceptions are stored and maintained over time (cf. Santoro 2000: 34–5).

survive, Philodemus depicts the gods as animate beings who are able to eat, move, breathe and talk.[56] In a famous passage of Book 3 (which has been made much more perspicuous by Holger Essler's re-edition), Philodemus explains that the gods have their venerable seats (ἕδη) in the heavens, apparently in the interstitial space between worlds (μετακόσμιον).[57] From there they perpetually send to humans the images producing their 'pure representations' (ἀκεραίους παρέχοντες ἀεί τὰς φαν[τ]ασίας) as blessed and imperishable aggregates. Yet, on their way to earth, the god images may also be defiled (παρεπιμολ[ύ]νονται) by their merging with other images from the heavenly bodies, coming to form 'perceptive compounds' (συμπλοκαί) which induce mankind to worship the stars.[58] Such a view is wholly consistent with Lucretius' caveat against false religious beliefs in the introduction to his treatment of celestial phenomena (6.68–79), where the reader is urged to 'take on (suscipere) with peaceful heart the simulacra which are messengers of the divine shape (divinae nuntia formae) and are borne into human minds (in mentes hominum) from the holy body of the gods (de corpore sancto)'. Philodemus corroborates his theory by referring to Epicurus' own pro-nouncements,[59] but idealists such as David Sedley are prepared to reconcile this textual evidence with their hypothesis as well, for they think that Epicurus' theological statements may have been intentionally ambiguous for the sake of 'the school's public reputation'. According to Sedley, Epicurus' forthright claim that there are gods 'may well also have misled certain of his own followers' into the realist error.[60] But it is hard to believe that such learned Epicureans as Philodemus, Cicero/Velleius

---

[56] That god is a living being (ζῷον) characterized by eternity and blessedness is unequivocally stated by Epicurus, Ep. Men. 123. In On the Gods 3, Philodemus includes nutrition (fr. 77), motion (col. 10.6–11.25), respiration and conversation in Greek (col. 13.20–14.13) among the gods' faculties (see the edition of Diels 1917, with the improvements of Arrighetti 1955, 1958, 1961). As for divine breathing and speaking, Philodemus reports the authoritative assertions of Hermarchus (fr. 32 in Longo Auricchio 1988: 67–8; 128–37).

[57] On the gods' celestial abodes, which according to Philodemus should be revered more than human-made temples, see col. 10.1–6 in the new edition of Essler 2009: 169; 195–200. A wide-ranging reappraisal of this and other ancient sources on Epicurean theology can be found in Essler 2011, who makes a strong case for the realist view. Epicurus, Ep. Pyth. 89, defines the μετακόσμιον as the 'interspace between worlds' (μεταξὺ κόσμων διάστημα) – what Cicero (Fin. 2.75; Nat. D. 1.18; cf. also Div. 2.40) translates as intermundia (see Obbink 1996: 7–8) – but the earliest occurrence of the Greek word in an Epicurean theological context is col. 8.33 of Philodemus' On the Gods 3 (Essler 2009: 166; 180).

[58] Col. 8.35–9.36. Cf. also Konstan 2011: 59–60.

[59] Epicurus' name is attested at col. 9.26, and a reference to On Nature 5 is likely to be implied at col. 8.14–15. Cf. Essler 2009: 174–5.

[60] Sedley 2011: 49–51.

and Lucretius – whom Sedley himself characterizes as a 'fundamentalist' –
were all misled.[61]

There is good reason to agree with David Armstrong that the idealist
(and innatist) interpretation of Epicurus' thought reflects 'the Cartesian
sense of isolated selfhood in the universe characteristic of every advanced
Western society since the late seventeenth century'.[62] As he points out,
both Lucretius and the other Epicurean sources show that 'there is a lot
more to the Epicurean universe than mere *res extensa*', indeed that 'it has a
permanent and secure place above and outside us for *res cogitans*'. In
defence of the idealists, it must be said that Epicurus' notion of an
extended mind receiving atomic films as messengers of truth sounds
anything but natural to modern readers, accustomed as they are to recognizing in interior conscience the 'messenger from Him, who, both in
nature and in grace, speaks to us behind a veil'.[63] The rise of rationalist
internalism has only further widened such cultural distance. Still, in order
to understand in depth Lucretius' didactic strategies, it is on Epicurus'
universe of distributed knowledge that we have to found our analysis.

Textuality and Symbol Grounding: *De Rerum Natura* as a Distributed Cognitive Artefact

It is generally recognized that Lucretius' main purpose in writing the *DRN*
is to change the mind of his addressee by gradually revealing to him the
true nature of things. Step by step, readers are involved in the process of
creation of the poem, which coincides with the making of an ethically
stabilizing Epicurean worldview.[64] As Lucretius' didactic work progresses,
both the internal and the external addressee – that is, both Memmius and
the Roman reader – are led to reshape their cognitive assets and their very
approach to cognition.[65] It is thus more than reasonable to expect that the

---

[61] Cf. Konstan 2011: 61. On Lucretius' Epicurean fundamentalism see Sedley 1998: 62–93. While
suspending judgement on Philodemus, Sedley 2011: 50 n. 60 acknowledges that Lucretius and
Cicero ('and therefore, quite possibly, Cicero's Epicurean source') assumed the realist
interpretation, but thinks that the doctrinal material transmitted by both authors tends to favour
idealism. Lucretius' belief that the gods are thin atomic bodies living outside our world emerges
beyond any doubt from 1.44–9, 5.146–55 and 6.68–79.

[62] Armstrong 2013.

[63] An influential definition of conscience by Cardinal John H. Newman (Newman 1875: 73),
incorporated into the *Catechism* of the Second Vatican Council.

[64] For the involvement of the reader compare the analyses by Taylor in Chapter 3 and Kennedy in
Chapter 13 of this volume.

[65] The importance of the communicative relationship between poet-teacher and addressee for the
literary construction of the *DRN* has been effectively pointed out by Mitsis 1993 and Conte 1994:
1–34. Mitsis, in particular, has shown how Lucretius exploits the co-existence of an internal and an

epistemological theory outlined so far plays a relevant role also in the poet's organization of his materials, arguments and images. Indeed, when trying to convert his reader, Lucretius seems acutely aware that Epicurus' universe of atoms, void and travelling *simulacra* is the backdrop to his didactic enterprise. The poet–instructor capitalizes on Epicurus' teachings about the mechanisms of knowledge transmission, carefully targeting his text towards the reader's mental life and imagery. Since, as every good Epicurean knows, the mental is strictly a product of external sense-impressions, the first and most basic device employed by the author to entice his audience is the transformation of immediately perceptible phenomena (when possible, of everyday experiences) into philosophically instructive insights. In a real sense, it is the text itself as a material source of knowledge that is entrusted with the task of impressing the reader's mind and leading it to a shared perception of truth.[66]

Over the past few decades, considerable research has been devoted to Lucretius' use of this didactic technique in the emblematic case of analogical arguments.[67] In the concluding section of this essay, I would like to suggest that a well-thought-out strategy of, so to speak, cognitive familiarization underlies the whole of the *DRN*, as this is construed by Lucretius as a distributed cognitive artefact aiming to comprehend (and ultimately to mirror) the atomic cosmos of both the author and his addressee.[68] Students of distributed cognition have shown that when several individuals engage in

external addressee to make his philosophical arguments more compelling. On the typically epic 'illusion that the poem is really only coming into being as it evolves before the readers' eyes' – which may be termed 'poetic simultaneity' – see Volk 2002: 6–24.

[66] On the Epicurean view of human artefacts as atomic bodies capable of impressing and enticing see Frischer 1982, according to whom the portraits of Epicurean philosophers were used for the 'passive' recruitment of disciples outside the Garden. Though from different perspectives, both Thury 1987 and Schiesaro 1994 have argued that Lucretius understood his text as a material entity giving body to (and complying with) the laws of the cosmos. Volk 2002: 103 has warned that 'it is risky business to build an interpretation on a mere hypothesis of Epicurean theory'. But the thorough study of Erler 1993 should sensitize us to the psychagogic value of texts in Epicurean communal life, and it cannot be wise to divorce Epicurus' gnoseology from his social ethics and praxis.

[67] See, e.g., Schrijvers 1978; Schiesaro 1990; Garani 2007; Tutrone 2012b; Taub 2012. The importance of analogical reasoning in Lucretian science is a consequence of Epicurus' own injunction (*Ep. Hdt.* 38–9) to investigate what is non-evident (ἄδηλον) by means of inductive inferences. According to Asmis 1984: 197–211, in the second and first century BC, the Epicureans put even more emphasis on the scientific role of inductions, as attested by Philodemus' treatment of 'transition by similarity' (ἡ καθ' ὁμοιότητα μετάβασις) in *On Signs*. Lucretius fully exploits the imaginative potential of empirical analogies, endeavouring to establish common ground between himself and his addressee: see now Taylor in Chapter 3 of this volume.

[68] For a narratological exploration of Lucretius' overarching poetic cosmos see Gale 2004. On the performative linguistic 'mechanisms through which Lucretius verbally creates and re-creates the natural and human worlds' see Shearin 2015, at ix.

dialogue by means of written or oral language, they constitute a 'dynamical' distributed system and activate a process of 'social symbol grounding'. According to Angelo Cangelosi, this is the process by which a shared lexicon of perceptually grounded symbols is developed and negotiated by a group of knowing agents who 'associate entities and states in the external (and internal) world with internal categorical representations'.[69] As Cangelosi observes, the faculty of grounding and sharing symbols is deeply connected with 'the double function of language as a social/communicative means and as an individual/cognitive capability', allowing us 'to internally represent the world we live in, to process such representations to generate new concepts and explanations, and to communicate with others about our knowledge of the world'. It is striking to see how closely such theoretical description corresponds with Lucretius' poetic praxis and the Epicurean account of knowledge formation. A faithful interpreter of Epicurus' 'externalist' canonic, Lucretius constructs his text as an extended cognitive device – what contemporary cognitivists would call an 'exogram' – simultaneously interacting with the reader's mental representations (or 'engrams') and the elements of physical reality.[70]

Epistemologically speaking, Lucretius' fundamental expectation is that the *DRN* will turn into an internalized cognitive artefact revealing the objective (though previously unrecognized) effects of Epicurus' physics on the addressee's experience. Atoms and *simulacra* are, of course, supposed to be there – both inside and outside the reader – long before the start of the poem, but it is only though cooperation with the poet-teacher that readers can realize how (and where) things really are. At the same time, far from restricting itself to an aseptic transmission of scientific knowledge, the *DRN* aspires to convey a new ethical code, radically transforming the addressee's understanding of society, history and the self. Inasmuch as it shows the inextricable entanglement of moral norms, mental skills and communal values underlying knowledge transfers, the *DRN* offers especially fruitful material for the so-called cognitive humanities.[71] In fact, after many years of

[69] Cangelosi 2008: 83–4, who specifies that 'communication can be achieved not only through speaking, but also through other more "stable" forms of communication, such as written texts, audio recordings or other social artefacts'. On the question of internal categorization and symbol productivity see also Harnad 1987, 1990, and Belpaeme, Cowley and MacDorman 2007.

[70] The distinction between the complementary realms of 'engrams' (the internal memory records of each individual) and 'exograms' (external symbol systems serving as infinitely expandable and continuously refinable storage devices) has been elaborated by Donald 1991: 269–360, who regards 'graphic invention', and hence ancient alphabetic writing, as a landmark in human cognitive evolution, strictly related to the historical emergence of 'theoretic culture'.

[71] For a stimulating introduction to the cognitive humanities see Garratt 2016.

research on animals, brains and computer models, some of the fiercest supporters of the distributed cognition thesis have argued precisely for the need to focus on contexts that, as John Haugeland wrote, 'have a history or belong to a tradition'.[72] Like the Renaissance memory arts studied by John Sutton, Lucretius' physical-ethical therapy bears invaluable witness to the historically developed 'ability to interiorize relatively stable forms of culturally sanctioned scaffolding in the quest for self-mastery'.[73]

According to Epicurus, however, self-mastery is generally achieved by committing one's philosophical education to an expert mentor.[74] At various points in the *DRN*, Lucretius solicits the faithful commitment of his pupil-addressee. In this respect, too, Epicurean and contemporary discourses on epistemology seem to converge, for, to cite John Haugeland again, 'we can't really have understood the human mind – and, in particular, with regard to its very distinctive capacity ... to seek objective truth – until we have understood its capacity for faithful commitment'.[75] On the one hand, Lucretius presents himself as a loyal disciple of Epicurus, the only real master validating the poem's content,[76] but on the other hand he asks his reader to engage in a very similar relationship of trust, attentiveness and allegiance.[77] This second relationship, which is at the core of the symbol grounding process, is continuously negotiated at the meeting point between text and cosmos, minds and bodies, inside and outside. For instance, when at the start of the poem the author addresses his dedicatee through an emotionally appealing second person singular, claiming that 'you yourself will seek to leave me, overcome at some point by the priests' frightening words',[78] a multi-faceted connection between internal and external dimensions is established. The anonymous external reader is surreptitiously invited not to share what would be an act of betrayal on the part of the internal addressee, while the image of future conflicting words intrudes into the work's didactic present.[79] The Roman *vates*

---

[72] Haugeland 2002: 29. According to Haugeland, Andy Clark's approach to cognitive phenomena is 'oddly impoverished' by its lack of attention to public language and socio-cultural norms.

[73] Sutton 2010: 208.   [74] See, e.g., the testimony of Sen., *Ep.* 52.3–4.

[75] Haugeland 2002: 35–6.

[76] The most eloquent evidence comes, of course, from the poet's eulogies of Epicurus in 1.62–79; 3.1–30; 5.1–54; 6.1–42. See Craca 1989.

[77] On the issue of philosophical allegiance in the Hellenistic and Roman worlds, with special regard to Epicureanism, see Sedley 1989b.

[78] 1.102–3 *tutemet a nobis iam quovis tempore vatum | terriloquis victus dictis desciscere quaeres.*

[79] In this initial section of the poem, the addressee's departure from Epicurean doctrine is considered plausible by virtue of the artifice of 'poetic simultaneity' (cf. n. 65 above). As philosophical novices, Memmius and the Roman reader behind him are still vulnerable to the nefarious influence of religious thought. Cf. Mitsis 1993: 123–8.

blamed by Lucretius are thought to perform their misleading speech acts outside the spatio-temporal arena of the text. Yet in some of the most literarily elaborate sections of the *DRN*, Lucretius depicts his own intra-textual discourse as the enlightening utterance of an inspired seer.[80]

For Lucretius, crossing the border between mind and world often means to encapsulate the addressee's cultural experience into the poem's didactic accounts. Framed in a cosmos of invisible bodies which take visible shape within the text, the cognitive background of readers is dramatically re-interpreted – but only in order to reveal its truest nature, unknown to the readers themselves. A simple but telling example can be drawn from the Book 4 treatment of sense-perception we referred to earlier. While explaining that smell is the result of slow and delicate *simulacra* approaching the nostrils, Lucretius contends that, very much as in the case of taste, 'different flows of scents suit different animals because of their shapes' (4.677–8).[81] A gallery of enticing images follows (4.678–83):

> ideoque per auras
> mellis apes quamvis longe ducuntur odore,
> volturiique cadaveribus; tum fissa ferarum
> ungula quo tulerit gressum promissa canum vis
> ducit, et humanum longe praesentit odorem
> Romulidarum arcis servator, candidus anser.

> Therefore, the bees in the air
> are attracted by the smell of honey at great distance,
> and vultures are allured by corpses. A pack of hounds
> sent ahead by the hunter leads him where the cloven hoof
> of wild beasts has stepped, and from afar the pure white goose,
> saviour of the Romans' citadel, detects the smell of humans.

Apiculture, hunting, necrophagy and Rome's mythologized history have been embedded into the poet's atomic argument, which assigns new meanings to a widely distributed imagery. In epistemological terms, this is a stratified conglomerate of imagery made up of both empirical acqui-sitions and culturally ingrained symbols. Beekeeping and hunting with game dogs were common practice in the Roman world (especially among

---

[80] See, e.g., the apologetic self-portraits of 1.921–50, 4.1–25 and 5.110–13, or the marked contrast between the Presocratic philosophers (first of all Empedocles) and the Pythia in 1.734–41. Empedocles' influence on Lucretius' self-conscious stance as the 'highest priest of Epicurean rationalism' has been beautifully captured by Hardie 1986: 17–22. See now Shearin 2015: 55–60.

[81] On Lucretius' olfactory theory and its ancient models (certainly including Epicurus, *Ep. Hdt.* 53, and the larger exposition in *On Nature* 3–4) see Koenen 1997.

owners of villas and country estates), but they were also traditional themes
of didactic epic. The most Lucretian poem of the Augustan age, Virgil's
Georgics, devotes an entire book to the practical and cultural value of
bees.[82] And from Xenophon to Grattius and Nemesianus, cynegetic
literature figures consistently in the didactic tradition.[83] Likewise, vultures
pouncing on corpses were a common sight on ancient battlefields, but the
dismemberment of dead bodies was also charged with symbolic resonance
(first of all as a paradigm of anti-heroic death) as early as Homer.[84] Even
more notable, Lucretius' allusion to the story of the geese that saved the
Capitol from the Gauls betrays a willingness to locate Epicurus' thought,
with all its anti-traditional overtones, appealingly within the familiar
background of Roman folklore and epic. By dedicating a whole hexameter
to the 'pure white goose, saviour of the Romans' citadel' (4.683), Lucretius
evokes in the minds of readers an array of patriotic narratives and estab-
lishes with them a relationship of *aemulatio*.[85] Indeed, whereas the most
popular versions of the myth emphasize acoustic details, reporting that the
sacred geese of Juno heard the Gauls and awoke the Roman garrison with
their honking and flapping of wings, Lucretius is unique in focusing on the
geese's sharp sense of smell.[86] Insofar as it raises the level of cognitive
attention, this distinctive choice enhances the persuasive potential of
Epicurus' olfactory theory. But, again, as a material device impacting on
the mind, the text appeals to both the cultural imagination and the
embodied experience of readers. The cultural memory of the Romans
was frequently rekindled by the direct vision of objects, monuments and
rituals.[87] As for the story of the Gauls' siege in 390 BC, we know from
Cicero that in Lucretius' day a pack of sacred geese was fed at public

---

[82] Bees, with their attendant ritual and mythological ramifications, are the subject of *Georgics* 4. It is
perhaps unnecessary to recall that honey symbolism plays a highly relevant role in Lucretius: see,
above all, 1.936–50 (cf. 4.11–25) and 3.9–13. On Virgil's reception of Lucretian poetry in the
Georgics see Gale 2000, who, among other things, notes that 'the miniature world of Virgil's bees
has parallels with the miniature world of Lucretius' atoms' (49).

[83] For a broad contextualization of ancient hunting literature see MacKinnon 2014.

[84] See Vernant 1991.

[85] Note also the use of the epic form *Romulidae*, which suggestively depicts the Romans as
'descendants of Romulus'. The term recurs in Verg. *Aen.* 8.638, and may well be of Ennian
origin. Cf. Bailey 1947: III.1262.

[86] Especially useful is the comparison with Livy 5.47.2–4 and Aelian *NA* 12.33. But see also Verg.
Aen. 8.655–8; Ov. *Met.* 2.538–9; Plin. *NH* 10.51; 29.57; Columella *Rust.* 8.13.1–2. It is significant
that no other ancient source apart from Lucretius refers to the geese's olfactory keenness. See
Koenen 1997: 171–2.

[87] I use the expression 'cultural memory' in the sense advocated by Assmann 2011. On the complex
function of memory in Roman public discourse see Gowing 2005.

expenses on the Capitol hill.[88] When the censors took office, their first
duty was to contract for the food of these meritorious animals.[89] And on
the anniversary of the siege, a goose was carried about on a sumptuous
litter with purple and gold ornaments, while dogs – the other protagonists
of Lucretius' animal scene – were crucified near the Circus Maximus to
commemorate their failure to announce the Gauls' assault.[90]

The interlacing of inner and outer dimensions, subjective experiences
and social customs, is essential for the making of a work which, since the
beginning, has presented its textual structure as an illustrative image of
the external world. No fewer than three times in the first two books of the
DRN, readers are invited to look at the letters on the page in front of them
to grasp the concept of atomic compound.[91] Building on the richly
ambiguous meaning of the word *elementum* (a translation of the Greek
στοιχεῖον), Lucretius overlaps the ideas of alphabetic letter and atom, and
argues that macroscopic bodies and microscopic particles stand in the same
relationship to one another as words and letters.[92] This all-embracing,
intellectually omnivorous poem strives to capture at the same time the soul
of the addressee and that of the author – both being material bodies which,
by means of the text, participate in a distributed cognitive venture. From
time to time, readers are urged to integrate the work's content by extrap-
olating additional arguments from their own experience. This is, for
instance, what Memmius is asked to do to understand the notion of void
(1.398–409): like a keen-scented hound, he has to follow in the poet's
'little footsteps' (*vestigia parva*), find arguments by himself, and thus
'extract the truth' (*verum protrahere*) from its 'blind lairs' (*caecas latebras*).[93]

[88] Cic. *Q Rosc.* 56.   [89] Cf. Plin. *NH* 10.51; Plut. *Quaest. Rom.* 98.
[90] Plut. *De fort. Rom.* 12; Ael. *NA* 12.33; Serv. *ad Aen.* 8.653. Another folkloric belief about animals is
re-used by Lucretius at 4.706–21, where the analogous physical principle that different visual
simulacra suit different species is demonstrated on the basis of the lions' alleged fear of cocks. On
Lucretius' ethno-biology and its intellectual background see Tutrone 2012a: 47–8; 73–80.
[91] Cf. 1.817–29, 2.686–99 and 2.1004–22. In all these passages, the poet's 'specular' reference to his
text is made conspicuous by the hexametric clause *nostris in versibus ipsis* ('in my very verses'). The
atoms–letters analogy surfaces also in 1.192–8 and 1.907–14 without reference to the composition
of the *DRN*. See also the three chapters in the next section of this volume.
[92] See Snyder 1980: 31–51, developing the so-called 'atomology' theory of Friedländer 1941.
Lucretius' argument has solid roots in Epicurean philosophy (*pace* Dalzell 1987), and the analogy
seems to go back to the founding fathers of ancient materialism, Leucippus and Democritus. See
also Dionigi 1988 and Armstrong 1995. An epistemologically engaging discussion of Lucretius'
'textualization of nature', bringing into dialogue ancient and modern constructions, is provided by
Kennedy 2002.
[93] For another similar case see, e.g., 6.527–34. On Lucretius' hunting imagery see Whitlatch 2014. As
Konstan 2004, 2006 has pointed out, an active and critical audience is envisaged by most ancient
authors, from Plato and Plutarch to Virgil and Ovid. Yet the specificity of the *DRN* lies in its
literary exploitation of Epicurus' gnoseological theory.

Convinced as he is that truth is the product of collaborative and 'stochastic' efforts, Lucretius is ready to inscribe into his extended artefact capti-
vating pieces of mythical wisdom such as the story of the Capitol geese.[94]
Alternatively, the image of the writing poet can be introjected into the text.
When claiming that dreams are the result of persisting atomic stimuli
determined by daily activities, Lucretius includes himself in his gallery of
dreaming types. The author confesses to seeing his image at night 'always
intent on investigating the nature of things and on exposing it in the native
idiom of Rome' (4.969–70 *nos agere hoc autem et naturam quaerere rerum* |
semper et inventam patriis exponere chartis). If readers, too, accept being
sucked in by the cosmic mirror of the poem, they will easily (and
beneficially) realize that the distinction between thoughts and beings –
res cogitans and *res extensa*, in Cartesian terms – is as evanescent as that
between writer and reader.

---

[94] On the Epicurean view of philosophical teaching as a 'stochastic art' (τέχνη στοχαστική), that is, as
a conjectural, situation-based technique, see Gigante 1983a: 62–7. Lucretius' pragmatic approach
to myth, poetry and other traditional forms of knowledge is much more in line with orthodox
Epicureanism than is usually recognized: see Obbink 1995b.

The Word and the World

The Word and the World

CHAPTER 5

Infinity, Enclosure and False Closure in Lucretius' De Rerum Natura

Donncha O'Rourke

In Lucretius, the philosopher's commitment to the finitude of life and the end of the world sits uneasily with the poet's ambition to perpetuate the teachings of Epicurus in immortal verse.[1] This paradox was appreciated by Ovid, whose own bid for *fama perennis* at the close of *Amores* 1 includes 'sublime Lucretius' among the poets who have secured everlasting fame through poetry[2] (*Am.* 1.15.23–4):[3]

> carmina sublimis tunc sunt peritura Lucreti,
> exitio terras cum dabit una dies;

The poetry of sublime Lucretius is destined to perish at that time when a single day consigns the earth to destruction.

In this witty yet respectful acknowledgement of Epicurean doctrine, Ovid sets Lucretius apart from those poets whose immortality goes unqualified by making his literary fame coterminous with the lifespan of the earth. Homer may have believed in κλέος ἄφθιτον (*Iliad* 9.413 'imperishable renown'), but the Epicurean could not (cf. *Ep. Hdt.* 74 φθαρτούς φησι τούς κόσμους, 'he says worlds are destructible').[4] As the commentators note, Ovid's pentameter invokes to this end the apocalypse as described at *DRN* 5.92–5 *maria ac **terras** caelumque tuere: | quorum naturam triplicem, tria corpora, Memmi, | tris species tam dissimilis, tria talia texta, | **una dies dabit exitio** ('behold the seas, earth and sky: their threefold nature and three*

For discussion or response to earlier drafts I warmly thank Fiachra Mac Góráin, Alex Hardie, Jason Nethercut and Marco Peru.

[1] For some responses to this paradox see Segal 1989, 1990: 180–6; Edwards 1993.

[2] On this couplet see McKeown 1989: 407–9 ad loc. In general on *Am.* 1.15 see Vessey 1981; Boyd 1997: 166–70.

[3] The translations in this chapter are my own unless otherwise noted. The text of Lucretius is that of Rouse and Smith 1992.

[4] On κλέος ἄφθιτον (not necessarily formulaic in Homer, but the phrase caught on) see Finkelberg 2007 with earlier bibliography. See also Garcia 2013, with the Appendix for the close semantic (but technically not cognate) relation of φθίνω and φθείρω.

bodies, Memmius, their three aspects so unlike, three such compositions, a single day will consign to destruction'). Ovid's allusion anticipates a tradition of Lucretius-interpretation that the chapters in this section of our volume take up, namely that the poem stands in a relation of analogy – on multiple levels and in varying degrees of proximity – to the universe it describes: the *DRN* presents an itself as an *imago mundi* beginning with creation in the Hymn to Venus and ending with destruction in the Athenian plague, and composed of *elementa* ('letters') whose arrangement complements that of the *elementa* ('atoms') that constitute the physical fabric of the world (see further in the Introduction, pp. 8–9, above). By way of this metapoetic analogy, the passage of Lucretius to which Ovid alludes might itself be taken to hint at the concomitant destruction of the *DRN*, invoking as it does the title of the poem, its *corpora* and its *texta*.[5]

As every Epicurean knows, the counterpart to the death and destruction contingent on the inevitable disaggregation of atomic compounds is the renewal guaranteed by the necessity that those same atoms, being of infinite number in the infinite universe that lies outside this *kosmos* or world (Lucretius' *mundus*), will reunite in new combinations (Epicurus, *Ep. Hdt.* 39, 41–2, 45, 54–5; *DRN* 1.215–64, 1.951–1051, 2.67–79, 2.569–80, 2.991–1022, 3.964–77, 5.247–60).[6] Indeed the *vis infinitatis* (as Cicero's Velleius hails it at *Nat. D.* 1.50)[7] enables the Epicurean to 'postulate accident on a staggeringly vast scale',[8] such that the *very same* atomic configurations can be expected, sooner or later, to recombine anew (*DRN* 3.847–60).[9] Alessandro Schiesaro has argued that the *DRN* sees itself implicated in this process of palingenesis elementally, at the level of its letters and its atoms.[10] While some modern readers have resisted this degree of equivalence between the word and the world of the *DRN*, the reconstitution of the text is an implication of the analogy that seems to have been familiar to Cicero (*Nat. D.* 2.93):[11]

---

[5] At the opening of the final third of the *DRN* (see Farrell 2007, esp. 78–85), it is tempting to see in *tria corpora* and *tria texta* a gesture to the tripartite organization of the poem as well as of the world it describes.

[6] On infinity in Epicurean physics see Furley 1981; Asmis 1984: 261–75, esp. 261–7 on the infinite universe; Giannantonini 1989; Sedley 2007: 136–9, 155–66; Bakker 2018. For the principal texts see Long and Sedley 1987: 1.44–6 (10 A, B, C). See further n. 15 below.

[7] For discussion of this phrase in its context see Kleve 1979a.

[8] Sedley 2007: 155. The point remains under discussion: see Bersanelli 2011: 200–1.

[9] The reconstitution of the individual is, of course, heavily qualified (cf., e.g., *DRN* 3.670–8): see Warren 2001.

[10] Schiesaro 1994.

[11] See Pease 1958: 780–1 ad loc. on the tradition of these objections prior to Cicero. For this passage in connection with the *DRN* see esp. Armstrong 1995: 224–5; cf. Snyder 1980: 35–6.

Hoc qui existimat fieri potuisse, non intellego, cur non idem putet, si innumerabiles unius et viginti formae litterarum vel aureae vel qualeslibet aliquo coiciantur, posse ex is in terram excussis Annales Enni, ut deinceps legi possint, effici; quod nescio an ne in uno quidem versu possit tantum valere fortuna.

As for anyone who supposes that this can happen [i.e. that atoms randomly collide to produce the world in all its variety], I cannot understand how he does not also believe that, if countless copies of the twenty-one letters of the alphabet, made of gold or whatever, were thrown together somewhere, it would be possible to reproduce from these, when shaken out onto the ground, a readable version of the Ennius' *Annales*; I'm not sure whether chance could pull off such a feat even for a single line!

So Balbus may scoff, invested as he is in Stoic providence, but for those who postulate a boundless universe with an unlimited supply of atoms, chance palingenesis is – according to what philosophers call the 'principle of plenitude' – an inevitability: in an infinite universe of infinite *elementa*, anything that *can* happen, *will* happen eventually – necessarily, not providentially (cf. *DRN* 2.522–80, 1048–89).[12] As far as the *Nachleben* of Ennius is concerned, the intertextual and ideological reconfiguring of the *Annales* in the *DRN* is signalled in Lucretius' rationalizing take on his epic precursor's self-presentation as the reincarnation of Homer (1.112–26), and in his own reproduction of Ennian 'originality' in the 'second proem' or 'apologia' later in the same book (1.921–50, cf. 4.1–25): it was Ennius 'who first brought down from pleasant Helicon a garland of evergreen foliage' (117–18 *qui primus amoeno | detulit ex Helicone perenni fronde coronam*) and sang 'in everlasting verses' (121 *aeternis . . . versibus*) about the ghost of 'ever flourishing Homer' (124 *semper florentis Homeri*) expounding to him a very unEpicurean nature of things; now it is Lucretius who ranges over the trackless haunts of the Muses where none before have set sole (1.926–7, 4.1–2 *avia Pieridum peragro loca nullius ante | trita solo*), drinking from the springs and plucking the flowers of Callimachean originality (1.927–8, 4.2–3) for a 'distinguished garland' (1.929, 4.4 *insignem . . . coronam*).[13] In the *DRN*, intertextuality is tantamount to palingenesis: as in nature, so in literature there is – to borrow a phrase – *nil novi sub sole*.

---

[12] On the 'principle of plenitude' in this connection see Bakker 2018: 56 with n. 60 and 58 with n. 69.

[13] See Gale 2001b on Lucretius' thematization of poetic succession through paronomasia in this passage and elsewhere in the *DRN*. On Lucretius' poetic admiration but philosophical rejection of his literary forbears see Gale 2007b, esp. 59–67 on Ennius, and 70–4 for the Callimachean dimension. For the former see also Gigon 1978; Nethercut 2014. For the latter see also Kenney 1970; Brown 1982.

Since the nature of things is contingent on infinity, it may be asked how this poem *On the Nature of Things*, to the extent that it doubles *as* the universe, can contain infinity within the limited confines of its text.[14] There is in addition the more purely philosophical question of the extent to which Lucretius can achieve didactic closure on a topic that is inherently open.[15] If closure is always provisional, as Don Fowler pointed out to Classicists not once but twice,[16] the problem will be especially gaping in the case of infinity. In the history of human thought, infinity is a concept that, perhaps more than any other, defies description, nurtures paradox, and generally makes the head ache.[17] Adrian Moore identifies a principal 'paradox of thought about the infinite' as follows: 'We appear to have grasped the infinite as that which is ungraspable. We appear to have recognized the infinite as that which is, by definition, beyond definition.'[18] In antiquity, the mind-bending implications of infinity were formulated in the *ad infinitum* paradoxes of Zeno, whose anti-teleological mischief was tackled most influentially by Aristotle in his denial of extracosmic space[19] and in his celebrated distinction at the level of number between the notion of an 'actual' infinity (impossible since one cannot have infinity 'all at once') and 'potential' or theoretical infinity (a temporal projection that cannot in practice be reached or traversed).[20] This was a solution of fundamental importance to Aristotle's worldview, as Jonathan Lear has noted: 'the possibility of philosophy – of man's ability to comprehend the world – depends on the fact that the world is a finite place containing objects that are themselves finite. And the possibility of philosophy is one possibility that Aristotle spent his life actualizing.'[21]

If Aristotle solved a problem, however, he also gave expression to an anxiety.[22] To sample just two responses from the later history of this anxiety, Boëthius associates unlimited numerical progression with evil

[14] The question is posed by Gale 2019 in a discussion of Lucretius' contribution to the tradition of name-puns and acrostics in didactic poetry.
[15] The major treatment of infinity in Lucretius is now Morenval 2017. Salemme 2011 is a detailed commentary on *DRN* 1.951–1117. See also Keyser 1919; Saint-Denis 1963; Avotins 1983; Clay 1983: 131–45; Segal 1990: 74–93; Kennedy 2013; Bakker 2018. Cf. Fitzgerald 2016a: 100–11 on Lucretius' celebration of nature's infinite variety.
[16] Fowler 1989b, 1997b. See also Grewing, Acosta-Hughes and Kirichenko 2013.
[17] See Moore 2001; Zellini 2004; Barrow 2005; Achtner 2011; Bersanelli 2011.
[18] Moore 2001: 12.　　[19] See Sorabji 1988: 125–59.
[20] From an ever-expanding bibliography see Lear 1979; Sorabji 1983: 210–13; Moore 2001: 34–44; White 2013, esp. 260–5. On Aristotle's cosmic teleology see Sedley 2007: 194–203.
[21] Lear 1979: 202. Cf. Furley 1981; Bakker 2018: 57 with nn. 65–6.
[22] For the following examples and others see Zellini 2004: 13–16.

itself (*Inst. ar.* 1.32 'malitiae dedecus'); and Hegel condemned the Aristotelian conception of potentially infinite progression as a 'false' or 'bad'
infinity ('die schlechte Unendlichkeit') that he saw symbolized in the
never-ending punishments in the underworld:[23]

> Prometheus, for example, is chained to a mountain in Scythia where the
> eagle insatiably devours his liver which ever grows afresh; similarly Tan-
> talus in the underworld is tormented by an endless unquenched thirst,
> and Sisyphus has always uselessly to trundle up anew the rock that
> continually rolls down again. Like the Titanic powers of nature them-
> selves, these punishments are the inherently measureless, the bad infinite,
> the longing of the 'ought', the unsatiated craving of subjective natural
> desire which in its continual recurrence never attains the final peace of
> satisfaction. For the Greek correct sense of the Divine, unlike the modern
> longing, did not regard egress into the boundless and the vague as what
> was supreme for men; the Greeks regarded it as a damnation and relegated
> it to Tartarus.

Hegel here takes up a way of reading Hades also witnessed in *DRN* 3,
where the eternal punishments of legendary convicts in the underworld
symbolize the pathologies to which non-Epicureans are condemned in real
life: Tityos is the lover in whose guts the vultures rummage 'for all eternity'
(3.986 *perpetuam aetatem*); to roll Sisyphus' rock is 'to seek power which is
empty and never granted, and therein forever to endure hard labour'
(998–9 *petere imperium quod inanest nec datur umquam,* | *atque in eo
semper durum sufferre laborem*);[24] the Danaids' vain attempt to fill their
perforated *vas* communicates in layman's terms the difference between the
two categories of pleasure, those that are 'katastematic' or enduring being
preferable to those that are 'kinetic' or transitory (1003-10).[25] Bound up
with the concept of infinity, then, are feelings of yearning and desire, but
also doubt and uncertainty, and even intimations of death. In *Lucretius on
Death and Anxiety*, Charles Segal has drawn attention to Lucretius' studied
association of infinity and death throughout the *DRN* as a response to
ancient criticism of Epicurus that saw scant therapeutic benefit in 'the
thought of the soul being poured into infinity as though into a gaping sea'
(Plut. *Non posse* 1107a ἡ ἐπίνοια τῆς ψυχῆς ὥσπερ εἰς πέλαγος ἀχανὲς τὸ
ἄπειρον ἐκχεομένης).[26] On Moore's view, the paradox of thought about

---

[23] Hegel, *Aesthetics* (I, II.ii, Ch. 1.2c), trans. Knox 1975: 1.466.
[24] The adjective *inane* associates Sisyphus' pursuit of power with the (infinite) void; cf. Hor. *Sat.*
1.2.113 with Gowers 2012: 113 ad loc.
[25] See Reinhardt 2002.　　[26] Segal 1990: 14–17, 74–93.

infinity is a function of human finitude with which all writing on infinity, including his own, is necessarily preoccupied:[27]

> The roots of this paradoxical nature lie in our own finitude (however construed). For it is self-conscious awareness of that finitude which gives us our initial, contrastive sense of the infinite and, at the same time, makes us despair of knowing anything about it, or having any kind of grasp of it. This creates a tension. We feel pressure to acknowledge the infinite, and we feel pressure not to. In trying to come to terms with the infinite, we are in effect trying to come to terms with a basic conflict in ourselves.

Not for nothing, then, does Ovid in the *Amores* recognize Lucretius', as well as his own, preoccupation with death and infinity. Lucretius, for his part, is required to instruct his reader in a topic on which an understanding of the nature of things is contingent, but which also threatens to engulf the principles on which the possibility of the good life is predicated.

∞

The introductory considerations above show the validity in antiquity as well as today of the remarks – often quoted in discussions of infinity – of German mathematician David Hilbert (1862–1943): 'The infinite has always stirred the emotions of mankind more deeply than any other question; the infinite has stimulated and fertilized reason as few other ideas have.'[28] This synthesis – or collision – of emotion and reason is especially pertinent in the context of a philosophy that seeks to avoid mental disturbance. Epicurus' surviving discussions of infinity in its various forms are, to be sure, more cerebral than emotional in manner (*Ep. Hdt.* 41–2, 56–7, 60, 72).[29] By contrast, Lucretius' Epicurus rises to a Promethean victory against the heavens (1.72–7):

> ergo vivida vis animi pervicit, et extra
> processit longe flammantia moenia mundi
> atque omne immensum peragravit mente animoque,
> unde refert nobis victor quid possit oriri,
> quid nequeat, finita potestas denique cuique
> quanam sit ratione atque alte terminus haerens.

75

---

[27] Moore 1993: xi, now reworded at Moore 2001: xvii. Compare Segal 1990: 17: 'There remains the very troubling tension that many people, both ancients and moderns, continue to feel between our finitude and the infinity of our own future non-being. The proof, based on the soul's mortality, that we do not experience infinity after death does not necessarily eliminate our anxiety about an infinite void stretching before us.'

[28] Quoted at, e.g., Moore 2001: 1 (as epigraph to the Introduction).

[29] On Epicurus' terminology see Morenval 2017: 31–63, comparing Lucretius at 63–154.

Thus the lively power of his mind prevailed, and he advanced far beyond the blazing ramparts of the world and traversed the immeasurable whole in mind and spirit, from where he victoriously reports to us what can come about, what cannot, *in fine* the reason why each thing's capacity is limited and its boundary-stone lodged deep.

Reason and poetry here join forces to trample religion underfoot (78–9 *quare religio <u>pedibus</u> subiecta vicissim | obteritur*). Form matches sense also in the enjambment of *extra | processit* (72–3), as the Greek hero discovers infinity in the manner of a triumphant general surveying newly conquered territory (*peragrare* is a t. t. of ordnance survey).[30] This is no dispassionate account of Epicurean enlightenment: Lucretius arrogates military language to a philosophy that advocates peaceful withdrawal, that relativizes Roman claims to predestination and world-power, and that rewrites knowledge and, with it, a system of sociopolitical power that enlists divine coopera-tion.[31] The ethical implications of the infinite universe are witnessed in the tears to which Alexander the Great was reduced upon hearing the Demo-critean Anaxarchus: 'Is it not worthy of tears that when there are infinite worlds (κόσμων ὄντων ἀπείρων) we have not yet become masters of even one?' (Plut. *De tranq. anim.* 466d; cf. Val. Max. 8.14.ext.2).[32] The universe is infinite, then, but this is not the *imperium sine fine* that Virgil's Jupiter prophesies to the Aeneadae (*Aen.* 1.278–9).[33]

This passage's claim to universal authority is not just politically contro-versial. It also straddles a major philosophical debate on the nature of the infinite, here encapsulated in the phrase *omne immensum* – a totality (*omne*) that is yet beyond measurement (*immensum*). This paradox elides rival views of infinity rooted in the Presocratic tradition: viewed as an all-encompassing whole (πᾶν), the infinite is absolute, perfect, perhaps even

---

[30] The classic discussion of this passage is Buchheit 1971. The analogy derives force from a possible pun on Epicurus' name, ἐπίκουρος meaning 'ally' or 'mercenary soldier': for this paronomasia in other passages see Snyder 1978: 229–30; Snyder 1980; Gale 1994: 137; O'Hara 1998. In the proem to *DRN* 3, the verb *suppedito* at 10 *suppeditas praecepta* ('you [Epicurus] supply precepts') and 23 *omnia suppeditat . . . natura* ('nature supplies everything') calques the verb ἐπικουρέω with the same pun in view.

[31] For a Foucauldian reading of this passage in the context of the *DRN* and the didactic tradition as a whole see O'Rourke 2019.

[32] On the ethical and theological repercussions of infinity see Warren 2004b. See also Giannantonini 1989: 25–6.

[33] See Schiesaro 2007a: 42, qualified by Kennedy 2013: 59–61. Alex Hardie brilliantly suggests (*per litteras*) that 'within *imperium sine fine* lurks a Graecising [created] 'etymology' *imperium | ἄ-πειρον*'. On the temporal and spatial dimensions of Virgil's *imperium sine fine* (though not explicitly related to the philosophical contexts discussed in the preceding essays of its volume) see Pavan 1989. See further n. 76 below.

divine; viewed, on the other hand, as unlimited (ἄπειρον), it is incomplete, imperfect and unattainable.[34] Duncan Kennedy has argued that Epicurus' mental apprehending of this 'immeasurable whole' *mente animoque* is informed by Aristotle's dismissal of 'actual' infinity in favour of a merely theorized 'potential' infinity.[35] As Kennedy argues, the phrase *mente animoque* qualifies Epicurus' claim to universal knowledge as being grounded in theory rather than practice – that is, in the provision of a *ratio* by which everything in the infinite universe can be explained, rather than in taking us through an explanation for every individual facet of the infinite universe. On the one hand, then, Lucretius here affords Epicurus a kind of post-Aristotelian 'get-out clause' that keeps the *DRN* safely in the realm of the potential rather than actual infinite; on the other hand, however, the ambition to proceed beyond the ramparts of the world to survey the 'whole immeasurable' ('all at once', as it were, rather than potentially and over time), couched as it is in imperialist language sugges-tive more of Aristotle's pupil than of Alexander's teacher, is a totalizing claim that throws down a challenge to Aristotle's redefinition of *apeiron* as 'not that which never has something outside it, but that which always has something outside it' (*Ph.* 3.6, 206b34–207a1). Lucretius' *omne immen-sum* conceptualizes infinity in a way that elides this distinction and imposes didactic closure where closure is at its most elusive.

The manoeuvring in this passage highlights at the start of the *DRN* not just Epicurus' ambition as a philosopher of the infinite, but Lucretius' as its poet. The rival conceptions of infinity that the *DRN* must represent, the *omne* and the *immensum*, correspond to the rival modes of enclosure distinguished by Umberto Eco in *The Infinity of Lists*.[36] Eco takes Homer's Shield of Achilles and Catalogue of Ships as paradigms for alternative modes of enclosure, demoting the self-contained wholeness of the former perhaps surprisingly in favour of the never-ending concatenation of the latter.[37] Homer's ancient readers would have subscribed to Eco's reading of the Shield as a totality, allegorizing it as they did as a composite expression of Empedocles' cosmic cycle (Heraclitus, *Quaest. Hom.* 49).[38] One such reader may well have been Lucretius, whose *DRN* begins with a gesture to the allegoresis of the Homeric Mars and Venus as Empedoclean

---

[34] See Morenval 2017: 13–27 and *passim*. From an immense bibliography see the overviews by Moore 2001: 17–33, esp. 17–19, 23–5; Zellini 2004: 1–37.

[35] Kennedy 2013, esp. 54–5.   [36] Eco 2009.

[37] Eco 2009: 8–35. It is not entirely clear how seriously Eco intends to valorize the list; for a classicist's perspective see Beard 2009.

[38] See Buffière 1956: 159; Hardie 1985, 1986: 340–1.

Strife and Love (Heraclitus, *Quaest. Hom.* 69.1–11; schol. *Od.* 8.267; Eustathius 1.298 *ad* Hom. *Od.* 8.267),[39] and enacts as a whole a cosmic cycle from creation to destruction, and back again, its *elementa* themselves subject to palingenesis, as we have seen. The *DRN*, then, may be said to embody the form demoted by Eco. It presents as its totalizing philosophy a closed system that enables all phenomena to be explained in like terms (what philosophers call the 'principle of uniformity'),[40] propounding (itself as) an infinite universe that, as Kennedy has argued, encapsulates a 'Theory of Everything' without having to explain everything, a model of knowledge based on compression rather accumulation, a 'cosmogram' rather than an encyclopedia.[41]

The first term of Lucretius' *omne immensum* thus seems to be well covered by the *DRN* in its pursuit of ataraxic closure.[42] At the same time, however, the Epicurean principle of multiple explanation (*Ep. Hdt.* 78–80, *Ep. Pyth.* 86; *DRN* 5.526–33, 6.703–11),[43] itself a corollary of the 'principle of plenitude',[44] creates in the *DRN* effects of the opposite kind, most famously in Book 3 where the accumulation of proof after proof for the soul's mortality really does begin to look as if it might go on (and on) *ad infinitum*.[45] Passages such as this deploy what Eco describes as a 'rhetoric of enumeration',[46] in particular in their use of anaphora, asyndeton,

[39] For the allegory see Buffière 1956: 168–72; Hardie 1986: 62. It is not clear if this allegory goes back to Empedocles himself, but it is generally agreed that Lucretius was aware of it: on the philosophical and literary aspects of the subtext see Furley 1970 and Sedley 1998: 16–32, esp. 27. See further Clay 1983: 22–3, 82–110; Gale 1994: 41–2, 71–2, 219–20; Garani 2007: 37–43.

[40] On the 'principle of uniformity' in this connection see Bakker 2018: 56 with n. 59.

[41] Kennedy 2013, esp. 63–7. Morenval 2017: 231–50, 419 makes the attractive suggestion that Epicurus' *Epitome* (cf. *atomos*) was likewise to be seen as a miniature of the massive *On Nature*. Henderson 2011 applies the term 'cosmogram' to Pliny's 'hyperlinked' *Natural History*, also listed (but for its list-like qualities) by Eco 2009: 153. On Pliny's lists see Doody 2010: 23–30, contrasting Lucretius at 23: 'This vision of a nature that can be broken into sections and catalogued, fact by fact, name by name, item by item, until all of it is listed, represents a new idea about what it is to know about the nature of things. In the *Natural History*, nature becomes exactly the sum of its parts, a catalogue of details that anyone can grasp, but that only Pliny has contained and organised.'

[42] But only 'seems': as the anonymous reader points out, *omne* is itself a less totalizing equivalent for πᾶν than *totum*, suggesting that there is 'a "cultural translatability" issue hidden here in full view'. On this view, the move from *totum* to *omne* at *DRN* 3.17–30 (quoted below) is instructive.

[43] On multiple explanation see Asmis 1984: 321–30 (on Epicurus); Hankinson 2013 (comparing Lucretius); Hardie 2009: 231–63 (Lucretius and his epic successors).

[44] See Bakker 2018: 59–63, with text to n. 12 above.

[45] This section ends with a (for Lucretius quite rare) catalogue of proper names spanning the mythological sinners in the underworld to historical celebrities who are no longer with us, including (last but not least) Epicurus himself (3.978–1044): see Kyriakidis 2007: 87–93.

[46] Eco 2009: 133–7. For Lucretius' use of rhetorical figures to convey the infinite see generally Morenval 2017: 354–425.

polysyndeton and tautology:[47] these figures are on display in (e.g.) Book 6 when, having accounted for thunder, lightning, waterspouts, cloud formation and the rainbow, Lucretius rattles off various other meteorological phenomena that could be explained according to the same principles (6.527–31):[48]

> Cetera **quae sursum crescunt sursum**que creantur,
> et **quae** concrescunt in nubibus, **omnia**, prorsum
> **omnia**, nix venti grando gelidae*que* pruinae
> *et* vis **magna** geli, **magnum** duramen aquarum,
> *et* mora quae fluvios passim refrenat aventis . . .

The other things that grow above and are produced above, and that grow together in the clouds, everything, absolutely everything, snow winds hail and icy frost and the great might of ice, that great hardening of water, and the retardation that everywhere reins in the eager rivers . . .

Despite the claim to totality and omniscience here, this open-ended congeries is closer to the *immensum* than to the *omne*. In such instances as these the text gestures to an infinity of a much less stable order, to inexhaustible progressions that cannot be contained or narrated to their end, not even if – as Homer put it – you had 'ten tongues and ten mouths, or a voice never to be broken' (*Il.* 2.489–90).[49] As Eco explains, invoking Aristotle's distinction, the list is 'an *actual* infinity, made up of objects that can perhaps be numbered but that we cannot number – and we fear that their numeration (and enumeration) may never stop'.[50] On this view, it is perhaps surprising to find that, as in Homer, this alternative mode of enclosure – emphasizing the *immensum* rather than the *omne* – is also represented in Lucretius' text.

The 'uneasy pleasure'[51] of Lucretius' lists, then, is to some extent at odds with the infinite totality conquered in Epicurus' universal triumph in *DRN* 1. If that passage elides the *omne* and the *immensum* in a way that closes down the inherent openness of Aristotle's potential infinite, the series of proofs for the infinite universe at the end of the same book tends in the opposite direction.[52] Here the principle of multiple

---

[47] Deutsch 1939 painstakingly compiles rhetorical figures in Lucretius, but only barely senses the significance of her labours at pp. 172, 175–6. Interpretative approaches are taken by Friedländer 1941; Snyder 1980; Dionigi 1988. Cf. Fitzgerald 2016a: 105–6.

[48] See Wills 1996: 131–2, 442, 284.

[49] See Sammons 2010 on the unstable authority of Homer's catalogues. At *DRN* 1.398–417 Lucretius encourages the addressee to adduce further proofs for the existence of void, threatening Memmius, if he demurs, with a never-ending series of his own.

[50] Eco 2009: 15.   [51] Eco 2009: 17.   [52] For detailed commentary see Salemme 2011.

explanation is such that the *DRN* might be said to reflect, and in so doing to enact, the infinite nature of things.[53] The most famous of these explanations provocatively Romanizes a thought-experiment attributed to Archytas of Tarentum (Eudemus apud Simpl. *in Phys.* 467.26–40 = fr. 47 A.24 DK)[54] as a Fetial rite that declares war on the idea of there being a limit to the universe (1.968–83, cf. Livy 1.32.12):[55]

> Praeterea si iam finitum constituatur
> omne quod est spatium, siquis procurrat ad oras
> ultimus extremas iaciatque volatile telum,   970
> id validis utrum contortum viribus ire
> quo fuerit missum mavis longeque volare,
> an prohibere aliquid censes obstareque posse?
> alterutrum fatearis enim sumasque necessest;
> quorum utrumque tibi effugium praecludit et omne   975
> cogit ut exempta concedas fine patere.
> nam sive est aliquid quod probeat officiatque
> quominu' quo missum est veniat finique locet se,
> sive foras fertur, non est a fine profectum.
> hoc pacto sequar atque, oras ubicumque locaris   980
> extremas, quaeram quid telo denique fiat.
> fiet uti nusquam possit consistere finis
> effugiumque fugae prolatet copia semper.

Furthermore, suppose for a moment all of space were finite: if someone ran right out to the farthest edge and threw a flying spear, does it, as you would have it, go where it has been sent, whirled with powerful force, and fly afar? Or do you think that something can prevent and block it? For you must concede and choose one or the other possibility. Each of them precludes your escape and obliges you to acknowledge that the universe stretches out without end. For whether there is something that prevents the spear and obstructs it from going where it has been sent and from lodging itself in an endpoint, or whether it is borne outside that, it did not start out from an end. In this way I shall follow along and, wherever you locate your farthest edge, I shall ask what ultimately happens to the spear. What will happen is that the end can nowhere exist and the opportunity for flight forever defers your escape!

---

[53] For this suggestion see Fratantuono 2015: 62, noting that the argument is longer still, given the lacuna after line 1013.

[54] For the argument and some ancient replies see Sorabji 1988: 125–8.

[55] Or, as Clay 1983: 137–40, at 40, suggests: 'The infinite universe of Greek atomism is approached as if it were an alien and hostile world lying beyond the *ager Romanus*.' Full discussion at Morenval 2017: 342–53; see also West 1969: 46–8. The allusion is disputed by Gottschalk 1975 and Salemme 2011: 44–5 ad loc.

In contrast to Epicurus' traversal of the whole infinite at the start of the book (*omne immensum peragravit*), Lucretius in effect subscribes here to Aristotle's numerical infinite as something than can never be traversed – but re-imagined in spatial terms the argument now subverts Aristotle's telos-oriented denial of actual infinity in space.[56] As at 1.72–3 above, the enjambments at 969–70 (*siquis procurrat ad oras | ultimus extremas*) and 980–1 (*oras ubicumque locaris | extremas*) audibly and visually accompany Lucretius as he demonstrates that there is no end-of-the-line in the universe.[57] By its very nature, this is an argument that has no conclusion – or better, its lack of conclusion is the argument, since the limited counter-argument takes refuge in a position that proves there is no escaping the infinite. Revelling in this paradox, Lucretius is prepared to make us concede his *QED* over and over again *ad infinitum*.

The emphasis at the beginning of *DRN* 1, then, is on the infinite as something that can be comprehended in its wholeness (*omne immensum*); by contrast, here at the end of the book, the emphasis is on the infinite as something that cannot be grasped. If the earlier passage imposes didactic closure on the question of infinitude, the end of the book is rather more open and, as such, potentially less conducive to *ataraxia*, as the reception history of this conception of infinity has tended to show.

∞

Returning at the end of the book to unpack the idea of the infinite universe introduced at its start, *DRN* 1 appears to organize itself in a neat ring-composition. Such an impression is merely temporary, however, since Lucretius' treatment of the topic spills over into *DRN* 2 with discussion of the atoms' perpetual motion (62–332) and inexhaustible supply (522–80), and culminates in the revelation that there is an infinite number of finite worlds just like ours (1023–1174). Comparing the finales of the six books of the poem, Müller finds that *DRN* 1 and 2 merge more closely than the other books, with a 'continuity of train of thought' in the reprise of the phrase *nunc age* at 2.62 after its previous occurrence at 1.953, where the theoretical discussion of infinity proper begins.[58] Lucretian infinity thus seems to run on *ad infinitum* not only at the end of *DRN* 1, but in

---

[56] Morenval 2017: 45 locates this 'glissement' between numerical and spatial infinity in Epicurus.

[57] Sharing the same root as ἐπίκουρος (see n. 30 above), *procurrat* here encodes Epicurus' name at another strategic juncture (cf. *DRN* 3.1042 *ipse Epicurus obit decurso lumine vitae*, with Gee in this volume, p. 195).

[58] Müller 1978: 201 (repr. in Gale 2007a: 237, whence the translation).

breaking the confines of that book with further expatiation on the topic in *DRN* 2. Comparable here is Ovid's thematically apposite straddling of the book division of *Metamorphoses* 1 and 2 with Phaethon's extramundial flight towards his father Sol/the sun,[59] a narrative that Alessandro Schiesaro reads as 'as a probing comment on Epicurus' metaphoric flight, and by extension on Lucretius' poetic and philosophical project'.[60] In general terms, then, but perhaps also quite specifically, we can take up Don Fowler's invitation to consider the ways in which the *DRN* – for all 'its belief in truth, in the discovery of correct ways to divide up the world rather than of simply persuasive or attractive ones' – is in fact less 'segmented' and more invested in Ovidian variety and continuum than might be expected.[61]

At the start of *DRN* 2 the continuum is presented in the 'distant views' over the sea and plain, these traditional images for the cosmos thus reinforcing the thematic continuity between the first two books, but revamped for Epicurean purposes in Lucretius' focalization of the philosopher's quasi-divine detachment from those imperilled by storm and warfare (2.1–6).[62] In the finale of the same book, Lucretius encourages the reader to open the mind to a startling new truth about nature – namely, that there is an infinite number of worlds (2.1023–89).[63] To prepare the reader for this revelation, Lucretius points out that the sky, constellations, moon and sun, which we take for granted, would affright us in just the same way were we to look upon them for the first time. Rather than banalizing nature, however, the shock of the new inversely draws attention to the wonder to be found in the familiar by an inquiring mind, even when that wonder is subject to rational explanation (2.1044–7):

> quaerit enim rationem animus, cum summa loci sit
> infinita foris haec extra moenia mundi,
> quid sit ibi porro quo prospicere usque velit mens
> atque animi iactus liber quo pervolet ipse.

For, since the sum total of space is infinite out there beyond these ramparts of our world, the spirit seeks to reason what there is yonder where the mind wants continually to look forth and where one's mental leap freely flies forth of itself.

---

[59] See Holzberg 1998, esp. 88–91 on this example.   [60] Schiesaro 2014: 75 and *passim*.
[61] Fowler 1995, quotation at 15.
[62] De Lacy 1964. See also Clay 1983: 243–4. On the infinite sea in Lucretius see Saint-Denis 1963.
[63] On this aspect of Epicurean cosmology see Asmis 1984: 310–15; Morenval 2017: 217–29. On the end of *DRN* 2 see Clay 1983: 239–50.

The phrase *animi iactus* ('mental leap') is to be understood as the Epicurean ἐπιβολὴ τῆς διανοίας, the epistemological process whereby the mind
apprehends abstract concepts or phenomena of which it can have no
immediate sensory experience, such as, in this case, a universe of infinite
worlds (or, as at 2.740, colourless atoms).[64] There is instructive similarity
between this passage, describing the mind's instinct to understand what is
'out there' *extra moenia mundi* by means of this *animi iactus*, and those at
the beginning and end of the previous book in which infinity is discussed:
Epicurus, too, proceeds *extra . . . moenia mundi* in mind and spirit (1.72–4
above), and the spear shot into infinity (1.970 *iaciatque volatile telum*) is a
thought-experiment that itself requires the same 'mental leap' as in this
section of *DRN* 2, in which it is the *animi iactus* that flies forward
(*pervolet*). The parallels between these passages point to infinity as a
concept that is necessarily beyond the reach of sensory experience, but
which can yet be intuited by the sublime mind. The sense of the sublime
here is confirmed retroactively by the similarity of (Ps.-)Longinus' meditation on the inspiration derived from the contemplation of nature, beauty
and the unknown (35.2–3):[65]

> What, then, did they see, those godlike men (οἱ ἰσόθεοι ἐκεῖνοι) who
> strove for the greatest things in their writing, and looked down upon
> precision in every detail? *Inter alia*, the following: that nature did not
> choose us, man, as a base and ignoble creature, but introducing us into life
> and into the whole universe (εἰς τὸν σύμπαντα κόσμον) as though into
> some great festival, to be spectators of its contests and the most aspiring
> competitors, she immediately implanted an invincible desire (ἄμαχον
> ἔρωτα) in our souls always for everything great and more numinous
> (δαιμονιωτέρου) than ourselves. Therefore the whole universe is not
> enough for the **mental leap** of human thinking and intellect, but our
> thoughts often pass beyond even the bounds of space (διόπερ τῇ θεωρίας
> καὶ διανοίας τῆς ἀνθρωπίνης **ἐπιβολῇ** οὐδ' ὁ σύμπας κόσμος ἀρκεῖ, ἀλλὰ
> καὶ τοὺς τοῦ περιέχοντος πολλάκις ὅρους ἐκβαίνουσιν αἱ ἐπίνοιαι), and if
> one were to contemplate life in the round, wheresoever it has a greater
> abundance in all things and is great and beautiful, quickly will one know
> for what we have been born.

---

[64] On this concept see Asmis 1984: 83–9, 124–6 with a review of earlier scholarship, and Schrijvers
1978: 102–6 (repr. in Gale 2007a: 277–80) in a discussion of Lucretian analogy; see also Tutrone in
this volume (p. 86).
[65] The comparison is noted by Russell 1964: 165–6, 167 ad 35.3 and, in the context of an extended
parallel between Ps.-Longinus, *Subl.* 35.2–5 and *DRN* 6.608–737, by Porter 2003: 214–19,
esp. 217 n. 65 and Porter 2007, esp. 174 (in both cases Porter hypothesizes a common source).
For a history of the literary and philosophical trope of the flight of the mind see Jones 1926.

The ἐπιβολή that here transcends the bounds of the universe attests a thought-process about the sublime that is also instantiated in Lucretius.[66] The invocation of the technical language of Epicurean epistemology in both contexts suggests that just as Lucretius' contemplation of infinity reaches out to the ineffable sublime, so the ineffable and the sublime habituate the mind to what the infinite is through the process of πρόληψις or preconception (Lucretius' *notities*).[67] Beyond the bounds of the finale to *DRN* 2, where the universe of infinite worlds is revealed, the same nexus of ideas recurs at the start of Book 3 to introduce Lucretius' 'infinite list' of proofs for the mortality of the soul. Here Lucretius celebrates as 'forever most worthy of eternal life' (3.13 *perpetua semper dignissima vita*) the teaching of Epicurus' 'divine mind' (15 *divina mente*) for the revelation it has imparted to him (3.16–18, 28–30):

> diffugiunt animi terrores, moenia mundi
> discedunt, totum video per inane geri res.
> apparet divum numen sedesque quietae
> . . .
> his ibi me rebus quaedam divina voluptas
> percipit atque horror, quod sic natura tua vi
> tam manifesta patens ex omni parte retecta est.

. . . the terrors of the mind take flight, the ramparts of the world part, and through the whole void I see things as they happen. Revealed is the majesty of the gods and their peaceful abodes . . . Thereupon from these things a certain divine pleasure and frisson grips me, because thus by your power nature is so manifestly laid out and in every aspect unveiled.

In this thrill of discovery, Lucretius follows in the footsteps of Epicurus who, as described in the proem to *DRN* 1, blazed a trail in mind and spirit beyond the *moenia mundi* (1.73) to uncover the nature of things. In so doing he takes us from *terror* to *horror*, from the fear of the unknown to the frisson of the sublime that intimates infinity itself.

∞

Lucretius' use of poetry to go where no one has gone before is canvassed in the famous programmatic lines that, as transmitted, occur both at *DRN* 1.926–50 and (with a few differences) as a 'proem in the middle' at *DRN*

---

[66] On the Lucretian sublime see Conte 1994: 1–34; Porter 2003, 2007; Hardie 2009; Most 2012; Schiesaro 2014, esp. 86–7.

[67] On *prolēpsis* see Asmis 1984: 21–3, 61–3. Morenval 2017: 289–90 not dissimilarly suggests that Lucretius creates in the reader feelings of desire in order to promote the sensation of the infinite sublime.

4.1–25. As well as signalling his elemental kinship to Homer and Ennius in the epic tradition, as discussed above, the terms in which Lucretius claims poetic originality are strikingly reminiscent also of Epicurus' trail-blazing peragrations through the infinite universe at the start of the poem (1.926–7, 4.1–2 *avia Pieridum peragro loca nullius ante | trita solo*, cf. 1.74 *omne immensum peragravit*):[68] as Diskin Clay puts it succinctly, '[t]he ἄπειρον of Epicurus and the *auia Pieridum* are one and the same'.[69] As far as the iteration of Lucretius' programme at *DRN* 1.921–50 is concerned, then, it is hardly incidental that it occurs immediately prior to the book's culminating exposition of infinity from line 951: Lucretius' sublime inspiration uniquely qualifies him to compose the poetry of the infinite.

The recollection of the start of *DRN* 1 here in its programmatic second proem sets up a ring-composition that imparts a sense of closure to the book prior to its finale on the infinity of the universe. This sense of an ending may have been all the more acute for the ancient reader who had Lucretius' Epicurean source-text in view: if David Sedley's reconstruction of Epicurus' *On Nature* is accurate, such a reader would have been familiar with the critique of rival theories of the elements, treated by Lucretius in the immediately preceding section at *DRN* 1.635–920, from the *end* of Epicurus' physical and cosmological exposition.[70] At any rate, an ending has been sensed here in *DRN* 1 by modern scholars,[71] as well as by the ancient reader who, probably in the early/mid-third century AD, inserted what our oldest manuscript *O* has transmitted as a transliterated Greek *capitulum* quoting Epicurus, *Ep. Hdt.* 41 τὸ πᾶν ἄπειρόν ἐστι· τὸ γὰρ πεπερασμένον ἄκρον ἔχει· ('the whole is infinite; for what is finite has an extremity') as a heading for the section beginning at 951.[72] The 'false closure' thereby created is, of course, entirely appropriate given that the finale which follows is about, precisely, the impossibility of ever reaching the end – an effect that, as argued above, spills over from the end of *DRN* 1 into the view of the boundless sea at the start of *DRN* 2, and from the

---

[68] For further connections between these passages see Gale 1994: 120 n. 82, 145–6 with n. 62. See also Clay 1983: 340 n. 190; Hardie 1986: 21; Segal 1989: 204, 1990: 180; Morenval 2017: 350.

[69] Clay 1976: 209 (repr. in Gale 2007a: 24).   [70] Sedley 1998: 123–6, 145–6, 190–2.

[71] Schrijvers 1970: 41–7 sees the second proem rounding off an ensemble of programmatic statements across the book; Müller 1978: 200 (repr. in Gale 2007a: 236–7) views it as a 'pause' after the doxography and before the conclusion; see also Piazzi 2011: 215, 219.

[72] See Butterfield 2013: 136–202, esp. 181–2. In this volume (pp. 37–9), Butterfield discusses the *capitula* that introduce the description of the eternal seats of the gods (1.44–9 and 2.646–51) with the first words of *KD* 1 Τὸ μακάριον καὶ ἄφθαρτον, 'The blessed and indestructible': insofar as ἄφθαρτος is a t. t. of atomism (*Ep. Hdt.* 41, 55, 74; cf. n. 4 above), this *capitulum* recognizes the atomic principle behind temporal infinity or immortality.

proof for infinite worlds at the end of that book to the *divina voluptas atque horror* of Lucretius' sublime insight at the start of *DRN* 3. Reading across this grandly denied closure, then, we pass from Lucretius' manifesto for philosophical poetry, concluding with an explicit reference to his verses and a resounding invocation of the title of the poem, to a new beginning that emphatically tells us that there is no *finis* (1.948–57):

> si tibi forte animum tali ratione tenere
> versibus in nostris possem, dum perspicis omnem
> naturam rerum qua constet compta figura.   950
>   Sed quoniam docui solidissima materiai
> corpora perpetuo volitare invicta per aevom,
> nunc age, summai quaedam sit **finis** eorum
> necne sit, <u>evolvamus</u>; item quod inane repertumst
> seu locus ac spatium, res in quo quaeque gerantur,   955
> pervideamus utrum **finitum** funditus **omne**
> constet an **immensum** pateat vasteque profundum.

... [I have chosen to expound Epicurean doctrine in poetry] to see if I might perhaps be able in this way to hold your attention in my verses, while you see right through the whole Nature of Things, the form in which it stands composed.

But since I have taught that the densest particles of matter fly through time eternally and without ever being destroyed, come now, let us unfurl what end there is or is not to their sum total; similarly, what has been discovered as the void, or the place and space in which all things happen, let us examine whether it is completely and utterly finite or opens out beyond measure and to a vast depth.

As Lucretius claims to break new ground poetically, so his text is about to break away from ring-composition and closure to enact a serial progression as proof after proof and line after line accompany the extension of infinite space. Read in this way, the allusion to the *volumen* that the reader unrolls as Lucretius unfolds his argument (954 *evolvamus*)[73] is all the more *ad rem*. It is only as we unfurl these further columns of text that we come to realize that this is not the end of the book, and in the process we learn that there is no end to the universe. When, therefore, Virgil's Jupiter unrolls the book of fate at *Aen.* 1.262 (*longius et volvens fatorum arcana movebo*, 'and, further unrolling the scroll of fate, [I] will disclose its secrets'),[74] he does so as a

---

[73] *OLD* s.v. 6. The allusion is suggested by Bailey 1947: II.762 ad loc.; Brown 1984: 191 ad loc.; Morenval 2017: 261. On the use of this image at *DRN* 1.144 see Kennedy in this volume (pp. 265–6).

[74] Here I adopt Mynors' punctuation and the translation of Fairclough/Goold 1999: 281. For Virgil's book-roll image see also Conington and Nettleship 1881 ad loc., and most subsequent commentaries; Austin 1971: 102 ad loc. concurs, but reminds the reader that Jupiter is also 'turning things over' in the mind (*OLD* s.v. 6b).

reader of the _DRN_, guaranteeing infinite empire to the Aeneadae ironically on Lucretian authority:[75] _his ego nec metas rerum nec tempora pono:_ | _imperium sine fine dedi_ (_Aen._ 1.278–9 'For them I set no limits, spatial or temporal: I have granted empire without end').[76]

The role of Lucretius' second proem in setting up this false closure might be taken to recommend 1.926–50 as the 'correct' setting for these lines in the poem. However, it might also be said that their repetition as a preface to Book 4 only reinforces the way in which they can masquerade as an epilogue to Book 1.[77] In this case the minor variations in the passages will conspire in their closural and apertural functions: at 1.949–50 _dum perspicis omnem_ | _naturam rerum qua constet compta figura_, the four words that follow the caesura in 950 look back over the cohesion of the universe and poem; the variation at 4.24–5 _dum percipis omnem_ | _naturam rerum ac persentis utilitatem_ ('while you comprehend the whole Nature of Things and perceive its utility') looks ahead to a book on sense-perception and epistemology.[78] The repetition, therefore, contributes to Lucretius' exploitation of the material text at the end of Book 1. If the never-ending poem really is of a piece with the universe it describes, such repetition should not surprise us either: in an infinite universe of infinite _elementa_, anything that can happen once is guaranteed to happen again. _Nil novi sub sole._

Repetition, again as Eco points out, is also one of the strategies deployed by the list as a means of conveying infinity, suggestive as it is of an inexhaustible reserve of material.[79] In the context of the seriatim arguments for infinity at the end of _DRN_ 1, repetition is witnessed at the level of individual words (1.998–1001, 1008–11):[80]

---

[75] In a different vein, cf. the Lucretian-sounding Horace at _Sat._ 1.3.111–12 _iura inventa metu iniusti fateare necessest_ | _tempora si fastosque velis evolvere mundi_ ('you have to admit that laws were invented through fear of injustice – if you should wish to unroll the calendar of world history') at the end of what can be read as a unitary mega-diatribe spanning the first three satires (see Gowers 2012: 16, 122 ad _Sat._ 1.2.1).

[76] Hardie 2009: 167, 173–9 locates in _imperium sine fine_ a meditation on the nature of things, culminating in the quasi-Lucretian spear-throw by which Aeneas brings Turnus to his knees and the epic to its debatable close (_Aen._ 12.919–26). See further Rimell 2015: 28–80, esp. 28–65. Cf. n. 33 above.

[77] Alternatively, 1.921–50 could be taken as prefatory to the finale without much weakening the closural and apertural signals in the lines that follow.

[78] Kyriakidis 2006 relates the repetition _cum variatione_ to Lucretius' position on the impossibility of _metathesis_.

[79] Eco 2009: 137 and _passim_. The didactic technique of repetition is made explicit at Epicurus, _Ep. Hdt._ 35–6, 83, _Ep. Pyth._ 84–5, 116. On different forms of repetition in Lucretius see Bailey 1947: 1.144–65; Dionigi 1988: 75–88; Buglass 2015. For the rationale see Clay 1983: 176–85; Schiesaro 1994: 98–100.

[80] Noted by Deutsch 1939: 44, 53.

> Postremo ante oculos res rem finire videtur;
> aer dissaepit collis atque aera montes,
> terra mare et contra mare terras terminat omnis;   1000
> omne quidem vero nihil est quod finiat extra.
> . . .
> Ipsa modum porro sibi rerum summa parare
> ne possit, natura tenet, quae corpus inani
> et quod inane autem est finiri corpore cogit,   1010
> ut sic alternis infinita omnia reddat.

Lastly, before our eyes thing is seen to limit thing: the air separates the hills and the mountains the air, the land ends the sea and conversely the sea all lands; but there is in fact nothing that limits the universe on the outside . . . The very sum of things, furthermore, is kept from setting a limit for itself by nature, which compels body to be limited by void, and what is void again by body, so that alternately in this way it renders everything infinite.

Lucretius' use of formal devices to reflect the world around the text features in these lines in the figure of polyptoton: the repetition of inflections of the same word represents a universe of infinite extension in which one thing cannot but be bounded by another, matter by void and void by matter, and so on *ad infinitum.*

Of course, Book 1 must come to an end somewhere, and when it does we find it still repeating itself on this microtextual level (1.1114–17):

> Haec sic pernosces parva perductus opella;
> namque alid ex alio clarescet, nec tibi caeca
> nox iter eripiet quin ultima naturai
> pervideas: ita res accendent lumina rebus.

These matters you will work out, then, led on with just a little effort: for one point will become clear from another, and blinding night will not steal your road to seeing the farthest reaches of nature. So things shed light on things.

In this closural *epiphonema*,[81] polyptoton conveys the domino-effect of deductive argumentation, but the idea also links in with the preceding discussion of the seriatim concatenation of matter and void. The goal, says Lucretius, is the *ultima naturai*, but since we now know those *ultima* can never actually be apprehended (or comprehended?), we might wonder if it is not the journey that is more important. In a way that this passage brings to mind, Immanuel Kant held that we cannot ultimately know anything, much less the infinite, since knowledge is always contingent on other

---

[81] See P. Fowler 1997, esp. 120–3 (repr. in Gale 2007a: 209–14) on these lines, their closural signals, and their connection to *DRN* 1.407–9 and 5.1454–7. See also Kennedy in this volume (pp. 267–8).

knowledge, such that discursive thought is itself an infinite regress,[82] an idea sometimes compared to Derrida's concept of *différance*, whereby meaning is endlessly deferred through the semantic web, as every term takes its meaning from another term, and so on *ad infinitum*. As Don Fowler observed in his discussion of the rather Ovidian lack of segmentation in the *DRN*, this tendency may be witnessed in Lucretius' complex etymologizing, through which '[t]he words of the poem are as subject to dissemination and deferral as any others'.[83] This presents what may be a rather perplexing state of affairs for a poem that aims to elucidate a philosophy that – according to the first rule of its *Canon* – demands precision of expression, and that had evolved its own terminology, precisely to avoid the infinite regress of meaning (*Ep. Hdt.* 37–8):[84]

> Πρῶτον μὲν οὖν τὰ ὑποτεταγμένα τοῖς φθόγγοις, ὦ Ἡρόδοτε, δεῖ εἰληφέναι, ὅπως ἂν τὰ δοξαζόμενα ἢ ζητούμενα ἢ ἀπορούμενα ἔχωμεν εἰς ταῦτα ἀναγαγόντες ἐπικρίνειν, καὶ μὴ ἄκριτα πάντα ἡμῖν <ἢ> **εἰς ἄπειρον** ἀποδεικνύουσιν ἢ κενοὺς φθόγγους ἔχωμεν· ἀνάγκη γὰρ τὸ πρῶτον ἐννόημα καθ᾽ ἕκαστον φθόγγον βλέπεσθαι καὶ μηθὲν ἀποδείξεως προσδεῖσθαι, εἴπερ ἕξομεν τὸ ζητούμενον ἢ ἀπορούμενον καὶ δοξαζόμενον ἐφ᾽ ὃ ἀνάξομεν.

> First of all, Herodotus, one must grasp the underlying meaning of words, so that by reference to these we can evaluate opinions, inquiries or conundrums, and lest all things go unevaluated for us in our attempt to prove them *ad infinitum*, or we end up with an empty vocabulary. For the primary concept in respect of each word must be scrutinized and need no further proof, if at any rate we are to have something to which to refer the inquiry or conundrum and opinion.

Whereas Epicurus here warns against language that risks spinning out εἰς ἄπειρον, Lucretius by contrast embraces the inevitable deferral of meaning precisely when seeking to explain the fundamentally inexplicable concept of infinity. For the *DRN* as a translation, this *différance* is inevitable, but its poetic form went further in a way that was not inevitable.[85] Scholarly discussion of Lucretius' contravention of Epicurus' strictures against poetry has tended to emphasize how poetic language elucidates, enhances, and makes more appealing the *obscura reperta* of Epicureanism; but it might

---

[82] For Kant's (explicitly acknowledged) relationship to Lucretius see Baker 2007: 284–5 with further bibliography; Adler 2012. Moore 2001: 84–95, esp. 86–7, locates Kant in the history of thought about infinity.
[83] Fowler 1995: 16. Cf. Morenval 2017: 284–5.
[84] On this passage and Epicurus' first rule of inquiry see Asmis 1984: 19–34.
[85] So also Morenval 2017: 285–7.

also be said that poetry's suggestiveness and elusiveness open a window onto the infinite. It seems no coincidence, therefore, that Lucretius makes his apologia for his choice of poetry as a medium for philosophy at precisely this juncture in the text. Not only do the physical properties of the Roman book-roll enable Lucretius to represent the nature of things as *omne immensum*, as we have seen, but the very language of poetry, right down to the letter, is capable of conveying the implications and consequences of infinity, and of communicating to mortal minds the sense of sublime detachment that will make them, as Ovid recognized in his reading of Lucretius, immortal.

CHAPTER 6

Lucretian Echoes
Sound as Metaphor for Literary Allusion in De Rerum Natura *4.549–94*

Jason Nethercut

Introduction

Midway through the fourth book of the *De Rerum Natura* (*DRN*), Lucretius offers a detailed account of acoustics and auditory phenomena. This account occurs in the context of his broader discussion of the atomic mechanics of sensory perception. For Lucretius, hearing, just like every other perception, results from our apprehension of atomic bodies interacting with our sense organs.[1] Of course if all potential obstructions to the flow of sound atoms are removed, we hear perfectly clearly (4.549–56):[2]

        Hasce igitur penitus voces cum corpore nostro

550   exprimimus rectoque foras emittimus ore,

        mobilis articulat verborum daedala lingua

        formaturaque labrorum pro parte figurat.

        hoc ubi non longum spatiumst unde illa profecta

        perveniat vox quaeque, necessest verba quoque ipsa

555   plane exaudiri discernique articulatim;

        servat enim formaturam servatque figuram.

Therefore, when we push these voices forth from deep within our body and send them straight out from our mouth, the dexterous tongue, craftsman of words, separates them apart and in turn the shaping of the lips gives them form. Therefore, when the distance is not far whence each of those voices departs and arrives to us, it follows that the words themselves also are heard clearly and are distinguished bit by bit. For each voice preserves its shaping and preserves its form.

In order to illustrate exactly how fundamental atoms are to the process of hearing, Lucretius adduces a number of examples in which the clarity of our hearing is affected negatively; in every instance, this misapprehension

---

[1] The most comprehensive account of Lucretius' discussion of acoustics is Koenen 2004. See also Zinn 2018.

[2] My text is that of Rouse and Smith 1992; all translations are my own.

results because some intermediate source has prevented the sound atoms from reaching our ears (4.557–62):

> at si interpositum spatium sit longius aequo,
> aera per multum confundi verba necessest
> et conturbari vocem, dum transvolat auras.
> ergo fit sonitum ut possis sentire neque illam   560
> internoscere, verborum sententia quae sit:
> usque adeo confusa venit vox inque pedita.

But if the distance set between should be further than is fitting, it follows that through much air the words are confused together and the voice is disrupted, while it flies across the breezes. Therefore, it comes to pass that you can perceive the sound and cannot differentiate what the meaning of the words is: so confused and entangled does the voice come to you.

It is in this context that Lucretius discusses the phenomenon of echo. For Lucretius, though an utterance must derive from one source, the atoms that make up the sound emanate into the universe upon articulation. As a result, one utterance will produce a large number of identical sound atoms, some of which may bypass those who could hear them. The image Lucretius uses to make this point is that of a herald speaking to an audience. This herald sends forth many voice atoms from his body, some of which must necessarily strike walls and other hard objects. These atoms then bounce back, returning the sound at a delay to the audience (4.563–71):

> Praeterea verbum saepe unum perciet auris
> omnibus in populo, missum praeconis ab ore.
> in multas igitur voces vox una repente   565
> diffugit, in privas quoniam se dividit auris,
> obsignans formam verbis clarumque sonorem.
> at quae pars vocum non auris incidit ipsas,
> praeterlata perit frustra diffusa per auras;
> pars, solidis adlisa locis, reiecta sonorem   570
> reddit et interdum frustratur imagine verbi.

Moreover, often one word sent from the mouth of a herald strikes the ears of all in a crowd. Therefore, one voice suddenly scatters into many voices, since it splits itself into all the separate ears imprinting on the words its shape and clear sound. But the part of the voices which does not fall on the ears themselves, having passed them by, perishes scattered in vain through the breezes. Part of them, having been hurled against solid places, is thrown back and returns the sound and sometimes deludes us with the image of a word.

Lucretius' description of the echo, then, arises organically from his atomic explanation of auditory perception.

What follows in our text, however, is an aside that, though connected to the preceding discussion of echo, is, in many ways, anomalous. Here Lucretius offers a first-hand account of his own experience hearing multiple echoes, which is then expanded with his report that unnamed rustics attribute the phenomenon to satyrs, nymphs, fauns and Pan (4.572–94):

Quae bene cum videas, rationem reddere possis
tute tibi atque aliis, quo pacto per loca sola
saxa paris formas verborum ex ordine reddant,
575   palantis comites cum montis inter opacos
quaerimus et magna dispersos voce ciemus.
sex etiam aut septem loca vidi reddere voces,
unam cum iaceres: ita colles collibus ipsi
verba repulsantes iterabant docta referri.
580   Haec loca capripedes satyros nymphasque tenere
finitimi fingunt, et faunos esse loquuntur,
quorum noctivago strepitu ludoque iocanti
adfirmant volgo taciturna silentia rumpi,
chordarumque sonos fieri dulcisque querellas,
585   tibia quas fundit digitis pulsata canentum,
et genus agricolum late sentiscere, quom Pan,
pinea semiferi capitis velamina quassans,
unco saepe labro calamos percurrit hiantis,
fistula silvestrem ne cesset fundere musam.
590   cetera de genere hoc monstra ac portenta loquuntur,
ne loca deserta ab divis quoque forte putentur
sola tenere. ideo iactant miracula dictis
aut aliqua ratione alia ducuntur, ut omne
humanum genus est avidum nimis auricularum.

When you see this clearly, you could give an account to yourself and others, how it is that throughout solitary places the rocks return in due order equivalent forms of words, when we look for our companions wandering among the dark hills and with a loud voice summon them scattered about. I have seen places return even six or seven voices, when you sent forth just one: thus did the hills themselves upon the other hills drive back and re-echo the words trained to come back. The locals imagine that goat-footed satyrs and nymphs inhabit these places, and they say that there are fauns, by whose clamour spreading through the night and joking games they declare that the soundless silence is commonly broken; and that sounds of strings come to life, and sweet songs of lament, which the pipe pours forth, struck by the fingers of the singers; and that the race of rustics hears far and wide, when Pan, shaking the pine-tree shrouds of his half-monstrous head, often runs over the open reeds with curved lip, so that the pipe does not cease from pouring forth the woodland Muse. They speak of other prodigies and portents of this kind, lest by chance they be thought to inhabit solitary places, deserted even by the gods. Therefore, they boast of marvels with words or they are induced by some other explanation, as the whole human race is all too eager for tall tales.

Scholars have long acknowledged that Lucretius finishes off his quite technical discussion of these sensory phenomena with a passage that is markedly poetic. Indeed, in these lines others have seen the influence of pastoral poetry, evocations of the Hylas story in Hellenistic poetry, and other engagements with myth that are fundamental to Lucretian poetics.[3] In what follows, I will take as my methodological first principle the idea that the form of Lucretius' poem mirrors its content, and I will suggest that these poetic elements, far from ornamental, ultimately reflect the content of the passage, functioning to reinforce the atomic explanation of echo that Lucretius advances. Relevant in this context is the fact that echo operates metatextually as a reflexive marker of allusion.[4] In this way, my analysis builds on the growing consensus in the scholarly literature that the poetic form of the *DRN* complements its philosophical content.[5] At the same time, I will argue that Lucretius' procedure in the echo discussion finds a parallel in the works of Philodemus of Gadara, whose arguments regarding poetics regularly reflect ideas taken from other branches in the Epicurean system. By juxtaposing Lucretius with Philodemus, I will suggest that the harmony between form and content on display in the Lucretian passage on echo displays his Epicurean orthodoxy when it comes to the poetic concepts of Form and Content.

Lucretius' Echo and the *Homeric Hymn to Pan*

There appear to be a number of allusions to earlier poetry in Lucretius' discussion of echo. These allusions fall into two groups: specific allusions to the *Homeric Hymn to Pan* (*HH* 19) and more general allusions to earlier poetry that represent Echo in anthropomorphic terms and as a consort of Pan. It remains an open question when the *Homeric Hymns* as we have

---

[3] For discussions of these lines see Bailey 1947: III.1249–51 ad loc. with earlier bibliography; Koenen 2004. For the pastoral associations of Lucretius' description see Fiscal 1947: 86–90; Gillis 1967. For the Hylas story see Hardie 1988: 77. For mythology and Lucretian poetics see Ackermann 1979: 107–19; Schrijvers 1983: 370–1 (= 1999: 38–9); Gale 1994: 133–8; Gigandet 1998: 286–302.

[4] See Hollander 1981; Hinds 1998; 5–8; Heerink 2015.

[5] Fundamental is Gale 1994, but see also Thury 1987 and the series of close readings in Schiesaro 1990. Cf. Schiesaro 1994; Fowler 1995; Kennedy 2000; Gale 2004; O'Hara 2007: 64–9.

them came to be compiled into a circulating corpus.[6] Scholars of Latin
poetry often have taken it for granted that Latin poets, especially those of
the Augustan period, allude, sometimes quite extensively, to the Hymns.[7]
But the fact remains that the evidence for a collection of Hymns as such is
not forthcoming in any direct way until much later. Regardless of the form
in which the Hymns were available in the first century BC, it seems
possible that Lucretius alludes to the *Homeric Hymn to Pan* at various
points in his description of echo. Such an allusion might make sense *a
priori* insofar as in this text we find the earliest narrative of Pan's birth and
parentage, as well as the earliest connection of Pan with the nymph Echo.
HH 19 therefore represented a repository of material for Lucretius to
demythologize in his explanation of the echo.[8] In fact, it may be that the
Hymn's opening lines lie behind his evocative (re)telling of the rustics'
fictions (4.580–4; *HH* 19.1–3):

> Haec loca capripedes satyros nymphasque tenere
> finitimi fingunt, et faunos esse loquuntur,
> quorum noctivago strepitu ludoque iocanti
> adfirmant volgo taciturna silentia rumpi.

The locals imagine that goat-footed satyrs and nymphs inhabit these places, and
they say that there are fauns, by whose clamour spreading through the night and
joking games they declare that the soundless silence is commonly broken.

> ἀμφί μοι Ἑρμείαο φίλον γόνον ἔννεπε, Μοῦσα,
> αἰγιπόδην, δικέρωτα φιλόκροτον, ὅς τ'ἀνὰ πίση
> δενδρήεντ' ἄμυδις φοιτᾷ χοροήθεσι νύμφαις.

Muse, tell me about the dear son of Hermes, the goat-footed one, two-horned,
lover of clamour, who wanders throughout the wooded glades together with
nymphs who are accustomed to the dance.

Long ago Schrijvers suggested in passing that Lucretius alludes to the Pan
Hymn in these lines.[9] In addition to a number of common elements in
these two passages – e.g., noise (*noctivago strepitu*; φιλόκροτον) and the
grouping of fauns and nymphs (*nymphas ... faunos*; ὅς ... ἄμυδις φοιτᾷ
χοροήθεσι νύμφαις) – Lucretius appears to provide a calque on Pan's

[6] See Faulkner 2011b with discussion of the *status quaestionis*. I follow Janko 1982: 185 in dating the
    Hymn to Pan between the late sixth and mid-fifth centuries BC. Cf. Fröhder 1994: 304–5; Càssola
    1997: 364; Germany 2005: 187; Thomas 2011: 169–71.
[7] See Hinds 1987; Barchiesi 1999; Syed 2004; Clauss 2016; Harrison 2016; Miller 2016; Keith 2016;
    Nethercut 2016, esp. n. 4.
[8] See Gale 1994: 133–6 for demythologization in Lucretius' description of echo.
[9] Schrijvers 1983: 370 (= 1999: 38).

epithet αἰγιπόδην used twice in the *Homeric Hymn to Pan* (19.2; 19.37) with his own *capripedes*. Ernout and Robin tell us that this is the first appearance of the adjective in Latin, while Ackermann adduces it as proof that Lucretius wants us to be thinking of specifically Greek mythological antecedents.[10] Of course αἰγιπόδης occurs in other texts before Lucretius, but even so it occurs very infrequently and generally not in narrative contexts resembling what we find in the Lucretius passage and the Pan Hymn.[11] In light of the evidence, one might agree with Schrijvers about this allusion. We can note too that an allusion to the Pan Hymn might be announced by the Alexandrian footnote, as three separate verbs of reporting occur in a span of four lines (*fingunt . . . loquuntur . . . adfirmant vulgo*).[12]

It is not only to *HH* 19 that Lucretius would appear to allude in these lines. Lucretius' description of Pan's piping seems to direct the reader back to a similar description in an epigram attributed to Plato (*DRN* 4.588–9; *Anth. Pal.* 9.823.3–4):

> unco saepe labro calamos percurrit hiantis,
> fistula silvestrem ne cesset fundere musam.

(Pan) often runs over the open reeds with curved lip, so that the pipe does not cease from pouring forth the woodland Muse.

> αὐτὸς ἐπεὶ σύριγγι μελίσδεται εὐκελάδῳ Πάν,
> ὑγρὸν ἱεὶς ζευκτῶν χεῖλος ὑπὲρ καλάμων.

When Pan himself modulates on his melodious pipe, throwing his moist lip over the yoked reeds

A number of verbal similarities and similarities of detail encourage the reader to see an allusion here: Pan (*Pan*, 4.586; Πάν) passes his lip (*labro*; χεῖλος) over the reeds (*calamos*; καλάμων) that form his pipe (*fistula*; σύριγγι). Most commentators have adduced this epigram in their analysis of this passage.[13] Given that Lucretius describes both the dexterity of Pan's playing (*calamos percurrit hiantis*) and the continuous outpouring of his tune (*ne cesset fundere*), one might be tempted to connect these lines back further to the *Homeric Hymn to Pan*, whose only simile describes Pan as the nightingale (*HH* 19.16–18):

---

[10] Ernout and Robin 1925–8: 239; Ackermann 1979: 111.
[11] αἰγιπόδης before Lucretius: *HH* 19.2, 19.37; Herodotus 4.25; *Anth. Pal.* 6.57.3, 9.330.2.
[12] For the Alexandrian footnote in Lucretius see Nethercut 2014: 448 and 2018.
[13] Representative is Bailey 1947: III.1251 ad 4.588. Regardless of its Platonic authenticity, this epigram must be earlier than Lucretius.

οὐκ ἂν τόν γε παραδράμοι ἐν μελέεσιν
ὄρνις, ἥ τ'ἔαρος πολυανθέος ἐν πετάλοισιν
θρῆνον ἐπιπροχέουσα χέει μελίγηρυν ἀοιδήν.[14]

Not even she could run past him in songs, the bird who among the leaves in flowery spring pouring forth her lament in addition pours forth her honey-voiced song.

In a separate discussion, Germany has also suggested in passing that Lucretius' description of Pan's piping *dulcis querellas* is evocative of the Hymn's characterization of Pan's music as νήδυμος (16), of the mournful song of the nightingale in this simile, and of the description of Echo's lament (21).[15] All of this evidence suggests that it is plausible that Lucretius combines allusions to the *Homeric Hymn to Pan* with allusions to other, earlier poetry about Pan in his description of the echo. It may even be that this combinatorial allusion functions correctively.[16] On such a reading, Lucretius implies that the simile in the *Homeric Hymn* contains the correct explanation of the phenomenon under discussion: rather than some impossibly hybrid musical deity, birdsong is the ultimate source of the nocturnal music the rustics hear.[17]

Lucretius' description may also engage more generally with earlier poetry that personifies Echo, who is often presented as a consort of Pan, a point that has been well documented in the scholarly literature on this passage.[18] Koenen has presented the evidence most cohesively that Lucretius takes over fragments 'from different literary stories and descriptions of the echo'.[19] Lucretius insinuates that Echo is one of the nymphs who accompany the satyrs with his use of the participle *iocanti* (4.582). Technically this

---

[14] I owe this suggestion to Matthew Carter, in a stimulating (but as yet unpublished) paper he presented on 'Hermes and Pan in the *Eclogues* and *Georgics*' at a conference on the Reception of the Homeric Hymns in Heidelberg on 24 June 2014. He went on to suggest that if Lucretius uses the *Hymn to Pan* in this passage and if, as seems likely, he uses the *Homeric Hymn to Aphrodite* as a source for the hymn to Venus which inaugurates the *DRN*, perhaps we have evidence that a collection of the Homeric Hymns was available to Roman poets in the generation before Vergil. On the nightingale simile in the *Homeric Hymn to Pan* see Thomas 2011: 155–8 and 168–9, who notices in it an allusion to the comparison of Penelope to the nightingale at *Od.* 19.518–22 and suggests that the figure of Echo in the *Hymn* 'may well be a symbol ... of *Hymn* 19's allusivity' (169). Cf. Germany 2005: 199–202, with further bibliography on the allusion to the *Odyssey* in *HH* 19.

[15] Germany 2005: 199.

[16] For the phenomenon see Thomas 1986 and his discussion of 'window reference'.

[17] This explanation will be corroborated later in *DRN* 5, when Lucretius connects the origin of human speech and music to birdsong. On the connection between the account of echo and the origin of music at *DRN* 5.1379–411 see Buchheit 1984: 143 and 147–54; Gale 1994: 134.

[18] For surveys of Echo/the echo in ancient literature see *RE* 5.1926–30 (Waser); Roscher 1.1213–14 (von Sybel); *RAC* 4.500–5 (Hermann). Cf. Hollander 1981: 6–15; Loewenstein 1984: 10–32.

[19] Koenen 2004: 716–17 with bibliography of earlier discussions.

participle describes the rustics' *ludus*, and so Echo is not actually present in this description. Of course, it is entirely appropriate for the mythological worldview that Lucretius is contradicting here that Echo is only sensed or heard and is not physically present. In any case, with this implicit person-ification of Echo, Lucretius participates in a developed tradition of poetry that conceptualizes Echo in anthropomorphic terms (e.g., Pindar *O.* 14.20, Euripides *Hec.* 1110–11 and Aristophanes *Thesm.* 1056–97).[20] Moreover, in associating Echo with Pan, Lucretius may allude to the myth of their union prominent in Hellenistic (and Imperial) literature. Callimachus, fr. 685 Pf. (*ap.* schol. Theocrit. ii.17) tells us that Iynx is said to be the daughter of Echo (and, it follows, Pan), while Moschus, fr. 2.1–2 Gow describes a complicated chain of love that intermingles Pan, Echo and a satyr, a detail that one might connect to Lucretius' *finitimi* and their mixing of satyrs, nymphs, fauns and Pan.[21] Even these general allusions to previous poetry, however, may ultimately go back to the *Homeric Hymn to Pan* (19.19–21), where echo (Echo?) is said to wail alone in the mountains.[22] Lucretius may thus implicitly provide us with a poetic archaeology for the story the *finitimi* tell, taking us, through his allusions in this passage, continuously back to the first appearance in the poetic tradition of this myth in the *Homeric Hymn to Pan*.

Form and Content in Epicurean Poetics

On the basis of the evidence explored in the previous section, the reader is encouraged to read what may be considered a tour de force of literary allusion in this passage, including window allusions that function to help the reader demythologize the wild stories of Lucretius' rustics. I want to suggest at this point that the combination of so many different allusions may serve another purpose, namely to illustrate in the realm of poetics the atomic explanation for the phenomenon of echo that precedes this passage. Crucial for my analysis here are the insights about the relationship between

---

[20] Important here too is Ennius, *Andromacha* 33 Jocelyn, which I take as coming from the *Andromeda* on the basis of its close verbal correspondences to Aristophanes, *Thesm.* 1065–72, itself a parody of Euripides' *Andromeda*. In other words, Ennius' fragment functions as a window allusion to Euripides' play of the same name via Aristophanes' *Thesmophoriazusae*.

[21] Again, for this line of argument, see Koenen 2004: 717. On Moschus fr. 2 Gow see Loewenstein 1984: 23; Kegel-Brinkgreve 1990: 47–8. On the close mythical association of Pan and Echo in later literature see Lucian *Dial. D.* 2.4, *Bis acc.* 12; *Anth. Plan.* 154, 156, 223; *CIG* 4538; Nonnus *Dion.* 16.289, 39.130; *Hymn. Orph.* 11.9; Polyaenus *Strat.* 1.2; Philostr. *Imag.* 2.11; Dio Chrys. *Or.* 6.20; most fully, Longus 3.23.

[22] See Germany 2005 and Thomas 2011: 168–9, both with further bibliography.

form and content in Epicurean poetic theory found both in the *DRN* itself
and in the treatise *On Poems* by Philodemus of Gadara, both of whom
posit a fundamental harmony between form and content. For Philodemus,
form and content are intricately connected, a change in one necessarily
altering the other.[23] Perhaps most famously, David Armstrong has suggested that this idea means that for Philodemus (and Lucretius)
'metathesis', or a changing of poetic word order in any poem, is impossible, because the new, changed phrasing would represent a completely
different poetic composition.[24]

But before I bring this evidence from Philodemus and Lucretius to bear
on the discussion of echo found in *DRN* 4, I turn to Lucretius' famous
atoms–letters analogy, which David Armstrong, among others, has argued
is central to the analysis of form and content in Epicurean poetic theory.
This analogy will also prove important to my argument below, so I will
quote here its most elaborate manifestation in the *DRN* (2.1013–22):

>   quin etiam refert nostris in versibus ipsis
>   cum quibus et quali sint ordine quaeque locata;
> 1015   namque eadem caelum mare terras flumina solem
>   significant, eadem fruges arbusta animantis;
>   si non omnia sunt, at multo maxima pars est
>   consimilis; verum positura discrepitant res.
> 1019   sic ipsis in rebus item iam materiai
> 1021   concursus motus ordo positura figurae
>   cum permutantur, mutari res quoque debent.

Indeed even in my verses themselves it makes a difference with what other letters
and in what order each letter is placed. For the same letters signify sky, sea, lands,
rivers, sun, the same too crops, trees, living creatures; if not all, yet by far the
greatest part are similar, but owing to their position the things sound different. So
in things themselves likewise when the meetings of matter, its motions, order,
position and shapes are changed, the things too are bound to change.

That Lucretius connects the atoms that make up all the compounds in the
universe with the letters that make up all the words in the verses of
the *DRN* has been taken as proof that he shares Philodemus' ideas about
the relationship between form and content. And it is important for our
understanding of this analogy that Schiesaro has argued that every analogical model in Lucretius that comprises elements taken over from perceiv-
able reality must necessarily maintain a causal relationship with the

---

[23] Armstrong 1995. See also Asmis 2004.   [24] See further Shearin in Chapter 7 of this volume.

unperceived generative bodies of nature.[25] While he extrapolates this generalization from the dust motes analogy, it should also, if it is valid (as I believe it is), be applicable to the letters–atoms analogy. If we do so apply this generalization, we can recognize that Lucretius encourages the reader to extrapolate a causal relationship between atomic activity and poetic activity. The shifting of letters, words and verses is the direct consequence of the shifting of atoms that make up these letters, words and verses.[26] It appears, then, that form and content are not only insep-arable from one another in Lucretian thought, but that they may be causally related. Any change in poetic form results from the shifting of the atoms that make up the formal aspects of a poem. At the same time this change in poetic form causes a concomitant change in the *res* – i.e. the content – that is signified by these formal aspects. Lucretius suggests, therefore, that form and content are inseparably and causally connected.

In drawing this connection between the theory of Philodemus and its counterpart in Lucretius' atoms–letters analogy, and Schiesaro's analysis of analogy in the *DRN*, I am aware that these two perspectives are potentially at odds. Most obviously, Philodemus does not derive his poetic theory from atomic activity, unlike Schiesaro. Philodemus, it appears, views the poet as someone who imposes formal order on the atoms, while Schiesaro's ideas would indicate that the atoms spontaneously create a poetic cosmos, in principle independent of any poet or creator. This tension lies at the heart of the *DRN*, which represents the atoms as haphazardly giving rise to the universe; the *DRN* itself, however, is the work of Lucretius who imposes order on his poetic material, according to his own understanding of the universe.

In any event, all this suggests that we are justified in seeing Lucretius' incorporation of so many allusions into the form of his discussion of echo as inseparably connected to – reflective, even, of – the content itself of the discussion. These multiple allusions to earlier poetry function as a metapoetic illustration of the atomic dynamics of his explanation. Just as the echo is explained as the separation of multiple atomic compounds from one originary conglomeration, so too does Lucretius encourage us to recognize the process of allusion, and specifically of combinatorial allusion, as the emanation of literary influences from one original text.[27] In this specific example, Lucretius' passage on the echo accommodates the

---

[25] Schiesaro 1990: 27–9.
[26] For a somewhat sceptical overview of this topic see Volk 2002: 100–5.
[27] Koenen 2004: 710 has suggested that the phrase *sonorem | reddit* (4.570–1) implies through a metapoetic evocation of an echo a connection between the sound (*sonorem*) and meaning of the text (*-rem | reddit*).

confluence of multiple allusions to the *Homeric Hymn to Pan*; not only does Lucretius make allusions to the Hymn, but he also includes intermediary texts that allude to the Hymn. Viewed in this way, Lucretius' passage functions metapoetically as one of the *loca sola* (4.573) that produce multiple echoes: allusions to the Pan Hymn reverberate throughout his description of Pan's music-making.[28]

Other metapoetic markers in this passage contribute to this picture. For example, the noun *corpus* (body, atom, poetry-book) features throughout the passage (e.g., 4.525–6, 549) and there are frequent references to poetry (e.g., 584 *querellas* and 585 *tibia*) and poetic production (579 *verba ... docta referri*). Moreover, Lucretius refers to his own experience (549–50 *cum corpore nostro | exprimimus* and 577 *vidi reddere voces*), which may anticipate the intertextual reception of his own work (cf. 604 *ex aliis aliae quoniam gignuntur*). On the other hand, Lucretius may be drawing our attention to the *intratextual* echoes in his discussion of echo, especially when we note line 577 (*sex etiam aut septem loca vidi reddere voces*), where 'seeing sounds' strikes the reader as unusual (although cf. 4.303 *quinque etiam aut sex ut fieri simulacra suërint*, where Lucretius describes the identical process of atomic reflection in the visual sphere).[29] I should add, too, that the appropriation of Lucretius' discussion of echo in poets like Vergil and Ovid reveals that Lucretius' metapoetic presentation of the phenomenon produced its own subsequent echoes along the way.[30] The discussion of echo, it turns out, illustrates how sounds echo about both from one text to another *and* within texts themselves. These later echoes of Lucretius are also new configurations, radically different from Lucretius' explanation of the phenomenon. Lucretius' ideas of metathesis thus find confirmation in the subsequent poetic reception of his echo passage.

[28] A further textual marker of this metapoetic gesture may been seen in the repetition of the noun *vox* (554, 559, 562, 565 [×2], 568, 576, 577) throughout the description of the echo, which may additionally hint at the multiple allusions contained in the passage. In this context, the description of Epicurus' *ratio* at 3.14–15 (*ratio tua coepit* **vociferari** | *naturam rerum*) is a relevant example in Lucretius where philosophical speech is described with the same root.

[29] See Hardie 1988: 75–6 for this comparison.

[30] Vergil alludes to this passage in *Ecl.* 1.1–5 (see, Van Sickle 1978: 88–9; Hardie 1998: 10–12; Breed 2000, esp. 11–14; Breed 2006: 13–14, 99–101; Fitzgerald 2016b, esp. 5); cf. *G.* 4.511–15 which shares much of the vocabulary of Lucretius' allusions to the nightingale simile in the Pan Hymn. Heerink 2015: 109–12 has recently suggested that Propertius has Lucretius in mind in his own version of the Hylas story at 1.20, while Ovid has this passage in mind throughout his Narcissus episode in *Metamorphoses* 3 (see Hardie 1988; Hardie 2002: 152–6; Tissol 1997: 15–17).

Epicurean Poetics in the Epicurean System

In demonstrating this connection between his account of perception and his poetics, Lucretius follows the Epicurean model established by Philodemus in which poetics harmonize with other areas of the philosophical system. While many questions remain surrounding Philodemus' theory, it seems quite clear that he insists that sound and sense in poetry are fundamentally connected. This is precisely the position inherent in the Echo passage in Lucretius. It will be useful to adduce this evidence from Philodemus in order to appreciate the orthodoxy of Lucretius' procedure in the case I have been analysing in this chapter. Philodemus' poetic ideas as we know them from his treatises *On Music*, *On Poems* and *On the Good King According to Homer* provide us with most of the information we have about post-Aristotelian poetic theory, which came even closer than Aristotle to articulating a real theory of poetry. This has become particularly clear from the reconstruction and interpretation of Philodemus' *On Poems*. It is difficult to know exactly what the motivations of the Euphonists and their opponents were regarding poetry, but these shadowy figures certainly seem to have been concerned with the same issues that are involved in serious aesthetic inquiry.[31] Moreover, theorists like Pausimachus of Miletus – the most radical of the Euphonists – were extremely rigorous in their discussions of the criteria for poetic excellence, submitting the poetry of Homer, Euripides and others to intense scrutiny in order to prove their own ideas.[32] Philodemus was heir to this post-Aristotelian tradition of poetic theory, even if he opposed it in some important ways. One might even surmise that Philodemus took up poetics precisely because the Euphonists and others raised issues in such a way as to seem to demand an orthodox Epicurean answer.[33] Indeed, throughout his poetic treatises Philodemus shows how the wrong-headed poetics of the Euphonists, 'Aristo' the Stoic, Crates of Mallos and others transgress the tenets of Epicureanism.[34] One might conclude that Philodemus felt

[31] The Euphonists discussed, among other things, the function of poetry, the role of genre and the role of diction in poetic excellence, all topics treated by (e.g.) Aristotle in the *Poetics*. See further, Janko 2000: 155–89. More recently, Janko 2011: 229 suggests that euphonic analysis of poetry had become in the Hellenistic period at least as important as Peripatetic literary criticism. Zinn 2018: 137–40 and 143–4 connects Lucretius' theory of sound to other areas of Lucretian Epicureanism including poetics.

[32] On Pausimachus and the Euphonists see Janko 2000: 165–89.   [33] See Janko 2011: 223.

[34] For example, Philodemus rejects Crates' claim that excellence inheres naturally in poetry (*On Poems* 5, col. 22.14–25) on the basis of orthodox Epicurean epistemology. We judge good poetry, Philodemus suggests, because there exist universal προλήψεις from which valid principles of

compelled to answer these philosophers in the way he imagined Epicurus would have done.

Following Epicurus, Philodemus claims that musical performances can be a source of pleasure. Delight in music should not be overindulged, for it quickly becomes tiresome and detracts from the most important source of pleasure: studying philosophy.[35] Poetry presents the same problems as music, yet Philodemus does assert that poetic composition can bring genuine pleasure, so long as one does not make a habit of it.[36] The detached relationship with poetry advocated by Philodemus is conducive to pleasure, a fundamental prerequisite for the *ataraxia* that is the main ethical aim of any Epicurean. Therefore, unlike music, poetry, far from hindering ethical growth, can actually help the Epicurean attain his highest ethical goal. In articulating his poetics in a way that resonates with Epicurean ethics, Philodemus connects poetics with the wider Epicurean system; Lucretius operates similarly by having his allusive poetics reflect his ideas about perception in the echo passage.

It is not just poetic performance that Philodemus connects to Epicurean ethics. He has far more to say about poetic composition, and his ideas are also fundamentally informed by his ethics.[37] Philodemus maintains, against the Euphonists, that the phonetic qualities of a poem cannot be divorced from their semantic function.[38] This is because the sound of a poem alone cannot produce pleasure, the most important effect of poetry.[39] At the same time, however, Philodemus denies that sound reinforces meaning, on the grounds that it is completely irrational (μ[αν]ι-κόν) to seek out any similarity of diction to the things that are indicated.[40] At this point, one may recognize an apparent contradiction in Philodemus' ideas. Presumably he rejects the possibility that sound reinforces meaning because to argue for such a relationship between sound and sense pre-supposes paradoxically the ability to separate the two, inasmuch as sound has to be reified in separation from sense to make any claims about how it may reinforce what is conveyed. At the same time, the idea that sound can

---

poetic judgment are derived. See further Mangoni 1993: 31; Rispoli 2005: 111; Janko 2011: 224. For a contrary view, however, see Pace 2000: 73–4.

[35] *On Music* 4, col. 37.8–39 Neubecker.   [36] Asmis 1995: 31–2.

[37] Attempts to determine a developed poetic doctrine in Philodemus, however, have been unsuccessful. See Mangoni 1993: 28; Arrighetti 2000: 20; Pace 2000: 74; Janko 2011: 223. Most recently, and most successfully, see McOsker 2015.

[38] *On Poems* 5, col. 13.32–14.2 Jensen. Philodemus also claims that the only acoustic feature of poetry that can produce pleasure is rhythm at *On Poems* 5, col. 26.36–27.3. For Philodemus' views on form and content see Asmis 2004.

[39] *On Poems* 5, col. 29.30–32.   [40] *On Poems* 5, col. 35.16–20.

reinforce sense may also imply the subordination of one to the other, given that sound must be granted a higher importance if it is to be purposefully modulated to coincide with the meaning of what is conveyed.[41] Viewed another way, of course, it could be that such a position presupposes the subordination of sound to sense, inasmuch as sense could be seen to govern what sounds are selected to convey an idea. In any event, the critical point is that regardless of how one views the situation, subordination must be presupposed. We should remember in all of this, however, that Philodemus' rejection of the idea that sound can reinforce meaning does not conflict with his broader view of the fundamental importance of both form and content for poetic excellence, as seen most specifically in his arguments about metathesis that I have discussed earlier. For Philodemus, form and content, sound and sense function symbiotically – a change in one produces a change in the other – but this relationship cannot be mutually reinforcing.[42] And in this, again, Philodemus achieves a measure of consistency and resonance with the wider Epicurean system that is mirrored in Lucretius' echo passage.

Returning now to the relationship between Philodemus' poetics and the broader Epicurean system, we can observe that he demands excellence of both form and content for poetic composition, while putting further stipulations on both. He maintains that diction (λέξις, i.e. Form) 'should imitate diction that also teaches what is useful', and thought (διάνοια, i.e. Content) 'should partake of thought that is intermediate between the thought of the wise and that of the ignorant'.[43] Philodemus grounds his requirement that diction teach what is useful (ὠφέλιμα) in Epicurus' complaint, which was shared to a degree by many earlier philosophers, including Plato, that Homer says many harmful things.[44] By demanding that good poetic form provide moral benefit, Philodemus carves out a place for poetry in Epicurean ethics. In requiring content to express ideas that are situated between those of the wise and those of the ignorant (τῶν χυδαίων), he predicates his notions of content on commonplace ideals.

---

[41] This, in fact, is the position of Crates of Mallos, the opponent Philodemus is addressing when he rejects the possibility that sound can reinforce sense.

[42] The nuances of Philodemus' theory in this respect are remarkable and would appear to conflict with what we find in Lucretius, who, in his famous honeyed cup simile, underlines the fundamental equivalence between form and content (honey and wormwood), while suggesting that his poetry elucidates his subject matter (*DRN* 1.933–4 *obscura de re tam lucida pango | carmina*); see, e.g., Gale 2007b: 72–3 and now Nethercut 2019.

[43] *On Poems* 5, col. 23.1–7. But see Hammerstaedt 2003: 308 for the suggestion that this indicates that good verse may be interpreted both superficially and in a deeper way.

[44] See Murray 1965; Richardson 1975.

This emphasis on the commonplace coincides with Philodemus' prerequisites for the judgement of poetry, prerequisites that are completely in line with Epicurean epistemology.[45]

Regarding the judgement of poetry, Philodemus argues against Crates' view that there is a natural goodness in poems and against the philosophical view that there are arbitrary regulations (θέματα) according to which a poem's excellence must be judged.[46] Rather, he maintains that there is a common judgement (κρίσ[ι]ν ... κοινήν) of fine and bad poems that does not vary from one group to another.[47] The basic aims (ἑστηκότες σκοποί) of poetic excellence exist whether one thinks so or not.[48] In this way, Philodemus bases the judgement of poetry on the epistemological truth of Epicureanism that all opinions are to be judged based on preconceptions (προλήψεις). These προλήψεις, common for all people, are formed empirically and naturally.[49] For Philodemus, therefore, the judgement of poetry – like all judgements we make – is subject to the constraints of Epicurean epistemology.

In addition to being interested in poetic theory, Philodemus practised philosophical literary criticism. He devotes an entire treatise, *On the Good King According to Homer*, to showing how Homer is a politically useful poet.[50] This treatise proves that Philodemus felt no need to isolate poetics, politics and ethics from each other. Whereas Epicurus, like Plato before him, expels Homer on the grounds that he says many harmful things,[51] Philodemus believes that Homer provides morally beneficial instruction for rulers. Moreover, in defending the ethical benefit that poetic content can confer, Philodemus argues that the moral truths inherent in poetry can only be accessed by the Epicurean sage, who alone has a properly philosophical understanding of the world. Here, Philodemus follows Epicurus' argument that only the wise man has the ability to speak correctly about poetry.[52] Philodemus, then, finds a way to contradict Epicurus' ethical critique of poetry, while at the same time maintaining orthodoxy with the founder's 'poetics', if we may call them that. By this manoeuvre, Philodemus is able to expand the parameters of Epicurean poetics, while basing this expansion on the teachings of Epicurus.

---

[45] See further Beer 2009: 106–17.   [46] *On Poems* 5, col. 22.14–25.
[47] *On Poems* 5, col. 22.25–34.   [48] *On Poems* 5, col. 22.35–23.11.
[49] On προλήψεις see Epicurus *Ep. Hdt.* 37–8; Cic. *Nat. D.* 1.44–5.
[50] See Murray 1965; Asmis 1991; and Farrell in Chapter 11 of this volume.
[51] Heraclitus, *Quaest. Hom.* 4 (= Epicurus, fr. 229 Usener) and 79, especially 4: ἅπασαν ὁμοῦ ποιητικὴν ὥσπερ ὀλέθριον μύθων δέλεαρ ἀφοσιούμενος; cf. *DRN* 1.102–35. See Asmis 1995: 16–17.
[52] Diog. Laert. 10.120.

All of this evidence, therefore, makes it clear that in all other regards Philodemus articulates his poetic theory with reference to the Epicurean system, striving at every turn to show how poetics must be congruent with the other areas of Epicureanism. When Lucretius uses literary allusion to the *Homeric Hymn to Pan* to reinforce the atomic explanation of echo, then, he would be conforming with Epicurean precedent in having an aspect of his poetics harmonize with atomic physics.

Conclusion

Lucretius' description of the echo proves to be a seminal passage in our understanding of how Lucretius appropriates earlier poetry and how this allusivity interacts with his Epicurean mission. At the same time, the fact that this passage concerns the nature of sound suggests that sound itself is a crucial element in Lucretius' larger poetics, a suggestion that we can triangulate with Lucretius' repeated analogy between the atoms that make up the universe and the letters that make up the *DRN* and with the arguments that others have made about sound and Lucretian poetics.[53] While my analysis implicitly sanctions the familiar idea that Lucretius uses the sound of his poem to reinforce the meaning of what he says, it also expands our understanding of this concept to include his practice of literary allusion. My argument thus suggests that one fruitful direction of future research on the *DRN* would be to connect Lucretius' allusion to earlier texts (an understudied area in Lucretian studies, especially compared to the robust study of allusion in Augustan poetry) with his insistence on the basic harmony between the form and content of the *DRN*. To put it another way, there would appear to be much more we can say about how Lucretius uses literary appropriation as a rhetorical tool in his exposition of Epicurean physics. The preceding analysis might serve as a starting point for a more systematic analysis of this issue.

---

[53] On the role of sound in Lucretius' poetics see Deutsch 1939; Friedländer 1941; Snyder 1980.

CHAPTER 7

Saussure's cahiers *and Lucretius'* elementa: *A Reconsideration of the Letters–Atoms Analogy*

Wilson H. Shearin

In memoriam TJM

> The universe signified long before people began to know what it signified.
>
> Claude Lévi-Strauss, *Introduction to the Work of Marcel Mauss*[1]

> If Saussure didn't publish the anagrams he deciphered in Saturnian poetry, it is because they cast aside academic literature.
>
> Jacques Lacan, *Radiophonie*[2]

Familiarity has rendered certain well-known passages of *De Rerum Natura* (*DRN*) difficult for the scholarly reader. It is easier to enumerate the ways in which these canonical lines have been read – and inevitably misread – than to wade through them with fresh eyes, free from the blinkers provided by their history of interpretation. One such passage – or rather one set of such passages – presents the well-known analogy between letters and atoms. 'Here and there in my very verses', the Epicurean poet writes near the end of his first book, 'you see many letters (*elementa*) common to many words, though you must still admit that verses and words are distinguished amongst themselves by both sense and singing sound (*sonitu . . . sonanti*). Letters (*elementa*) can do (*queunt*) so much with only their order (*ordine*)

Various institutions and interlocutors aided me during the lengthy gestation of this chapter. I am grateful to them all. Joe Farrell, Duncan Kennedy, Damien Nelis and Eva Noller (as well as others I have now forgotten) helped me with the topic in Edinburgh. Joshua Katz shared his work on Saussure. Jennifer Ferriss-Hill, Hugh Thomas, Hanna Golab, Han Tran, John Paul Russo and James Townshend prodded me to think harder in Miami. Margaret Foster, Jonathan Ready and Cynthia Bannon inspired me to rethink the chapter on a visit to Bloomington. Finally, Donncha O'Rourke has been an incredibly patient and perceptive editor. This chapter would not exist without his tactful aid and prodding.
[1] Lévi-Strauss 1950: L (50): 'L'Univers a signifié bien avant qu'on ne commence à savoir ce qu'il signifiait' (cited at Agamben 2011: 67; translated at Lévi-Strauss 1987: 61).
[2] Lacan 1970: 58: 'Si Saussure ne sort pas les anagrammes qu'il déchiffre dans la poésie saturnienne, c'est que ceux-ci jettent bas la littérature universitaire' (cited as an epigraph to Lotringer 1973).

altered.'[3] Playing upon the double sense of *elementum* as both 'letter' and 'atom', this passage and other similar ones scattered throughout the poem assert that the manner in which letters create words is fundamentally analogous to how atoms create worlds. A long history of scholarly interpretation has made this analogy the basis for several theories of reading.[4] In revisiting two of these theories here – and then in supplementing them with a third theory, developed through consideration of the anagrammatic 'readings' of Swiss linguist Ferdinand de Saussure – I aim to defamiliarize.[5] If, with the aid of Saussure, I am able to make the all-too-familiar connection between letters and atoms seem strange, this defamiliarizing, it is hoped, may render obscured elements of the *DRN* more visible. In the ensuing discussion, I highlight gaps, omissions and emphases in existing readings of the letters–atoms analogy, yet my aim is less to cast these theories aside or to advocate a new, 'correct' reinterpretation of the analogy than to suggest that past readings have won their interpretative insights at the cost of moments of unnecessary blindness. The well-known analogy may, in other words, buttress theories (or aspects) of reading other than those that have been alleged.[6]

As a way into the scholarly conversation – and into three atomist theories of reading – let us turn first to the words of Alessandro Schiesaro, who poses the question at hand with remarkable clarity. Considering the letters–atoms analogy, he writes:

[3] *DRN* 1.823–7 *quin etiam passim nostris in versibus ipsis | multa elementa vides multis communia verbis, | cum tamen inter se versus ac verba necessest | confiteare et re et sonitu distare sonanti. | tantum elementa queunt permutato ordine solo . . .* I quote here only the lines referring to 'letters', but the preceding and following lines – with the term *primordia* – make the connection to atoms explicit. For the other Lucretian passages comparing letters and atoms see *DRN* 1.192–8, 907–14; 2.688–99, 1004–22. Unless otherwise noted, the Latin text follows that of Munro 1886; translations are my own.

[4] The association of letters with atoms certainly predates Lucretius, and in fact seems to be a long-standing atomist link. See, e.g., Armstrong 1995: 211–12. The crucial texts are from Aristotle (*Metaph.* 1.4, 985b12–19; *Gen. corr.* 1.2, 315b6–15). Diels 1899 and Burkert 1959 provide useful discussions of both *elementum* and στοιχεῖον, the Greek term used to link letters and atoms. Volk 2002: 100–5 offers an extensive bibliography on – and discussion of – the analogy. See also the Introduction (pp. 8–9) and Tutrone (p. 99) in this volume.

[5] Here I characterize Saussure's anagrammatic practice as 'reading' (in quotation marks), as it is not entirely similar to the other theories considered: it is not an attempt to interpret the letters–atoms analogy to support a specific reading practice. That said, it certainly is reading in the sense of being a careful consideration of Lucretius' letters and words. (I thank Jon Ready for his thoughts on this point.)

[6] It is worth pointing out that, in reviewing two prominent interpretations of the letters–atoms analogy, I in no way take myself to have covered all existing – or even all important – treatments of that analogy. The two interpretations I review are above all useful for demonstrating what Saussure can contribute to existing discussions of the analogy.

Like many Lucretian analogies this one requires a careful investigation of its status, since the term 'analogy' itself . . . does not in fact clarify what type of relationship is established between the two elements of the analogy. *What exactly does it mean, **in terms of Lucretian epistemology and physics**, that the letters we use are like the atoms that compose the whole universe?*[7]

Schiesaro's words are worth quoting precisely because they render explicit the (otherwise largely implicit) rules that have governed past scholarly interpretation. That is, atoms, of course, resemble letters in a number of ways – both are fundamental building blocks of a sort; yet the challenge is to elaborate this analogy in a way that is both sufficiently Lucretian ('in terms of Lucretian epistemology and physics') and sufficiently practical as a theory of language or reading.[8] While all the theories considered here draw upon aspects of the *DRN* to authorize their interpretations, in their practical application they may also obscure important aspects of Lucretian and Epicurean thought.

Sound (*sonitu ... sonanti*)

I begin with arguably the most famous (and, in terms of scholarly writing, most productive) parsing of the analogy.[9] Over seventy years ago now, Paul Friedländer articulated what he called 'atomology' as a theoretical licence for close attention to the sounds of Lucretius' poem. Friedländer links wordplay to atoms chiefly on the basis of a repeated Lucretian example connecting *lignum* and *ignis*, or, in Cyril Bailey's rendering, 'beam' and 'flame'.[10] 'Do you see', Lucretius asks, again near the end of his first book, 'that the same first-beginnings, changed a bit amongst themselves, create both *ignes* and *lignum*? So, too, with the very words. Their letters have been changed a bit amongst themselves, when we mark

[7] Schiesaro 1994: 84 (emphasis added). Noller 2015: 145 offers insightful consideration of these remarks.

[8] By 'practical', I mean that the force of the letters–atoms analogy must be sufficiently grounded in Lucretius' actual, 'practical' use of letters, however one parses it theoretically.

[9] In this section, I focus on Friedländer 1941, which is generally considered theoretically foundational for studying sound- and wordplay in Lucretius. There are, though, several other works that focus on this topic (generally in a more empirical mode), e.g., Deutsch 1939 and Snyder 1980. David West, too, has spilled much ink on this topic, although he firmly rejects Friedländer's 'atomology': see, e.g., West 1969: 94–114 (based in Varronian etymology), West 1982, West 1991.

[10] Friedländer (1941: 17) coins the term thus: 'The basis for this (sit venia verbo) atomology was laid early in the poem. In his polemic against Anaxagoras Lucretius had stated that one should find small particles of fire in wood, *in lignis ... ignis* (891–2), if the theory of the *homoeomeriae* were right. And again (901): *non est lignis tamen insitus ignis*. The similarity of sound failing to support the wrong doctrine of Anaxagoras does support the orthodoxy of Democritus and Epicurus.' For Bailey's rendering see Bailey 1947: 1.223.

ligna and *ignes* with different names' (1.907–14). While the repeated letter cluster *ign-* (and the sounds associated with this cluster) certainly endorses Friedländer's study of the sonic texture of the *DRN*, it is unclear that his focus is entirely underwritten by any theoretical passage of Lucretius. As we have already seen, sound (*sonitu*) does appear in the letter–atom passages as a feature that distinguishes verses and words, but Lucretius' expressed interest falls much more clearly upon the nature of letter combinations and how such combinations mimic atomic ones. Of course, when read aloud, letter combinations have sonic properties – Friedländer himself stresses that *elementa* are both letters and sounds[11] – yet Lucretius seems to imagine a reader (1.907 *iamne vides* 'do you see'), one who gazes into the text, rather than an auditor.[12] The *DRN*, moreover, regularly presents Lucretius himself as a writer. In his proem, for example, the Epicurean poet asks Venus to be his ally 'in writing verses' (1.24 *scribendis versibus*), and this passage is not unique.[13] In short, if we allow that – whatever else they may be – *elementa* are also written marks and that a full account of their properties, in combination or otherwise, must take note of this status, then a certain blindness inheres in Friedländer's technique: he unabashedly privileges the spoken voice over the written *elementum*.[14] While this observation in no way vitiates Friedländer's perceptive detection of alliterative patterns and their effects, from a theoretical standpoint his reading practice may be better grounded in Dionysius of Halicarnassus' *De compositione verborum* or the lost annals of euphonist criticism than in the letters and atoms (that is, *elementa*) of Lucretius, at least as they are portrayed in the surviving *DRN*.

Order (*permutato ordine*)

More recently, David Armstrong, Stratis Kyriakidis and others, following the pioneering work of Nathan Greenberg, have read Lucretius as a complement to Philodemus, developing a theory that travels under the name of 'the impossibility of metathesis'. According to this principle, the

---

[11] See, for example, Friedländer 1941: 17: 'The "letters" – *this name covering at the same time what we call letters and sounds* – are the elements of language, a limited number producing the abundance of words and verses.' (Emphasis added.)

[12] I thank Donncha O'Rourke for suggesting this point to me.

[13] *DRN* 1.24–6 *te sociam studeo* **scribendis versibus** *esse | quos ego de rerum natura pangere conor | Memmiadae nostro* … Cf. *DRN* 4.969–70 *naturam quaerere rerum | semper et inventam patriis exponere* **chartis**. See Lowrie 2009: 32–4 on writing in Lucretius.

[14] This critique of Friedländer owes something to Derrida 1967 and his concept of *logocentrisme*. See, for example, Derrida 1967: 11.

link between letters and atoms is first and foremost about verbal arrangement and its physical qualities. As Kyriakidis writes, on this theory the
poem is ἀμετάθετον: 'the transposition of verses (or their minor components, the words or even the letters) in a poetic work should be considered
impossible for the reason that the metathesised elements affect the whole
poem and its thought, thus creating a different poetic work'.[15] In analysing
Lucretius, Kyriakidis thus stresses the prominence of Latin terms such as
ordo and *positura* in the letter–atom passages. He reproduces in his reading
one of these passages, drawn from the end of the second book, and he
highlights words that characterize both position and atomic movement
within the discussion (*DRN* 2.1013–22):

> quin etiam refert **nostris in versibus ipsis**
> cum quibus et quali sint ordine quaeque locata;
> namque eadem caelum mare terras flumina solem
> significant, eadem fruges arbusta animantis;
> si non omnia sunt, at multo maxima pars est
> consimilis; verum positura discrepitant res.
> sic ipsis in rebus item iam materiai
> [intervalla vias conexus pondera plagas]
> **concursus motus ordo positura figurae**
> cum permutantur, mutari res quoque debent.[16]

Moreover, **in my very verses** it matters
with which <*sc.* other letters> and in what sort of order each has been placed;
for the same things signify *caelum mare terras flumina solem*,
the same <signify> *fruges arbusta animantis*;
if they are not all the same, nevertheless much the greatest part is
entirely similar; but the things (*res*) differ by their positioning (*positura*).
So now in the case of material things themselves, it is likewise:
[intervals, passages, connections, weights, blows]
pressing together, movement, order, positioning, shapes,
when these are changed, things too ought to transform.

Unlike Friedländer's atomology, this theory clearly attends to the written
letter and its textual placement. It has, moreover, clear evidentiary support
within the *DRN*, which not only discusses ideas such as *ordo* and *positura*
but also, as scholars have noted, bears the structuring stamp of rhetorical
and poetic teaching. Yet this insight, I suggest, comes at a cost. While the

---

[15] Kyriakidis 2006: 606–7. Kyriakidis draws upon earlier work by Armstrong (1995) and Greenberg
(1955). See also Nethercut in this volume (pp. 131–4).
[16] The text here follows Rouse and Smith 1992, which follows Lachmann in deleting line 1020; the
translation is my own.

passage that Kyriakidis cites from the second book appears to stress order, position, and location, the one from the first book with which we began arguably places an equal emphasis on possibility, potentiality, and creative power. 'Letters **can do** (*queunt*) so much', Lucretius remarks there. Similarly, the full variety of things 'can be created' (*queant . . . creari*) from the actions of 'first-beginnings', or atoms. Such comments are not adequately incorporated into the metathesis theory, which – particularly in its reading practice – uses atomic arguments chiefly to underwrite the careful interpretation of minute, fixed textual features.[17] This theory largely treats the creative power of letters as if it has gone dormant: our job as critics is to examine the well-wrought artefact remaining from a now-lost creative moment.[18] But such a theoretical position is not inevitable: there are ways to read power and potentiality back into letters, and here, I suggest, the anagrammatic readings of Ferdinand de Saussure can offer assistance.

The Power of *elementa* (*tantum elementa queunt*)

Saussure's anagrams have always seemed scandalous, and not simply because – in countless examples from nearly one hundred surviving notebooks – they fail to embody what is usually meant by anagram, that is, the rearrangement of the letters in a given word or words to form another word or phrase.[19] Admittedly, their scandal derives in part from the author himself. In the 1960s and early 1970s, when excerpts from the previously unpublished anagrams first began to appear, Saussure was known quite simply as the father of structuralism. He was a scholar who conceived of language through theoretical constructs such as *langue*, the abstract system of language internalized by speakers, and *parole*, the individual act of speech.[20] Yet the anagrams bear no resemblance to such theorization: they are decidedly more empirical. In them, rules seem to shift constantly and recede in the face of

[17] Kyriakidis, for example, uses the principle to explain the minute alterations between *DRN* 1.926–50 and the proem to Lucretius' fourth book.

[18] In fairness to Armstrong, he begins his discussion of 'the impossibility of metathesis' with a discussion of the magical, performative power of the alphabet (1995: 210–11). And elsewhere he even includes discussion of Saussure (1995: 229–30). Yet – while there are a number of minor differences – my chief point is that the reading practice that has resulted from Armstrong's incredibly learned discussion is one that places more emphasis on order than on the power of letters to create and denote new words.

[19] The standard English treatment of the anagrams remains Starobinski 1979, but see now Katz 2013, with his extensive bibliography. For the Lucretian anagrams specifically, Gandon 2002 is essential (with many plates of Saussure's *cahiers*) and Gandon 2006 offers theoretical observations.

[20] On *langue* and *parole*, see Saussure 1972: 36–9. A discussion of Saussure with a literary-critical bent is Culler 1986.

ever more empirical evidence. Language, at times, even seems to outstrip and befuddle its greatest systematizer. The anagrams thus bring to life a new Saussure, one whose readings 'deconstruct' his own structural linguistics.[21]

Another, related source of scandal is that Saussure's anagrams often seem arbitrary and unintended. It is not that there is no method to his investigations, but rather that the anagrams themselves often resemble faces in clouds or inkblot tests. Constant doubt reigns over what design, if any, lurks behind them. Yet this scandal may make them, if anything, more useful for unlocking the *DRN*. Absence of design is hardly alien to Epicureanism, which not only studied and espoused anti-teleology, the lack of providential order, on a cosmic level but also – at least through its critics – pondered the possible textual implications of this doctrine. In Cicero's *De natura deorum*, for example, a Stoic puts forward the hostile suggestion that adherents of cosmic anti-teleology ought to believe that Ennius' *Annales* could be constructed from a chance collocation of letters upon the earth.[22] While Saussure's reading practice is far from the complete casuistry Cicero describes, as we shall see, it puts into play similar questions.

What, then, are the details of Saussure's anagrams? How precisely do they provide us with a more 'creative' understanding of written letters? Perhaps the best way in is simply to read along with Saussure as he scrutinizes a few lines of the *DRN*. Let us begin, then, as Lucretius often does himself, with Epicurus:[23]

"Epicurus"

... sed **E**o magi**S** acrem
inritat animi virtutem, effringere ut arta

---

[21] See Katz 2015: 113–15 for a balanced discussion of the various scholarly traditions of interpreting Saussure. As Katz notes, there are at least two different traditions of speaking of 'two Saussures' (typically, a linguistic one and a literary-critical one); and indeed, there are even those who would speak of 'three Saussures'. Katz himself prefers a unified Saussure: 'I see Saussure's three visions of language ... as reconcilable within one very special person of unusual linguistic agility' (115).

[22] Cic. *Nat. D.* 2.93 *hoc qui existimat fieri potuisse, non intellego cur non idem putet, si innumerabiles unius et viginti formae litterarum uel aureae uel quales libet aliquo coiciantur, posse ex iis in terram excussis Annales Ennii, ut deinceps legi possint, effici: quod nescio an ne in uno quidem versu possit tantum valere fortuna.* ('Whoever believes that this <*sc.* the world being formed by the chance meeting of atoms> could happen, I do not understand why this same man would not think that, if the countless forms of the twenty-one letters, whether golden or whatever kind you wish, should be cast together somewhere, that from these letters, just tossed out upon the ground, the *Annales* of Ennius can be fashioned so that they then can be read. As for which, I do not know whether chance (*fortuna*) could make this happen even with one single verse.') For discussion of this passage in relation to Lucretius see also O'Rourke in this volume (pp. 104–5). For further consideration of textual anti-teleology see Shearin 2012.

[23] Translated from Gandon 2002: 330–2.

natURaE Primus portarum claustra CUPIret. (*DRN* 1.69–71)

Mannequin [Eo magiS] (69)

...

Detail of Syllables

E- : beginning of *mannequin*. It is certain, moreover, that the group of
   words *effringer(e) ut* [*E -ig -ru-*] alludes to the word, but without being a
   fixed part of the anagrammatic process.

EP- : *naturaE Primus*. This *ep-* is placed in such a way before the vowels
   i- u-, and with *-ur-* on its other side that the connection with
   epicurus may be felt immediately.

-PI-} *cu-pi-ret*.} Either the *r* or the *E* which follow add to the effect.
-CU-}

-UR- : *nat-ur-ae primus*.

-RU- : *porta-ru-m claustra*. The *p* which precedes as well as the *c* of *claustra*
   play an accompanying role.

-US : It would suffice, after the group -RU-, to add the final S of the
   mannequin. Nevertheless, the -US- of *primus* is in such good position
   after the preceding anagrammatic material that everything invites us to
   take it as forming its own group.

...

It [*sc.* this anagram] is one of those which seems to arrive at this game:

E : *Eo magis, Effringere.*
P : *Primus Portarum.*
I : *Inritat.*
C : *Claustra Cupiret.*
U : *Ut*
R : *– In-Ritat* ?
U : (See below.)
S : *Sed*

Perhaps, in this game, consonantal V is not distinguished from the vowel
(*u*) – with the result that one ought to add *uirtutem* to *ut* here.

Both in Lucretius and elsewhere, the Saussurean process of anagrammatic reading often concerns a proper name.[24] Here, in the opening
book, where Epicurus appears for the first time, Lucretius praises his
philosophical master, but precisely not by name: instead, he is simply

---

[24] In fact, it appears that Saussure's fascination with anagrams arose out of his research into Saturnian
verse. In these investigations, he first developed the notion that Latin poems could be built around a
theme, regularly a proper name. See Joseph 2012: 487–9.

the *Graius homo* who stood up against *religio*. Saussure thus identifies Epicurus as the 'theme-word', or *mot-thème*, which has been woven cryptically into Lucretius' text. This identification, it must be admitted, is, if contextually motivated, also somewhat arbitrary (i.e., why Epicurus and not *religio*? Moreover, why – when the surrounding lines also discuss Epicurus – is his name woven specifically into these three?), yet the rest of the reading process unfolds as an attempt to justify it. First, to confirm the presence of this 'theme-word', Saussure also identifies a *mannequin*, a little box or basket, a portion of text whose beginning and end – typically its first and last letters – coincide with those of the theme-word.[25] The *mannequin* is, in Saussure's eyes, a strong clue to the otherwise hidden anagrammatic process. In the present instance, he locates *eo magis* in line 69, which begins with E and ends with S just like the name Epicurus. Then, the true hunt begins. Armed with both his theme-word and his confirmatory *mannequin*, Saussure searches furiously for two-letter segments of Epicurus' name throughout the chosen three lines, also allowing single letters at both the beginning and end of the name. His hunt here is successful: it turns up the single letter E as well as the pairs EP, PI, CU, UR, RU, and US. In addition, Saussure uncovers a further confirmation of these lines' cryptic obsession with the name of Epicurus: there are, it appears, words beginning with each letter of the philosopher's name. Initial E, P, I, C, U, and S are obvious. Perhaps, too, he suggests, one can take U as the first letter of *virtutem* and seize the internal R from *inritat* to have a full complement of the letters in the Samian philosopher's name.

Granting that there is arbitrariness in Saussure's procedure, granting even that its own author was never convinced of its validity, we can nonetheless effectively place it into dialogue with the theories (atomology, metathesis) we have examined to this point. In the first instance, the procedure is (unlike Friedländer's) clearly a theory of the written letter. While in his personal communications and notebooks the Swiss linguist was apt to speak of his project as based in the analysis of syllables, as we have already seen, this is simply not the case: his anagrammatic reading practice finds individual letters as well as letter pairs – and many of these pairs simply could not be detected by the ear. In the example just

---

[25] See Gandon 2002: 387, where he defines the *mannequin* as a 'portion of the text whose beginning and end correspond to those of the theme word'.

considered, Saussure splits a diphthong and crosses a word boundary to find the pair EP in Epicurus. Moreover, his reading practice also explicitly grants an excess of signification – a certain potentiality or power, then – to letters: in Saussure's anagrams, letters *cannot be presumed to signify only in the words in which they are found.* While their position and order still matter deeply, letters signify by creating connections between, across, and in combination with the letters of other words. And it is worth pointing out that this excess of signification is inscribed into the theory. So long as we allow Saussure his 'theme-word', the rest of his reading practice, which is built around the search for this hidden term, follows, if not logically, at least directly from this concession. By definition, then, Saussure's anagrammatic letters point, or at least *can point,* beyond themselves.

Yet it may be thought that the form of power I here ascribe to letters is fairly banal. Wordplay, sound-play, puns, all of these phenomena rely upon a similar excess of signification, upon letters doing more than it may seem. And indeed, to the extent he theorized the problem, Saussure himself conceived of the letters in his anagrams as doing something beyond pointing covertly to a hidden name. Saussure once wrote the following to his friend and former student Antoine Meillet:[26]

> It is likely that the different sound games of verse come from the anagram, which in the end is nothing more than one of these games. ... one understands the superstitious idea which could suggest that for a prayer to be efficacious, it would be necessary that the very syllables of the divine name were mixed into it indissolubly. One would, so to speak, bind God to the text, or even if one introduced the name of the devotee and the name of the god at the same time, one could create a bond between them that the divinity was not, so to speak, any longer free to reject.

The purpose of the anagram, and of the 'theme-word' behind it, thus is clear: to grant a text, through divine sanction, performative power or efficacy, an ability to accomplish actions seemingly beyond the typical power of mere words.[27]

[26] Letter from F. de Saussure to A. Meillet, 23 September 1907: Benveniste 1964: 114.
[27] Saussure's interest in divine names, it is worth noting, hardly begins with this letter. There is a much earlier fragment (published as Lévi-Strauss 1972, apparently from 1894) where he proclaims: 'le *nom* est bien le principe décisif, non de l'invention des êtres mythologiques ... mais de l'instant où ces êtres deviennent *purement* mythologiques'. Saussure's interest (apparently spurred by consideration of W. D. Whitney) at this point seems to be in the linguistic mechanisms of abstraction – how, that is, names come to refer to non-tangible, non-earthbound entities. For Saussure's engagement with the American linguist Whitney see Joseph 2012: 409–13.

This interpretation of the anagram of Epicurus' name fits well with other anagrams found in Saussure's surviving notebooks. Although it is unnecessary to review further anagrams in the same detail as the first, one in particular perhaps hints at a similarly performative backdrop:

> I, 1 seq. Afrodītē-Ap(h)rodītē
>
> **A**eneadum genetrix, hominum **DI**vomqu**E** voluptas,
> alma Venus, caeli subter labentia signa
> quae mare navigerum, quae terras **FR**ugiferentis
> concelebras, per **TE** quoniam genus omne animantum
> concip**IT**ur, vis**IT**que ex**OR**tum lumina solis
>
> *Mannequin*: [**A**eneadum genetrix hominum divomqu**E**]

Here, in the opening lines of the poem, Saussure finds scattered about – not letters comprising the name Venus – but ones making up Afrodite, spelt with the letter F. The *mannequin*, beginning with A and ending with E, occurs in the first line. The segmented letters and letter pairs are fairly banal, and Saussure does allow the reversed syllable OR in place of the expected RO. What is perhaps most interesting in all of this, though, is the interpretation given to the passage by Jean Starobinski, the scholar initially responsible for making Saussure's anagrams available to a broader audience. Starobinski writes:[28]

> In the admirable preamble of *De rerum natura*, Ferdinand de Saussure discerns the obsessive presence of Aphrodite's name. The invocation to Venus is constructed on the Greek name of the goddess ... **Everything happens as if the poet had wished, in the very act of composition, to demonstrate a fecundity and productive power for which the name of Aphrodite was the wellspring.**

While Starobinski does not mention Saussure's idea of binding spells, his characterization of the anagrammed name again seems to grant letters a performative or productive power – first and foremost, an ability to generate further words from the name of Aphrodite. But it is of course hardly irrelevant that Venus and Aphrodite, goddesses of love, lust and procreation are strongly linked with creative power themselves.

To return, then, to the letter–atom analogy with which we began, I have been placing Saussure into dialogue with existing interpretations of the letter–atom passages to show, ultimately, the greater *productive* and *performative* power that the Swiss scholar attributes to *written*

---

[28] Starobinski 1979: 57 [1971: 79]. (Emphasis added.)

letters. Even if his anagrams are not directly concerned with interpreting the letter–atom passages, they offer what can only be called a rather atomic model for understanding how letters may be dispersed throughout a text and still combine to create significance. Moreover, by placing letters into a performative religious context in which they bind or otherwise act efficaciously, Saussure begins a dialogue which may be useful for the project I outlined initially – defamiliarizing the letter–atom comparison.

There are no doubt those who would balk at bringing Lucretius into discussions of religious ritual, particularly on the basis of what seem to be unsubstantiated speculations about the origins of an ephemeral phenomenon.[29] Yet my interest here is in performativity, a linguistic structure, or rather a structure that is part linguistic, part religious, philosophical, and cultural. This structure may be revealing for Lucretius' efforts in connecting letters and atoms, even if it is wholly false, or at least wholly unverifiable, with regard to Saussure's anagrams. Earlier in the chapter I suggested that *queunt* in the first letters–atoms passage pointed to a sense that letters, like atoms, have significant creative powers. Through Saussure, we have now identified two ways in which written letters may have such creative powers. First, they may, though atomically dispersed through a text, point beyond themselves by combining in creative ways. This sense of creativity does not strike me, in the Lucretian context, as particularly novel. The wordplay studied by Friedländer, although it fails to consider fully the properties of written letters, demonstrates a similar phenomenon. Yet the second way in which Saussure views letters as possessing creative power – that is, by acting performatively and binding the divine to the text – perhaps casts a different light on the *DRN*.

But how, more exactly, is this claim relevant to the Lucretian comparison of letters and atoms? It is all very well to suggest that letters in some ancient contexts may possess, or at least have been ascribed with, a performative power associated with divinity, yet where is divinity in the letters–atoms passages? While a full account of the divine in

---

[29] It is perhaps worth noting that Lucretius does appear, at least at times, to draw upon religious ritual in shaping his poem. The discussion at *DRN* 1.958–1001 (on the unbounded nature of the universe) has been thought to conjure up Fetial ritual. Bailey 1947: II.767 attributes the idea to Bignone, referring the reader to *Aeneid* 12.266 (where Tarrant 2012: 156–7 likewise suggests a reference to fetial ritual). See, too, Shearin 2015: 82–8 (on fetial ritual) and O'Rourke in this volume (p. 113). With regard to proper names, Lucretius' practice (at least *vis-à-vis* Epicurus) is remarkable: Epicurus seems to be a virtual *nomen sacrum* for the Latin poet. (See Shearin 2015: 118–24.)

Epicureanism is beyond the scope of the current essay, one way of reading Epicureanism as a school of thought is to suggest that atoms take the place of the divine. In other ancient philosophical systems, the world arises from (and is structured by) a divine mind; in Epicureanism, by contrast, it arises merely from (chance collisions of) atoms. Similarly, in the realm of language, if properly divine speech, in the fullness of its authority, creates in being spoken – for example, Jupiter's act of *fari* paradigmatically creates one's *fatum*, or fate – then perhaps we should see performativity and linguistic creativity as a central point of the connection between letters and atoms. Atoms are regularly characterized in the *DRN* as *semina, genitalia corpora,* or *primordia*: speech closely associated with them could plausibly also have such generative power. In the opening paragraph of this chapter, I highlighted *queunt* in the first passage to indicate that Lucretius' analogy between letters and atoms is centrally, if not exclusively, concerned with ideas of creativity, possibility and power. Yet this is not the only place in the letter–atom passages where performativity may be glimpsed. When, for example, Lucretius says at *DRN* 2.1015–16 that *eadem caelum mare terras flumina solem* | *significant* ('the same <things> *significant* [denote? make into signs/ names?] *caelum mare terras flumina solem*'), does he mean that the same letters 'denote' these things, as the Rouse–Smith Loeb has it, or rather that the same letters performatively name them, making these words into signs?[30] An attractive feature of taking Lucretius' point to be that letters have performative (or naming) power is that it avoids the need to explain why the poet selects words that obviously *do not* have the same letters: how can one say that the same letters denote *caelum* and *terras*? The words appear to share only two letters. If, on the other hand, one takes the Epicurean's point to be that letters (however composed) have *the power* of denotation, then it does not matter which words are chosen. Letters (composed somehow) simply are able to perform a denotative function. Likewise, when Lucretius mentions *positura* in the very next sentence, asserting *positura discrepitant res*, does he mean that words differ due to the position of their letters or rather that their sense differs due to the performative ability of letters to posit? *positura elementorum*, in other words, may be a subjective as well as an objective genitive; and *positura* may refer not so much to fixed position or order as to the

---

[30] A central problem of the *DRN* is, of course, the (performative) creation of a new Latin philosophical vocabulary; it thus makes sense that Lucretius would theorize language's creative power. See Farrell 2001: 39–51.

creating and positing power of this ordering.[31] Even if these readings only sow seeds of doubt rather than inspire full conviction, I hope now – both in my meanderings through Saussure and elsewhere – to have created the suspicion that one should, in any full interpretation of the letter–atom passages, make more room for performativity, the creative power of letters, alongside their position and sound. In so doing, I hope to have rendered the all-too-familiar a bit less so.

---

[31] A parallel for this sense of *positura* occurs at Propertius 4.3.37–8, where the word must mean something like the 'positing' of god: *cogor ... pictos ediscere mundos,* | *qualis et **haec docti** sit **positura dei*** ... ('I am compelled ... to learn maps by heart, of what sort is this positing of a learned god').

PART IV

Literary and Philosophical Sources

CHAPTER 8

Arguing over Text(s): Master-Texts vs. Intertexts in the Criticism of Lucretius

A. D. Morrison

Introduction: Reading the *De Rerum Natura*

There is a long history in Lucretian scholarship of finding conflict in the *DRN* between its philosophical argument or content and aspects of its poetic form. Epicurus himself may have been hostile to some common aspects of much poetry (such as myth or figurative language),[1] and there is good evidence for wider Epicurean reservations about poetry, at least as a vehicle for education or instruction.[2] Famously, M. Patin argued for a submerged, self-contradictory sympathy in the *DRN* for the theological, teleological view of the world which it ostensibly attacks, betrayed in part by its imagery and poetic descriptions of nature and the universe.[3] More recent criticism has, as Monica Gale has described,[4] moved away from seeing such conflict or contradiction between the Epicurean content of the *DRN* (or its Epicurean project to deliver *ataraxia*) and its poetic form. Rather, something of a synthesizing consensus has developed, which sees

I am very grateful to Alison Sharrock, Donncha O'Rourke and Jenny Bryan, whose many helpful suggestions have greatly improved this chapter.

[1] See Epicurus, *Ep. Hdt.* 38 (Epicurus' requirement that the primary meaning of every term should be clear), frr. 568–9 Usener = Diog. Laert. 10.121 b4, b2 (only the wise man can properly discuss poetry and would not pursue it as an activity) and fr. 163 Usener (the injunction to avoid παιδεία in all its forms). Recent scholarship has developed a more nuanced picture of the attitude of Epicurus to poetry, suggesting that far from seeing Epicurus as espousing a blanket hostility to it (Heraclitus *Quaest. Hom.* 4, 79; Plut. *Non posse* 1092c–1094d), we should make room for the possibility of poetry being acceptable from an Epicurean perspective as able to provide pleasure to its audience (see Asmis 1995: 20–1; Obbink 1995b: 189–94). On Epicurus' reservations about poetry see Gale 1994: 14–18, 2001a: 16–18; on Epicurean hostility to myth Obbink 1995b: 206 n. 58, with several examples.

[2] Cf., e.g., Plut. *De tranq. anim.* 465f (on Epicurus). Fragments of Philodemus (e.g., *On Poems* 5 col. 29.17–19 κἂν ὠφελῇ | κα[θὸ πο]ήματ' οὐκ ὠφε|λεῖ, 'even if they [i.e. poems] benefit, they do not benefit as poems') suggest a conception of poetry which allows for an ethical usefulness which is incidental but does not form its central function. See further Asmis 1995: 26–32; Janko 2000: 8–9.

[3] Patin 1868: 1.117–37. On Patin's long shadow in Lucretian scholarship see Gale 1994: 1–2, 2007a: 3. See further Goldschmidt in this volume (pp. 55–7).

[4] See Gale 1994: 1–5, 2007a: 3–17.

the *DRN*'s poetic form and Epicurean argument as working towards the same goal and analysable from the same perspective.[5]

It is this synthesizing, harmonizing perspective which Don Fowler adopted in his important discussion of literary and philosophical approaches to the *DRN*'s intertexts,[6] where he explored 'the way in which they [i.e. its intertexts] contribute to the master argument of the *De rerum natura*'.[7] But Fowler also focused attention in that essay on the different communities of readers of the poem, suggesting that the conflict often discerned between poetic form and philosophical content in the *DRN* might be seen in part not as an intrinsic property of the text itself (as something objectively 'in' the poem, in a manner analogous to its form in dactylic hexameters or its containing an account of Epicurean physics)[8] but 'in terms of an opposition between the differing practices of two interpretative communities', by which he meant (very roughly) philosophers and literary critics. I return to the topic of form vs. content at the close of this article, but first I shall pursue Fowler's insight into the importance of readers and reading practices for what critics discern in the poem, because there exist (I suggest) some crucial differences in some important ways in which the *DRN* is read and criticized by different readers (or reading communities). By focusing on different strategies of reading employed in examining the *DRN* we can uncover key elements of the attitudes of different readers which may in part explain some of the perceived conflict in the poem, but also suggest that the recent synthesizing critical perspective on the *DRN*, which views its poetic form and its philosophical content as working harmoniously together, may have

---

[5] Good examples of such 'harmonizers' include McLeod 1963; Minadeo 1969; Baron 1986 (who provides a useful survey of such approaches at p. 29, nn. 1 and 2) and especially the influential survey by Classen 1968 of how poetic and rhetorical strategies in the *DRN* promote its Epicurean doctrine. The synthesizing, harmonizing consensus extends to the majority of recent approaches to Lucretius, including those which discern in the *DRN* the deliberate use of non-Epicurean imagery or language to promote the poem's Epicurean purpose: e.g., on the use of myth by Lucretius, see Gale 1994; Campbell 2002, 2003: 180–4. For Gale Lucretius' use of myth 'far from exemplifying the conflict of philosophy and poetry ... constitute[s] Lucretius' most triumphant reconciliation of those old enemies' (1994: 5). See also Anderson 1995 (a review of Gale 1994) on what he terms 'Unitarians' who credit Lucretius 'with a unifying conception and a creative rhetoric that ... largely succeeds in its effort to make the *DRN* an integrated poem of Epicurean exposition'. On the appropriation in the *DRN* of other modes of discourse (e.g., theological language) see Kennedy 2000.

[6] Fowler 2000b.   [7] Fowler 2000b: 155.

[8] Such a presence 'in' the text is the assumption of many critics (cf., e.g., Wormell 1960 and see Gale 1994: 1 n. 2 for further examples), though some critics have located the conflict not primarily in the text but in its author (as more than merely a periphrasis for the poem): see, e.g., Patin 1868: 1.127: 'Le sentiment religieux est si naturel chez l'homme, qu'il se fait jour, par moments, à travers les doutes du sceptique, les négations de l'athée.'

overlooked (or forgotten) some important differences between the poem's readers (and their reading strategies), and also some crucial characteristics of Lucretius' poem itself.

In particular, I shall examine some important differences to be found in some common ways of reading the *DRN*'s relationship with other texts, since they allow us to see more sharply the different perspectives from which the *DRN* itself is approached by different readers. These ways of reading should be viewed as tendencies or common patterns in the ways the *DRN* is read from different perspectives, which we might call (for reasons which will become clear) 'master-text' and 'intertextual' modes of reading. The former is more common among philosophers analysing the *DRN*, but it is very clear that not all philosophers read the *DRN* in this way (or indeed in the same way as one another), while the intertextual mode is common among literary critics, but it is equally true that not all such critics share this critical approach. Without wishing to reduce the plurality of reader-reception, then, I hope to identify some important differences in *common* modes of reading the *DRN*.[9] These modes of reading are also, I should stress, *not* code for a particular theoretical school or for particular authors (although I will point to particular examples which I think are especially instructive for illustrating the interpretative tendencies I discuss); this chapter is not meant as polemic. In part this should point us toward the need for a plurality of approaches to texts such as the *DRN*, a notion to which I shall also return, but these differences in modes of reading are related to aspects of the text being read (and how it relates to other texts). Examining these modes of reading will allow us to perceive more clearly some key characteristics of the *DRN*, not least the remarkable character of an Epicurean philosophical poem, its oddity as well as its brilliance.

Master-Text(s)

The 'master-text' mode of reading is so called because in such a mode a given text (in our case, the *DRN*) is related in strong fashion to another text on which it is in many ways dependent, and against which it could (theoretically, at least) be checked. As we shall see, the precise nature and identity of this 'master-text' can vary, according to the purpose or use to which the text being so read is put, but master-text readings share the

[9] One might also view these modes as two extremes of a spectrum on which the majority of reading practices for Lucretius might be located. These modes might themselves be employed or approached by one critic at different times or with reference to different texts with which the *DRN* develops a relationship.

characteristic of making the text they are reading in some manner subordinate to another, different text. Such readings have long been widespread in the scholarship on Lucretius: one might characterize the long history of the investigation into the *DRN*'s (especially philosophical) 'sources' as being in large part an argument about *which* is the correct master-text against which to check the poem.[10] Examples abound, but one of the clearest is provided by Carlo Giussani,[11] whose view of the *DRN*'s dependence on Epicurus' (lost) μεγάλη ἐπιτομή was very influential (not least on Bailey).[12] Giussani focuses on the question of which of Epicurus' works provided the 'guida e fonte' for Lucretius' poem, an approach Joseph Farrell has characterized as having the goal of identifying a model wherein the poet's role or contribution would be greatly diminished.[13] Such a reading strategy can be described as employing a strong 'master-text' model in which the *DRN* is subordinated to another text, since Giussani's method was to reject the master-texts other critics had proposed, such as the *Letter to Herodotus*, on account of the differences between the order and arguments in the *DRN* and the putative alternative master-texts. Lucretius, on this view, cannot have used, e.g., the *Letter to Herodotus* as his 'guida e fonte' since, if he had done so, there would be no divergence from the model in terms of the argument and its sequence.

Master-text readings of the *DRN* are not, however, confined to nineteenth-century *Quellenforschung*: they are also visible in more recent (and more sophisticated) investigations into the Epicurean material on which Lucretius was building, where we can still see the employment of particular, specific Epicurean texts as 'concrete' instances of master-texts for the poem, and also in some attempts to place Lucretius in a wider Epicurean philosophical context, where the master-text is more general and diffuse than a particular model-text, but the critical approach involved nevertheless displays some of the same tendencies towards the subordination of the *DRN* to another text against which it can be checked. I shall first examine two recent examples of 'concrete' master-texts for the *DRN*, before turning to an example of a more general and diffuse Epicurean master-text reading which well illustrates some representative tendencies in this mode.

The *DRN* offers us, it should be emphasized, many reasons for reading Lucretius as a conduit or vessel for the teaching of Epicurus himself. For

---

[10] See Bailey 1947: 1.22–31 for an overview of the investigation of Lucretius' sources, with the important reservations of Clay 1983: 21–35 and Farrell 2007: 76–8.
[11] Giussani 1896: 1–11.   [12] See Clay 1983: 29–30.
[13] Farrell 2007: 77. See also Clay 1983: 21–30 on this tendency.

example, the poem makes explicit Lucretius' status as a follower at the beginning of Book 3: 3–4 *te sequor, o Graiae gentis decus, inque tuis nunc | ficta pedum pono pressis vestigia signis* ('I follow you, O shining light of the Greek people, and firmly place my footsteps in the tracks you made').[14] Lucretius further characterizes himself in this passage as composing his poetry directly from the work of Epicurus, comparing himself to a bee (a common image for a poet)[15] feeding as though from the golden words of Epicurus himself (3.11–12). Tennyson's Lucretius characterizes himself in the same way: 'I prest my footsteps into his' (Tennyson, *Lucretius* 118).[16] It is no surprise, therefore, that Lucretian scholars have taken this self-characterization seriously. Among the most important to have done so recently is David Sedley, whose *Lucretius and the Transformation of Greek Wisdom* relates the *DRN* strongly to the content (and order) of Epicurus' (largely lost) *On Nature*,[17] which he views as 'Lucretius' sole Epicurean source', and which he began by following very closely ('almost mechanically'), before developing a structure for the entire poem which Sedley regards as 'radically revised' when compared with its Epicurean model, but which was only completed for the first three books. For the latter three books, in contrast, Lucretius 'had plans which can still to some extent be discerned from his proems, but which he did not live to put into operation'.[18]

For the purposes of this chapter, I am not concerned with the merits or demerits of the case that Sedley makes for reading the *DRN* as strongly as he does against *On Nature*;[19] rather I am using his argument as a prominent example of a 'master-text' reading. Very frequently Sedley subordinates the *DRN* to the reconstructed *On Nature* and/or to a putative *DRN* 2.0 (that is, the revised version of the *DRN* which, according to Sedley, Lucretius did not complete).[20] Sedley's conception of the character of Lucretius' dependence on Epicurus can be illustrated by his 'cardinal rule':

---

[14] On this passage and the complexities in the relationship between Lucretius and Epicurus as depicted in the proem of Book 3 see Konstan 1988. For the Latin text of Lucretius I have used Rouse and Smith 1992. Translations are my own, except where indicated.

[15] See Bailey 1947: II.989; Kenney 2014: 76 ad 3.11–13. Examples include Pind. *Pyth.* 10.53–4; Pl. *Ion* 534a; Hor. *Carm.* 4.2.27.

[16] In that poem Lucretius passes by his wife 'to turn and ponder those three hundred scrolls | left by the Teacher, whom he held divine' (vv. 12–13).

[17] Sedley 1998: 68 argues that at *DRN* 3.9–13 Lucretius announces that he depends exclusively on Epicurus, to the exclusion of other authorities.

[18] Sedley 1998: 134.

[19] On Sedley's view of the relationship between the *DRN* and *On Nature* see Clay 2000a: 265–7.

[20] See Butterfield 2013: 272–3 on the question of the state of revision of *DRN* and its consequences for editors.

The cardinal rule in the second half of the poem is this: **if you want to make sense of a puzzling sequence of topics adopted by Lucretius**, since he demonstrably has not completed his own reorganisation of the material, **ask why *Epicurus* should have ordered it in this way.**[21]

Here we can see the master-text approach used in the interpretation of the *DRN* itself: a critic puzzled at the sequence of events in the second half of the poem should refer this sequence not to (as it might be) the internal logic of the *DRN*, but to *another, different text*, the *On Nature*, since on Sedley's view the second half of the poem reflects the order of that text, because the poem has not yet been revised. There is then here also a subordination of the *DRN* as we have it to a further text, the revised *DRN* 2.0, which would have the 'proper' (i.e. Lucretian) order.

Instructive too is Sedley's interpretation of the topic of ghosts as it appears in *DRN* 4: this is prominent at the beginning of that book (4.26–41), but Lucretius then devotes 'only' eleven lines to the topic later (4.757–67), which Sedley interprets as insufficient from an Epicurean point of view:

Are the images of the dead which invade our dreams ones which emanated from those same people before they died, even centuries ago? . . . And how are waking visions of ghosts – referred to explicitly in the proem – to be explained? **These are important questions for an Epicurean to be able to answer . . . Above all, Lucretius owes his readers a well-reasoned assurance (which was certainly forthcoming from other Epicureans, and almost certainly from Epicurus himself) that such images could not actually be alive.**[22]

This is part of Sedley's argument that the latter three books of the *DRN* have not been revised, in contrast to the earlier three: the text of the *DRN* as it stands is therefore being compared with and checked against a putative *DRN* 2.0 (its own contents, argument and emphasis derived in part from 'other Epicureans'). I do not wish to claim that (philosophical) master-text readings such as this one are confined to readings of the *DRN*,[23] but it seems clear that this is the mode of reading being employed by Sedley. A reading strategy which subordinates the text it examines to other texts can be usefully contrasted with the critical attitude often

---

[21] Sedley 1998: 151; cf. Clay 2000a: 268–9. In this and other similar quotations the bold indicates my own emphasis.

[22] Sedley 1998: 149–50.

[23] A clear example of a master-text reading from another area of ancient philosophy is provided by Gregory Vlastos' approach to the early, 'Socratic' dialogues of Plato, for which the *Apology* operates as a 'check' and 'touchstone' (Vlastos 1971: 3–4) for Socrates' philosophy.

adopted to some other, probably unrevised texts, such as Virgil's *Aeneid*. The *Aeneid* contains over fifty examples of 'half-lines',[24] which are metrically incomplete hexameters, such as *munera laetitiamque dii* (*Aen.* 1.636), and are 'an obvious sign of the poem's lack of final revision'.[25] But modern critics of the *Aeneid* do not (for the most part) move from this fact to attempts to supplement them or speculation about what revisions would have taken place had Virgil lived to complete his poem.[26] Rather, critics focus on their effect in the text as constituted,[27] as Austin demonstrates, arguing that there is 'no valid reason for supposing that such lines were a deliberate innovation in technique, although they are sometimes accidentally effective in themselves'.[28] Here, in contrast to Sedley's approach to the *DRN*, the focus of critical attention is on the final condition of the unrevised poem.

Another important aspect of the master-text mode of reading is the notion of the *DRN*'s 'reader' with which Sedley is operating. He makes regular reference to the poem 'owing its readers' particular arguments or pieces of Epicurean doctrine: examples include the discussion of the images of the dead in Book 4 (see above), and especially the description of the plague at Athens at the end of the poem (6.1138–286). It is such readers whom Sedley has in mind when he argues that Lucretius must have intended to revise the end of the *DRN* in part because of the unsettling effect the current ending has on its readers.[29] Sedley argues that the end of the poem is missing a crucial part of the Epicurean *tetrapharmakos*,[30] and that this is part of a debt or obligation to the poem's readers: 'What Lucretius **still owed his readers** was Epicurus' explanation of how tolerance of physical pain depends on our mental attitude to it.'[31] Because this

---

[24] See in general on these half-lines Sparrow 1931; Walter 1933. Goold 1970: 151–2 provides a convenient list and argues strongly that Virgil did not intend to leave them incomplete.

[25] Hardie 1994: 105.

[26] Cf., however, the discussion of Miller 1909 who does record some attempted supplements of the lines, and Steele 1910, who suggests the difficulty of completing some of the half-lines effectively. Several Renaissance continuations of the *Aeneid* were attempted (on the most famous, the fifteenth-century 'thirteenth book' by Maffeo Vegio, see Buckley 2006), but the desire to supplement and complete the epic contrasts sharply with modern critical approaches to the poem.

[27] Indeed, a few have argued that such is their effectiveness that some may be intentional (cf., e.g., Baldwin 1993: 148–51), which is an idea at least as old as Abraham Cowley, as Baldwin demonstrates (1993: 144–5).

[28] Austin 1977: 71 ad 6.94. He gives the examples of 1.534, 2.66, 4.44. See also the sensible comments of Camps 1969: 129–31.

[29] On the end of the *DRN* see (e.g.) the different views of Sedley 1998: 160–5 and P. Fowler 1997 (the latter arguing for several important closural features at the end of the poem, and for the close of the *DRN* as a 'test' for the reader, for which cf. Clay 1983: 250–66).

[30] See Long and Sedley 1987: 25J, *KD* 1–4.   [31] Sedley 1998: 163.

element is missing, Sedley deduces that Lucretius meant to include it in a revised *DRN* (*DRN* 2.0).[32] This forms another variety of master-text approach, since here the *tetrapharmakos* can be used to check what should have been included in a revised *DRN*, but does not function as a strong model (for the poem as a whole) in the manner of the *On Nature*.[33]

Here the reader of the *DRN* (as conceived of by Sedley) is in some sense *also* subordinate to the master-text or texts – Sedley's reader expects particular items or arguments to be included in the poem. The term 'reader' is (of course) a distinctly malleable and pliable one, able to cover a wide range of meanings:[34] Sedley does not make explicit his theoretical perspective on the reader, but he appears to assume a considerable overlap between the reader(s) implied or constructed by the poem[35] and the poem's flesh-and-blood, historical readers in the first century BC (and perhaps later), whom he assumes would have wanted the same outcome as that assumed for the poem's implied readers (*ataraxia*).[36] But it is most important for our purposes to note that this putative reader is emphatically one who reads the poem primarily for its Epicurean content rather than its form. The reader Sedley assumes seems motivated, at least in part, by the therapeutic potential of the *DRN* to transform his experience and deliver him *ataraxia*.[37] This conception of the reader who focuses very much on the *content* of the *DRN* implies some limitations to the recent synthesizing consensus on the poem discussed above, in that the primary interest of this reader appears to be the philosophical therapy the *DRN* espouses, rather than the poetic form which it takes. For such Epicureans (or would-be Epicureans) the fact that the *DRN* is a poem seems hardly to matter.

---

[32] See especially Sedley's use (1998: 165) of Epicurus' letter to Idomeneus (Diog. Laert. 10.22) and its profession of philosophical detachment from physical pain, which Sedley sees as indicative of the content of the intended close of *DRN* 2.0.

[33] See further below on the wider philosophical system as the master-text.

[34] For orientation on the thorny problem of the variety of readers posited by different critical approaches to didactic poetry see Sharrock 1994: 6–17, with particular reference to the *DRN* at 12–13, 15–17.

[35] Such readers are clearest in such passages as 1.136–45 to Memmius, where Lucretius' aim 'to spread out clear lights before your mind' (144 *clara tuae ... praepandere lumina menti*) is explicit, and also in the repeated lines (first at 1.146–8) on the necessity of dispelling mental terror and darkness through the *naturae species ratioque* ('the appearance and law of nature').

[36] Sedley 1998: 91–3 allows that some of Lucretius' readers will have known more than Lucretius about some philosophical (e.g., Stoic) positions. On the role of Memmius see n. 73 below.

[37] N.b. esp. the repeated declarations of the need to dispel with reason *terrorem animi tenebrasque* (1.146–8, 2.59–61, 3.91–3, 6.39–41). For the therapeutic potential of the *DRN* see Nussbaum 1994: 140–91; Kilpatrick 1996; Vieron 2013: 120. On the wider therapeutic dimensions of Epicureanism see Gigante 1975; Nussbaum 1986.

That this master-text mode of reading is persistent and widespread in Lucretian studies is clearly demonstrated by the recent book by Francesco Montarese (*Lucretius and his Sources*).[38] Montarese's is an avowedly master-text approach following in the footsteps of Sedley,[39] and argues in detail for Lucretius' dependence on a lost Epicurean work for his attack on various Presocratic physical theories at *DRN* 1.635–920. As Sedley does, Montarese allows for some (limited) adaptation by Lucretius of his Epicurean source material,[40] but he still makes the *DRN* largely subordinate to the content and arguments of its master-text. The master-text approach is explicitly a methodological assumption, one which is not limited to the *DRN* but applies more widely to Latin philosophical works of the period: 'Roman philosophical authors of the second and first centuries BC were **accustomed to follow Greek originals closely**, and sometimes simply translated those models';[41] 'Cicero, **and presumably any Roman writing philosophy in Latin in the first century** BC, would have found it natural to use Greek sources, and **might have done little more than translate his Greek source** into Latin'.[42] Such an approach leads Montarese (as it does Sedley) to view Lucretius' 'original composition' as consisting in only a small proportion of the poem, chiefly the prologues to each of the books, 1.398–417, 1.716–33 (praising Empedocles and Sicily), 1.921–50, 4.1037–287 (at least in part) and possibly 2.600–60 (Magna Mater).[43]

Not all master-text readings, however, focus on a particular model-text. In a distinct, separate type of master-text reading, we do not explicitly find either a particular source text (such as the *On Nature*) or a putative revised text. But there remains in such cases some subordination of the *DRN* to a different text, one other than the *DRN* as now constituted, akin to the employment of the *tetrapharmakos* by Sedley (see above). In this species of master-text reading, the master-text is something like the wider philosophical system (in the case of the *DRN*, of course, this is Epicureanism).[44] This

---

[38] Montarese 2012.
[39] As explicitly acknowledged at Montarese 2012: 9: 'The indebtedness of this study to David Sedley's book ... will be apparent to the reader: he has pointed the way. I follow the approach he has adopted.'
[40] See esp. chapter 4 of Montarese 2012.   [41] Montarese 2012: 5.   [42] Montarese 2012: 6.
[43] See Montarese 2012: 18–19. Sedley 1998: 134 has a similarly restricted view of Lucretius' 'original compositions', confining them to 'the proems, the poetic manifesto at I 921–50 (and IV 1–25), at least the bulk of the *magna mater* passage (II 600–60), the ethical diatribes which close books III and IV, and the concluding account of the Athenian plague'.
[44] See Sharrock 2013: 4–6, 9 on the focus on the 'system' in much philosophical work on Lucretius and some of its interpretative consequences. This focus on the philosophical system, and hence on a species of master-text, appears to be relatively widespread in some approaches to ancient philosophy

system too has to be reconstructed from a variety of texts (the *DRN* itself features heavily, not without problems of circularity), but the crucial point from our perspective is that the system can be used to check interpretations of the *DRN*.[45] Such readings in effect harmonize the *DRN* with other Epicurean texts. A good example is provided by David Konstan in his discussion of the diatribe against death in Book 3, in particular Lucretius' treatment of the mourners of a dead father (3.904–11):[46]

> 'Tu quidem ut es leto sopitus, sic eris aevi
> quod superest cunctis privatu' doloribus aegris;
> at nos horrifico cinefactum te prope busto
> insatiabiliter deflevimus, aeternumque
> nulla dies nobis maerorem e pectore demet.'
> illud ab hoc igitur quaerendum est, quid sit amari
> tanto opere, ad somnum si res redit atque quietem,
> cur quisquam aeterno possit tabescere luctu.

905

910

'You, in truth, as you are in the sleep of death, so you will be for the rest of time, free from all troubling pains; but we have wept inconsolably next to you, now turned to ash by the horrifying pyre, and no day will ever take the eternal sorrow from our hearts.' It should be asked of this person: what is so exceedingly bitter that, if things return to sleep and rest, someone should pine away with eternal grief?

Konstan acknowledges the grumpy tone Lucretius takes to the mourners of a dead father here: '**Lucretius is a tad gruff with these grumblers as well**, as he poses the rhetorical question: "what is so bitter about something returning to sleep and quietude, that a person can waste away in eternal mourning [*luctus*]?" (3.909–11). It would seem that, whatever Epicurus' attitude, **Lucretius has little patience with grief for the**

---

more broadly: for example, all four of the 'genres' of the history of philosophy identified by Rorty 1984 are (broadly speaking) directed at the philosophical views of individual philosophers, rather than particular texts, in a way which suggests the primary focus is a philosopher's wider system of thought (or hypothetical engagement with modern philosophers or philosophical problems) rather than the reading of an individual text.

[45] Donncha O'Rourke suggests to me that the distinction between the concrete and more abstract varieties of master-text reading are reminiscent of the Contean distinction between types of intertext, specifically 'modello-esemplare' (where a particular passage serves as a model for a later text) and 'modello-codice' (where a broader text serves as the representative of a genre or type for a later text and provides a matrix of possibilities against which one can read the later text). Sedley's analysis of the *DRN* would be more like the modello-esemplare (the specific text, *On Nature*), whereas Konstan focuses more on the broader modello-codice of Epicureanism. It is worth noting, however, that in master-text readings the distinctive characteristic is the subordination of the target-text to the source text, which is not present in intertextual approaches (see further below). For Conte's approach to intertextuality see Conte 1985: 121–2, 1986: 31; Hinds 1998: 41–3.

[46] Konstan 2013.

deceased.' But Konstan also adverts to the concern of other Epicureans with providing consolation (cf., e.g., Plut. *Non posse* 1101a5–b1 reporting Epicurus' attitude to grief; Philodemus, *On Death* col. 25.2–9 Henry),[47] and this leads him to play down the uncompromising tone of Lucretius' words to the mourners:

> Here, he is censuring, not the immediate sense of loss … but rather the idea that grief is insatiable and interminable. That reproach, as I have mentioned, is **a commonplace in virtually all consolatory literature**, and I believe that we may take **this passage in Lucretius** as evidence that the Epicureans too adopted such an attitude.[48]

Here the literature of consolation, and especially the views of other Epicureans about grief and consoling mourners, are used to modify interpretation of the *DRN*: the *prima facie* impatience of the poem with the mourners depicted is read as rather more accommodating, because of the other texts invoked as a check or key to the description of mourning. Here too, then, we have a 'master-text' reading, though of a different kind from that employed by Sedley. This reading also assumes an Epicurean reader (again encompassing both the poem's implied reader and his real-world analogues), or at least one mainly focused on the therapeutic potential of the poem. Konstan's reader looks to the *DRN* for the same type of consolation as one would find in other Epicurean texts, and this leads him to argue that the *DRN* itself provides similar consolation.

Intertext(s)

Such master-text readings which employ other texts as keys or checks (in different ways) on the *DRN* are strikingly different from one of the most prominent approaches to reading Latin literature, including the *DRN*. This is the 'intertextual' mode, which one might describe as the dominant critical type of reading employed today for Latin (and much Greek) literature.[49] There is, of course, more than one kind of intertextual

---

[47] On Philodemus' view here see Konstan 2013: 204, Morrison 2013: 228. Cf. also Demetrius Laco *PHerc.* 1013 col. 18.1–4 πῶς οὐ]κ ἄτοπον τὸ λέγε[ιν] ὡς Ἐπίκουρος τἀποθνήσκειν οὐ παραμ[ε]μύθηται, 'Surely it is strange to claim that Epicurus has not provided consolation from dying?' (trans. Henry 2009: xvi–xvii).

[48] Konstan 2013: 206–7.

[49] For Baraz and van den Berg 2013: 1 intertextuality has been prominent 'since Conte first reconceived Giorgio Pasquali's *arte allusiva* in terms of Julia Kristeva's intertextuality and helped establish a dominant model for the study of Latin poetry'. See further D. Fowler 1997a: 13–20; Hinds 1998: 17–51; Baraz and van den Berg 2013: 1–3. On Pasquali's 'arte allusiva' see Pasquali 1942; Thomas 1986: 171–2; Pucci 1998: 13–14.

reading: not all those involved in the practice of intertextual reading either do it the same way or think that they are doing things in the same way: the books of Hinds, Edmunds and Pucci (for example) show how much variation there can be between different practitioners of such readings, not least when they come to articulate their theories of intertextuality.[50] But I do want to claim that again we can discern broad tendencies in these intertextual readings, and that these are different in character from those we identified in master-text readings.

My first example of intertextual reading is Tobias Reinhardt's article on the end of *DRN* 3 and Plato's *Gorgias*, especially its closing eschatological myth (523a–527e), which functions as a final demonstration of how Callicles is wrong to prefer a life of unjust pleasure, since the damage this will do to his soul will be obvious in the underworld. I have chosen this piece in particular because some of the language Reinhardt uses to describe the *DRN*'s relationship to the *Gorgias* recalls some aspects of the master-text approach I outlined above, but is, in fact, importantly different. Reinhardt compares the *DRN*'s relation to the *Gorgias* to that of a commentary on a primary text:

> **[J]ust as a scholarly commentary has little in the way of internal textual logic of its own but, in following 'the text' and dividing it up into lemmata, receives its structure in virtue of its being a commentary on something, so the end of Book 3 would appear as a less-than-coherent jumble of passages unless the reader provides one by reading it against a certain model.** And in obvious analogy to scholarly commentaries ancient and modern, we can identify the social and psychological aims this commentary serves: the final part of Book 3 acknowledges the impact made by Platonic dialogues and the *Gorgias* in particular in the Hellenistic era, **attempts to police the persuasive vigour of this work, gives the reader guidance** so that he may not misinterpret the *Gorgias* but rather **see what makes sense in it and what should be rejected**, and, finally, is one element in Lucretius' broader strategy of **inviting and manipulating the reader** to become a member of the kind of close-knit, sect-like community which distinguishes the Epicureans from the other Hellenistic schools.[51]

The relationship Reinhardt suggests here is, however, not one where we should conceive of the *Gorgias* as a master-text against which we can check the interpretation of the *DRN*. Rather, the *DRN* (on Reinhardt's view) acts

[50] See Hinds 1998; Pucci 1998; Edmunds 2001. On the range, variety and significance of intertextual readings see D. Fowler 1997a: 14–34 and 2000b: 139–40.
[51] Reinhardt 2004: 43–4.

as a control on and guide to the *Gorgias*, providing the means by which to distinguish what is worthwhile from what is to be discarded: the *DRN* is in fact meant to modify our reading of the *Gorgias*. Its 'secondariness', then, is in the manner of a response or a correction.[52] The structural and organizational problems in what Reinhardt calls the 'microstructure' (2004: 27) of the end of *DRN* 3 form therefore an *intertextual cue* to look outside the *DRN* and to its polemical relationship with the vision of the underworld in the *Gorgias*.

The *Gorgias* is recalled in order (as Reinhardt puts it) 'to contest this link between pleasure conceived as contentment and the prospect of getting away lightly in a final judgement': the *DRN* employs the end of the *Gorgias*, using the content and context of the final myth, but modifies it and appropriates it for a different purpose in the *DRN*. This is the hallmark of intertextual relations (at least as widely practised and theorized by readers of Latin poetry): the lack of subordination of text B (the receiving or target text, or hypertext) to text A (the source text or hypotext).[53]

The focus of Reinhardt's reading remains the *DRN* as constituted now; it is not harmonized with a model text or wider philosophical system. The reader of the *DRN* posited by such a reading has recourse to a wider range of texts than Sedley's more focused Epicurean reader whose reference points are principally other Epicurean texts (or positions). Reinhardt's reader is still interested in the shape of the argument in the *DRN*, but the operation of this argumentative, persuasive drive involves competing non-Epicurean texts. Such a reader reads the poem with a large number of potential intertexts in mind – a reader more akin, perhaps, to the readers of other Latin poems without an explicit Epicurean programme.

My second intertextual example is my own reading of Lucretius' criticism of the mourners of a dead father (*DRN* 3.894–911: see above) against the words of the Homeric Hector to Andromache imagining her future slavery and wishing to be dead before the fateful day (*Il.* 6.450–65). As in the other examples in this chapter I am not concerned with the merits of the case, but in the approach taken: the Iliadic intertext recalled here on this view makes Lucretius even more uncompromising in his attitude to mourning:[54]

---

[52] On such 'corrections' see Thomas 1986: 185–8.
[53] Cf., e.g., Genette 1997: 2–6 on 'hypertextuality' between texts, which is marked by this lack of subordination.
[54] The multiple parallels are detailed and discussed in Morrison 2013, esp. 216 n. 9.

The Iliadic echo reminding us of the perspective of the dead man, furthermore, makes it particularly arresting when Lucretius responds to his imagined mourners that the dead man has no desire for *tot praemia uitae* ('all these prizes of life') after his death (Lucr. 3.899), and comments that the failure to realise this means they do not free themselves *animi magno . . . angore metuque* ('great anguish and fear of mind', 3.902–3) . . . Now that we know (having read book 3) that we are made up of body and soul (*anima*), both of which are mortal and made up of atoms (Lucr. 3.417–829), and that on the separation of body and soul at death both cease to exist (Lucr. 3.323–36), so that sensation also ceases (Lucr. 3.838–42), **Lucretius proposes that we should accept that the typical behaviour of mourners (and, through the Iliadic intertext, the pain Hector feels now about a future in which he will not exist) are mistaken** and themselves evidence that they cannot rid themselves of attitudes which stand in the way of the achievement of *ataraxia*.[55]

Here again the relationship to the other text is not one of subordination: the Iliadic intertext does not determine the meaning of the *DRN* passage; rather it is the interaction between the two texts which creates a particular effect on the reader of the *DRN*. Here too (as for Reinhardt) the reader envisaged for the *DRN* has a broader set of potential reference points than standard Epicurean *topoi* or teachings (such as the *tetrapharmakos*). Texts such as the *Iliad* are 'in play' for such a reader, as they would be for a reader of Virgil's *Aeneid*, for example. Again, this points us towards a different conception of the reader of the *DRN* from that we have observed in master-text readings, again with consequences for interpretation of the poem as a whole.

Before we examine these consequences in detail, it is worth noting a further aspect of intertextual approaches to texts such as the *DRN*. Intertextual reading is not interested solely in the presence in the *DRN* of other texts but also in the reception of the *DRN* by other texts. Studies of this kind continue to flourish: one can cite as a prominent recent example the examination by Alessandro Schiesaro of the engagement with Lucretius in Ovid's *Metamorphoses*,[56] which is in turn part of a broader acknowledgement of the importance of the *DRN* for Augustan and later poets.[57] A good example of this importance is the use made of the *DRN*, in particular of the 'mourners' passage (3.894–6 *Iam iam non domus accipiet*

---

[55] Morrison 2013: 218.
[56] Schiesaro 2014; for Ovid's explicit reference to Lucretius in *Am.* 1.15 see O'Rourke in this volume (pp. 103–4). On Augustan engagement with Lucretius see also Giesecke 2000.
[57] On the reception of Lucretius by later Latin poets see in general Hardie 2009; on the reception of the *DRN* in Virgil's *Georgics* see also, e.g., Gale 2000.

te laeta neque uxor | optima, nec dulces occurrent oscula nati | praeripere et tacita pectus dulcedine tangent, 'No longer will your happy home or excellent wife greet you, nor will your sweet children rush to snatch kisses and touch your heart with heartfelt sweetness') by Horace in his famous Postumus ode (*Carm.* 2.14.21–4):[58]

> linquenda tellus et domus et placens
> uxor, neque harum quas colis arborum
>   te praeter invisas cupressos
>   ulla brevem dominum sequetur.

... you will have to leave your land and your house and your pleasing wife, nor will any of these trees that you cultivate follow their short-term master except the hated cypresses.

These lines seem clearly to recall the *DRN*'s characterization of the mourners' bewailing of the dead man's lost home and wife, but again put it to a different purpose: Horace's poem suggests that the traditional torments of the underworld await, and so life should be enjoyed. The resemblance between Horace and Lucretius has long been noticed,[59] but a good example of an explicitly 'intertextualist' reading is that of Edmunds:

> In book 3 of *DRN*, Lucretius counters the fear of death by showing that the soul is material and does not survive death. The lines just quoted [*DRN* 3.894–6] are what mourners say, who believe that there is some part of you left to regret these things. Lucretius argues against the mourners. But Horace's speaker uses the mourners' point of view in order to persuade Postumus – implicitly – to enjoy life because death is to be feared. The allusion to Lucretius, if intentional on the part of the speaker, obliges the reader to imagine a background. For example, the Horatian speaker might be challenging the known adherence of his friend Postumus to the views of Epicurus as expounded in Lucretius. It would also be possible to understand the allusion as communication between the implied poet and the reader. Ultimately, the reader in fact will decide, and the decision will depend on how he manages to integrate the allusion into his reading.[60]

I would want to add that here *Odes* 2.14 looks back to Lucretius' own appropriation of Hector's fears for his wife's future when he is dead in *Iliad* 6, and restores the sense that such a separation is painful and fearful. Horace thus returns to the natural, unEpicurean fear of death arising (in this case) from the division between loved ones, and does so in part

---

[58] Trans. Edmunds 2001: 72. See in general on this ode Anderson 1968; Nisbet and Hubbard 1978: 222–41; Roberts 1991; Paschalis 1994–5.
[59] See, e.g., Nisbet and Hubbard 1978: 234–5.   [60] Edmunds 2001: 73.

by reactivating some of the original context and emotion from the Iliadic intertext Lucretius had earlier appropriated. Therefore the Horatian reading of the *DRN* implicit in the ode has the potential to point us to awkward or disruptive elements present in the *DRN* through its intertexts:[61] the intertextual readings of Reinhardt and Morrison above have largely read the poem's relations with other texts as promoting (or at least not contradicting) its Epicurean message, but careful readers of Lucretius such as Horace, Virgil and Ovid are able to indicate problematic aspects of its intertexts,[62] such as the possibility that an exposition of Epicurean physics may not, in fact, be sufficient to dispel a fear of death fundamental to the human condition.

Here too it is worth considering the reader of texts such as Horace's ode which such intertextual readings assume (or construct): such a reader has as potential reference points, or 'texts in mind', both the *DRN* and the *Iliad* (as well as a still broader range of texts, including Greek lyric and Greek epigram). All of these texts can be activated and utilized in the creation of meaning by *Ode* 2.14. In the next section we shall take a closer look at the readers envisaged by the different modes of reading we have examined, in order to uncover the consequences for our interpretation of the *DRN* of these different modes of reading.

Consequences and Conclusions: Readings and Readers

It is clear that there are key differences in the modes of reading and criticizing the *DRN* which we have studied. Master-text readings subordinate the *DRN* to other texts, whether these are strong models on which the poem's content or structure is based (such as Epicurus' *On Nature*), or a more diffuse conception of a master-text such as the wider Epicurean system of thought, against which the *DRN* can be checked or measured. In some cases, as we have seen, gaps between the *DRN* and its master-text can be eliminated by positing a *DRN* 2.0, which in turn conforms more closely to the master-text. The reader envisaged by such readings is primarily interested in Epicureanism, or perhaps especially in becoming an Epicurean or in benefitting from the rewards the *DRN* promises

[61] See Fowler 2000b: 155, who comments on the (in that article unexplored) 'potential for disruption' of the *DRN*'s intertexts. As he says, 'in another mood, I might wish to go further down that road than I have done here'.

[62] For Ovid's 'remythologizing' of Lucretius in the Phaethon episode at *Met.* 1.747–2.400 see Schiesaro 2014, esp. 73–87, 94–6, where he argues that Ovid highlights structural and logical problems in Lucretius' employment of the Phaethon story at *DRN* 5.396–415.

(in *ataraxia* as a goal).[63] Accordingly, the main reference points for such a reader are other Epicurean texts or other formulations of Epicurean doctrine, with which they are either familiar or from which the material they expect to be in the *DRN* can be reconstructed. This contrasts sharply with the intertextual mode which assumes a much wider range of potential reference points for a putative reader of the *DRN*, encompassing (e.g.) Plato or the *Iliad*, i.e. texts beyond a narrow Epicurean curriculum. These texts, in turn, are not conceived of as dominating the *DRN* or determining its meaning; rather, they can be mobilized by the *DRN* as part of its complex literary texture, in order to emphasize particular aspects, correct the other text, or complicate the reading of the poem (or, as part of its Epicurean project, to challenge alternative beliefs or positions, such as those found in Plato's *Gorgias*). The reader envisaged by the intertextual mode resembles much more closely the readers of Latin literary texts envisaged by critics of other Latin poets such as Virgil or Horace.

The differences in approach and underlying critical framework of these differing modes of reading the *DRN* do lead to real differences in interpretation (they are not simply 'theoretical' in the pejorative sense which opposes this to 'practical'). The different approaches affect how, for example, one reads the end of the *DRN*, or one's views of how uncompromising or sympathetic certain parts of the poem are, such as the diatribe against death and its treatment of the mourners.

Both the differences in approach and the consequences of differences in interpretation should give us pause when considering the recent synthesizing consensus on the poem. But acknowledging differences between different critics in reading practices and theoretical assumptions should not be seen as a cause for dismay (or lead to a sort of critical divorce between different kinds of reader).[64] Rather, it is best to see the range of approaches as valuable within a pluralist conception of how one should approach texts as complex as the *DRN*. Malcolm Heath, for example, has warned of the dangers of consensus and the value of critical disagreement on classical texts, and the importance of disagreement for pointing towards underlying methodological differences.[65] These differences in turn can be encompassed within a pluralist conception of how to read texts.[66]

---

[63] On the *DRN*'s orientation towards its readers see Tutrone in Chapter 4 of this volume.
[64] For example, tensions between textual-critical and literary-critical approaches are discussed by Butterfield in Chapter 1 of this volume.
[65] See Heath 2002, esp. 9–38 and also cf. Sharrock 2013: 3–4 on the importance of recognizing a plurality of approaches to Lucretius.
[66] Cf. Heath 2002: 57.

Nevertheless, perhaps there is room to see some lack of fit between the philosophical content and the poetic form of the *DRN*, which is the subject with which we began. In part it is possible to see some of the internal conflict discerned by some in the poem as a result of the different ways in which the *DRN* can be read, both as an intertextually dense poem and an expression of Epicurean philosophy. Some of the tension, then, in the *DRN* between form and content is a product of different modes of reading, that is differences *in us* as readers of the text (and in the readers we construct for the poem as hermeneutic devices, as we have explored). But here I would like to advert to a crucial aspect of the *DRN* (and the relationship between form and content) which our investigation helps us to see more clearly (and which the synthesizing consensus perhaps obscures) and that is the *oddity*, the strangeness of putting Epicurean philosophy into the form of six books of hexameter verse. The form of the poem as a vehicle for its Epicurean content is in fact remarkable and unparalleled,[67] a fact which is sometimes obscured or overlooked when the poem is assimilated with other, prose texts of Epicurus. Lucretius has been characterized as out on his own and exceptional among his contemporary Epicureans with regard to his attitude to Epicurus' teaching,[68] but he is most exceptional when considered as an Epicurean *poet*. As noted above, there is good reason to think that Epicurus himself was at least wary of poetry,[69] and furthermore good reason to think that Epicureans more generally were not in favour of poems with the didactic form and purpose of the *DRN* (the poems of Philodemus make a striking contrast in this regard).[70] Some critics regard writing such a poem as a 'next step',[71] given the views of poetry we find expressed (or implied) in Philodemus, but this is to underestimate (in my view) the revolutionary character of the *DRN*, and to perceive as incremental something which is in fact very different in kind. The writing of poetry to entertain (as exemplified by the epigrams of Philodemus) and the interpretation of Homer as providing starting points for ethical discussion (as in *On the Good King According to Homer*) are agendas fundamentally different from that of writing a long didactic epic on Epicurean physics. In this connection we need to take seriously Lucretius' comments on poetic originality at 1.921–34, especially the claim that 'I traverse the Pierides' trackless haunts, never before trodden by the foot of anyone' (926–7 *avia Pieridum peragro*

---

[67] There are other philosophical poems, of course, such as that of Empedocles, but the *DRN* is unique as an *Epicurean* philosophical epic.
[68] See Sedley 1998: 91–3.   [69] See n. 1 above.   [70] See n. 2 above.
[71] Cf., e.g., Janko 2000: 9 'It was left to Lucretius to take the further step of composing a poem which taught the true philosophy of Epicureanism.'

loca nullius ante | trita solo),[72] not only for his achievement of bringing Epicureanism into verse, but for the poetic ambitions this has satisfied (cf. in particular 1.923 *laudis spes magna*, 'the high hope of fame', and 1.924–5 *suavem . . . amorem | Musarum*, 'the sweet love of the Muses').

Given the exceptional nature of the poem, we should also ask ourselves what kind of reader did the *DRN* in fact enjoy. What type of reader was Memmius, for example, to whom the poem is explicitly directed?[73] Are we to conceive of him as reading the poem in the hope of *ataraxia*, in the manner of Sedley's reader, or would he have read the poem at least as much for its artistry and complexity? The reader constructed by the poem is in places one explicitly portrayed as one whose mental state would benefit from reading it (cf., e.g., 1.102–6 on Memmius' fears as likely to be stirred by priests; 1.127–35 on the need properly to explain dreams and visions), but that he is addressed in a hexameter poem also implies not only that this form is the honey to sweeten the medicine (as at 1.931–50), but also that such a reader reads the poem also for its qualities as a poem, which in turn are not simply the set-piece displays of virtuosity, such as the invocation of Venus, but its metre, diction, broader use of language, imagery, intertexts, engagement with myth, and so forth. There is good reason to think that the Memmius constructed by the *DRN is* interested in Epicureanism,[74] but it is also clear that aspects of the poem and its poetic form anticipate and accommodate different types of reader including those reading the poem with different motivations. What of Virgil, for example, who engages so closely with the *DRN* (cf., e.g., *G.* 2.490–2)?[75] Or Cicero (not an Epicurean), who writes to his brother that Lucretius' poems are *multis luminibus ingeni, multae tamen artis* ('having many flashes of inspiration, but also much skill', *Q Fr.* 2.10.3)?[76]

---

[72] 1.926–34 are repeated, not accidentally, at the beginning of Book 4 (1–9). On this repetition see further O'Rourke in this volume (p. 120).

[73] On the issue of Memmius as the addressee of the *DRN* and his function in the poem see (e.g.) Classen 1968; Kleve 1979b; Townend 1978; Keen 1985; Baron 1986: 10–13. Particularly useful on Memmius and his relationship to the wider readership of the poem are Clay 1983: 212–34; Sharrock 1994: 15–17; Mitsis 1993. See further Farrell in Chapter 11 of this volume.

[74] See esp. Lucretius' underlining of Memmius' merits and the expectation of his pleasant friendship as spurs for the production of the poem: 1.140–2 *tua me virtus tamen et sperata voluptas | suavis amicitiae quemvis efferre laborem | suadet.* Cf. however the view of Mitsis 1993 that Memmius is presented as a didactic *nepios*. The interest in Epicureanism of the Memmius within the *DRN* is a distinct question, of course, from that of the identity and receptiveness (or hostility) to Epicureanism of the historical Memmius.

[75] On Virgil's use of the *DRN* see (e.g.) Hardie 1986; Farrell 1991; Gale 2000.

[76] Thus the paradosis, as printed by Shackleton-Bailey, though the text of the letter has been disputed and various emendations proposed: Cicero may have denied Lucretius' genius (*ingenium*) but allowed him skill, if the emendation *non multis luminibus ingenii, multae tamen artis* is preferred. See Shackleton-Bailey 1980: 190–1.

Such readers may well have read the *DRN* in a manner closer to that employed by readers of Virgil's *Aeneid* or the *Odes* of Horace.[77] The *DRN* encompasses and enables readers with different aims and desires, which is one of the hallmarks of great literature. Some readers will have enjoyed the poem for the pleasure it produces as an aesthetic object (as some Epicureans, and perhaps even Epicurus himself, allowed was possible);[78] others will have approached the poem primarily for its therapeutic or philosophical potential (and many readers will have combined these and other motivations). We can best do justice to the richness and complexity of the *DRN* if we acknowledge the different readers our various readings and critical approaches assume, and therefore the types of text we make the *DRN* speak to and against, rather than obscuring the differences between them. Indeed, the more types of reader one sees in the *DRN*, the greater the plurality of approaches required and the less monologic the poem will seem. To this reader, at least, the poem itself accommodates far more than one type of reader and does so with a striking degree of complexity, for which our criticism of the poem needs to allow.

---

[77] This is not to deny Virgil's Epicurean connections and associations, on which see in general Armstrong, Fish, Johnston and Skinner 2004, but to recognize that his interest in a hexameter poem would also have been that of a poet.

[78] See Asmis 1995: 20–1, on the basis of Plut. *Non posse* 1095c–1096c.

CHAPTER 9

Lucretius and the Philosophical Use of Literary Persuasion

Tim O'Keefe

Lucretius makes no pretence to producing original philosophical arguments – instead, he is presenting Epicurus' arguments in an attractive form
in order to spread his healing gospel to an audience of Romans. So one of
the primary focuses of attention when looking into Lucretius' use of his
philosophical sources has been to discern what exactly those philosophical
sources are. Obviously, the ultimate source of most of Lucretius' arguments is Epicurus himself, but this leaves open the question of Lucretius'
proximate sources. Does he sometimes draw on later Epicurean texts, ones
that debated the precise meaning of Epicurus' own doctrines and engaged
in disputes with Academic sceptics and Stoics? Or does Lucretius draw
exclusively on Epicurus himself?

In the first part of this chapter, I will review this *Quellenforschung* and
argue that, in the case of the *De Rerum Natura* (*DRN*), this debate will
likely be inconclusive and fruitless, notwithstanding exciting new discoveries of texts from Herculaneum or elsewhere. In the second part of the
chapter, I will turn to a consideration of how Lucretius, in the way he
appropriates and presents his philosophical sources, might be considered
original philosophically and not just poetically. Drawing a parallel with
recent reconsideration of Cicero as an original philosopher, I will sketch
out how Lucretius' presentation of his arguments is philosophically distinctive, even though the arguments themselves are derived from others.

Tradition: Lucretius' Philosophical Sources

The search for Lucretius' philosophical sources has a long history, but
the touchstone for recent discussions is David Sedley's *Lucretius and
the Transformation of Greek Wisdom* (Sedley 1998), which argues that

I'd like to thank Donncha O'Rourke, Hal Thorsrud, and the readers for Cambridge University Press
for their valuable feedback on this chapter.

Lucretius' only philosophical source is Epicurus' *On Nature*. We can usefully divide the debate into two broad camps of opinion: that Lucretius is working exclusively from Epicurus' own texts (or, in Sedley's terms, 'Lucretius the fundamentalist'),[1] and that Lucretius also draws on later sources ('Lucretius the *au courant*').[2]

One can look into the question of Lucretius' sources for its own sake, just because one is curious as to what they are; but in theory, discovering Lucretius' sources could have intellectual value beyond merely satisfying this intellectual curiosity. Our understanding of an argument can be shaped by knowing the context in which it was produced.[3] For instance, Lucretius argues that the world was not created by the gods for our benefit, because it is far too flawed (*DRN* 5.195–234, cf. 2.167–82). It is common and understandable to read this argument as a contribution to the 'Problem of Evil', i.e. as a challenge to the existence of God as traditionally understood in Judeo-Christian theology: a maximally great being, who is omnipotent, omniscient and all-good.[4] We can legitimately ask how Lucretius' argument *would* apply to such a god, but we anachronistically distort the argument if we view it in itself as an attempt to show that such a god does not exist, because such a god was not part of the intellectual landscape in either Epicurus' or Lucretius' time. Instead, Plato's craftsman god of the *Timaeus* and the Stoics' immanent cosmic deity are wise and perfectly good, but they fall short of omnipotence, needing to exercise their power within the limitations of matter.[5] If, then, we were able to ascertain (for instance) that one of Lucretius' arguments is aimed at the Stoics in particular, this might help improve our understanding of Stoic theology.

Before looking in detail at the content of the *DRN* itself, there is little reason to assign a higher prior probability to either the fundamentalist or *au courant* position. We have no reports on the sources for the *DRN*, either from Lucretius himself or others, and next to no information about

[1] Sedley 1998, esp. Chapter 3 (pp. 62–93), is the primary exponent of the 'fundamentalist' position, although Furley 1966 is also important for debunking claims that Lucretius is responding to Stoic influence.
[2] See, e.g., Asmis 1982; Clay 1983; Schrijvers 1999.
[3] A representative example of trying to do this in the case of Lucretius is Algra, Koenen and Schrijvers 1997.
[4] For instance, the early church father Lactantius reports the Epicurean arguments in such a way (Lactant. *De Ira Dei* 13.20–2), and David Hume quotes Lactantius' report when he attributes the problem of evil to Epicurus (*Dialogues Concerning Natural Religion*, part 10).
[5] For instance, when trying to reconcile God's providential care for us with the evils in the world, the Stoic Chrysippus claims that god made our skulls as (relatively) thin and fragile as they are because, if he had made them any thicker, we would be stupider (Gell. *NA* 7.1.1–13).

Lucretius' life. The *DRN* itself shows that Lucretius was a devoted adherent of Epicurus familiar with the ways of Rome's upper classes,[6] and he was plugged in enough to the Roman *literati* that Cicero obtained a copy of his poem and admired its quality (*Q Fr.* 2.9.3). Even from this scant information, it seems more likely that Lucretius had some commerce and familiarity with other Epicureans of his time and place, and hence could have drawn upon their texts and engagement with other philosophical schools, rather than toiling in isolation with access to nothing but Epicurus' own texts. Also, Epicureanism stresses the importance of friendship with like-minded people in obtaining a pleasant life, and Lucretius cared enough about his wider society that he wrote the *DRN* in order to try to bring more people into the Epicurean fold. Although possible, it would be anomalous for a committed Epicurean with an evangelical streak to wall himself off from local Epicureans.[7]

However, even if we grant this conjectural case for Lucretius' involvement with other contemporary Epicureans, it does not follow that he utilized any texts post-dating Epicurus. The proems in the *DRN* show that Lucretius idolizes Epicurus, and, as James Warren notes, Lucretius does not seem particularly interested in extended dialectical engagement with other philosophical schools; rather, his goal is to put forward the saving message of Epicurus as effectively as he can, and he engages with others on only a limited basis where doing so helps advance Epicurus' own position.[8] So even if Lucretius had access to more recent material and was aware of later Epicureans' disputes with the Stoics and Academic sceptics, it would be consistent with his aims to work exclusively with Epicurus' own texts when explaining Epicurean physics.

Turning to the *DRN* itself, the most obvious problem with ascertaining its sources is that we have access to almost none of the texts of either Epicurus or subsequent Epicureans that plausibly could be its sources to compare it against. The only complete texts by Epicurus we have on physics and celestial phenomena are the *Letter to Herodotus* and *Letter to Pythocles*, summary overviews too compressed to have been Lucretius'

---

[6] See Gale 1994: 89–90 for a brief review of the evidence that the poem is written 'in terms appropriate to a cultured and aristocratic audience'.

[7] For more on Epicureanism around the time of Lucretius see Sedley 2009; for a list of Romans who were (or might have been) Epicureans and the evidence for their allegiance see Castner 1988.

[8] Warren 2007: 21–2. As Warren notes, this lack of engagement includes philosophers prior to Epicurus, such as Plato and Theophrastus, that Epicurus himself engaged with. The major exceptions are Lucretius' refutations of Heraclitus, Empedocles and Anaxagoras in *DRN* 1.635–920. I discuss them below.

source. We have only bits and pieces recovered from Herculaneum of Epicurus' magnum opus, *On Nature*, and the text is for the most part highly fragmentary. The only later Epicurean for whom we have substantial texts is Philodemus, also recovered from Herculaneum. Although these texts are also incomplete and often fragmentary, we possess portions of several treatises that are in far better shape than what we currently have from Epicurus' *On Nature*.[9] However, these treatises generally deal with ethical topics that aren't covered at any length by Lucretius. Moreover, given how extensively Lucretius reworks material for his own poetic ends, it would probably be challenging to conclude with confidence that Lucretius was working from some treatise, even if further portions of Epicurus' *On Nature* or of Philodemus dealing with the same topics as the *DRN* were deciphered to the point where we could compare them.[10]

It is worth noting that even if we could make a match between a passage of the *DRN* and a potential source text, this may not settle the overall question of whether Lucretius is an Epicurean 'fundamentalist' or philosophically *au courant*. Let us presume for a moment that we were able to match a stretch of the *DRN* to a newly discovered and deciphered text from Epicurus' *On Nature*. That would be exciting, but it would not prove that Lucretius draws exclusively from Epicurus throughout the *DRN*.[11] The comparable scenario regarding Philodemus initially appears a little different: if we found a text of Philodemus that closely followed what Lucretius was saying, wouldn't that be enough to show that Lucretius at least sometimes

---

[9] See Gigante 1995 for a history of the recovery of the Herculaneum papyri. Some of the more complete and prominent treatises are Henry 2009, Konstan, Clay and Glad 1998 and Tsouna 2012, with facing Greek and English text. See Essler 2017 for an excellent compilation of modern editions of Philodemus.

[10] Challenging, but not impossible. The publication of the Strasbourg papyrus of Empedocles led David Sedley to issue a limited retraction (Sedley 2003b) of his earlier claim that Empedocles is only a poetic and not a philosophical source for Lucretius, as Lucretius does draw from Empedocles in a few places in his account of biology. In doing so, Sedley shows the careful linguistic work needed to ascertain that Lucretius is drawing from a particular text.

[11] Similar considerations apply to Sedley's claim that the overall organization of the *DRN* mirrors the organization of the first fifteen books of Epicurus' *On Nature*. (See chapter 4 of Sedley 1998, pp. 94–133, for Sedley's reconstruction of the overall plan of *On Nature*, and chapter 5, pp. 134–65, for his argument that Lucretius follows *On Nature*.) Sedley's case is conjectural – both because we are often unsure of the exact contents of *On Nature*, as Sedley admits, and also because Sedley claims that Lucretius was part way through a radical reorganization of the *DRN* upon his death to explain why the *DRN* closely follows the order of *On Nature* in some places and not in others. However, even if we grant that the initial organization of the *DRN* as a whole was modelled after *On Nature* prior to a partially completed reworking of its structure, that is consistent with Lucretius drawing upon other texts at particular points in the poem, e.g., in his discussions of why the world is not providentially organized for our benefit, or of the origins of species and the development of society. For further discussion of Sedley's approach see Morrison in this volume (pp. 161–4).

uses a later Epicurean as a source? Before drawing that conclusion, however, we would first need to rule out the possibility that each of them is drawing independently from a third source, such as Epicurus.

In the near-absence of such potential source texts, another way of trying to ascertain Lucretius' sources is to infer what they are from the content of the *DRN* alone. For instance, let us imagine that in his description of perception, Lucretius had included a detailed refutation of the doctrine that some (but not all) of our sense-impressions accurately and infallibly represent the objects they are from, and that such 'graspable' impressions form the foundation for our knowledge. We could conclude that such a refutation of a Stoic theory would have been drawn from later Epicurean polemics against the Stoics, even if we did not have access to the source Lucretius was using.

However, the *DRN* as we actually have it contains no such passages. It used to be thought that many of Lucretius' arguments were aimed against the Stoics, but David Furley has shown convincingly that these arguments could equally be aimed at philosophers preceding Epicurus (philosophers from whom the Stoics themselves probably drew).[12] For instance, Lucretius' argument that the flaws in the world show that it was not made by the gods for our benefit could apply in equal measure to the god of the Stoics and to the demiurge in Plato's *Timaeus*, and we have good reason to believe that the *DRN* specifically engages with the *Timaeus* in places.[13] Likewise, Lucretius' anti-teleological arguments that organs such as the heart have no function and that their apparent functionality should instead be attributed to a process of natural selection (4.823–57; 5.783–877) apply equally against the Stoics, Plato and Aristotle. To give a non-Stoic example, Lucretius argues that anybody who does not have confidence in the trustworthiness of the senses would have no basis for action (4.500–10). We know that precisely this charge was made against the Academic sceptic Arcesilaus by Colotes, a younger compatriot of Epicurus (Plut. *Adv. Col.* 1120c–d). But Epicurus himself made the same argument against Democriteans whose denial of the existence of sensible qualities like sweetness led them also to deny that the senses were trustworthy.[14] As we have it, Lucretius' argument could be drawn from either Colotes or from Epicurus, or again from some later Epicurean writing against the academic sceptic Carneades.

---

[12] Furley 1966.

[13] See Solmsen 1953 for an argument that Lucretius' account of the growth and decline of the cosmos draws upon and modifies the cosmology and biology of the *Timaeus*, and De Lacy 1983 for many other examples of Lucretius' engagement with the *Timaeus* and other Platonic dialogues.

[14] A recent overview of the texts and issues is Lee 2011; see O'Keefe 1997 for my own interpretation.

Given Lucretius' goals and approach in the *DRN*, absence of evidence for an *au courant* Lucretius should not be taken as evidence for his absence. As James Warren notes, Lucretius' overriding goal is to have his readers accept Epicurus' saving message, not to give an overview of the merits and demerits of various philosophical positions, and 'he will consider un-Epicurean ideas only if by doing so he can clarify the Epicurean truth or head off dangerous misunderstandings'.[15] Lucretius very seldom refers to philosophers other than Epicurus – besides referring to Democritus on three occasions (3.370–95, 3.1039–41, 5.621–36), his only extended engagement is with Heraclitus, Empedocles, and Anaxagoras, each of whose physical theories Lucretius brings in for (relatively) detailed refutation in *DRN* 1.635–920.[16] This exception to Lucretius' general practice can be explained by noting, as Warren does, that they represent 'the range of alternative conceptions of the fundamental elements of the universe' – i.e. monist, finite pluralist, and extreme pluralist – and that refuting their views suffices, in Lucretius' eyes, for refuting similar ontologies.[17] His usual procedure against other philosophers is to issue more generic 'catch-all' arguments, as Gordon Campbell dubs them – ones that can target both Platonist and Stoic providentialist theologies, teleological biologies of various stripes, and the positions of all of those who cast doubt on the senses as sources of knowledge.[18] Given this procedure, we would equally expect to find the sorts of arguments we do find in the *DRN*, whether or not Lucretius is drawing from Epicurus himself or from a later source.

Similar considerations of Lucretius' purposes undercut one of David Sedley's positive arguments for Lucretius either being ignorant of or deliberately ignoring all philosophical and scientific developments after Epicurus.[19] Sedley notes that Lucretius' argument regarding the nature and location of the mind entirely ignores medical advances after Epicurus' time, which had established that, if the mind has some seat in the body, that seat is in the head and not the chest. In fact, Lucretius specifically says that it would be equally ridiculous to suppose that the mind is in the head as in the feet (3.788–93). Unlike Lucretius, later Epicureans such as Demetrius of Laconia struggled with how to reconcile these advances with their respect for Epicurus' authority.[20]

---

[15] Warren 2007: 21.   [16] For the Latin text with a detailed commentary in Italian see Piazzi 2005.
[17] Warren 2007: 27.   [18] Campbell 1999.   [19] Sedley 1998: 68–72.
[20] For more on Epicurean reverence of their master and how it led to an unwillingness to contradict him see Sedley 1989b. However, this reverence did not make later Epicureanism philosophically stagnant, as demonstrated by the chapters in Fish and Sanders 2011.

This argument does have some weight, but I am not entirely convinced. First of all, even if we concede that Lucretius was ignorant of this particular issue, which had been debated by some contemporary Epicureans, I do not think we have enough information on how prominent it was in the general educated public to conclude that somebody ignorant of it must thereby have been ignorant of all philosophical and scientific advances post-Epicurus. (For example, Cicero, who never seemed to miss an opportunity to ridicule Epicurus for his mulish ignorance and later Epicureans for their slavish devotion to their master, did not criticize contemporary Epicureans for insisting that the *animus* is located in the chest.) And if Lucretius was aware of this debate, it is one that contemporary Epicureans were apparently divided on how to resolve, and getting into the weeds of such an unresolved intraparty dispute would derail Lucretius from his primary goal, which is to establish that the mind is a material organ and hence mortal. So if Lucretius decided simply to ignore one contentious contemporary dispute for that reason, this would not give much evidence of an across-the-board policy to ignore all post-Epicurus material.

So the question of Lucretius' philosophical sources is inconclusive and will probably remain so, because the evidence we have and that we might obtain is equally likely on either the fundamentalist or *au courant* positions. But I think that little hangs on answering the question, other than satisfying our intellectual curiosity. Let us imagine that, because of further discoveries from Herculaneum, we are able to establish conclusively the source for Lucretius' anti-providential argument from the flaws of the world – that it is drawn either from a stretch of Epicurus' *On Nature* that had been engaging with Plato's *Timaeus*, or from one of the recent Epicurean handbooks of theology that Cicero used when composing *De natura deorum*, which have the Stoics as one of their main targets. What difference would it make? In either case, Lucretius is still putting forward a rather general argument against the notion that our world is the creation of a god who is powerful, wise and loving, which is precisely where we stood before the discovery. The 'catch-all' character of Lucretius' arguments, which makes it difficult to ascertain their sources, also means that finding their precise sources doesn't much matter for understanding them. It also means that, even if we were able to establish that a recent Epicurean handbook was the source of Lucretius' arguments, this discovery would probably add little to our understanding of Stoic theology.

Furthermore, even if we could establish that Epicurus himself is Lucretius' only philosophical source, it does not follow that Lucretius' arguments target only contemporaries and predecessors of Epicurus. As an educated Roman, Lucretius was surely aware of Stoicism, and there are some places in the *DRN* that are plausibly taken to refer to the Stoics.[21] At 5.22–54, Lucretius favourably compares Epicurus' revelations to the deeds of Heracles, who was one of the heroes to the Stoics. At 2.600–60, Lucretius first enumerates the ways in which the Earth has been regarded as a divine Mother before warning against the dangers of allegorically applying traditional myths to natural processes, a Stoic practice which contemporary Epicureans criticized, as in Cic. *Nat. D.* 1.40. Lucretius' audience also knew of the Stoics and the Academic sceptics, and this knowledge will have mediated their reception of the *DRN*. In that context, if Lucretius came across an argument in Epicurus that criticized Plato's *Timaeus* based on the flaws of the world, and used that argument in his own poem when arguing that the world is not the creation of a benevolent deity, then Epicurus' argument thereby becomes a rebuttal of Stoic theology, too. Likewise, if Lucretius drew upon an 'inaction' argument against scepticism by Epicurus, one that was directed at sceptical atomists like Metrodorus in particular, that argument would thereby also become an argument against the Academic sceptics.[22]

Innovation: Lucretius and the Psychology of Philosophical Persuasion

In this section, I turn from the question of what precisely Lucretius' philosophical sources were to the question of how Lucretius' use of these sources in his poetry may establish him as a distinctive philosopher in his own right. Lucretius has been considered a great poet, and a vital source for the philosophy of Epicurus, but not as a philosopher in his own right. The obvious reason for not considering Lucretius as a philosopher is that he says he is indeed following in the footsteps of his master Epicurus and transmitting his doctrines (*DRN* 3.3–4, 5.55–6). But I do not think that this bars us from considering Lucretius as a distinctive philosopher. Before making my case regarding Lucretius, let me briefly sketch out an instructive parallel case, that of Cicero.

Like Lucretius, Cicero was long treated mainly as a source of information for the arguments and positions of other philosophers, such as Arcesilaus, Carneades, the Stoics and the Epicureans. As with Lucretius,

---

[21] These examples are from Campbell 1999. See also Gee in Chapter 10 of this volume.
[22] Fowler 2000b: 140 makes a similar point. See Fowler 2000b for more on the relationship between source-texts and reception in understanding Lucretius' literary references.

this reductive assessment of Cicero as a philosopher arises from his claim that his philosophical dialogues did not contain much original argumentation (*Att.* 12.52.3).[23] Instead, when composing them, he used the handbooks of various schools as his source for arguments, translating them into Latin and supplying a dramatic setting and conversation between spokesmen representing the various schools.[24] But there has been an increasing trend towards treating Cicero as a significant philosopher in his own right. This trend has developed in at least three distinct ways.

The first way is to claim that Cicero has staked out significant philosophical positions and arguments of his own, and not merely transmitted the positions and arguments of others. In his *On Laws*, for instance, Cicero presents a theory about the relationship of law to ethics that is indebted to the Stoics but is still very much his own, and one that has a significant impact on the Natural Law tradition.[25] This line of argument is not promising when it comes to Lucretius, as he says at *DRN* 3.1–30 that he is not trying to compete with Epicurus in discovering anything new, but is transmitting the golden truths that have been revealed to him by Epicurus, his 'father' (9 *tu pater es*).[26]

The second way is to claim that while Cicero's basic philosophical positions may often be drawn from others, if we attend to the specific manner in which he articulates them, given his own social standing and interests, we shall see that the exact content of these positions is distinctive. For instance, Cicero harshly criticizes the Epicureans for subordinating virtue to pleasure, and the basic shape of his critique is appropriated from the Stoics.[27] However, Pamela Gordon has argued that, for Cicero, *virtus* is not merely generic human 'virtue', but a particularly Roman ideal

---

[23] Striker 1995 contains a good summary of the reasons for not thinking highly of Cicero as a philosopher, along with useful pushback against them, and Schmidt 1978–9 gives an account of how Cicero fell into philosophical disrepute, after previous esteem, on account of his unoriginality.

[24] It is worth noting that Cicero himself (correctly) considered his coinages for Greek philosophical terms – 'teaching philosophy to speak Latin' as he put it (*Tusc.* 2.3) – to be among his most important contributions.

[25] A good recent article on this topic is Asmis 2008b. For an excellent recent example of presenting Cicero's philosophy as a whole on its own terms, without attempting to titrate out what is original from what is not, see Woolf 2015.

[26] Volk 2002: 107–12 argues that Lucretius is 'paradoxically' claiming not to compete with Epicurus *as a poet*. She cites the imagery used in 3.3–8, comparing Epicurus to a swan and a racehorse, animals symbolizing poetic activity. But the wider context of *DRN* 3.1–30 makes it clear that Lucretius is praising Epicurus for illuminating the blessings of life (3.2) and as a discoverer whose reasoning proclaims the nature of things and drives away our terrors (3.9–17), and it is in this arena that Lucretius is not competing with Epicurus but merely imitating him.

[27] He criticizes the Epicureans on this basis in many places, but the most sustained critique is in *Fin.* 2, especially *Fin.* 2.45–77.

linked, both etymologically and conceptually, to *manliness*. For Cicero, identifying pain as the greatest evil is not merely immoral but 'emasculating and effeminate'.[28] For Lucretius, this line of inquiry is more promising than the first: for instance, it could be argued plausibly that in the particular way he depicts the horrors of civil strife (1.29–43, 3.48–93, 5.1120–50, 6.1282–6), Lucretius puts a distinctive spin on the Epicurean ideal of security from danger.

The final way is to look not at the particular arguments and positions within Cicero's works but at the literary form he uses to present them. Cicero writes dialogues in which the spokesmen for various philosophical schools put forward their arguments on topics such as the nature of the gods and the highest good, and while these dialogues consist mainly of long stretches of exposition, the participants do get to question and criticize one another. Cicero's use of the dialogue form is not merely a convenient and user-friendly way of transmitting various arguments to his Roman audience. It reflects his own conviction as an Academic sceptic that a person should engage in inquiry by undogmatically considering all of the pertinent arguments on a topic. Cicero also often puts himself within his dialogues as a character, where he expresses his own opinions about the strengths and weaknesses of the positions articulated – not in order to convince his audience to agree with him by an appeal to his authority, but to show that, as an undogmatic Academic, he is still free to give his provisional assent to whatever seems to him to be the most reasonable position after engaging in inquiry. If we look merely at the arguments and positions within Cicero and ignore his manner of presenting them, we will miss something important about Cicero as a distinctive philosopher.[29]

This last is the kind of case I will pursue in respect of the *DRN*: the way Lucretius uses poetry to present Epicurean arguments is as *philosophically* significant as the way Cicero uses the dialogue to present the arguments of various schools. As is well known, Lucretius himself explains his choice of poetry to express his arguments by comparing himself to a doctor (1.935–50, 4.10–25): in order to persuade a child to drink some nasty-tasting medicine, a doctor will smear the lip of the cup with honey; likewise, says Lucretius, many people find attending to philosophical arguments unpleasant, and so he coats the healing message of Epicurus in poetry in order to make it go down more easily. Working through

---

[28] Gordon 2012: 111 in a chapter (pp. 109–38) on Cicero's gendered polemics against the Epicureans.
[29] For a good brief explanation of Cicero's use of the dialogue form along these lines see Annas 2001: x–xvii. For in-depth consideration of Cicero's use of the dialogue form see Schofield 2008.

explanations of how magnets work or demonstrating the atomic basis for hunger can be tedious and difficult, but the aesthetic pleasure of reading well-crafted poetry helps keep you going. On this model, the persuasive work is done entirely by the arguments, with the poetry playing only an ancillary role of helping you attend to the arguments.

However, this view of what Lucretius accomplishes with his poetry risks selling him short. The *DRN* is filled with literary and rhetorical methods of persuasion. Without giving a complete catalogue of these, let us note a few salient examples before considering their philosophical significance.

Using Vivid Imagery to Evoke Emotions

One of the primary tasks of the *DRN* is to get its readers to abandon their allegiance to traditional Greco-Roman religion. The opening of the poem contains a full-throated condemnation of the evils such religion has caused (1.80–101). But Lucretius does not merely list these evils and explain how religion causes them; instead, he gives a heartrending description of the sacrifice of Iphigenia by her father Agamemnon in order to appease the anger of Artemis. This description evokes pity for Iphigenia and indignation at Agamemnon, so that the reader shares Lucretius' outrage.[30] Another example occurs in Lucretius' description of sex. The Epicureans hold that sexual intercourse never helped anybody, and a person is lucky if they are not harmed by it (Diog. Laert. 10.118). Lucretius condemns in particularly strong terms romantic infatuation, which distorts a person's judgement and leads to the neglect of duty. In the course of his denunciation, Lucretius presents a disturbing description of frenzied, infatuated lovers having sex, in which they intermingle their saliva and crush lips with teeth, making their consummation seem repellent and disgusting (4.1037–191).[31]

Raising and Redeploying Powerful Cultural Tropes

Lucretius uses a wide range of metaphors in his eulogies of Epicurus. One of the more surprising is that Lucretius describes the theoretical intellectual

---

[30] Morrison 2013 shows how Lucretius evokes emotions here and in other passages describing death, and he explains how the evoked emotions are supposed to help persuade his readers to accept the Epicurean message.

[31] That Lucretius condemns romantic love and depicts the sex of infatuated lovers in a repellent way does not entail that he similarly condemns all forms of love or sex. See Arenson 2016; Brown 1987: 60–100, and the sources in n. 41 below.

activities of Epicurus, who investigated the causes of natural phenomena, in terms of the deeds of epic heroes (1.62–79): when we were grovelling in the dust under the weight of traditional religion, Epicurus dared to raise his eyes to challenge it. He boldly burst through the gates of nature and roamed throughout the cosmos in order to cast down traditional religion at our feet and liberate us from it.[32] Elsewhere Lucretius maintains that what Epicurus has done for us is far greater than any of the deeds of Heracles (5.22–54). In these passages, then, Lucretius evokes the awe and admiration we feel at the courageous actions of epic heroes and redirects them toward a quite different object. Another surprising comparison by Lucretius is his extended description of the earth as a mother-goddess, awesome and worthy of respect – a metaphor he defends using, even though he immediately adds that the metaphor is dangerous and literally false, as the earth is not divine and not sentient (2.594–660). Here, then, Lucretius evokes the feelings of awe people have towards the earth conceived of as a mother-goddess and redirects them towards the earth as understood by the Epicureans – as a non-sentient and non-purposive conglomeration of matter.[33]

Ridicule

Besides eliminating the fear of the gods, the other main task of the *DRN* is eliminating the fear of death. This is done by showing that death is annihilation, and hence not bad for us. One of Lucretius' targets is the Pythagorean and Platonic theory of there being a soul which survives the death of the body and lives again when it unites with a new body, in a cycle of reincarnation. Lucretius presents a wide array of arguments against the theory, but he also mocks it. He says that it is ridiculous to imagine innumerable immortal souls gathering around a pair of rutting animals, jostling one another in order to be the first one in when new life is conceived; he then suggests that maybe the souls avoid this conflict by agreeing to a 'first come, first served' policy (3.776–83). Here, Lucretius would discredit the theory of transmigration by making it look silly.[34]

---

[32] For detailed consideration of this metaphor see Buchheit 1971. For further discussion of this passage in this volume see O'Rourke in Chapter 5 (pp. 108–10, 118), Shearin in Chapter 7 (pp. 146–8), Asmis in Chapter 12 (pp. 257–8) and Kennedy in Chapter 13 (pp. 279–80).

[33] For a much more in-depth treatment of Lucretius' usage of these mythological tropes that partially overlaps with the approach taken in this chapter, see Gale 1994, esp. 129–55. See Taylor 2016 for a detailed examination of how Lucretius uses allusions to comedy and tragedy in the theatre, including the sacrifice of Iphigenia, in his mission to relieve his readers of false and damaging beliefs.

[34] See Gellar 2012 for much more on Lucretius' use of ridicule and satire.

That Lucretius uses such literary and rhetorical methods of persuasion is, I trust, uncontroversial. But this still leaves open the question of their philosophical significance. It might be thought that Lucretius' use of non-rational methods of persuasion such as appealing to emotions and ridicule is non-philosophical, or perhaps even anti-philosophical. After all, the appeal to pity is a fallacy, and concluding that the doctrine of transmigration is false because a mocking and unfair depiction of it makes it seem silly would be invalid.

If this charge that Lucretius is anti-philosophical is warranted, he would be guilty of the same intellectual crime that Martha Nussbaum accuses the Epicureans generally of committing.[35] Nussbaum claims that the Epicureans are willing to use effective but irrational methods of persuasion. This willingness is based on their therapeutic conception of argumentation, combined with their hedonistic conception of the human good. Epicurus holds that philosophy produces mental health (*SV* 54), and the Epicureans compare philosophy to medicine, as we have seen above: just as the value of medicine derives entirely from its effectiveness in driving out bodily disease, so too the value of a philosophical argument derives entirely from its effectiveness in driving out diseases of the mind (Porph. *Ad Marc.* 31). But the Epicureans conceive of happiness as consisting in freedom from pain, especially freedom from fear, regret and other forms of mental turmoil. Unlike Aristotle, the Epicureans do not think that being rational is *per se* a good thing for a human being, and so an Epicurean has no reason to respect the rationality of her interlocutors, if using irrational means of persuasion is effective at promoting their peace of mind.[36] Nussbaum claims that, if we look at the actual practices recommended and followed by the Epicureans, we will see that they are in fact willing to violate the norms of rational discourse for the sake of therapeutic effectiveness.[37]

---

[35] Nussbaum 1986.

[36] Similar considerations underlie the Epicurean doctrine of 'multiple explanations'. To have peace of mind, we must have absolute confidence that cosmological and meteorological phenomena are not due to the will the gods, and physics supplies us with the arguments we need to exclude the gods from the cosmos (*Ep. Hdt.* 76–8). However, knowing the exact explanation of these phenomena does not much matter, as long as we know that there is *some* sort of natural explanation (*Ep. Hdt.* 79–80; *Ep. Pyth.* 85–8). Because of this, the Epicureans are content to go through lists of possible explanations of things like eclipses without settling on which one is correct (*Ep. Pyth.* 92–115; *DRN* 5.592–770), as knowledge is not *per se* valuable. For more see Hankinson 2013.

[37] Some of these practices include threats of shunning, informing on wrongdoers, and encouragement of an uncritical adulation of authority figures. Nussbaum's main source for such practices is Philodemus' treatise *On Frank Criticism*, although she draws upon Epicurus himself and Lucretius too. Tsouna 2007: 91–118 offers a useful overview of Philodemus' treatise, and argues against some of Nussbaum's characterizations of Philodemus' therapeutic practices.

But a willingness to use rationally dubious methods of persuasion, even if it initially seems warranted, does not fit with other important commitments of the Epicureans, and of Lucretius in particular. One of Lucretius' repeated refrains is that we must study the underlying principles of nature in order to dispel the terrifying darkness that covers our minds (1.146–8, 2.59–61, 3.91–3, 6.39–41),[38] and Epicurus thinks that only the wise person is unshakably persuaded of anything (Plut. *Adv. Col.* 1117f). So if I believe that transmigration is false, but I have that conviction only because a mocking description of the cycle of rebirth made the doctrine seem silly, such a conviction will not serve as the secure foundation for the peace of mind that I need. Instead, I must understand the reasons why the *animus* is material, and hence mortal, which will include understanding the reasons for rejecting the doctrine of transmigration. Lucretius does not merely mock the doctrine of transmigration; he also gives arguments against it.

The question, then, is whether we can reconcile Lucretius' use of the literary and rhetorical methods of persuasion outlined above with his insistence that we need to have a reasoned understanding of the workings of the world in order to secure happiness. Happily, I think that Epicurean ethical views generally, and Lucretius' views on human psychology in particular, enable precisely this reconciliation.

The Epicureans believe that, as members of a sick society, we have absorbed false beliefs and misguided attitudes that make us suffer. We think that money and social status are the keys to happiness, and we envy the unscrupulous businessman who manages to get ahead. We revere jealous and capricious gods who are not worthy of such reverence. Lucretius adds to this the observation that we do not know ourselves well, that we are often driven by subconscious beliefs and desires. The man who recoils in horror at the thought of his body being torn limb from limb by a pack of wild dogs may believe that he believes that death is annihilation, but his horror shows that unconsciously he still has some unacknowledged belief that a part of him survives his death (3.870–93). Another man is bored, restless and dissatisfied, dashing back and forth from his mansion to his country home – he does not know the cause of his illness, an illness rooted in his fear of death (3.1053–75).[39]

---

[38] I see no need to explain the repetition of these lines by saying that the *DRN* is unfinished. Instead, Lucretius deliberately deploys these lines as a *leitmotif* to reaffirm the fundamental justification for the poem as a whole. On these lines and those which precede see also Taylor in Chapter 3 and Kennedy in Chapter 13 of this volume (pp. 69, 268).

[39] For more on the topic of Lucretius on unconscious motivation see Jope 1983.

These false beliefs and misguided attitudes, ones that are often subconscious, get in the way of accepting the healing message of Epicurus. Lucretius himself worries that Memmius might view Epicureanism as impious and sinful – and Epicureanism does indeed run counter to popular Roman views on the nature of the gods and the place of pleasure in the good life (*DRN* 1.80–3). I propose that Lucretius uses literary and rhetorical methods of persuasion to counter such beliefs and attitudes so that his reader will then be open to the arguments he presents. Viewed in this way, these methods do not displace argumentation; instead, they work together with it. Let me briefly discuss how this would work in the examples I have given above.

A typical Roman, even if they do not believe in the literal truth of all of the traditional stories about the gods, probably has a reflexive and deep-grained reverence for the gods as traditionally depicted.[40] They will be aware of the mythical stories such as Agamemnon sacrificing Iphigenia, but they've never been bothered much by them. (The same may be said in our culture of Yahweh ordering the Jews to commit genocide against the Canaanites.) In order to break through this harmful cultural conditioning, Lucretius vividly portrays what this mythical story really involves, in order to bring home its horror. The emotional reactions of pity and indignation that Lucretius' poetry produces are apt, and they do not produce an ungrounded and irrational belief in the evils that religion causes. Instead, they help counter an irrational complacency that the reader had before, a culturally induced deadening of their sensibilities.

Similar considerations can explain Lucretius' mockery of transmigration. Many people probably approach the doctrine of transmigration with a misplaced sense of respect and reverence. The idea that the soul could move from life to life can seem sublime, and befitting the dignity of the soul. Making fun of the doctrine helps to deflate this misguided sense of awe, lessening a person's emotional attachment to the doctrine, and hence rendering them more open to the arguments Lucretius offers against it.

---

[40] The religious positions of Romans at this time were a complicated mix, and picking out typical religious views is not easy. See Gale 1994: 85–98 for more on the topic. She concludes that belief in the literal truth of 'superstitious' myths regarding the gods may have been widespread among the lower classes, although it is hard to tell, but seemed to be relatively rare among the elite. However, even the elites generally regarded historical myths (e.g., about the deeds of the founders of Rome) as accurate. But even among the elite, the traditional stories regarding the gods were generally treated with respect as an important part of civic *religio*. Lucretius would have been strongly opposed both to a belief in the literal truth of such myths and to an attitude of respect towards such myths as cultural touchstones.

In the case of romantic love, maudlin popular celebrations of it will lead people to view it with a sentimental attachment, and a person in the throes of infatuation may even think of the consummation of their love in quasi-divine terms, as in Aristophanes' myth of erotic reunification in Plato's *Symposium*. Lucretius' harsh and debunking depiction of infatuated lovers as frenzied and dissatisfied animals acts as a corrective to such attitudes.[41]

There is also a broad strain of anti-intellectualism in Greek and Roman culture, which often celebrates virile men of action and accomplishment, while pitying the impractical philosopher with his head in the clouds. Callicles' denunciation of philosophy as unfitting for a grown man (Pl. *Grg.* 484c–486d) and the story of Thales falling into a well as he was gazing at the stars (Diog. Laert. 2.4–5, Pl. *Tht.* 174a) exemplify such an attitude. For Lucretius, this gets things deeply wrong: while he would have some sympathy for criticism of otherworldly philosophers who disdain the material world, the intellectual work of Epicurus has a tremendous practical impact. Accordingly, in his poetry Lucretius evokes the trope of the epic hero and redirects the admiration it elicits to a more appropriate object.

Finally, Lucretius' depiction of the earth as mother-goddess is only one of a number of passages in which he surprisingly deploys the figures of traditional religion or otherwise personifies nature: the most conspicuous example is the invocation of Venus at the start of the poem (1.1–43); in Book 3, nature herself chastises those who fear death (3.931–77). Of course, Lucretius is doing multiple things by deploying these images, and he need not have a single set of purposes across all of these passages. But one purpose he might have, in line with the view I have been sketching here, is to help convince his reader that atomism need not lead to the disenchantment of nature.

Many people view nature with a combination of wonder, awe and fear. Unless we have a proper account of the nature of things, these feelings can be dangerous, leading us in our ignorance to attribute the workings of the world to the gods (*DRN* 5.1183–240). For most of his audience, these feelings are now bound up with false religion or with viewing nature anthropomorphically. While Lucretius argues that the earth and celestial bodies are not sentient or divine (5.110–45), he shares his audience's feelings of wonder before nature and thinks they are perfectly appropriate. At *DRN* 2.1030–7, Lucretius says that nothing more marvellous than the

---

[41] For detailed (and contrasting) assessments of Lucretius' condemnation of romantic love see Nussbaum 1994: 140–91 and Gordon 2002.

spectacle of the sun, moon and stars can be imagined, but familiarity has deadened us to its wonders, and at 3.28–30 he says that having the workings of the world revealed to him by Epicurus fills him with a 'divine pleasure' (*divina voluptas*) and a 'shuddering' or 'trembling awe' (*horror*).[42] By evoking the feelings of awe bound up with traditional tropes like viewing the earth as our mother, and transferring them to the dancing of atoms in the void, Lucretius helps blunt one possible source of resistance to accepting Epicureanism: the sense that the Epicurean view of the world is cold, mechanical and shorn of wonder.[43] To evoke these feelings in the course of explaining the Epicurean worldview is much more effective than just giving an argument for the conclusion that there is no impropriety in believing that the heavenly bodies are insentient and at the same time beholding them with awe.

Whether Epicurus is Lucretius' only philosophical source or he draws upon others, the way in which he uses his philosophical sources is informed by an understanding of human psychology and of the point of philosophical argumentation. As noted above, Epicurus stresses that the point of philosophical arguments is to help heal people from the psychic diseases of false beliefs, empty desires, and destructive emotions. Philodemus, in his *On Frank Criticism*, discusses in detail how an Epicurean pedagogue will take into account a person's particular psychological profile when interacting with them.[44] In his *On Anger* he says that sometimes imagery is more effective therapeutically than argumentation: a person prone to harmful bouts of anger may not appreciate how badly off they are if their philosophical 'doctor' merely reasons to them about the effects of anger, whereas if the doctor brings the badness of anger before their eyes via a vivid depiction of its effects, he will make them eager to be treated.[45]

But Epicurus' *On Nature* and the works we have of Philodemus are standard philosophical treatises. Philodemus describes how a pedagogue may use imagery as a tool of persuasion, but he doesn't employ this tool

---

[42] On the sublime in these and similar passages see further O'Rourke in this volume (pp. 115–17).

[43] For more on this topic see O'Keefe 2003: 57–60. Good overall considerations of Lucretius' non-theistic conception of the 'sublime', and how it connects to the history of the sublime, are Most 2012 and Porter 2007.

[44] For instance, he will have to decide whether to use mild or stringent reproofs and how much praise to mix in alongside criticism, and these decisions will be based on both his experience of how a person's age, social standing and gender affect the way they react to criticism, and on his knowledge of the individual. For more detail see Tsouna 2007: 91–125.

[45] *De Ira* IV 4–19. For more on this technique see Tsouna 2007: 204–9, and more generally on the treatise *On Anger*, pp. 195–238.

much in what we have of his writing. Epicurus does show some sensitivity for communicating his ideas effectively to a wide audience: the *Principal Doctrines* are handy for memorizing especially important points of Epicurean dogma, and Epicurus notes that the *Letter to Herodotus* was composed as a summary of the main points of Epicurean physics for those unable to work through the long treatises (*Ep. Hdt.* 35–6). Yet the *Letter to Herodotus* is a strictly unadorned presentation of doctrines and arguments, and moreover one that is at points desperately obscure for any audience of beginners. In his use of literary and rhetorical methods of persuasion alongside his argumentation, Lucretius alone among the Epicureans shows a sensitivity for needing to present his arguments in a way that also takes into account the biases, stereotypes, and other psychological factors that hinder his audience from accepting the healing gospel of Epicurus. In this respect, the *DRN* is a more effective embodiment of Epicureanism than anything written by Epicurus.

CHAPTER 10

The Rising and Setting Soul in Lucretius, De Rerum Natura 3

Emma Gee

Stars and Souls

As disciples of the Epicurean worldview, we must draw the unsettling conclusion that even Epicurus is mortal (*DRN* 3.1042–4):[1]

> ipse Epicurus obit decurso lumine vitae,
> qui genus humanum ingenio superavit et omnis
> restinxit, stellas exortus ut aetherius sol.

Epicurus himself died, once his life's light had run its course; even though he surpassed the human race in intellect, and put everyone in the shade, like the incandescent sun does the stars, once it's risen.

Lucretius configures Epicurus' life as the 'course' of a great flaming heavenly body: at his birth (rising), he obliterated the stars, other human intellects.[2] When his life had followed its course to the end (*de-curso*), those other intellects – unseen until then because, like stars by the light of the sun, they were obscured by the dazzling brightness of Epicurus' mind – appeared as do stars at their first helical rising, tentatively twinkling out from their previous bright obfuscation.

Epicurus' mind is analogous to the most prominent and most symbolic of the heavenly bodies, the sun. The minds or souls of other human beings are like the other stars. This passage on Epicurus' death is merely the climax of the coupling between souls and stars that, in fact, is a running analogy *throughout* the exegesis of the soul in Book 3 of the *De Rerum Natura (DRN)*. In what follows I shall draw out this analogy as it appears elsewhere in the book, and explore its meaning in the light, as it were, of

Thanks to Donncha O'Rourke, the *divina mens* of this volume, and to the readers at Cambridge University Press, especially 'Reader B'.

[1] Text of Lucretius from Bailey 1947. All translations in this chapter are my own.

[2] For the etymology ('atomology') of Epicurus here (*currere* being cognate with ἐπίκουρος, 'ally' or 'mercenary soldier') see Snyder 1978: 229–30 and 1980: 108. See also O'Rourke in this volume (p. 114 n. 57).

Epicurean philosophy, but also in relation to philosophies which Lucretius, as an Epicurean, was seeking to eclipse.

Kinship between souls and stars is a prominent idea in the intelligent-design philosophies of antiquity, Platonism and Stoicism.[3] Its definitive statement is in Plato's *Timaeus*, where each soul is said to originate from the star designated for it by the demiurge, to which it will eventually return after its temporary embodiment in this life (*Ti.* 41d4–42d5). Writing only a few years after Lucretius' *DRN*, Cicero in the *Somnium Scipionis* neatly stitches together Platonism and Stoicism to form his exposition of the connection between souls and stars (Cic. *Rep.* 6.15):[4]

> And to these people a soul (*animus*) was given from out of those everlasting fires which you call the stars and planets (*sidera et stellas*), which, rounded and spherical, charged with divine mind (*divinibus animatae mentibus*), complete their orbits and whorls with astonishing swiftness.

Cicero combines the best of both worlds, harmonizing his translation of Plato's *Republic* with the concepts of Stoicism. As in Plato, the *animus* is lent to people from the heavenly bodies. But Cicero's heavenly bodies are animated by a divine mind which looks suspiciously Stoic. *Divina mens*, a collocation Cicero will often give his Stoic speaker in the *De natura deorum*, is almost a *terminus technicus* used to designate the divine creative principle of the Stoic universe.[5] Soul, by virtue of its heavenly kinship, necessarily partakes of order, sharing in the harmony of the spheres, as expounded by Cicero in the *Somnium Scipionis*, as well as sharing in the harmonizing *divina mens* of Stoic thought.

None of this applies, of course, to Lucretius. Lucretius' soul is not a singular guiding intelligence, analogous to the Stoic *divina mens*, but a more disparate entity. When Lucretius refers to the *animus* and *anima* it is always implied that we are to take them as a complex, i.e. as differentiated entities of mind and soul acting together as a unit.[6] His most characteristic expression when describing them is the conjunctive *animi natura animaeque* (e.g., 3.212), which I translate as 'the nub of the intelligence and the

[3] Thom 2006: 62: 'The notion of kinship between gods and humans was widely established in antiquity' – except, of course, in the atomist traditions.
[4] My translation. The *De re publica* was written between 54 and 51 BC and made public in 51 (see Zetzel 1995: 1–3). Cicero's knowledge of, indeed admiration for, the *DRN* is clear from the famous letter of 54 BC, *Q Fr.* 2.10 (9), no. 14 ed. Shackleton Bailey 1980. See Sedley 1998: 1; Gee 2013: 61; Henderson 2016: 453; Morrison in this volume (p. 175).
[5] Cf., e.g., *Nat. D.* 2.80 *efficitur omnia regi divina mente atque prudentia*, 'it's brought about that all [the heavenly bodies] are ruled by divine intelligence and providence'.
[6] Lucretius describes the mind-soul complex at *DRN* 3.136–60. On Epicurean views of the '*animus–anima* complex' see Gill 2006: 46–66.

soul'. They are the two things which, in conjunction with the body, make us who we are. The mind takes precedence in terms of control (3.138–9):

> sed caput esse quasi et dominari in corpore toto
> consilium quod nos animum mentemque vocamus.

But that power of reasoning we call intelligence and mind is – so to speak – the head, in that it is in charge throughout the body.

The soul is the vital force distributed throughout the body responsible for sensation. Most importantly, the mind and soul are mortal: they are born, and they die (3.417–8 *nativos animantibus et mortalis | esse animos animasque*). On the latter point, Lucretius is emphatic (e.g., 3.543 *mortalem tamen esse animam fateare necesse*, 'But you have to admit that the soul is mortal').

Lucretius as an Epicurean reacts against the Platonic and Stoic understandings of the soul and the universe.[7] In Platonism the soul is designed by the gods to mirror a universe which is an expression of intelligent design. In Stoicism the soul is the rational part of mankind, akin to the heavenly bodies, themselves made of πῦρ τεχνικόν, designing fire, the principle which orders the universe.[8] Lucretius' opposition to these ideas doesn't mean there is *no* connection between soul and universe, however. In a sense, from the Platonic and Stoic perspective of the soul's uniqueness, there is *too much* of a connection, since in Epicurean thought the boundaries between soul and the rest of the world are blurred. Epicurus said ψυχὴ φύσις τις εἶναι, 'the soul [is] nature', or, '*a* nature' (fr. 32 Arrighetti). This is not 'nature' as we use the word, for instance of the 'nature' of a person, but 'an organic growth' like a plant that grows and dies.[9] For Lucretius, as an Epicurean, souls and stars share the same nature, but not in the Platonic or Stoic sense. They are not 'akin' in the sense of sharing rationality and immortality, rather they are made of the same material components.

If Lucretius' soul is not a microcosm of any intelligent-design system of order, neither is Lucretius' universe, nor his stars. In Epicurean astronomy, the configurations of the heavens are temporary, idiosyncratic and causally indeterminate.[10] Astronomy is good, for the Epicurean, *not* because of any

---

[7] It is an established view that both Epicurus and Lucretius are reacting against the Platonic tradition: see Arrighetti 1973: 602–3; Sedley 1998: 75–8, 152–3. Although Lucretius does not explicitly name the Stoics, his arguments very often imply them, as I have illustrated in Gee 2016.
[8] On the stars in Stoicism as πῦρ τεχνικόν see Thom 2006: 77.
[9] Arrighetti 1973: 321 with discussion at 624.
[10] See Epicurus, *Ep. Hdt.* 76b, quoted and discussed in Gee 2016: 115.

divine providence which it evinces, but by virtue of the very fact that more than one explanation is possible for phenomena; we just don't know, for instance, why some stars move more slowly, some more quickly, or whether eclipses of the sun and moon are produced by the interposition of another heavenly body or by extinction of the one in question. It is the act of speculation – not ruling things out *prima facie*, not worrying about finding a definitive cause or the apparent *lack* of a system – which provides reassurance.

Lucretius' take on astronomy is set out in *DRN* 5. His agenda is to convince us that the stars are *not* divine or immortal (5.302–5):[11]

> sic igitur solem lunam stellasque putandum
> ex alio atque alio lucem iactare subortu
> et primum quicquid flammarum perdere semper;
> inviolabilia haec ne credas forte vigere.

So you have to think that the sun, moon and stars throw out their light from now one, now another wellspring, and that they always shed whatever part of the fire comes first: in case you believe that these things flourish impregnable.

For Lucretius, the sun, moon and stars are ephemera: they arise anew each day and each day decay. This is a far cry from their Stoic role as 'designing fire'. Like the soul, Lucretius' heavens are mortal, their guiding forces often invisible or ineffable, not susceptible to a unitary explanation. In fact, in the *DRN* the motions of the heavenly bodies are often open to multiple explanations (e.g., the movements of the sun at 5.614–20; and of the moon at 5.705–30).[12]

Since everything in Lucretius' Epicurean universe shares the atomic nature of everything else, the special similarity between souls and stars is all the more worth marking, given how much is made of a connection between stars and souls in opposing traditions. It is these opposing traditions which concern us as here, since, paradoxically at first sight, they provide Lucretius' target in his polemical revision of the connection between souls and stars.

Despite a certain orthodoxy which decrees that Lucretius' work was not informed by contemporary debates between the Hellenistic philosophical schools,[13] it has been shown fairly conclusively that the *DRN* starts out by

---

[11] On Lucretius' astronomy see Gee 2013: 57–80.
[12] On Epicurean multiple explanations, including of astronomy, see Hardie 2009: 232 and 234; Hankinson 2013.
[13] See Sedley 1998: 65: 'Does the *De rerum natura*, the most brilliant philosophical composition to survive from its period, reflect the highly charged philosophical atmosphere of mid first-century BC

engaging with Cleanthes' *Hymn to Zeus*.[14] In this central Stoic text we find the idea of the interconnectedness of mankind and god, i.e. of soul and cosmos (since, for the Stoics, the human soul is made of creative fire, and god is also the fiery creative force of the world, the κοινὸς λόγος or πῦρ τεχνικόν). In particular, line 4 of the *Hymn* says something like 'for we have our origin in you [Zeus], bearing a likeness to god' (ἐκ σοῦ γὰρ γενόμεθα θεοῦ μίμημα λαχόντες).[15] The connections between this *Hymn* and the hymnic opening of the *DRN*, then, signal Lucretius' response to a text which is an evangelical pronouncement of ideas about mankind and the universe which are apparently in stark opposition to his own. Opinion differs as to the nature of these connections, but whether they are accounted for as thematic similarities or verbal borrowing,[16] they produce the effect of a competitive *aemulatio* in Lucretius' approach to Cleanthes.

The heavens in Lucretius will prove to be a particular node of opposition to Stoicism, but Lucretius' hymn to Venus begins by referring to the heavens in deceptively 'Cleanthean' terms.[17] The allegorical reading of Venus required by Lucretius' hymn presents the same problem as the *Hymn to Zeus*,[18] where a prayer section (lines 32–9) sets up an ambiguity between Zeus as an abstract cosmic principle, who can't be addressed in person, and Zeus as a traditional god, with divine ears.[19] For Cleanthes 'the whole universe, spinning around the earth, truly obeys you (*sc.* Zeus) wherever you lead' (7–8 σοὶ δὴ πᾶς ὅδε κόσμος ἑλισσόμενος περὶ γαῖαν | πείθεται ᾗ κεν ἄγῃς), just as Lucretius addresses 'fruitful Venus, you who under the sliding signs of heaven fill up the navigable sea, the crop-heavy earth' (1.2–4 *alma Venus, caeli subter labentia signa | quae mare navigerum,*

Italy? Amazingly, it does not.' This position is reflected particularly in Sedley's section on 'Contemporary Stoicism' (pp. 82–5). *Contra* see Clay 2000: 260; Gee 2016: 135. See further O'Keefe in Chapter 9 of this volume.

[14] First noted by Munro 1886, ii.31. See further Asmis 1982 and Campbell 2014.

[15] This reading is adopted by Long and Sedley 1987: ii.326, whose text I follow; the translation is that of Thom 2006. On the textual problem of the line see Thom 2006 ad loc. For a full text and translation of Cleanthes' *Hymn* see also James 1972; Gee 2000: 81–4.

[16] For the former see Asmis 1982: 468; Thom 2006: 28 (where, nevertheless, four parallels are adduced). For the latter view see Campbell 2014, noting inter alia that lines 1–3 of the *Hymn to Zeus* are 'nearly exactly parallel' to Lucretius, with the address to the god (unusually) displaced to the beginning of the second line.

[17] On Lucretius' astronomy in opposition to Stoicism see Gee 2013: 81–109. It is a commonplace of Stoicism that the heavens are evidence of a divine plan (cf., e.g., Cic., *Nat. D.* 2.4, 2.16).

[18] Asmis 1982: 458. Cf. Campbell 2014: 55: 'Lucretius can be seen to be turning the tables on the Stoics but at the same time using a Stoic technique of allegorising.' For Lucretius' approach to allegory see *DRN* 2.655-60.

[19] See Thom 2006: 25. Asmis 2007 shows how the hymn reconciles the mythological and philosophical Zeus.

quae terras frugiferentis | concelebras). *Labentia* carries the same force as ἑλισσόμενος: both terms describe the motion of the heavenly bodies as they 'slide' across the sky.[20]

Universality is present in both writers, but it plays out differently: for Cleanthes 'it is right for all mortals to address you' (3 σὲ γὰρ καὶ πᾶσι θέμις θνητοῖσι προσαυδᾶν), whereas for Lucretius 'every living thing' owes its existence to Venus (4–5 *per te quoniam genus omne animantum | concipitur*). Lucretius' *genus omne* is opposed to Cleanthes' μοῦνοι (5), which, as Thom puts it (2006 ad loc.), emphasizes the 'exclusive position of humans in nature': humans *alone* are like god.[21] For Lucretius, mankind is *not* special: both the world and the soul are φύσις τις, 'some kind of growth', in Epicurean terms, and both will die.[22] Similarly, just as for Cleanthes nothing can happen without Zeus (15 σοῦ δίχα), so for Lucretius nothing arises without Venus (22–3 *nec sine te quicquam dias in luminis oras | exoritur*); both gods bring concord (18 ἀλλὰ σὺ ... ἐπίσ-τασαι, 'but you ... put in order'; cf. 31–2 *tu sola potes tranquilla pace iuvare | mortalis*);[23] Cleanthes' Zeus loves the unlovable (19 οὐ φίλα σοὶ φίλα ἐστίν, 'even the unloved is dear to you'), just as Lucretius' Venus makes all things *amabile* (23). Venus' is not the ordering love of Cleanthes' god, however, but a tough love altogether more raw than its Stoic counterpart.

It appears, then, that polemical engagement with Stoicism is visible from the outset of the *DRN*. Such engagement continues, I argue, throughout the poem, often in the form of appropriation and overwriting of material from opposing ideologies.[24] In other words, Lucretius' engagement with other philosophical schools occurs consistently on the *intertextual* level. It is my thesis here that Lucretius invokes the well-known parallelism between souls and stars by drawing verbally on another (contemporary) Stoicizing text on the stars, the *Aratea* of Cicero. This work left a deep and indubitable mark on the *DRN*.[25] Often, allusions to the *Aratea* form the verbal

---

[20] *Labor* is a *terminus technicus* for the motion of the stars, their smooth 'sliding' motion from East to West across the sky: e.g., Ov. *Fast.* 1.2 *lapsaque sub terras ortaque signa*. Aratus, *Phaen.* 531 uses the Greek verb ἑλίσσω (with similar force) of the shape of the celestial globe across which the heavenly bodies move.

[21] On the unique place of mankind in nature see Cic. *Nat. D.* 2.140 and 153.

[22] See p. 197 above.

[23] The *Hymn* contains a 'polyptotic repetition of forms of σύ/σός' (Thom 2006 ad *Hymn* 3); so too Lucretius' hymn of forms of *tu*.

[24] See Gee 2016.

[25] For the arguments see Gee 2000: 70–91; Gee 2013: 57–109 and the list of parallels in Appendix B (pp. 189–231); more recently, Gee 2016.

backbone of Lucretius' descriptions of the soul.[26] Such allusions frequently occur in aggregation.[27] We 'see' Cicero's stars through Lucretius descriptions of soul, like looking at the night sky through a permeable membrane or a sheet of cellophane. We read the words in Lucretius' arrangement; but through those words shines a previous context, Cicero's text. A poetic figure emerges from the connection between the two texts. In recalling the original context, the Aratean 'sky' beyond Lucretius' verbal membrane, we are led to infer that the soul (about which we are reading) is like the stars (which we recall from the intertextual context).

We can call this 'intertextual metaphor', metaphor created by intertextuality. It is, if you like, second degree metaphor, not actually stated as 'x is y', but present in the substrate layer of the text, glimpsed through words borrowed from another context.[28] 'Intertextual metaphor' arises from a binary interaction: Lucretius' text interacting with Cicero's text, and the reader's interaction with the resulting compound text, or, to put it another way (a) the allusive construction of the text, and (b) the process of recollection of the original context in reading.[29]

But there's a catch. Lucretius' is a polemical text; his soul is, as we've seen, constructed *in opposition* to the traditions which habitually link souls and stars. So 'intertextual metaphor' implies 'intertextual polemic'.[30] Such polemic functions by first appropriating, then redeploying, material from an earlier text affiliated to an opposing tradition,[31] or as Hardie puts it, 'Lucretius' peculiar tactic of getting inside his opponents' positions and then evacuating them of their prior content to refill them with Epicurean doctrine'.[32] This is exactly how I think Lucretius is treating Cicero's *Aratea* – a translation of a text which is, at least in its reception, a manifesto of Stoic cosmology, namely Aratus' *Phaenomena*.[33] He colonizes its

---

[26] In an aside in my book on Aratus and the Roman Aratean tradition, I go so far as to say that 'Human identity [in Lucretius] is thematized intertextually through the stars' (Gee 2013: 207).

[27] What I mean by 'aggregation' of parallels is when a text uses repeated allusion to point to another text. As Edmunds puts it, in cases where 'an extensive intertextual program is at work . . . in such large-scale programs, the continuous relation between C[ontext]1 and C2 is operative even in the absence of quotation . . . The continuous relation between C1 and C2 provokes a heightened awareness for quotations and more intense scrutiny when they appear' (Edmunds 2001: 140).

[28] I first use the term 'intertextual metaphor' in this way in Gee 2016: 140.

[29] On allusion as metaphor see Conte 1986, e.g., 38: 'In the art of allusion, as in every rhetorical figure, the poetry lies in the simultaneous presence of two different realities that try to indicate a single reality.'

[30] On 'intertextual polemic' see Gee 2016; also Gee 2013: 66–9, especially 67.

[31] See especially Gee 2016: 135–6.   [32] Hardie 1986: 11; cf. Campbell 2014: 33.

[33] See Lewis 1992. On Aratus' Stoicism see Gale 1994: 50 ('the *Phaenomena* is heavily influenced by early Stoicism'); Hunter 1995; Kidd 1997: 10–11. Fantuzzi and Hunter 2004: 226–7 are cautious. On Cicero's *Aratea* and Stoicism see Gee 2001.

material in the service of the Epicurean vision of the soul. Souls may be like stars, he seems to say, but they are not like *those* stars, the ones you know so well from Stoicism.

The Soul

Verbal reference to a Stoic text has philosophical consequences. As with the opening intertextuality with Cleanthes' *Hymn*, it sets up an expectation in the reader of a philosophical view which will not be fulfilled. Rather it will be replaced. This strategy of intertextual 'swerve' is part of Lucretius' protreptic technique throughout the *DRN*.[34] In the present case, we are most interested in references which set up a pattern for how we understand the soul, since, as we have seen, the soul is radically different in Epicureanism and Stoicism. My thesis is twofold: (i) that the mortal soul's passage from life to death in *DRN* 3 is figured as stellar, through recall of the movements of the stars embedded in the text by reference to Cicero's *Aratea*; and (ii) that this sets up a difficulty or paradox, both in respect of Cicero as a source text, and also in respect of the intelligent-design philosophy it espouses. As representative examples of this strategy I will study two passages from the *DRN*:

(1)   *DRN* 3.208–45: the elements of the *animus*
(2)   *DRN* 3.824–51: reassembly of our atoms over the course of time.

In both of these passages there are multiple allusions to Cicero's *Aratea*, illustrating how Ciceronian reference occurs in aggregation in the *DRN*. Where there is an aggregation of Ciceronian echoes connected with a particular theme, I call this phenomenon 'thematic reference'.[35] We'll see that Lucretius consistently gives astral imagery to souls through reference to Cicero's *Aratea*, but in the service of a philosophy which denies both the role of the stars and the soul as part of a greater world order.

(1)   DRN *3.208–45: The Elements of the* Animus

In this passage Lucretius describes how the *animus* consists of *aura*, *vapor* and *aer*, plus one other element too tenuous even to name. References to

[34] Gale 1994 has shown, for instance, how Lucretius both adopts Empedocles and substitutes his own view (see esp. pp. 59–74).
[35] Explored, in a different context, in Gee 2016. There I show how Lucretius' aggregative or recurring allusions to Cicero's description of the Dog Star act as a thematic signifier of 'the impossible' (*adunata*) in Epicurean cosmogony. Here, obviously, the theme is soul.

the *Aratea* are underlined in the text and in the passages of the *Aratea*. In each case, I offer a brief interpretation of the significance of the shared lexical elements in the light of their respective contexts in source and secondary texts.

> haec quoque res etiam naturam dedicat eius,
> quam tenui constet textura quamque loco se
> contineat parvo, si possit conglomerari,   210
> quod simul atque hominem leti secura quies est
> indepta atque animi natura animaeque recessit,
> nil ibi libatum de toto corpore cernas
> ad speciem, nihil ad pondus: mors omnia praestat
> vitalem praeter sensum calidumque vaporem.   215
> ergo animam totam perparvis esse necessest
> seminibus, nexam per venas viscera nervos;
> quatenus, omnis ubi e toto iam corpore cessit,
> extima membrorum circumcaesura tamen se
> incolumem praestat nec defit ponderis hilum.   220
> quod genus est Bacchi cum flos evanuit aut cum
> spiritus unguenti suavis diffugit in auras
> aut aliquo cum iam sucus de corpore cessit;
> nil oculis tamen esse minor res ipsa videtur
> propterea neque detractum de pondere quicquam,   225
> nimirum quia multa minutaque semina sucos
> efficiunt et odorem in toto corpore rerum.
> quare etiam atque etiam mentis naturam animaeque
> scire licet perquam pauxillis esse creatam
> seminibus, quoniam fugiens nil ponderis aufert.   230
>   Nec tamen haec simplex nobis natura putanda est.
> tenvis enim quaedam moribundos deserit aura
> mixta vapore, vapor porro trahit aëra secum.
> nec calor est quisquam, cui non sit mixtus et aër.
> rara quod eius enim constat natura, necessest   235
> aëris inter eum primordia multa moveri.
> iam triplex animi est igitur natura reperta;
> nec tamen haec sat sunt ad sensum cuncta creandum,
> nil horum quoniam recipit mens posse creare
> sensiferos motus et mens quaecumque volutat.   240
> quarta quoque his igitur quaedam natura necessest
> attribuatur. east omnino nominis expers;
> qua neque mobilius quicquam neque tenvius exstat,
> nec magis e parvis et levibus ex elementis;
> sensiferos motus quae didit prima per artus.   245

Another point proves what a tiny tuft the nature of the mind is, and how little space it would take up if you balled it all together (210): as soon as the covering of tranquil death is spread over a person, and the nub of the intelligence and the soul depart, nothing that amounts to even a single drop is visibly distilled from the body, in look or in weight. Death offers us everything intact, apart from a sense of life and warmth (215). So the *animus* must be made of incredibly small particles, integral to veins, guts, tendons, because when the totality of it has left the whole body, there's not even a chip off the body's contour, or the tiniest fraction of weight gone (220). It's the same when the aroma of wine has dissipated, or when a whiff of sweet perfume fades into the air, or when the quintessence of anything absconds from the physical substance. The substance itself doesn't seem visibly diminished because of it, and there's not even a slight reduction in mass (225), obviously because countless tiny particles make up the quintessence and savour of things in their intact state. So keep on and on reminding yourself that the mind- and soul-entities are made of inconceivably tiny particles, which even when they decamp take no weight with them (230). But that's not to say that [the *animus*] is made of only one thing. Someone in the process of dying emits a little puff of breath and heat, and the heat has air mixed in. You can't have heat that's not mixed with air. Because heat-particles are very diffuse (235), lots of air-particles must move about among them. And so we see that the mind is made of three things. But at the same time you have to understand that these three things put together can't cause sensation. None of them can fine-tune the motion you need for perception, whatever the whorls of thought are (240). So you have to add a fourth kind of thing. This one is completely name-free. Nothing's more evasive and gossamer, or made out of elements smoother and lighter. In a flash it drives the hit of sensation along the limbs (245).

(i)   *DRN* 3.218 *e toto iam corpore cessit*; 223 *de corpore cessit*
      Aratea 462 *toto cum corpore cedit*

The Ciceronian passage is *Aratea* 459–62, part of the *sunanatolai* and *sunkataduseis*, the 'simultaneous risings and settings', where the poet explains which stars rise and set together:[36]

> inde Sagittipotens superas cum visere luces
> institit, e[t]mergit Nixi caput, et simul effert
> sese clara Fides et promit pectore Cepheus.
> fervidus ille Canis toto cum corpore cedit . . .

When Sagittarius begins to see the lights in the sky, that's when the head of Engonasin emerges, and at the same time the bright Lyre unveils itself and Cepheus reveals his chest. That blazing Dog sets, taking his whole body with him . . .[37]

---

[36] On *sunanatolai* and *sunkataduseis* see Kidd 1997 ad Aratus, *Phaen.* 559–68.

[37] I thank here the Cambridge University Press reader who suggested that Canis is the whole constellation of the Dog, rather than, as I first thought, the Dog-star in the nose of the constellation of the Dog; I originally took these lines to mean that his nose sets first, followed by his body (*toto . . . corpore*).

Cicero had previously mapped the constellations in static position relative to one another. In this section of the *Aratea* we see a number of constellations moving together, as a *system*. The visible movement of one constellation gives information about the movements of a lot of other constellations, whether or not they happen to be visible at the time. The Ciceronian passage is about the setting of Canis, the constellation of the Dog; in Lucretius the argument is about the evanescence of the soul. Lucretius too is talking about a system: the *animus* can be understood as part of a system based on the nexus of particles of various kinds. As the stars move systematically, so the recession of the *animus* from the whole body at the moment of death reveals a system predicated on the existence of unbelievably tiny particles. In Cicero's Aratean system, what is visible gives the clues to what is invisible; so too in Lucretius what is visible (in this case, the fact that the body is no longer alive) gives the clue by which we understand the invisible make-up of the soul.

(ii)   *DRN* 3.242 *omnino nominis expers*
        Aratea 170 *expertis nominis omnis*

The context in Lucretius is the unnamed fourth element in the soul; in Cicero it is the residue of unnamed stars which surround the identifiable constellations (*Aratea* 170–2):

> et prope conspicies, expertis nominis omnis,
> inter Pistricem et Piscem quem diximus Austri
> stellas, sub pedibus stratas radiantis Aquari.

But nearby you'll see, all name-free, some stars between Pistrix and what's called the Southern Fish, broadcast under the feet of glittering Aquarius.

The earliest appearance of this three-word combination is in Cicero; it occurs in these two texts alone.[38] In each author, the phrase occurs in the same part of the hexameter, with the interchange of three lexical elements.[39]

Ciceronian reference to the nameless elements in the heavens becomes in Lucretius a description of a nameless element in the human soul. Furthermore, Lucretius uses his verbal raw materials to create a form of wordplay redolent of the atomic exchange which makes up the Epicurean universe, a quasi-anagrammatic combination of repeated letters, *om, in, omn, nom, nin,*

---

[38] I have consulted the online *Bibliotheca Teubneriana Latina* (De Gruyter) here and in what follows.
[39] See Gee 2013: 100–2.

min, etc.[40] The visual form of the words almost forms a pattern but ultimately misses the mark. The groupings of letters are like the fourth element of the soul – suggestive of a system but ultimately slippery and evasive.

The allusion is significant, in that Lucretius imitates an expression in Cicero which describes what is there almost a unique phenomenon – one that therefore stands out to the reader: the *limits* of the ability to classify. The 'fourth *natura*' (*DRN* 3.241) is the clearly present but unclassifiable element in Lucretius' system, just as the unnamed stars are in Cicero's. In the Epicurean universe, the principles of classification which inform the Stoic or Stoicizing universe of the *Aratea* break down. Lucretius chooses a bit of his source where this is, uncharacteristically, almost happening. He accentuates what in his model is a rare tendency.

This intertextual strategy can be even more clearly illustrated from another passage of *DRN* 3 on the soul. At 3.316 we find the near-exact repetition of an entire line from the *Aratea*:[41]

> *DRN* 3.316 *quorum ego nunc nequeo caecas exponere causas*
> *Aratea* 234 *quarum ego nunc nequeo tortos evolvere cursus*

Here Lucretius is discussing the ineffability of the many possible permutations of personality (3.314–18):

> inque aliis rebus multis differre necessest
> naturas hominum varias moresque sequaces;
> quorum ego nunc nequeo caecas exponere causas
> nec reperire figurarum tot nomina quot sunt
> principiis, unde haec oritur variantia rerum.

Human personalities and their contingent behaviour must also differ in many other respects. At this point I can't explain the latent causes or find a name for every possible constellation of elements which give rise to such rainbow characteristics.

The context of the borrowed Ciceronian line is the description of the Long Year (*Aratea* 232–6):

> hae faciunt magnos longinqui temporis annos,
> cum redeunt ad idem caeli sub tegmine signum;
> quarum ego nunc nequeo tortos evolvere cursus:
> verum haec, quae semper certo [e]voluuntur in orbe
> fixa, simul magnos edemus gentibus orbes.

---

[40] For verbal patterning and the atomic universe see Friedländer 1941; Snyder 1980: 31–51; Schiesaro 1994; Volk 2002: 100–5, summarizing the earlier debate. See further Shearin in Chapter 7 of this volume.
[41] See Gee 2013: 103–4.

[The planets] effect Great Years of extended span when they return to the same star-sign under the canopy of heaven. I am not now able to unroll their sinuous courses; but I shall proclaim at large the great orbits of those fixed stars which roll round in a predictable course.

The Long Year is the complete cycle in which the planets diverge from one another and eventually return to the same relationship with one another. As I show elsewhere, the planets in the Aratean tradition are 'unspeakable', because of their irregularity of motion. Aratus leaves them out entirely, apart from a *praeteritio*, and Cicero follows him here.[42] As with Cicero's planets, instruments of the long year, so with the determinants of character in Lucretius: we see their effects but we can't set forth their causes. Lucretius throws up his hands at the possibility of describing their infinite nuance, with a near-exact quotation of this entire line of Cicero. Again, Lucretius has drawn our attention to one of *a very few* instances of inexplicable phenomena in the *Aratea* to make his point. The inexplicable, a marginal phenomenon in Cicero, becomes key in Lucretius.

Most revealing is Lucretius' substitution of *caecas* for *tortos*. In Cicero the courses of the planets are 'convoluted'; in Lucretius the causes of personality are just straightforwardly 'hidden'. Lucretius adapts the Ciceronian line to a prevalent theme in the *DRN*, that of obfuscation and blindness.[43] In Book 1 alone, for instance, Lucretius deploys the adjective *caecus* (which can mean both 'blind', i.e. 'purposeless' like Richard Dawkins' 'Blind Watchmaker', and 'unseen') at least six times: of the hidden particles (*corpora caeca*) of wind (277 and 295); of atoms in general (328 *corporibus caecis*); metaphorically of the hiding-places (*caecas . . . latebras*) from which Truth must be drawn out (408); of the sneaky nature (*naturam clandestinam caecamque*) of the Primary Bodies (779); of the bodies themselves, *primordia caeca* (1110), and finally, in the book's closing lines, of 'obscuring' night, *caeca nox*, as a metaphor for unenlightenment (1115–16). By changing one word, Lucretius has adapted Cicero's profession of the planets' inexplicability to his own anti-teleological vision of a nature driven by unseen forces.

(2)   DRN 3.824–51: Reassembly of Our Atoms over Time

Each soul–mind complex is a one-off entity arising from a chance coalescence of atoms at a particular time. Even if the same coalescence were to happen again, we (as we are now) wouldn't know about it:

---

[42] Gee 2013: 112–15; 118–21.   [43] Cf. Campbell 2014: 53–4.

praeter enim quam quod morbis cum corporis aegret,
825   advenit id quod eam de rebus saepe futuris
macerat inque metu male habet curisque fatigat
praeteritisque male admissis peccata remordent.
adde furorem animi proprium atque oblivia rerum,
adde quod in nigras lethargi mergitur undas.
830   Nil igitur mors est ad nos neque pertinet hilum,
quandoquidem natura animi mortalis habetur.
et velut anteacto nihil tempore sensimus aegri,
ad confligendum venientibus undique Poenis,
omnia cum belli trepido concussa tumultu
835   horrida contremuere sub altis aetheris oris,
in dubioque fuere utrorum ad regna cadendum
omnibus humanis esset terraque marique,
sic, ubi non erimus, cum corporis atque animai
discidium fuerit quibus e sumus uniter apti,
840   scilicet haud nobis quicquam, qui non erimus tum,
accidere omnino poterit sensumque movere,
non si terra mari miscebitur et mare caelo.
et si iam nostro sentit de corpore postquam
distractast animi natura animaeque potestas,
845   nil tamen est ad nos qui comptu coniugioque
corporis atque animae consistimus uniter apti.
nec, si materiem nostram collegerit aetas
post obitum rursumque redegerit ut sita nunc est
atque iterum nobis fuerint data lumina vitae,
850   pertineat quicquam tamen ad nos id quoque factum,
interrupta semel cum sit repetentia nostri.

Even aside from the fact that [the soul] gets sick when the body is ill, it's often crushed with undefined misgivings about the future, suspended in an uncomfortable state of fear, eroded by anxieties, eaten away by guilt over things badly done in the past. That's not to mention idiosyncratic mindstorms and blackouts, or what happens when it's submerged in murky apathetic depths. So death is nothing to us, it is completely irrelevant (830) when you consider that the essence of the intelligence is mortal. Just as time past doesn't hurt us – say, when the Carthaginians converged into battle from all sides; then the whole world rocked on its foundations with the shockwave of war and everything under the sky's wide mantle trembled and convulsed (835), and it was unclear which of the two sides would wind up in charge of all humanity on land and sea – so, when we cease to exist, when the body–soul nexus from which our individual identity is formed splits apart, you've got to believe that nothing will have any effect on us – not even if earth collapsed into sea and sea into sky – because we won't exist then (840), so we will have no capacity to feel. And even if the essence of the intelligence and the thrusting soul should feel anything after it's been drawn out of our body, that's nothing to us, because as individuals we're fitted together from the knit and intertwine of body and soul (845). Not even if Time were to gather up our components after we die and reassemble them exactly as they are now, and the light of life were given to us once more – even this achievement would have no relevance for us (850) once the data of our Selves had been lost.

(i)   *DRN* 3.825 *saepe futuris*
      Prognostica fr. 3.2 *saepe futuros*

This is the earliest occurrence of the collocation *saepe futur-*, which occurs only in Lucretius and Cicero among first century BC texts. It therefore looks like a Ciceronian collocation Lucretius has borrowed.

Lucretius is talking about wrong-headed misgivings about the future. The Ciceronian passage comes from his translation of Aratus' weather-signs, at *Prog.* fr. 3.1–4, a description of impending storm:[44]

> atque etiam ventos praemonstrat saepe futuros
> inflatum mare cum subito penitusque tumescit,
> saxaque cana salis niveo spumata liquore
> tristificas certant Neptuno reddere voces . . .

And the sea often blows its fanfare for winds to come when the swell rises suddenly out of the deep, and the rocks, splashed pale with the snowy spray of salt, compete to echo Neptune's haunting song . . .

The interaction of Lucretius' text with Cicero's creates a storm metaphor in Lucretius' description of the soul's turmoil. The image arises by recollection of the storm context in Cicero. Depression in Lucretius becomes like a shipwreck or tsunami.

Lucretius' reader will have been primed to make this connection by the proem of the previous book, which invites us to look down with sublime insouciance upon those struggling in the sea-storm of their non-Epicurean lives (*DRN* 2.1–2).[45] Furthermore, the allusion also has a prolative function. The intertextual metaphor prepares the reader for an actual verbal metaphor of submersion in the ensuing lines at *DRN* 3.829 *adde quod in nigras lethargi mergitur undas*, 'consider also what happens when [the soul] is submerged in murky apathetic depths'. The fully realized metaphor develops out of, and confirms, the hint given a few lines earlier in the allusion to Cicero's *Prognostica*. Weather in Cicero becomes, in Lucretius, a metaphor for the moods of the human psyche.

---

[44] For further parallels with the *Prognostica*, which Lucretius certainly knew well, see Gee 2013: 200, 216, and Appendix B *passim*.

[45] A favourite Epicurean metaphor: see Fowler 2002: 28–37.

(ii)   *DRN* 3.829 *mergitur undas*
       Aratea 381 *mergitur unda*

Furthermore, Lucretius' watery metaphor for depression is *itself* a further
echo of the *Aratea*. *Aratea* 381 is the earliest instance of the collocation
merg- und- in verse. The context in Cicero is the simultaneous setting of
various constellations (*Aratea* 379–84):[46]

> non pauca e caelo depellens signa, repente
> exoritur pandens inlustria lumina Virgo.
> cedit clara Fides Cyllenia, <u>mergitur unda</u>
> Delphinus, simul obtegitur depulsa Sagitta,
> atque Avis ad summam caudam primasque recedit
> pinnas, et magnus pariter delabitur Amnis.

Virgo chases more than a few signs out of the sky as she rises, proffering her bright
lights. Mercury's Lyre defers to her, the Dolphin is submerged in the sea, the
Arrow is driven away and engulfed, the Bird departs as far as the end of its tail and
its wingtips, and the great River slips at the same time over the horizon.

The shared expression occurs in a list of many verbs of lapsing, subsidence
and evanescence in this passage of Cicero: *cedit, mergitur, obtegitur* (obfuscation again), *recedit, delabitur*. In Cicero the stars set in a landslide; in
Lucretius, it is the submersion of the soul as it slides down the slippery
slope of psychopathology. The metaphorical 'setting' of the soul engulfed
by the blackness of depression is figured by allusion to the setting of the
stars in Cicero.

(iii) *DRN* 3.849 <u>atque iterum</u> nobis fuerint data <u>lumina vitae</u>
       Aratea 287 <u>atque iterum</u> sol <u>lumine</u> verno

Here the allusion is tight: there are three shared lexical elements, and one
with slight *variatio* (Lucretius' *vitae* for Cicero's *verno*). Lucretius discusses
the idea, originally Stoic, that the universe might be destroyed and reas-
sembled in an identical state to how it is now.[47] The context in Cicero is
the celestial circles, the 'skeleton' of the armillary sphere, the underpinning
structure of the universe. The Lucretian resonance is with Cicero's description of the equator, the most central of these circles (*Aratea* 285–92):

---

[46] On Lucretius' use of a different part of this passage see Gee 2013: 85.

[47] The identical reassembly of the universe is possible for Epicurus and 'easily credible' for Lucretius:
'In its original, cyclic, guise the idea was Stoic' (Kenney 2014: 196 ad 3.847–51; and cf. 3.856). See
further O'Rourke in Chapter 5 of this volume. On the lines immediately following this passage see
Schiesaro 1994: 101: 'The Stoic belief in palingenesis and numerical identity is one of the polemical
targets of Lucretius' passage.'

> hosce inter mediam partem retinere videtur   285
> tantus, quantus erat conlucens Lacteus orbis,
> in quo autumnali atque iterum sol lumine verno
> exaequat spatium lucis cum tempore noctis.
> hunc retinens Aries sublucet corpore toto,
> atque genu flexo Taurus conititur; ingens   290
> Orion claro contingens pectore fertur;
> Hydra tenet flexu, Creterra et Corvus adhaerent ...

Midway between [the Tropics] is stretched another circle of the same circumference as the Milky Way. When the sun is on this circle at the autumn and spring equinox day and night are the same length. Aries straddles this circle and lights it up with his whole body; Taurus kneels on it with bent knee; massive Orion touches it with his chest as he flies along; the Hydra fastens [the Equator] with his coil, the Crater and the Raven are attached to it ...

In the *Aratea*, the celestial circles are the main area in which celestial order is revealed. The joining-up of the different elements in the sky forms one coherent system. Lucretius' passage is also about systematization. But in this case a *negative* answer is returned vis-à-vis system: *even if* the whole soul–body assemblage could notionally be rebuilt – like reconstructing a disassembled celestial orrery such as the Antikythera mechanism – such reassembly would be meaningless, because the 'self' is relative to the idiosyncratic circumstances surrounding each temporary assemblage. In the final analysis, Lucretius negates the significance of system in the face of contingency. The fact that he evokes the most definitive example of system in Cicero is part of his polemical strategy.

Souls and Stars

A little more can be said about system in this passage. Lucretius repeats the hexameter-end formula *uniter apti* at *DRN* 3.839 and 846 (quoted on p. 208 above). This is a favoured line-end collocation in Lucretius, occurring *only* in the *DRN*, but occurring there four times (3.839, 3.846, 5.537, 5.558). It is significant that, of the four occurrences, there are two each in Books 3 and 5 – the books which deal with, respectively, the soul and the stars. Both times in Book 3 *uniter apti* refers to the ὁμούρησις (connection) between soul and body.[48] Lucretius' collocation 'joins' the soul with the stars by verbal echo *intratextually*, in a way which is suggestive of further connections.

---

[48] For Epicurean ὁμούρησις see fr. 34.17 Arrighetti (Arrighetti 1973: 332 and 629).

If we wish, we can see another Ciceronian reference here, to Cicero's own use of the participle *aptus* at the line-end, in the same passage just examined in the preceding reference. Thus at *Aratea* 243 we get *vinctos inter se et nodis caelestibus aptos*, again of the celestial circles, which, as we've seen, form the all-important framework of the universe.[49] Both the soul–body nexus and the celestial circles represent the foundation of a whole, be that the universe or the human entity.

Given that Cicero's passage on the celestial circles has been shown to be at stake later in this passage, it is not impossible, to my mind, that we can recall it here too, and that *apti* at the line-end can foreshadow the connection later made by more explicit Ciceronian collocations. The argument from aggregation (n. 27 above) might support this view. Even if we aren't convinced that a one-word correspondence amounts in this case to intertextual allusion, it is still fruitful to consider Lucretius' own emphasis on joining as it emerges through the repeated formula in his text.

We've seen that body and soul are joined in one – *uniter apti* – at *DRN* 3.839 and 846. In arguing that air must be present in the earth in Book 5, Lucretius draws an explicit analogy with the body and soul (5.556–8):

> nonne vides etiam quam magno pondere nobis
> sustineat corpus tenuissima vis animai
> propterea quia tam coniuncta atque <u>uniter apta est</u>?

Don't you see also how the gossamer structure of the soul sustains our body, even though [the body is] very heavy, because it is so deeply implicated and joined into one with it?

In his analogy, Lucretius draws on the formula he originally used of the soul in Book 3: there soul and body were *uniter apti*; here the soul is deeply implicated with the body, *uniter apta est*. Near-direct verbal recall of the prior discussion in Book 3 reinforces the analogy.

In the same passage of Book 5, the connection was made even more explicit intratextually, by recall of a whole line, *DRN* 3.325/5.554 *nam communibus inter se radicibus haerent*, 'for they are entwined together by the roots', i.e. of the soul and body (Book 3), and of earth and air (Book 5). An identical line is used of both the soul and the world.

Intratextual recall of the soul in the description of the world does not end there. Consider the disposition of elements in the cosmogony at 5.449–57:

---

[49] On Lucretius' recall of this passage in *DRN* 5 see Gee 2013: 77–8.

> Quippe etenim primum terrai corpora quaeque,
> propterea quod erant gravia et perplexa, coibant   450
> in medio atque imas capiebant omnia sedis;
> quae quanto magis inter se perplexa coibant,
> tam magis expressere ea quae mare sidera solem
> lunamque efficerent et magni moenia mundi.
> omnia enim <u>magis</u> haec e <u>levibus</u> atque rotundis   455
> seminibus multoque minoribu' sunt <u>elementis</u>
> quam tellus.

So surely all the particles of earth, because they were heavy and intertwined, first converged in the middle and all took up the lowest locations; and the more they clustered together intertwined, the more they squeezed out the particles which made sea, stars, sun and moon and the casing of the great heaven. For all of these were made of much smoother and rounder elements than the earth.

The heavenly bodies are made 'more of smooth and round particles' (*magis ... e levibus atque rotundis | seminibus*) which are much smaller than the elements (*elementis*) which make up earth. Thus they are much more volatile. Here we are back to the Fourth Element of the soul, composed of particles than which nothing else is smoother or lighter (*DRN* 3.243–4 *qua neque mobilius quicquam neque tenvius exstat, | nec <u>magis</u> e parvis et <u>levibus</u> ex elementis,* see p. 203 above). The heavenly bodies, the threefold verbal echo tells us, are to the rest of the universe as the fourth element of the soul is to the other parts of the soul–body complex.

There are (we may not now be surprised to know) also intratextual connections between Lucretius' account of death, and the heavenly bodies in Book 5. In Lucretius' account of death (p. 203 above), one cannot see anything substantial subtracted from a corpse (3.213 <u>nil ibi</u> <u>libatum de toto corpore cernas</u>, 'nothing that amounts to even a single drop is visibly distilled from the body'). In Book 5, distance cannot add anything to, or subtract anything from, the sun's perceptible size (5.568–9 <u>nil</u> illa his intervallis <u>de corpore libant</u> | flammarum, nil ad speciem est contractior ignis, 'nor do these [lights] lose any force of flame from their body despite these distances, and the fire is no smaller in appearance').[50] Again, there are no fewer than three shared lexical elements. The imperceptible subtraction of something from the body is

---

[50] Likewise, in these same passages of Books 3 and 5, compare 3.229–30 *scire licet perquam pauxillis esse creatam | seminibus* ('we're permitted to know that [the mind- and soul-entity] is made of inconceivably tiny particles') with 5.590–91 [594–5] *scire licet perquam pauxillo posse minores | esse* ('we're permitted to know they're smaller [than they look] by an inconceivably tiny difference') from the end of the same passage on the sizes of the sun and moon.

EMMA GEE

like, Lucretius seems to say, the imperceptible diminution in size of fires seen from a distance. Both are mysteries to our perception. The common element is the subtraction of a modicum of heat and light. As the sun, so the human entity. We recall the death of Epicurus with which this essay began. His soul in its setting was not just *like* the sun: it was implicated with the sun in an ontological way.[51]

Conclusion

Lucretius designs his verbal universe to make us see that the nature of the soul is the same as that of the heavenly bodies. The fact that the soul and the stars share words on two levels – through allusion, in the description of the soul, to a text on the stars, and through recall of the soul through language it shares with the description of the stars – indicates an important truth: that they share the same atomic make-up. But it is precisely this concept which means that Lucretius' text is poised in an adversarial relationship with the texts on which it draws linguistically for the letter-atoms of the soul and stars in the *DRN*, namely Cleanthes' *Hymn* and Cicero's *Aratea*. His reassembly of the lines and half-lines of his Stoic sources is a rebuilding of the human entity, and the universe, along Epicurean lines.

Lucretius is working within an ideology which opposes intelligent design. In Plato, the soul is providentially embedded in the cosmos (*Ti.* 30b7–c1 οὕτως οὖν δὴ κατὰ λόγον τὸν εἰκότα δεῖ λέγειν τόνδε τὸν κόσμον ζῷον ἔμψυχον ἔννουν τε τῇ ἀληθείᾳ διὰ τὴν τοῦ θεοῦ γενέσθαι πρόνοιαν, 'Thus, then, in accordance with the likely account, we must declare that this Cosmos has verily come into existence as a Living Creature endowed with soul and reason owing to the providence of God', trans. Bury 1952). In Lucretius, we have the world *and* the soul, which share a material make-up but are unconnected in any teleological way. For Lucretius, no matter how glorious and substantial humanity and the universe are, they are both destined for dissolution and reaggregation. Human matter is recycled into, among other things, stellar matter, and vice versa, and it is on this fundamental level, rather than on that of shared *design*, that the connection between soul and stars exists. In Lucretius textual material pertaining to the stars is recycled into textual material pertaining to the body and *mortal* soul. Even Lucretius'

---

[51] On analogy and ontology in Lucretius see Schiesaro 1994.

own text will in time break down and be recycled, just as the elements of Cicero's text have been recycled as part of the atomic make-up of the *DRN*.[52] Our ability to unmask the serial making – and unmaking – of the universe emerges from melding intertextual with philosophical readings of Lucretius' text.

[52] On the 'palingenesis' of the *DRN* see Schiesaro's seminal article of 1994.

PART V

Worldviews

CHAPTER 11

Was Memmius a Good King?

Joseph Farrell

In this chapter I examine Lucretius' *De Rerum Natura* (*DRN*) as a work of ethical instruction, specifically with regard to political involvement, in the light of Philodemus' essay *On the Good King According to Homer*. My purpose is to contribute to the ongoing discussion of Lucretius' relationship to his Epicurean contemporaries. My approach will be to focus on the writers' respective addressees, Memmius and Piso.[1] In Section 1, I outline how these men, though broadly similar in some respects, differ as individuals. In Section 2, I argue that the lessons offered to Memmius and Piso, being appropriate to each man, also differ accordingly. In Section 3, I explain on the basis of these contrasts why I believe Lucretius takes a different view from Philodemus regarding participation in politics.

I

Comparing L. Calpurnius Piso Caesoninus and C. Memmius is possible and fruitful because the resemblances between them are real and obvious. Born into plebeian *gentes* that became prominent in politics during the third and second centuries BC, the two men were of a similar age and participated fully in the complex and dangerous politics of their times. In addition, both had intellectual interests and cultivated friendships with men who devoted most of their energy to literature and philosophy. Epicureanism was important to each, as well, though probably in rather different ways.

---

[1] Although the *libellus* containing the treatise does not name the author, experts agree that Philodemus is by far the person most likely to have written it; the name of Piso appears in the dedication (Gigante 1995: 63–4, with further references). The identity of Lucretius' addressee as C. Memmius L. filius, pr. 58 (*RE* 8), is less certain, though most of the doubt, which stems from the traditional reading of Cic. *Fam.* 13.1, has now been removed by Morgan and Taylor 2017 (see further in section 2 below). On the question of date see below, n. 44.

Against this background, some differences stand out in high relief.

First, in regard to family, the Calpurnii Pisones were *nobiles*, having produced their first consul in 180 and then six more over the following century, including the *proavus* and *avus* of Philodemus' addressee.[2] Piso's father served as quaestor in 100, and so qualified for the senate. He may not have pursued higher office, perhaps deciding to weather those politically turbulent times by lying low and letting others represent the family's interests.[3] Meanwhile, the Memmii, after four generations as senators, had not yet succeeded in becoming *nobiles* by attaining the consulship, instead producing mainly tribunes, along with a few men who reached the praetorship.[4] One former praetor nearly became consul in 100.[5] On the eve of his all but certain election, however, he was beaten to death by a mob led by one of his competitors.[6] After this man's assassination, there seems to have been no member of the *gens Memmia* in the senate for over three decades.

Next – and in view of their family histories, not surprisingly – Piso and Memmius had very different careers. Piso seems to have raced through the *cursus honorum*: he was quaestor in 70, aedile in 64, praetor in 61, and consul in 58.[7] From 57 to 55 he was proconsul of Macedonia.[8] Ultimately, he became censor in 50.[9] Memmius' official career is less well attested, in part because it was decidedly less distinguished. We do not know the year of his birth, but he cannot have been much younger than Piso, and he may

[2] They are (* denotes the great-grandfather and grandfather):
C. Calpurnius C. f. C. n. Piso, *RE* 62, cos. 180
C. Calpurnius Piso, *RE* 82, cos. 175
L. Calpurnius C. f. C. n. Piso Caesoninus, *RE* 87, cos. 148*
C. Calpurnius Piso, *RE* 73, cos. 139
Q. Calpurnius C. f. C. n. Piso, *RE* 86, cos. 135
L. Calpurnius L. f. C. n. Piso Frugi, *RE* 96, cos. 133
L. Calpurnius (L. f. C. n.) Piso Caesoninus, *RE* 88, cos. 112*

[3] Quaestor and senator: cf. Lintott 1999: 68–9. It is possible that Piso's father (*RE* 89) forsook politics not only for personal safety, but to profit from the munitions trade during the Social War (Cic., *Pis.* 87). The other family members who held magistracies between 100 and 70 include: L. Calpurnius Piso Frugi (*RE* 98), tr. pl. 89, pr. 74 (according to *MRR*; Syme 1955: 58 believes that the tribune and the praetor are different men and suggests that the latter was in fact Piso's father); L. Calpurnius Piso (*RE* Supb. 3.231, cf. 98), pr. or propr. before 90; and C. Calpurnius Piso (*RE* 63), cos. 67 (and therefore pr. by 70).

[4] For a stemma see Sumner 1973: 87. Cicero (*Brut.* 136) records that Memmius' uncle Gaius (*RE* 5, tr. 111) and his father Lucius (*RE* 13, monetalis c. 110) were energetic and even fierce prosecutors who only seldom spoke for the defence; see Sumner 1973: 87–90.

[5] C. Memmius (*RE* 5), tr. pl. 111, pr. 104 or 103.   [6] *MRR* 1: 574.

[7] Piso's early career is conveniently summarized by Nisbet 1961: v–vii.

[8] On Piso's proconsulship see Nisbet 1961: 172–82; Brennan 2000: II.535–7.

[9] *MRR* 2: 247–8.

have been a bit older.[10] It is often said that he was tribune in 66, but we have no definite knowledge of the offices he held before his praetorship in 58, three years after Piso.[11] The following year he was governor of Bithynia and Pontus.[12] He was a candidate to be consul in 53, but was defeated in circumstances that I will discuss below; and that was the end of his political career.

A third difference between Piso and Memmius involves each man's ability to form advantageous alliances and to negotiate the hazards of political life. Piso, scion of a wealthy and well-connected family, evidently felt sufficiently confident in these advantages to marry a woman of less distinguished lineage.[13] Memmius married Fausta, daughter of Sulla Felix, probably after the dictator's death in 78, when she and her twin brother Faustus were being raised in the house of Sulla's former lieutenant, L. Licinius Lucullus.[14] Just how much these relationships advanced or encumbered Memmius' career is an interesting question. Political success when Piso and Memmius were starting out depended on one's relationship to a different Sullan protégé (and rival of Lucullus), Cn. Pompeius Magnus. It is not surprising, then, that in the late sixties Memmius turned against Lucullus in order to curry favour with Pompeius. After prosecuting Lucullus' brother *de peculatu*, Memmius publicly opposed granting Lucullus a triumph and then prosecuted him, also *de peculatu*.[15] When neither of these efforts succeeded, Memmius tried a different approach. In a letter dated 20 January 60 BC, Cicero informed Atticus that the yearly festival of Iuventas would not be taking place, 'because Memmius had initiated Lucullus' wife into his personal cult', and that 'Menelaus', taking the news badly, divorced her; but, whereas the original Paris had offended Menelaus alone, the modern one insulted 'Agamemnon', as well.[16] This is universally interpreted as meaning that Memmius ('Paris') had seduced the wives of both Luculli ('Menelaus' ≈ Marcus, 'Agamemnon' ≈ Lucius). Such goings-on were hardly unheard of among the Roman elite, nor were they always politically motivated. But it seems remarkable that Memmius should choose this way to embarrass Lucullus, who must have approved Memmius' own marriage to Fausta, in order to curry favour with Pompeius.[17]

---

[10] As praetor in 58 Memmius cannot have been born later than 99/98; we have no indication that he was elected *suo anno* (cf. Sumner 1973: 8 n. 2) as Piso seemingly was (Nisbet 1961: v). Consul in 58, he was presumably born in 102/101.

[11] Ryan 1995.   [12] Brennan 2000: II.405.

[13] As is implied by Cicero, *Pis.* fr. ix, admittedly a hostile source: cf. Nisbet 1961: 53–4 ad loc.

[14] Sumner 1973: 88, with further references.   [15] Plut. *Luc.* 37.1–3.   [16] *Att.* 1.18.3.

[17] Plut. *Cat. min.* 29.3.

Later, after Pompeius formed a coalition with Caesar and Crassus, the
trick was to steer the ship of one's ambition by the shifting definition of
mutual interest among these warlords, until their alliance gradually
dissolved. Piso recognized this: in 59, when Caesar was consul, Pompeius
married Julia, Caesar's daughter, Caesar married Calpurnia, Piso's
daughter, and Piso was elected to be consul in 58.[18] But Memmius, as
praetor that same year, spent his time in office denouncing Caesar's
consular acts in 59.[19] Eventually, he changed course and somehow
patched things up with Caesar and, again as was noted above, was able
to stand for election as consul of 53, with the support of both Pompeius
and Caesar. But Memmius' candidacy was a disastrous scandal. Cicero
again, writing to Atticus on 1 October 54 BC (4.17.2), recounts a senate
meeting in which Memmius read out the text of an actual contract
stipulating that, in return for four million sesterces, the consuls of 54 would
rig the elections to ensure that Memmius and Cn. Domitius Calvinus
would succeed them. Memmius revealed this agreement, Cicero writes, on
Pompeius' advice, but without anyone else's knowledge; and Caesar upon
learning about it was highly displeased. Memmius bore the consequences,
losing the election while Domitius, despite his involvement in the plot,
won.[20] Memmius' bad luck continued: in 53, the new consuls presided
over a famously chaotic election that had to be postponed when one of the
candidates, T. Annius Milo, murdered one of his competitors, P. Clodius
Pulcer.[21] The following year, 52, thus began with an interregnum followed
by the election of Pompeius as sole consul.[22] Among the reforms he
enacted was a *lex de ambitu* that allowed for *ex post facto* prosecution of
crimes as far back as the year 70 BC; and under this statute Memmius was
tried and convicted for attempting to buy the election two years before.[23]
Memmius tried to retaliate by using the same law to indict Metellus
Scipio, a candidate in the most recent election and thus implicated in
the chaos that led to Pompeius' sole consulship. More to the point,
Pompeius had just married Metellus' daughter, Cornelia Metella. So,
Memmius struck back for his own conviction by charging Metellus under
the same *lex Pompeia* that produced his own conviction. When Pompeius
used influence to get his new father-in-law acquitted, Memmius resorted
to the tactic he had employed against Lucullus on Pompeius' behalf and

[18] Plut. *Pomp.* 48.3, *Caes.* 14.4–5, *Cat. min.* 33.4, App. *B Civ.* 2.14, Dio Cass. 38.index, 9.1, 13.2.
[19] Cic. *Q Fr.* 1.2.16, Suet. *Iul.* 23.1, *Ner.* 2.2, *Schol. Bob.* 130, 146, 151 Stangl.
[20] Cic. *Att.* 4.15.7 and 17.2, *Q Fr.* 3.1.16, 2.3, 3.2 with Sumner 1982.
[21] For a clear account of these elections see Gruen 1969.   [22] Plut. *Pomp.* 54; Dio Cass. 40.45–50.
[23] Cic. *Att.* 13.49.1, 10.4.8; Asc. *Mil.* 36; App. *B Civ.* 2.20–5.

tried to seduce Cornelia *per litteras*; but she rebuffed him and showed the letter to Pompeius.[24] At this point, Memmius decided there was nothing for it but to go into exile, which he spent in Athens.[25] There is no evidence that he ever returned, and by 46 he was dead.[26]

Meanwhile, throughout these troubled times, Piso continued to prosper. As censor in 50, he moderated the behaviour of his colleague, Ap. Claudius Pulcher, and attempted to mediate between the increasingly estranged Pompeius and Caesar. When Caesar marched on Rome in 48, Piso, like many senators, left the city in protest, but maintained a neutral stance and managed to keep up good relations with his son-in-law during and after the civil war. Piso also played a role in the struggle over Caesar's legacy, even if he did not long outlive the dictator.[27] Without question, therefore, Piso was by far a more distinguished, influential, and successful figure than Memmius.

As men of letters, too, Piso and Memmius present rather differently.

Piso's sumptuous villa at Herculaneum offers exceptionally articulate and coherent evidence in this domain.[28] Its sheer scale and luxurious furnishings prove that it could only have belonged to a man of the highest culture who possessed the means to celebrate that culture in the fullest measure. Among its contents was the most extensive library that has come down from the ancient world; and the remains identified to date consist almost entirely of Epicurus' and Philodemus' writings, including the essay *On the Good King*. This villa is therefore assumed by most to have belonged to Piso and perhaps to have been home to an Epicurean

---

[24] Suetonius (*Gram. et rhet.* 14.1) does not specify which of Pompeius' five wives was involved, but Kaster (1995: 173 ad loc.) answers that question convincingly. The anecdote clearly belongs to a period when Memmius was willing to risk insulting Pompeius, who had supported Memmius in the consular election of 54.

[25] Cicero, stopping in Athens on his way to Cilicia in the middle of 51, wrote a letter (*Fam.* 13.1) to Memmius, who had left for Mytilene the day before. Some have inferred that Memmius was changing his place of exile, but there is no confirmation of this. On the contents of this letter see below, n. 38.

[26] Cicero (*Att.* 6.1.23) also records that Memmius' cousin, C. Scribonius Curio, worked as tr. pl. in 50 to recall Memmius, but it is not known whether he was successful, nor whether Memmius was recalled with other exiles during Caesar's dictatorship in 49 (Caes. *B Civ.* 3.1.3–5, Suet. *Iul.* 41, Plut. *Caes.* 37.1). At *Brut.* 247, written in 46, Cicero speaks of Memmius as dead. On Memmius' exile in general see Kelly 2006: 194–5.

[27] Conveniently summarized, again, by Nisbet 1961: xiv–xv.

[28] This is not the place for a detailed discussion of the villa, particularly in relation to Cicero's comments on Piso's taste in an invective context. Nisbet (1961: 186–88) and Sider (1997: 9–15) give judicious accounts of the evidence regarding Philodemus' relationship with Piso and on the villa's role in it.

community with Philodemus at its centre.[29] An epigram addressed to Piso
by Philodemus makes an impression that it is fully compatible with
evidence from the villa.[30] In short, in his cultural pursuits Piso seems to
have taken seriously the teachings of the Garden, when a more relaxed or
eclectic approach might have been more typical of his class.

Our evidence concerning Memmius is harder to evaluate. He was
certainly a man of literary interests. Cicero (*Brut.* 247) considered him a
talented though undisciplined speaker and a devotee of Greek literature
who disdained Latin, though he did write Latin poetry.[31] Ovid (*Tr.*
2.243–4) and the younger Pliny (*Ep.* 5.3.5) mention his erotica, and what
little survives looks to be on other subjects.[32] He was still being read in
Gellius' time, but was thought by some critics to be *durus*.[33] In addition,
Memmius may have been a patron of Catullus and Cinna, who went to
Bithynia and Pontus as members of his cohort and are also thought, for
reasons that require no rehearsal here, to have shared certain aesthetic
ideals. But Catullus says nothing at all about Memmius' poetry, and
nothing unambiguous about him as a patron. Indeed, he only mentions
Memmius in terms that are anything but laudatory.[34] It is true that
Catullus uses invective as a form of homosocial bonding, but to call one's
praetor an *irrumator*, as he does in poem 10, seems an extreme form of
indirect praise. Still, Catullus' posture as a disappointed profiteer who
made no money in Bithynia is not only self-serving, but amounts to an
implicit claim that Memmius administered his province without exploitation. But even so, Catullus writes about Memmius only as someone
potentially helpful to him in business or politics. We therefore cannot
say that Memmius was a literary patron of Catullus or Cinna, or that he

[29] Gigante (1995: 79) argues from Philodemus' *Epigr.* 29 Sider that the philosopher lived in Piso's villa, but Sider (1997: 10–11 and 154; cf. 167) disputes this. It is important to remember that most of what is believed about the connections between Piso, this villa, and any teaching that Philodemus may have done there, are matters of inference – plausible inference, to be sure – and not definitely attested fact.

[30] *Epigr.* 27 (Sider 1997: 152–60 = *AP* 11.44, 23 GP); cf. Sider 1995. A second epigram addressed to Piso (38) does not seem to be genuine (Sider 1997: 199–202). Cicero (*Pis.* 70) claims that Philodemus wrote a great deal of poetry both to and about Piso; Nisbet (1961: 131–2) suggests that *Pis.* 67.13 is a satirical adaption of an epigram on a banquet given by Piso.

[31] See Courtney 1993: 233, Hollis 2007: 90–2.

[32] On the erotica, cf. the following note. Hollis 2007: 92 remarks that one fragment (45 in his edition = 1 Courtney) appears to be from a serious context.

[33] The critics in question are the snobbish *Graeci plusculi* quoted by Gellius (*NA* 19.9.7), who respect the love poetry of Catullus and a bit of Calvus' as well, but disparage Laevius, Hortensius, and Cinna along with Memmius. *durus* is the same word used by Quintilian to characterize Gallus (*Inst.* 10.1.93).

[34] Catull. 10.9–13, 28.9–10; on the latter poem see the following note.

shared their literary ideals in any simple sense.[35] Mainly, he was a more powerful 'friend' of them both who accepted them (perhaps on the recommendation of intermediaries) as members of his cohort; and that is all we know.

There is little to connect Catullus with Lucretius in any personal way, apart from the fact that they both name Memmius. But while it is easy to exaggerate the differences between these poets, differences there are, and they further undermine the possibility that Memmius was at the centre of a sodality based on shared literary ideals. Catullus was committed to a self-consciously 'new' Latin poetry modelled on that of Alexandrian poets, Callimachus above all, while Lucretius, though hardly unfamiliar with modernist poetics, affected a deliberately archaizing style reminiscent of Ennius.[36] If Memmius was the patron of them both, then his taste was notably eclectic. And even if Catullus' hellenizing style might have appealed to a man who preferred Greek literature to Latin (and who wrote erotic poetry himself), the aggressively latinate *DRN* insistently presents itself as a translation of Greek philosophy.[37] Why offer such a poem to a man like those who, according to Cicero (*Fin.* 1.4; cf. *Acad.* 1.4–6), thought putting philosophy into Latin a waste of effort because anyone interested could read it in the original Greek?

Finally, there is the question of Memmius' relationship to Epicureanism. This used to be thought a stumbling block to identifying Lucretius' addressee with the praetor of 58; but that problem may now have been solved. The evidence is, yet again, a letter from Cicero (*Fam.* 13.1), this one to Memmius himself on behalf of Patro, then leader of the Epicurean community at Athens, whom Cicero and Memmius met when Patro came to Rome some years previously. Memmius now owned a property in Athens on which stood the ruins of a house once owned by Epicurus himself. It is unclear what plans Memmius had for this property, but Patro wanted whatever was left of the house, by then a ruin, to remain as a memorial to the master. Cicero favoured this plan and urged Memmius to make over at least the part of the property connected to Epicurus. So far, so good; but here the problem arises. In an effort to persuade Memmius,

---

[35] Poem 28 provides the best example, in which Catullus commiserates with his friends in Piso's cohort, Veranius and Fabullus, and apostrophizes Memmius, complaining that members of both cohorts have been thoroughly ill-used by their more powerful friends.

[36] On Lucretius' familiarity with the literary avant-garde see Kenney 1970 and Gale 2007b.

[37] Lucretius' observations on the difficulty of translating Greek concepts into Latin verse and on the obscurity of his sources in contrast to the brilliance of his own poetry are found at *DRN* 1.136–45 and 921–34 ≈ 4.1–9. For discussion of these lines see Goldschmidt in this volume (pp. 50–55).

Cicero disparages Patro's philosophical beliefs and uses other language that
has led virtually all readers to think that he expected Memmius to object to
Patro's Epicureanism. It would be puzzling indeed if Lucretius had
addressed his poem to a pathological anti-Epicurean. However, in a careful
and convincing explication of this letter, Llewelyn Morgan and Barnaby
Taylor argue that Memmius was not a bigot, but simply a man of the
world, seriously interested in the philosophy of the Garden, but unwilling
to retire from worldly affairs in order to pursue the life of a fanatical
devotee.[38] Memmius' attitude, Morgan and Taylor suggest, would be
typical of the Roman political and social elite, whose lives demanded a
certain flexibility in the ways they acted on their philosophical beliefs.

With this, we come to the heart of the matter. In his essay *On the Good
King According to Homer*, Philodemus offers Piso advice on how to participate ethically in political life, particularly as that life was practised at Rome
in the mid-first century BC. The essay is not a piece of technical philosophy, and yet it has seemed odd that an Epicurean teacher would write to a
pupil in such a way as, if not to encourage, at least to permit political
activity. As Jeffrey Fish has recently explained, however, we need not think
that total withdrawal from politics, even if it was a stated ideal, was
absolutely required of all adherents, even in the time of Epicurus himself.[39]
Nor must we suspect Philodemus of hypocrisy, flattery, or any other form
of apostasy in writing *On the Good King* and addressing it to Piso. The
question is, what about Lucretius and Memmius?

If we assume that Lucretius' relationship to Memmius is essentially like
that of Philodemus to Piso, then the lessons that Lucretius offers Memmius
would seem peculiarly unwelcome.[40] But Philodemus and Lucretius
occupy very different positions from one another in relation to their
addressees. Specifically, we are speaking of the difference between a Greek
philosopher who had immigrated to Italy from Gadara, and in all probability, a Roman citizen of equestrian rank. Piso was Philodemus' Roman
patron, and Philodemus was his client, in the fullest sense of both words.[41]
The philosopher may have been largely or even entirely dependent upon
Piso for financial and every other kind of practical support. There is no
evidence that he ever became a Roman citizen, so he may have had no legal
standing without Piso's patronage. Even his fame and influence as an

---

[38] Morgan and Taylor 2017.   [39] Fish 2011.
[40] In Sections 2 and 3 I explain this point in detail.
[41] This is disputed by Allen and de Lacy 1939, but sustained by Gigante 1995: 50; cf. Sider 1997:
5 n. 11.

Epicurean teacher may have been as much Piso's achievement as his own, because without the material and social advantages afforded by someone like Piso, Philodemus might have accomplished very little. Lucretius' situation is entirely different. In the strictly intellectual life of this period, linguistic and cultural differences are relatively unimportant; but at the intersection of intellectual and social life, relations among Roman citizens were conceived quite differently from those between Romans and their Greek dependents. Thus, as we have seen, Catullus addresses and speaks of his more powerful *amici*, whether real or potential, with a liberty that no Greek writer would have used.[42] If Lucretius had viewed Memmius as a patron or potential patron of the sort that Piso was to Philodemus, and had treated him with the same deference, he would stand in marked contrast to Catullus by putting himself in such a subservient position. If we add this observation to the fact that Piso and Memmius also differ from one another in all the ways outlined above, particularly as regards the question of ethical behaviour in the political realm, then to expect the relationship of Lucretius and Memmius to resemble that of Philodemus and Piso makes very little sense. By the same token, an expectation that the same message is being delivered to both addressees seems to me highly implausible. I will defend and develop this position in the second section of the chapter.

2

The traditional view is that Lucretius died, pen in hand, in 55 BC. This is perhaps compatible with the idea that Lucretius planned to present the *DRN* to its addressee on the occasion of his election to the consulship of 53 – an election that Memmius actually lost in disgraceful fashion – but that the poet did not live to finish his tribute.[43] G. O. Hutchinson, however, has argued convincingly that the traditional date is based on unreliable external evidence, while evidence internal to the poem points to a date of 50 or 49 instead.[44] His argument has much to do with

---

[42] See n. 35 above. Besides Memmius (poem 28) and Piso (28, 47), prominent men whom Catullus abuses by name (or transparent pseudonym) include Caesar (57, 93), Mamurra/Mentula (29, 57, 94, 105, 114, 115), Clodius/Lesbius (79), and perhaps Cicero (49), Caelius (58, 100; cf. Rufus, 69 and 77) and Vatinius (14, 53, 54).

[43] 'Perhaps' because this perspective assumes that Lucretius staked a lot on Memmius' winning the election and even composed the opening of his poem well in advance of the event. This is a quite different strategy from the one that Vergil would follow in the *Georgics* or Horace in the *Epodes*, for example.

[44] Hutchinson 2001; cf. Schiesaro 2007a: 53–4. For a critical view of Hutchinson's arguments see Volk 2010, seconded with additional arguments by Krebs 2013.

Lucretius' insistence that a dangerous political situation demands Memmius' attention. This language, Hutchinson believes, fits the prospect of civil war in 50 much better than anything that was happening five years earlier.[45] But C. Memmius the failed consular candidate was in exile at the later date. Hutchinson notes that he may have been recalled, and even have participated and perhaps died in the civil war; but we have no record of such things. Hutchinson therefore admits the possibility that Lucretius' addressee was a different Memmius, while preferring to believe that it is the praetor of 58.[46] I am inclined to accept Hutchinson's arguments in favour of down-dating the poem, and to agree that the identity of 'the addressee scarcely poses an insuperable obstacle to the dating'.[47] To the extent that I differ from Hutchinson, it is mainly in finding that his proposed date tends to confirm the identity of Lucretius' Memmius as the failed consular candidate and political exile, because it makes what Lucretius has to say to him more forceful and pointed.

Lucretius' opening address to Venus, like all effective overtures, relates to every aspect of the poem that follows.[48] In particular, it launches a pair of argumentative arcs that span major architectural units, namely, Books 1–4 and Books 1–6 of the *DRN*.[49] These units exemplify what Lucretius represents elsewhere (1.931–50 ≈ 4.6–25) as the 'honeyed cup' effect. The opening of the poem draws the reader in with a ravishing display of appealing images and ideas that eventually give way to an unappealing but beneficial message that is disillusioning in the truest sense of the word, because it reveals the original image of Venus to be, in fact, an empty illusion. This is most graphically true in the movement from Book 1 to the diatribe against love and sex in Book 4, where the statement *haec Venus est nobis* (4.1058) redefines the goddess as nothing more or less than the human sex drive.[50] In a similar way, the scenes of catastrophic death and destruction with which the poem ends look back to the opening passage in an especially challenging illustration of the principle that nature allows nothing to be born unless it is 'assisted' by the death of another (1.262–4). So important are these ideas to Lucretius' teaching, in an ethical sense as well as every other,

---

[45] For further remarks on this question see the Introduction to this volume (p. 13).
[46] Specifically, C. Memmius tr. pl. 54 (*RE* 9): Hutchinson 2001: 159.   [47] Hutchinson 2001: 159.
[48] A useful introduction to the enormous scholarship on the proem is Gale 1994: 208–23, supplemented by Sedley 1998: 1–34.
[49] On the architecture of the poem see Farrell 2007, with further references.
[50] On the redefinition of Venus between Books 1 and 4 see Brown 1987: 91–9.

that his decision to begin as he does cannot have depended on any single factor, including his choice of addressee. That said, both of these ideas have a special relevance to C. Memmius.

With the poem's opening words, *Aeneadum genetrix*, Venus is defined as a political symbol; and in the mid-first century BC, this aspect of Venus' significance was prominent indeed. After next developing the idea of Venus as an allegory of human and divine pleasure (1 *hominum divomque voluptas*) and then of nature's fecundity (2–20), the poet asks Venus to assist him in writing for Memmius, whom she has always wished at every moment to be endowed with every distinction and to excel in every way (21–7). She must therefore overwhelm Mars so that the world may be at peace, and that Lucretius himself might have the calmness of mind to compose his poem at a time of such trouble, when Memmius cannot fail to present himself to his country's service (28–43). Here Lucretius returns to Venus' political significance while presenting Memmius as an almost heroic figure, a favourite of the goddess and a man of great importance to the state.[51] If Lucretius had composed this passage in the mid-fifties, perhaps with a view towards Memmius' reaching the consulship and, at last, ennobling his family forever, such a panegyric might have struck readers as seriously intended, even if it is wildly overstated. In keeping with this possibility, Venus' support might be thought to depend on the memory of some affinity with Venus claimed by members of the *gens Memmia* in the past.[52] Conceivably, Memmius' marriage to Fausta, daughter of Sulla Felix, a.k.a. Sylla Epaphroditos, could have been taken as evidence of Venus' favour, at least at one time.[53] But Memmius divorced Fausta, no later than 55, perhaps because he had discovered her

---

[51] Scholars have inferred that Venus had such relevance to the *gens Memmia* as a whole, thanks to her appearance on coins struck by L. Memmius in 106 and by (probably) his sons L. and C. Memmius in 87 or 86 (Crawford 1974: nos. 313 and 349). But these issues specify that the *monetales* were members of the *tribus Galeria*, whereas the issues of other Memmii (Crawford 1974: nos. 304, 427) do not; nor do these other issues refer to Venus. The inference of Taylor 1960: 233–4 that those who do not specify their tribe (or depict Venus) belonged to the *tribus Menenia* is accepted by Sumner 1973: 86 and by Crawford 1974: 321, who comments, 'It is remarkable that the use of Venus as a coin type ... is more assiduous in the coinage of the less important branch of the Memmii.' The Menenian branch produced the majority of Memmian office holders, including Lucretius' presumptive addressee.

[52] It can be inferred from Vergil's derivation of the name Memmius from that of Aeneas' companion Mnestheus (*Aen.* 5.117) that the Memmii boasted of their Trojan ancestry. Vergil does not, of course, suggest that they were actually descended from Venus, nor does Lucretius acknowledge such a claim, if that is indeed what the coinage of the Galerian Memmii (see previous note) actually means.

[53] On Sulla and Venus see Plut. *Sull.* 34, App. *B Civ.* 1.11; Keaveney 2005: 95–9, 135.

affair with one L. Octavius.[54] Not that there was much advantage in
staying married to Fausta: Memmius' ambitions now depended on the
support of Pompeius, who had far outgrown his status as Sulla's *quondam*
protégé, and of Caesar, never a friend of Sulla. And yet, under the alliance
of Pompeius and Caesar, Venus remained a potent emblem of Memmius'
political hopes. Pompeius, emulating Sulla and greatly outdoing his former
patron, had recently founded the cult of Venus Victrix as an emblem of his
own unprecedented success.[55] As for Caesar, of course, the entire *gens Iulia*
claimed descent from Iulus, son of Aeneas, son of Venus, a pedigree that
Caesar would one day celebrate by founding his own cult of Venus
Genetrix.[56] In the mid-fifties, then, the goddess might be seen as an
allegory of the alliance between Pompeius and Caesar, which was embodied in the mortal sphere by Julia, a living descendant of Venus, pregnant in
54 with the child of Pompeius and the grandchild of Caesar.[57] In this
sense, the poet's hope for philosophical *amicitia* with Memmius is congruent with the political *amicitia* between Rome's two most powerful men,
on which in turn depended Memmius' personal ambitions, not to mention any hope of peace for the state and, in effect, for the entire world.

On the other hand, if Lucretius composed his address to Memmius in
50 or 49, the situation was very different. As Hutchinson notes, the
friendship between Pompeius and Caesar was rapidly dissolving, and civil
war was approaching fast.[58] Julia had died in premature labour along with
the child whose birth might have prevented the breach between *gener* and
socer that by then was inevitable.[59] Rather than a symbol of the coalition
on which Memmius' advancement depended, the image of Venus' ascen-
dancy over Mars now represented the fading hope of avoiding a complete
breakdown of the coalition and of Roman society as a whole – although
just how Venus might prevent this in any practical sense is hard to guess.
Meanwhile, the country's urgent need of Memmius' service at this difficult
time has to be read as something other than conventional flattery of
Memmius' ambition in the language of duty and service. Indeed, Memmius' advancement no longer enters into it: his campaign to be consul had
ended in failure, disgrace, and exile. The state may have needed him in

[54] Fausta's affair with Octavius is briefly mentioned by Valerius Maximus (6.1.13). The date must be
inferred from Asconius' comment on *Scaur.* 46 that at the time of Scaurus' trial in 54, T. Annius
Milo had married Fausta *ante paucos menses*, and by implication soon after her divorce from
Memmius.

[55] Hanson 1959: 43–55; Kuttner 1999.   [56] Weinstock 1971: 80–91.

[57] The principal ancient sources are Plut. *Pomp.* 53 and *Caes.* 23.5–7.

[58] Hutchinson 2001: 150–3.   [59] Plut. *Pomp.* 53, Vell. Pat. 2.44, 47.

some sense – Lucretius' use of the verb *desse* (1.43) is urgent, and poignant in this context – but what, in any practical sense, was Memmius in a position to do?

In any case, the Venus proem is the hopeful starting point of arguments that end in disillusionment. In political terms, the promise held out in the proem reflects possibilities that may have existed in 55, but that had fallen away by 50, and certainly by 49 or 48. One might call Memmius an exemplary figure in this regard. From almost becoming the first man in his family to reach the consulship, he found himself a political exile instead. And it all happened under the sign of Venus, the most multivalent political symbol that existed in mid-first century Rome.

In most respects, Venus was a symbol that belonged to other, more powerful politicians than Memmius. But in one sense, Memmius himself might be more personally associated with the goddess. The movement from the ravishing *Aeneadum genetrix* of Book 1 to the diatribe against love and sex in Book 4, while offering an important general lesson for any reader about salubrious and deleterious attitudes to Venus, might contain a more particular lesson for Memmius himself in the same respect.[60] After all, Memmius twice and perhaps three times tried to use *stuprum* as a political tool.[61] His first, apparently successful attempt in 61 or 60 took place several years before the traditional date of the *DRN*. The second, when he perhaps took advantage of Fausta's adultery to divorce her and make up his quarrel with Caesar, would have occurred in about 55, at about the traditional date of the *DRN*. And the third, unsuccessful attempt – the second in which Memmius played the role of *moechus* instead of cuckold – was in 52, after the traditional date, but before the one proposed by Hutchinson. In any case, Lucretius' redefinition of Venus has pointed relevance to Memmius' career and character vis-à-vis his venereal ethics; and the later the date one is willing to accept, the more pointed that relevance becomes, in its political import, in terms of personal ethics, and because of how it all ended for Memmius.

Thus Memmius' sexual mores are closely related to his political career; more specifically, his failure to seduce Cornelia is closely entwined with his disappointed exit from the political stage, and from Rome itself. At the beginning of Book 2, Lucretius famously reflects with satisfaction on the

---

[60] On Lucretius' attack on misconceived love see O'Keefe in this volume (pp. 187, 192).
[61] Hutchinson 2001: 158 mentions Memmius' affairs along with several other embarrassing points in stating the case against the praetor of 58 as Lucretius' addressee.

pleasure to be had from occupying the citadel of philosophy, from which one may look down upon those who wander in search of the true path (2.9–13):

> despicere unde queas alios passimque videre
> errare atque viam palantis quaerere vitae,
> certare ingenio, contendere nobilitate,
> noctes atque dies niti praestante labore
> ad summas emergere opes rerumque potiri.

[A place] from which you might watch others go randomly astray, and in their wandering seek the path of life, making trials of talent, contests of distinction, striving night and day with consummate effort to reach the pinnacle of wealth and power and to take charge of human affairs.

Whatever one may think about Memmius' talent (*ingenium*), *nobilitas*, as I have said, is a quality that he signally lacked; nor did he ever reach the pinnacle of achievement or take charge of affairs in the fullest possible sense.[62] He was never consul, in fact failing spectacularly in his attempt to gain that office; and in seeking revenge for his failure, he alienated his former supporters and brought upon himself the necessity of fleeing the city.

A famous passage of Book 3 is relevant here, as well. In it, Lucretius explains the mythological torments of the underworld as allegories of ordinary afflictions endemic to human life (978–1023). Tantalus' punishment represents superstition, that of Tityos enslavement to sexual passion, Sisyphus labours to push the boulder of political ambition, and the Danaids to fill the vessels of insatiable desire for pleasure. Likewise, Cerberus, the Furies, Tartarus, and all the other terrors thought to lie beyond the grave are just fears that torture the man of guilty conscience, who lives in terror of discovery and punishment. The first and last of these myths, Tantalus and Cerberus et al., apply widely to a human propensity to superstitious fear. Tityos, Sisyphus, and the Danaids, on the other hand, represent human foibles that are still typical, but also more particular. Kenney makes clear that these myths represent irrational desire, greed, and ingratitude, respectively, and that Lucretius represents each general category by naming a specific instance of it. Regarding Tityos, instead of all desires he focuses on lust, writing *sed Tityos nobis hic est, in amore iacentem | quem volucres lacerant atque exest anxius angor* (992–3 'but Tityos is right here before our eyes, the man whom 'vultures' rip apart and gnawing

---

[62] See Fowler 2002: 61–2 ad loc. on *ingenium* and *nobilitas* as characteristics of the *novus homo* and the hereditary aristocrat, respectively.

anxiety devours as he lies prostrate in love'), before opening the image to a more general interpretation, *aut alia quavis scindunt cuppedine curae* (994 'or worries caused by some other appetite tear to pieces').[63] Similarly, as Kenney notes, Sisyphus represents 'a specific type of *avaritia*, political ambition', and the Danaids 'a type of ingratitude', but one that is here conflated with 'an inability to be satisfied, ἀπληστία' (1003–4 *animi ingratam naturam pascere semper | atque explere bonis rebus satiareque numquam*).[64] Lucretius' exploitation of these mythical punishments to illustrate pathologies that afflict us in life, not death, is therefore traditional, but his specific interpretation of these particular myths is distinctive. Of special interest is the conjunction of uncontrolled sexual appetite, unfulfilled political ambition, and a repetitive persistence in failed strategies to satisfy such appetites and ambitions. This conjunction is almost painfully appropriate to Memmius, the most prominent member of a family that for generations had failed to reach the consulship, and a man who, despite enjoying the support of Pompeius and Caesar, attempted to ensure victory by employing illegal measures that would lead to his prosecution, conviction, and exile, and who would then, seeking revenge, repeat a tactic that had apparently worked against Lucullus years before, trying but failing to seduce Pompeius' wife.[65]

After his conviction in 52, Memmius quit Rome for Athens, where he remained for at least a few years.[66] Hutchinson is the most recent of those who have pointed out that 'Lucretius' remarks on exile might seem unfeeling (3.48–58), though not entirely relevant to Memmius.'[67] Lucretius' depiction of exiles as 'men put to flight, far from the eyes of men' and 'afflicted with every misfortune' (3.48–50 *longeque fugati | conspectu ex hominum ... | omnibus aerumnis adfecti*) is no literal description of Memmius' situation at Athens, where we know he was a rich property owner. But these are conventional ideas that characterize the experience of any and all exiles. And when he specifically mentions exiles who have been

---

[63] Thus Kenney (2014: 210 ad 3.984–94) speaks of 'L.'s choice of love as the irrational desire, κενή ἐπιθυμία, *par excellence*', and notes (ad 994) that '*curae* must be understood of irrational desires in general'.

[64] Kenney 2014 ad 995–1002, 1003–10.

[65] Fish 2011 argues that Lucretius' allegory of the frustrated politician is not relevant to Memmius because we have no record that he suffered electoral defeat on a yearly basis. That is true enough, but I do not believe it is necessary or advisable to take Lucretius so literally here. Fish's documentation of a turning point in the interpretation of this passage, from an earlier consensus that it did have to do with repeated, fruitless attempts to gain a particular office year after year, to one in which the nature of the *cursus honorum* itself is indicted, is illuminating; but it seems to me that the more recent interpretation is in fact relevant.

[66] Cf. nn. 25 and 26 above.   [67] Hutchinson 2001: 158.

'befouled by a disgraceful accusation' (3.49 *foedati crimine turpi*), he speaks very directly to Memmius' situation as a man convicted of electoral bribery.[68] So, to this extent, Lucretius' remarks on exile, however unfeeling, also have pointed relevance to Memmius.

If that is so, it is reasonable to ask whether the place of Memmius' exile is also relevant to Lucretius' concerns. The poem ends at Athens, in two senses. Its final book begins with a hymn to Athens as the pinnacle of civilization, the consummation of a process of human development that Lucretius carefully tracks in the latter part of the previous book, and also as the adoptive home of Epicurus; but it ends with the graphic depiction of that same city in the grip of a plague that threatened to destroy it utterly.[69] As we have seen, while resident in Athens, Memmius had some dealings with the local Epicurean community, but of a kind that suggest that he was not in complete sympathy with their devotion to Epicurus' most rigid teachings. To such a man, the proem of *DRN* 6 may have seemed rather out of tune. The same must be true of the poem's end, which depicts the devastation of the city that Memmius had chosen as presumably the most pleasant place to spend his exile. It has been suggested that Lucretius chose to conclude the poem as he did by way of giving his reader a kind of final examination: if he could read Book 6 with equanimity, then he would have made considerable progress towards attaining a measure of *ataraxia*.[70] Such a test would be peculiarly appropriate to Memmius, either to measure how far he had come or to provide a graphic illustration of how far he had to go. That is because, as was noted above, the end of the poem looks directly back to the beginning. The relationship involves both inversions (e.g., Venus, fecundity, and birth are answered by plague, morbidity, and death) and more straightforward reminiscences. Among the latter are the phrases *patriai tempore iniquo* and *talibus in rebus* in Book 1 (41, 43) and *tempore tali* in Book 6, possibly in the poem's final line (1251).[71] In the latter passage, the phrase refers to the circumstances of the plague that afflicted Athens during the Peloponnesian War; in the former, it concerns the troubles that beset the Roman Republic in the mid-first century BC – specifically, according to Hutchinson, the civil war that

---

[68] Just a few lines later, Lucretius returns to the theme of criminal behaviour, this time linking it specifically to political ambition. In fact, he repeats the words he uses at the beginning of Book 2 when he describes the satisfaction of looking down from the citadel of philosophy to see others *noctes atque dies niti praestante labore | ad summas emergere opes* (2.12–13 = 3.62–3)

[69] Praise of Athens, 6.1–42; Plague of Athens, 1138–286 followed by the transposition of 1247–51 proposed by Bockemüller 1873–4; cf. Fowler 1997.

[70] Clay 1983: 250–66; Fowler 1997: 138.   [71] Cf. n. 69 above.

was imminent by 49.[72] Here, then, would be another link between the poem's exordium and its peroration. Yet another would be its addressee, living as an exile in Athens at a time of civil war: for the phrases just cited from Book 1 occur in a prayer to Venus on behalf of Memmius as well as of the poet himself (1.41–3):[73]

> nam neque nos agere hoc <u>patriai tempore iniquo</u>
> possumus aequo animo nec Memmi clara propago
> <u>talibus in rebus</u> communi desse saluti.

For <u>at this time of trouble for our country</u>, neither I myself can perform this act [i.e. write my poem] with untroubled mind, nor <u>at such a pass</u> can Memmius' brilliant offspring desert the common weal.

Hutchinson's argument – that the circumstances here envisioned by Lucretius fit the early stages of the war between Caesar and Pompeius better than any other time – is compelling. Though he does not say it in so many words, he seems tacitly to accept that Lucretius acknowledged Memmius' duty to take part in the war and perhaps even approved of it, however provisionally. Noting that C. Scribonius Curio, Memmius' cousin and tr. pl. in 50, was working on a scheme to recall his relative, Hutchinson suggests that this may have happened, that Memmius may have fought on the side of the senate and Pompeius, and that he perhaps died in the war. This is all possible, but also quite conjectural, since we do not know whether Curio's effort succeeded.[74] In fact, we have no further information about Memmius until 46, when Cicero mentions him in *Brutus* as though he were already dead.[75] It is thus equally possible, and requires us to posit no dramatic change in Memmius' situation, to assume that Memmius never returned to Rome, and that Lucretius, if he completed the *DRN* in the early 40s, as Hutchinson argues, addressed his poem to a man who was living in exile at Athens. If so, then his observation that Memmius could not desert his fatherland in its hour of need will have possessed a certain mordant quality, and the connection between the crisis of a civil war threatening Rome in the near future and

---

[72] Hutchinson 2001: 150–3. On the plague as a metaphor of civil war see Schiesaro 2007a: 55–8, with further references.

[73] For discussion of these lines see also Butterfield in this volume (pp. 22–3, 26–7). The first-person plural *possumus* might be read with reference to the argument of Taylor in Chapter 3 of this volume.

[74] In 48, Caesar caused measures to be enacted that would permit the return of those exiled under Pompeius in 52 (Caes. *B Civ.* 3.1.3–5, Suet. *Iul.* 41.1, Plut. *Caes.* 37.1, App. *B Civ.* 2.48, Dio Cass. 41.36.2, 42.24.2), and these measures might have affected Memmius; but if so, we do not hear of it.

[75] Cf. n. 26 above.

the crisis of the plague that had struck Athens long ago, at the start of the greatest war fought among the Greeks, will gain further point. As Lucretius' ideal reader, Memmius at the beginning of the poem will indeed have felt some duty to take part in his country's greatest crisis during his own lifetime, or maybe will have seen some opportunity in doing so; and he will presumably have been gratified by Lucretius' acknowledgement of whatever necessity or desire his addressee may have felt, in spite of Memmius' frustration at being unable to fulfil it; but if Memmius read the poem attentively and Lucretius' teaching was effective, by the end Memmius should have been able to read about the destruction of the city in which he was actually living, or of Rome, or any city, with perfect detachment.[76]

3

With this we may turn to the question posed by the title of this chapter. Was Memmius a good king? There are several ways to answer the question, all of which agree in general, while individually allowing different inferences.

We might first view the problem through the lens provided by Philodemus. Clearly Philodemus was prepared to say that Piso already was or might become a good king. Certainly his essay implies that, as an Epicurean teacher, Philodemus felt that such a thing was possible. The good king would not be the same thing as an Epicurean sage, but he would be ethically superior to a poor king while also being a serious Epicurean. In dedicating his treatise to Piso – possibly, as has been suggested, on the occasion of his consulship in 58 – Philodemus may have been offering instruction to guide Piso's handling of this high office; but in view of Piso's extensive experience in government by that time, it seems more likely that the treatise was a tribute to Piso's success in reaching the consulship without abandoning his Epicurean principles.[77] That is, rather than presuming to teach Piso how to become a good king, Philodemus was in effect assuring his patron that he actually was one. But could Philodemus have said the same thing about Memmius? It is true that when Philodemus composed his treatise, Memmius' career had not gone to pieces. He had

---

[76] Lucretius could be seen as offering a kind of consolation to Memmius, but in the form of a 'tough love' exhortation to face his own reversals and those of the state in the spirit of a true Epicurean. There might be a further implication not only that Memmius himself might face both disasters with equanimity, but that if he and other cultivated dabblers among the power elite took Epicurean ethical teaching more seriously, such disasters would be far less likely to occur.

[77] On the occasion of the treatise see Murray 1965: 179–80.

not yet suffered an electoral defeat (so far as we know), or been convicted of bribery or gone into exile. On the other hand, he had, very likely for political reasons, seduced the wife of his former supporter, Lucullus; and in contrast to Piso, it is hard to believe he did not yet feel the kind of contempt for more committed Epicureans that Cicero later expected him to feel. Philodemus would have had no reason to reassure Memmius that he was a good king, and perhaps no reason to think that Memmius would appreciate the compliment, particularly if it came from him.

But was Lucretius prepared to consider Memmius a good king, either in fact or potentially? This seems extremely unlikely. In the first place, the *DRN* is not a treatise on kingship theory, and its *obiter dicta* do not encourage the inference that Lucretius agreed with Philodemus' ideas on that subject.[78] Here it may be important that, whereas Philodemus follows many other philosophers in finding positive ethical exempla among heroes who fought in the Trojan War, Lucretius never does this. The first time he mentions these heroes (1.86 *ductores Danaum delecti, prima virorum*), he condemns their behaviour in absolute terms as representing the damage that religious superstition can cause (1.101 *tantum religio potuit suadere malorum*). After this, he mentions the Trojan War only twice more. Again in Book 1, he asserts that, as a mere accident of history, it has no direct relevance to us (1.464–77) – provocatively, no doubt, in a poem that addresses Venus as *Aeneadum genetrix*, the divine parent of the Trojan hero whose descendant, Romulus, founded Rome. In doing so, moreover, he slyly suggests that the behaviour of the Trojans offers negative ethical exempla, since he blames the destruction of Troy on Paris' abduction of Helen (1.464–5 *Tyndaridem raptam belloque subactas | Troiiugenas*; cf. 473–7). Lucretius' only other mention of the Trojan War occurs much later and strengthens his earlier point about its unimportance by relegating it, along with the Theban Wars of the Seven and the Epigoni, to the most remote past (5.326). On the whole, then, Lucretius is not especially interested in the Trojan War, and finds only negative ethical exempla in the behaviour of the heroes who fought on both sides of it. Moreover, his uniformly negative reading of Homeric ethics, including his spectacular denunciation of Agamemnon for the sacrifice of Iphigenia and his subsequent denial of the entire war's relevance to us, stands in sharp contrast to Philodemus' effort to find positive ethical lessons in Homer.[79] Notably,

---

[78] Cf. Sedley 1998: 62–93 and 2009: 40–45; Barbour 2007: 150–1; Farrell 2016. On political engagement among Roman Epicureans see Benferhat 2005.

[79] On Lucretius' indictment of Agamemnon see further O'Keefe in this volume (pp. 187, 191).

Lucretius bases his contempt for heroic values on two intrinsic principles
of Epicureanism, its rejection of conventional religious piety based on fear
of the gods, and its conception of past events as having no relevance to the
present. In contrast, Philodemus' lessons about Homeric kingship have
little connection to Epicureanism as such. It is almost as if Lucretius were
not only rejecting kingship theory in general, but implicitly reproaching
Philodemus for indulging in it, rather than concentrating on the explication of core Epicurean doctrine.

Lucretius' ethical perspective, then, both explicitly and implicitly,
would seem to be sceptical of kingship theory in general. But what about
his attitude towards Memmius himself? Much like Philodemus when he
addresses Piso, Lucretius treats Memmius as an exceptionally important
person. When he refers to his addressee as *Memmiadas* (1.26), affecting a
Greek patronymic in the style of Homer, he places Memmius on the
same plane as Scipio Africanus, whom he calls *Scipiadas* (3.1034) – in
another passage on the insignificance of past events. Elsewhere he is
Memmi clara propago (1.42) and *inclute Memmi* (5.8), the epithet *inclutus*
being otherwise reserved for Venus (1.40) and Epicurus (3.10). Such
manner of reference and address implicitly credits Memmius with heroic
ancestry and exceptionally high personal accomplishment. Lucretius
further expresses concern that it will be impossible for Memmius to find
time to read his poem, because his services are urgently needed to address
the crisis in which the republic finds itself (1.41 *patriai tempore iniquo*).
In view of all this, anyone might conclude that Lucretius did regard
Memmius as an important person and addressed him as one ought to
address a member of the Roman senatorial class. If that is so, then
whatever Lucretius may have thought of kingship theory in general,
one would have to suppose that he held Memmius personally in some
considerable esteem, precisely as a member of the governing elite and as a
man of great personal accomplishment.

In fact, this is most unlikely. As we have seen, Memmius was much less
distinguished than Piso. He was not from a family of *nobiles*. He himself
never attained the consulship. At the time when Lucretius wrote, whether
this was in 55 or after 50, Memmius had either not yet attempted to reach
this office or had tried and failed to do so, scandalously and spectacularly.
In those offices that he did hold, he accomplished nothing remarkable. In
view of Memmius' quite ordinary record, Lucretius' treatment of him
seems a bit thick. Moreover, it does not square, at all, with what Lucretius
says elsewhere about political life in general. And, as we have seen, what he
says about the vanity of holding military commands, the futility of having

repeatedly to run for successively higher offices, electoral failure, and political exile, not to mention the conjunction of these themes with those of personal failings such as lustfulness and an inability to be satisfied – all such passages read either as embarrassing lapses in tact or else as exceptionally direct and pointed lessons, when one remembers that the poem is addressed to Memmius in particular.

In my view, Lucretius was fully aware that many of his ethical lessons were especially applicable to Memmius. Indeed, I would not exclude the possibility that Lucretius chose Memmius as his addressee precisely because Memmius' behaviour reflected so badly not just on himself but on the entire Roman political class, particularly in their relaxed attitude towards living the philosophies that they claimed to espouse. In personal terms, Lucretius and Memmius may have been 'friends', in some sense, although that need mean little more than that they were not enemies. When Lucretius expresses a hope that they might enter into true *amicitia* (1.141), he is no doubt referring to Epicurean friendship in the fullest sense; but this does not mean that Lucretius was unaware what a distant possibility this actually was. And that is the main point. It may well be that Memmius was an ideal addressee because he was so much in need of the lessons that Lucretius had to teach. By the same token, Memmius' indifferent record as a politician, especially in view of his behaviour as a 'bad king', would have identified him as precisely the kind of person who had the most to gain from Epicurean therapy.

There is one sense in which Philodemus' ethical writings relate more directly to Lucretius' teachings. Not surprisingly, the relationship involves a characteristic Lucretian twist. Lucretius, as we have seen, addresses Memmius in laudatory terms, in spite of Memmius' quite modest record of accomplishment – and, depending on when exactly Lucretius wrote, in spite of the disastrous way in which Memmius finished his career. On the other hand, in addressing subjects like lust and political ambition, although he does not name Memmius in those passages, he risks indicting him in particular. The two essays of Philodemus that are relevant here are those *On Flattery* and *On Frank Criticism*. Unlike *On the Good King*, these treatises concern fundamental elements of Epicurean ethics. Philodemus' essay in kingship theory is specifically tailored to the vanishingly small audience of those who were or who might become Roman senators. Flattery and frank criticism, on the other hand, were concerns for anyone who might wish to live as an Epicurean, since the one is an obstacle and the other an essential means to ethical improvement. Lucretius, smearing honey on the rim of the cup, flatters Memmius, not just in a way to which any Roman senator was probably accustomed, but perhaps even going deliberately too far, and then offers bitter lessons more applicable to Memmius than to anyone else. This is not to say that Lucretius specifically follows Philodemus' advice on flattery and frank criticism, but rather that he makes use of these important Epicurean concepts and applies them in his own characteristic way.

In sum, it seems to me abundantly clear that Memmius was not, in fact, a good king; nor can I see any reason why either Philodemus or Lucretius would have considered him such. I further believe there is reason to suspect that Lucretius differed from Philodemus on whether it was really possible to be a good king, i.e. an active member of the Roman political class, or at least for such a person also to be a good Epicurean in the fullest sense. It thus seems possible that, whereas Philodemus clearly did consider Piso a good king and a good Epicurean, potentially and probably in fact, Lucretius may have demurred. In any case, it is not surprising that Lucretius, rather than writing an essay meant to honour its addressee as a good king, addressed his poem to a bad king who desperately needed conversion from a life of political ambition to the one of philosophical detachment that was available to all Lucretius' readers.

CHAPTER 12

A Tribute to a Hero: Marx's Interpretation of Epicurus in his Dissertation

Elizabeth Asmis

Marx wrote his doctoral dissertation 'Über die Differenz der demokritischen und epikureischen Naturphilosophie' between 1840 and March 1841. It was to be the first part of a comprehensive new study of Epicurean, Stoic, and Sceptical philosophy. As it turned out, Marx completed only the Epicurean part of his project. His failure to obtain an academic post, together with his turn to journalism and immersion in politics, pre-empted his plan. But there is also another reason, internal to his dissertation, why he might no longer have been eager to complete the project.

Marx concluded in his dissertation that Epicurus was 'the greatest Greek enlightener (Aufklärer)';[1] and he likened him to a Prometheus, proclaiming that 'human self-consciousness is the highest divinity'.[2] In Marx's dissertation, Epicurus is the high point of Greek philosophy. Alluding to Hegel's lack of enthusiasm for Hellenistic philosophy, Marx claimed that 'the death of heroes resembles a sunset, not the bursting of a frog who has inflated himself'.[3] For Marx, Epicurus is the final hero of Greek philosophy, representing its sunset in its greatest splendour.[4] Stoicism, by contrast, falls prey to superstition. There was little point, so it would seem, in going on to study the rest of Hellenistic philosophy.

Marx's dissertation has received much attention from students of Marxism.[5] There has been very little attention, on the other hand, from

I am very grateful to Donncha O'Rourke for helping me to improve this chapter and to students in various classes for vigorous debates on the issues.

[1] *MEGA* 1.1: 57; *CW* 1: 75. [2] *MEGA* 1.1: 14; *CW* 1: 30. [3] *MEGA* 1.1: 22; *CW* 1: 35.

[4] For Lucretius' use of this image in respect of Epicurus see Gee in this volume (pp. 195–6).

[5] Detailed treatments of the dissertation are by Sannwald 1957; Hillmann 1966; Gabaude 1970. Shorter treatments are by Kolakowski 1978 1.100–7; Baronovitch 1984; Fenves 1986; McCarthy 1990: 19–55; Stanley 1995 (who provides a useful overview of previous interpretations); Browning 2000; Schafer 2003 (with an excellent summary of the argument), 2006; McIvor 2008.

students of ancient philosophy.[6] This chapter addresses this gap. My aim is, in brief, to place the dissertation within the history of scholarship on Epicureanism in order to show both the originality of Marx's interpretation and the insights it brings to the study of Epicurus. To the classicist, the overwhelming impression is that Marx departs very far indeed from the evidence; there is much that seems odd or distorted. Marx himself took pride in his scholarship, and, I think, rightly so. He paid close attention to the original texts and took into consideration the scholarship of his day. It has been said by way of excuse that he had only faulty or incomplete evidence available to him. But this is not the basic reason for his innovations. As a follower of Hegel, Marx used Hegelian concepts to interpret Epicureanism as a stage in the unfolding of philosophical insight. At the same time, Marx believed that he had good evidence to place Epicureanism at a much higher stage of development than Hegel or anyone else had recognized before. The result is an evaluation that highlights with special urgency the problems that Epicurus tried to answer and still demand attention from scholars today.

I shall, therefore, look closely at the ancient evidence to gauge not only how far Marx departs from it but also what there is in it that made Marx so enthusiastic. Lucretius has a large part in Marx's interpretation. Marx read his poem, *De Rerum Natura* (*DRN*), closely. The entire poem is structured around the theme of freeing humans from the oppression of the gods; and, as I shall argue, this focus provides a framework for Marx's analysis. Lucretius also furnishes Marx with the underlying evidence for his interpretation: his depiction of the atomic swerve ('declination') as the cause of human freedom. By interpreting the swerve as the principle of human self-consciousness, Marx holds it responsible, ultimately, for the victory of humans over superstition. Hegel does not once refer to Lucretius in his evaluation of Epicurus' philosophy. Marx underpins his celebration of Epicurus as the greatest Greek 'Aufklärer' by citing at length Lucretius' homage to Epicurus as the conqueror who raised humans to the sky.

Hegel proposed in his *Lectures on the History of Philosophy* that all three post-Aristotelian philosophies adopted self-consciousness, as exemplified by the wise person, as their basic 'principle'. He attributed abstract individual self-consciousness (consisting of sensation) to Epicureanism, abstract universal self-consciousness (consisting of thought) to the Stoics,

[6] Among classical scholars, Bailey 1928 first drew attention to Marx's dissertation in a short article, in which he commended him for his scholarship. Recently, Lezra 2016 has focused on Marx's early encounters with Lucretius; Porter forthcoming offers a close analysis of the dissertation.

and the negation of both to the Sceptics. Yet Hegel saw little progress here. In all three cases, he thought, the 'one-sided' focus on the subject marked the end of the 'speculative greatness' of Plato and Aristotle.[7] By withdrawing into itself, self-consciousness became indifferent to reality. Hegel was especially critical of Epicurus. He dismissed most of his theories as superficial and not worth bothering about; and he went so far as to express relief that the bulk of Epicurus' voluminous writings were lost.[8] On the other hand, he did praise Epicurus' 'enlightened' opposition to superstition;[9] and he described his ethics as lofty.[10]

In his dissertation, Marx expresses admiration for Hegel's entire history of philosophy as 'amazingly-great and bold'; it marks the beginning, he says, of the history of philosophy as a whole.[11] Marx also describes Hegel's treatment of the three Hellenistic systems of philosophy as generally correct. At the same time, he justifies his proposal to offer a new treatment on two grounds: there is need of a more detailed treatment than Hegel was able to provide; and Hegel's speculative point of view prevented him from seeing the great importance of Greek philosophy after Aristotle. In taking this approach, Marx was much influenced by the Young Hegelians, especially Bruno Bauer, who sought to add fresh insights to Hegel's conclusions by elevating the principle of human self-consciousness.[12] In particular, Marx accepted Hegel's classification of Epicureanism as a philosophy of abstract individual self-consciousness. From this starting point, he developed Epicurean self-consciousness in an entirely new direction.

This chapter will focus on three topics treated in the dissertation: the difference between Democritus' and Epicurus' methods of philosophy; the swerve of the atom; and the so-called 'meteors', or heavenly bodies. Marx treats the first topic in Part I of the dissertation, headed 'Difference of the Democritean and Epicurean Philosophy of Nature in general'. This part

---

[7] Hegel *Werke* 1833: XIV.423–9; *Lectures* 1995: II.232–6. (I cite the 1833 edition as the one that Marx presumably read; existing English translations are based on subsequent editions.)

[8] Hegel *Werke* 1833: XIV.477 (so *Vorlesungen* 1996: VIII.119): 'Gottlob, dass sie nicht mehr vorhanden sind.' See Porter forthcoming for a detailed discussion of Hegel's view of Epicurus.

[9] *Werke* 1833: XIV.498–9; *Lectures* 1995: II.297–8. Cf. *Vorlesungen* 1996: VIII.128.

[10] Hegel *Werke* 1833: XIV.497–9, 513 (cf. *Vorlesungen* 1996: VIII.128, 134; partly in *Lectures* 1995: II.297–9). Hegel was also willing to call Epicurus the discoverer of the empirical science of nature, as practised in his own time (*Werke* 1833: XIV.497; *Lectures* 1995: II.297); but this is not entirely complimentary. He ignored Epicureanism altogether in his *Phänomenologie des Geistes*, which contains two sections on Stoicism and Scepticism.

[11] *MEGA* I.1: 13–14; *CW* I: 29–30.

[12] Rosen 1977 argues in detail for the influence of Bauer on Marx. Cf. Hillmann 1966: 226–8; McLellan 1969: 69–73; McIvor 2008: 428.

originally had five subsections; the last two are no longer extant, except for the notes. Part II follows up by treating the differences 'in particular'. It has five subheadings, beginning with the swerve of the atoms and ending with the 'meteors'. The intervening sections are on qualities, the difference between principle and element, and time. The dissertation ends with a sequel ('Anhang'), which is preserved only in fragments. In addition, there are seven notebooks, entitled 'Vorarbeiten'; these preliminary studies constitute an important supplement to the dissertation as we have it.[13]

Despite the lost parts, it is clear that the dissertation has a unified theme. Part I sets up an opposition: Democritus is a sceptical empiricist, who attributes everything that happens to the necessity of material causation; Epicurus retreats dogmatically into the serenity of self-consciousness, attributing everything to chance. Part II then constructs a continuous argument. Beginning with the claim that the Epicurean swerve ('declination') turns the atom into a principle of abstract, individual self-consciousness, it ends with the emergence of this principle as a force that annihilates the divinity of the heavenly bodies and thereby destroys the reality of nature as a whole. This is the culminating achievement of Greek philosophy; for it is the victory of abstract individual self-consciousness over superstition.

The Difference between Democritean and Epicurean Philosophy of Nature

In the first part of his dissertation, Marx issues a challenge to a view that had been passed on to his time from antiquity: this is the accusation that Epicurus simply took over Democritus' atomism, except for making a few, arbitrary changes for the worse.[14] By contrast, Marx sees the two thinkers as diametrically opposed.[15] This opposition will serve him, in the second part of the dissertation, as a basis for arguing that Epicurus made a huge advance on Democritus. Marx identifies three main contrasts: they concern ontology, scientific practice, and causation. First, he claims, Democritus held that what we perceive by the senses is merely 'subjective seeming'

---

[13] The first four Notebooks are dated to summer 1839. Notebook 4 is devoted entirely to Lucretius Books 1–3; Notebook 6 begins with a reading of Books 4 and 5 of Lucretius. The remaining Notebooks deal primarily with Diogenes Laertius (including Epicurus' extant three letters), Plutarch and Cicero.

[14] *MEGA* I.1: 23–5; *CW* I: 36–8. Cicero sets out the accusation at *Fin.* 1.17–21 and *Nat. D.* 1.66–73.

[15] *MEGA* I.1: 25–32; *CW* I: 38–45.

('subjektiver Schein'); Epicurus assigned objective reality ('objektive Erscheinung') to things that appear to the senses. Second, Democritus searched endlessly for the causes of sensory appearances; Epicurus withdrew into inner tranquillity. Third, Democritus attributed everything that happens to necessity; Epicurus replaced necessity by chance. In short, sensory illusion, empirical inquiry, and necessity are on one side; sensory certainty, personal serenity, and chance are on the other. As Marx observes, there is a certain 'Verkehrtheit' ('upside-down-ness') in this set of oppositions.[16]

Modern scholars are inclined to agree basically with Marx on the first contrast: Democritus did indeed doubt the reality of what appears to the senses, whereas Epicurus insisted that the senses put us in touch with objective reality.[17] For the rest, Marx adds interpretations of his own. Using Hegelian concepts, he claims that Democritus' atom does not come into 'Erscheinung' – that is, does not become 'manifest' – as the objective content of appearances, since the latter are merely subjective impressions.[18] It follows that the atoms, too, lack reality, leaving Democritus to explore nothing but sensory appearances. Paradoxically, Democritus becomes an empiricist, forever driven to investigate appearances in order to find the truth behind them, without ever succeeding. As an empiricist, moreover, Democritus attributes everything that happens to a necessary process of causation. Epicurus, by contrast, is guided by an ethical principle: he aims for serenity (*ataraxia*) as the goal of life. As a result, he has contempt for empirical investigation. Exalting the freedom of self-consciousness as the ruling principle of existence, he ends up attributing everything that happens to chance.

There is a lot to unpack in these oppositions; and Marx does so in the second part of his dissertation. Before we turn to his detailed explanations, however, let us consider each contrast from the point of view of modern scholarship. First, the evidence about Democritus' ontology is indeed confusing, as Marx points out. Two key pieces of evidence, said to be in Democritus' own words, are the following. The first (cited in part by Marx)[19] is: 'By convention, there is sweet, bitter, hot, cold, colour; but in truth, there are atoms and void.'[20] The second (not cited by Marx) is an accusation addressed by the senses to the mind: 'Wretched mind, after

---

[16] *MEGA* 1.1: 32; *CW* 1: 45.
[17] For Democritus see Barnes 1979: 11.257–62; Kirk, Raven and Schofield 1983: 411; Taylor 1999: 216–22. For Epicurus see n. 23 below.
[18] *MEGA* 1.1: 27; *CW* 1: 40.   [19] *MEGA* 1.1: 26; *CW* 1: 39.   [20] DK 68 B 9, cf. 125.

taking your proofs from us, you overthrow us; the overthrow is your downfall.'[21] In agreement with Aristotle, historians of philosophy have traditionally interpreted these texts along the following lines: Democritus responded to Parmenides' conceptual analysis of being by positing both being (in the form of atoms) and non-being (in the form of void).[22] This is an initial assumption, it has been thought, made by Democritus for the purpose of saving sensible reality. The second text has been thought to subvert this assumption by affirming the logical consequence that what appears to the senses is unreal; it follows that the atoms too are unreal.

Influenced by Hegel's conceptual analysis of being, Marx imputes the same initial assumption to both Democritus and Epicurus; he then draws a sharp distinction by imputing scepticism to Democritus and dogmatism to Epicurus. In the case of Epicurus, however, there is ample evidence for an altogether different method of argument. Instead of positing the existence of both atoms and void as an initial assumption, Epicurus adopted the empirical method of relying on sensible reality as a means of inferring what else there is.[23] Accordingly, he inferred the existence of atoms and void by a chain of reasoning based on the observation of perceptible things. Modern scholars are roughly agreed that Epicurus used empirical reasoning of this sort, although they differ on how extensively he used it. It is possible, moreover, as I have argued elsewhere, that Democritus also used an empirical method of inference.[24] Evidence is provided by the second text just cited: the mind takes 'proofs' for the existence of atoms and void by drawing inferences from sensible appearances, then is defeated by its defeat of the senses. In general, it appears that Democritus may well have agreed with Epicurus in substituting an empirical method of inference for a conceptual analysis of being. The difference is that Democritus ended up denying the reality of the phenomena and therefore also the reality of the atoms, whereas Epicurus affirmed the reality of both.

As the basis of his second and third contrasts, Marx introduces an Epicurean ethical principle: this is the claim that the human soul aims for serenity as its goal. As Marx sees it, this principle not only curtails scientific inquiry, but also entails that everything happens by chance. Epicurus has indeed often been accused of tailoring his physics to suit his ethics, without regard for logical consistency. Marx saves him from this

[21] DK 68 B 125.
[22] See, for example, Kirk, Raven and Schofield 1983: 408–15; Curd 1998: 180–4; Taylor 1999: 160–9.
[23] Long and Sedley 1987: 1.94–6 provide a brief overview. For a detailed discussion see Asmis 1984.
[24] Asmis 1984: 333–50.

charge by embedding ethics within his system of logic. This is a Hegelian move. As Marx will argue in the second part of the dissertation, Epicurus implanted self-consciousness at the very foundation of his physics in the form of the atomic swerve. The upshot is that Marx recognizes no fault in Epicurus' logic. In opposition to Epicurus' traditional detractors, Marx insists again and again that his reasoning is entirely consequential, even though (in the manner of Hegel) it generates contradictions. The only problem, according to Marx, is that Epicurus' logic stops short: it ends in an impasse, unable to resolve a final contradiction. But this is the way of philosophical progress; and, far from reflecting badly on Epicurus, it marks a high point in Greek philosophy.

There is also another way of saving Epicurus' logic, which owes nothing to Hegel. As just mentioned, Epicurus looked to sensory appearances as evidence for what is hidden. In some cases, he held, the evidence is sufficient to show that there is just one underlying explanation. This applies to basic truths, such as the claim that the universe consists of bodies and void, that there are indivisible elements (the atoms), and so on.[25] In some cases, on the other hand, the evidence is insufficient to show a single cause. In these cases, we look for multiple explanations, any one of which is possible, by finding analogies with what we perceive by our senses.[26] The latter is the method that applies to events in the heavens, whose causes are too distant for us to observe; examples are the rotation of the heavenly bodies, eclipses, phases of the moon, thunder, lightning, and so on. The discovery of multiple explanations in these cases is both necessary and sufficient for our peace of mind. For they confirm, as already entailed by single explanations, that everything in the world happens without any intervention by the gods. By contrast, to pick out single explanations for these events is to resort to 'myth'.[27]

As Epicurus believed, this is a scientifically sound method of inference. The only restriction is that one must stop investigating at the point where it threatens to disturb tranquillity. This is not to abandon the method, but to abandon endless investigation. It is an injunction that applies to all human activities, not just the investigation of nature. There is a limit to every pursuit, beyond which it threatens to produce more pain than pleasure. Scientific investigation serves indeed as a means to serenity, but serenity does not determine the truths it comes up with. Instead, the

---

[25] *Ep. Pyth.* 86. [26] *Ep. Pyth.* 85–8 and *Ep. Hdt.* 78–80.
[27] Epicurus *Ep. Pyth.* 87, 104 and 116.

principle of serenity stops the investigation at the point beyond which the investigation would defeat its own purpose.

To sum up so far, Marx agrees, in the first place, with the traditional view that Democritus denied reality to sensible things, whereas Epicurus assigned reality to them. On the second contrast, Marx is partly in agreement with scholarly opinion: unlike Democritus, Epicurus did put a limit to scientific investigation for the sake of serenity. Marx differs, on the other hand, from modern scholars by viewing the goal of serenity as a criterion of scientific truth. There is fundamental disagreement with scholarly opinion on the third contrast. True, Epicurus introduced chance into atomic theory by introducing the swerve. But this does not, according to Epicurus, prevent natural events from happening in accordance with the necessity of general laws.[28] It is a basic tenet of Epicureanism that there are strict limits to what a thing can and cannot do.

We turn now to the second part of the dissertation.

The Swerve ('Declination')

Ever since antiquity, the swerve of the atoms has generated both enthusiasm and scorn. Marx is its most ardent defender. As Lucretius explains (2.216–93), it is a random deviation from the straight downward fall of the atom; and it accounts for both the collision of atoms and free volition (2.256–7 *libera ... voluntas*).[29] Epicurus' ancient opponents saw it as a scandalous infringement of the principle that everything has a cause. A second difficulty, which is still debated vigorously today, is: how can a random movement account for free will?

Marx answers both problems by constructing a Hegelian line of thought. In sum, he views Epicurus as offering a conceptual analysis of the atom, according to which the swerve inheres in the atom as its formal principle. The swerve, therefore, is itself a cause, inhering in the very structure of what there is. Further, the swerve, as completed by the movement of repulsion, is the first form of self-consciousness. Ultimately, as Marx will argue in his section on the 'meteors', the swerve emerges as human self-consciousness, asserting its freedom from the gods.

---

[28] See Long 1977.

[29] The swerve is not mentioned in any of Epicurus' extant writings; but scholars are generally agreed that it was introduced by Epicurus. (Sedley 1983: 13 suggests that it was a late addition, presented in the closing books of Epicurus' work *On Nature*.) Marx himself leaves it open in his Notebooks (Notebook 1, *MEW* Suppl. Vol. 1, part 1: 42–4) whether Lucretius derived his interpretation of the swerve as a 'movement of the self' (*selbstische Bewegung*) from Epicurus; he says that this does not matter. At 2.257, *voluntas* is a generally accepted emendation for mss. *voluptas*.

How does Marx support this interpretation? Marx begins by drawing a new contrast between Democritus and Epicurus. Democritus, he claims, recognized two movements of the atoms: the fall of the atom in a straight line, and repulsion. Epicurus added a third movement, the swerve.[30] Marx then argues in detail for the difference the swerve makes.[31] Epicurus, he explains, started out with a concept of the atom as mere being, without any determination. This concept is attended by its negation, non-being, which is identified with the void. Situated within the void, the atom is a mere point that loses its individuality by becoming a straight line in its downward movement in the void. The fall turns the atom into relative being, determined by the void. This is the material *Dasein* ('being-there') of the atom; and it consists of a movement of 'non-independence' (*Unselbstständigkeit*).

This, then, is the first type of atomic movement. Because it negates the individuality of the atom, there is need of another movement. This is the movement of the swerve, by which the atom deviates from the straight line. The swerve is the *lex atomi*, or formal principle of the atom. As such, it represents the real 'soul' of the atom – not a mental content (as some interpreters supposed), but a principle of independence. The atom is now conceived as abstract individuality. This concept must in turn be realized (*verwirklicht*) by a third movement. This is repulsion, by which the atoms enter into a relationship with other atoms. The repulsion unites the materiality of the atom, which is represented by its fall, 'synthetically' with its form, which is represented by the swerve.[32] The result is, in actuality, the 'first form of self-consciousness', that is, a form of abstract individual self-consciousness.[33]

This is an entirely new interpretation, generated by the use of Hegelian logic, but without precedent in Hegel or any other thinker. Marx further surprises the reader by claiming that the swerve is a law that pervades all of Epicurean philosophy, depending on the area of activity.[34] Just as the atom liberates itself from – that is, deviates from/avoids (*ausbeugt*) – its relative existence as a straight line, so Epicurean philosophy deviates from/avoids the constraint of *Dasein* by the concept of abstract individuality. Examples are the avoidance of suffering and confusion by *ataraxia*, the avoidance of

---

[30] *MEGA* 1.1: 33; *CW* 1: 46. Marx has ancient testimonies for imputing to Democritus a downward movement in a straight line. This view, however, depends on the assumption that Democritus, too, recognized up-and-down directionality in an infinite universe. This is something that Epicurus maintained, but there is no evidence that Democritus took this view. It is much more plausible to take Democritus as positing just one movement, repulsion, which has been occurring for an infinite time.

[31] The full argument is at *MEGA* 1.1: 35–9; *CW* 1: 48–53. For detailed discussion see Schafer 2003: 130–5.

[32] *MEGA* 1.1: 39; *CW* 1: 52.   [33] Ibid.   [34] *MEGA* 1.1: 37; *CW* 1: 50–1.

pain by pleasure, and the gods' avoidance of the *Dasein* of the world by their separation from it. In Marx's words, the Epicurean swerve altered the 'entire inner construction of the atomic realm'. Whereas Democritus recognized only the material existence of repulsion, Epicurus was the first to recognize its 'essence' ('Wesen').[35] In short, the swerve turned a materialist philosophy into a philosophy of freedom.

What underpins this interpretation is a familiar Hegelian type of progression, applied to ancient atomism: the individuality of the atom is first negated by its fall, and this negation is then reconciled 'synthetically' (in Hegel's own terminology, it is *aufgehoben*) by the movement of the swerve, which assigns a new type of individuality to the atom, that of abstract individual self-consciousness. This type of individuality, moreover, underlies all of reality. By contrast, scholars of antiquity have traditionally seen the swerve as an aberration, not a causal principle; and they are far from assigning to it the cosmic importance that Marx does. What is there, then, that prompted Marx to see so much more? Granted that he is swayed by Hegelian logic, to what extent can the ancient evidence be taken to support the direction he takes?

Let us go back to Lucretius' two arguments for the occurrence of the swerve. The first is that the atoms would never collide if they always fell straight downward 'by their own weight' (2.218 *ponderibus propriis*). Just as Marx supposes, Lucretius refers to the swerve as 'another' cause of movement, besides collision and weight (2.285–6). It appears, then, that Lucretius recognized three causes of movement: weight, as the cause of a straight downward movement; the swerve, consisting of a minimal deviation from the straight line, as the cause of collision as well as free will; and collision (repulsion), scattering the atoms in all directions. Notably, Lucretius views the swerve as a cause, not as something that lacks a cause. Marx sets up his solution by eliminating weight from the initial concept of the atom. (He will introduce weight, along with all other qualities, at a later point in the argument.) With this obstacle out of the way, he saves Epicurus from infringing causation by viewing the relative existence of the atom in the void as its material cause and the swerve as its formal cause. He integrates repulsion within this causal duality by viewing it as the 'realization' of the swerve.

It can hardly be denied that there is an unbridgeable gulf between Epicurus' view of causation and the one that Marx imputes to him. One might well wonder, however, whether there is a way of saving Epicurus

---

[35] *MEGA* i.i: 39; *CW* i: 53.

that does not depend on an anachronism. What I have in mind is the idea that it lies in the very nature of the atom to swerve. On this view, nature accommodates chance as something that inheres within itself: natural bodies do not always move perfectly straight downward as a result of their weight, but their straight movement is interrupted randomly by a minimal deviation. In other words, weight normally causes the atoms to move straight downward, but it gives way at times to random deviations. In contrast with Marx, therefore, who viewed the swerve as a formal principle, it is possible that Epicurus viewed it as an element of chance in the operation of nature. On this view, too, the swerve is a cause; for it too inheres within the nature of a thing.

The swerve has traditionally been taken to be an oblique motion; and this is how Marx took it. The view I have proposed can accommodate a random oblique motion. But there is another possibility; and this fits my proposal especially well. Here, we need to bring in another unique Epicurean theory, which is very well attested.[36] This is the theory that the atom is a continuum made up of minimal parts. A minimal part has no extension of its own; instead, these parts merge with one another in such a way as to form a continuum with extension. An atom may consist of just a few minimal parts or a huge number. Now consider a straight downward motion. Lucretius specifies that the atom swerves 'by no more than a minimum' (2.244 *nec plus quam minimum*). This wording suggests a minimal part, such that the atom deviates sideways by just a minimum, then immediately continues in a straight downward movement. The straight downward motion is interrupted for just an instant, then resumes again. On this view, the swerve is a momentary discontinuity – a kind of wobble in the downward movement of the atoms – rather than an oblique motion. Through continued displacements, an atom will sooner or later meet with another atom.[37]

What makes this alternative especially attractive is that chance is kept within the strictest possible limits. One might still object that even the tiniest irregularity cannot happen by chance; there must be a reason why it happens just when it does. Against this objection, one might offer the reply: what happens in nature does not happen with mathematical precision. This is nothing new – Plato, Aristotle, the ancient mathematicians were all agreed. But the point suits the Epicureans especially well. Their theory of minimal parts offers a way of admitting minimal imprecision into the happenings of nature. Nature is indeed governed by general laws; but

[36] Epicurus *Ep. Hdt.* 56–9; *DRN* 1.599–634, 2.478–99.　　[37] See Asmis 1970: 4–20.

these laws contain within themselves a minimal degree of chance. This is far from Marx's way of integrating the swerve within the world. Yet there is some common ground: the belief that Epicurus did not make up theories at random. There is no need to leave the ancient critics with the last word: Epicurus' own theory suggests a response.

Lucretius' second reason for positing a swerve is that, without it, there would be no free volition (2.256–7 *libera ... voluntas*); for the swerve breaks the necessity of an unbroken chain of causation. He cites two kinds of observation as evidence: racehorses initiate movement from within their minds when they rush forth from their stalls; and we resist forces from outside by a movement from within (2.263–83). On the latter point, Lucretius says that there is 'something in our breast' (2.279–80) that can resist compulsion. Marx draws attention to this claim as evidence for a connection between the swerve and consciousness.[38]

In modern scholarship, there is a long-standing interpretation, proposed by Bailey (1928), that a random motion at the level of the atoms becomes, in the complex of the mind, a voluntary or purposive movement.[39] Scholars have proposed a variety of ways in which this can happen. Sedley has argued for a process of radical emergence, by which the mind can exercise control, from the top down, over the movements of the atoms.[40] Others reject emergence of this kind: they assign causal power to the atoms as such, acting on the basis of their own powers as united in a complex.[41] On either interpretation, the mind is subject to deviations that provide paths for action; in the case of the human mind, these deviations provide alternatives between which one can choose.[42] Some scholars have rejected Bailey's interpretation altogether by denying any occurrence of the swerve in a voluntary movement.[43]

Marx, then, offers his own solution to two basic problems about the swerve that have puzzled readers from antiquity: what accounts for it? and how does it account for human freedom? Marx answers both questions at once with a strikingly bold interpretation: he transforms what others decried as a causeless movement into a formal cause; and, by doing so, he makes the swerve the basis of human freedom. As we shall see in the final section of this chapter, the end result is a dissolution of the physical world.

---

[38] *MEGA* 1.1: 36; *CW* 1: 49.   [39] See Bailey 1928: 318–20.   [40] Sedley 1983: 40–9.
[41] So Asmis 1970, 1990; Fowler 1983; Purinton 1999.   [42] Bobzien 2000 rejects this position.
[43] Furley 1967 first gave impetus to this view: he argued that all that is necessary to free the mind from the necessity of fate is a single swerve, occurring in the complex of the mind at some point in one's lifetime.

The 'Meteors', or Heavenly Bodies

In Marx's interpretation of Epicurus, the principle of self-consciousness reaches a climax in the theory of the 'meteors', or heavenly bodies, as set out in the final section of his dissertation. Marx continues to build up to this conclusion in the intervening three sections that follow the swerve. Briefly, he argues in the second section that Epicurus' ascription of qualities to the atoms, including weight, contradicts the concept of the atom.[44] Conceptually, the atom is an abstract individual, distinguished by matter and form, but without any qualities. Marx elaborates this point in the third section, where he differentiates between the concept of the atom as a principle (*archē*) and the reality of the atom as an element (*stoicheion*), or substrate, of the world of appearances.[45] Through the ascription of qualities, the atom is alienated from its concept, so as to pass over into the existence, *Dasein*, of appearances. Abstract individuality remains in the domain of the concept: it is 'freedom from Dasein, not freedom in Dasein'.[46] In the fourth section, Marx argues that time belongs to the domain of *Dasein* as its form.[47]

The stage is now set for the resurgence of abstract individual self-consciousness. Marx begins his section on 'meteors' with a double contrast: as he now proposes, Epicurus' philosophy stands in contrast not only with Democritus' atomism, but also with the whole of Greek thought, both ordinary and philosophical. The Greeks, Marx says, were united in believing that the heavenly bodies are immortal deities, moving forever in the same way. In worshipping them, moreover, the Greek philosophers worshipped their own spirit (*Geist*).[48] Rebelling against this consensus, Epicurus tears down the heavenly bodies by dissolving them into abstract possibility. He does so by abandoning the method of single explanations for a new method, that of multiple explanations. This method, according to Marx, assigns to the heavenly bodies the abstract possibility of operating in any way at all, behaving now in one way, now in another, so long as there is an analogy with what occurs here on earth. What makes this possibility abstract, instead of real, is that real circumstances, which restrict the range of possibilities to just a single, necessarily realized possibility, are left out of consideration. It follows that the

---

[44] *MEGA* 1.1: 40–4; *CW* 1: 53–8. For the history and implications of this distinction see Kennedy in Chapter 13 of this volume.
[45] *MEGA* 1.1: 44–8; *CW* 1: 58–62.   [46] *MEGA* 1.1: 47; *CW* 1: 62.
[47] *MEGA* 1.1: 48–51; *CW* 1: 63–5.   [48] *MEGA* 1.1: 51–2; *CW* 1: 66–7.

heavenly bodies lack internal unity; they are mere abstractions, deprived of concrete being.[49]

This interpretation of multiple explanations is remote from Epicurus' own methodology. As previously noted, Epicurus viewed multiple explanations as alternatives between which we cannot decide because we lack sufficient evidence. Circumstances are nonetheless such that only one of the possibilities can happen; in short, Epicurus posited real possibility. His theory is a logically consistent extension of his use of single explanations, and it takes nothing away from the concrete reality of the heavenly bodies.

How, then, did Marx come to take a different point of view? His line of reasoning is especially complex, or, as Marx himself puts it, especially enigmatic. In the first place, Marx places an ethical principle in control of Epicurus' epistemology. We already saw him doing this in his general analysis of the differences between Democritus and Epicurus. As Marx now points out, Epicurus claimed that a belief in the divinity of the heavenly bodies brings the greatest confusion to the human soul. This is indeed a basic Epicurean tenet. But Marx now adds to it a consequence that is unique to his interpretation: Epicurus, he says, inferred that 'since the eternity of the heavenly bodies would disturb the ataraxy of self-consciousness, it is a necessary, stringent consequence that they are not eternal'.[50] Epicurus previously deduced the non-eternity of the heavenly bodies from the atomic structure of the universe; he did not put a moral law in charge of what happens. In agreement with his moral mandate, Marx now maintains, Epicurus changed his methodology from single to multiple explanations, thus depriving the heavenly bodies of the unity of concrete entities. Marx views this change as a breakdown of Epicurus' methodology.

As Marx himself points out, however, the moral mandate does not yet provide a full explanation. For, as Marx concedes to traditional scholarship, Epicurus already had a way of eliminating the eternity of the heavenly bodies without resorting to multiple explanations. As accidental combinations of atoms, they necessarily come into being and are destroyed. This is sufficient, Marx says, to counter the superstition of the Stoics or anyone else. Why, then, did Epicurus make such a drastic change to his method?

Here Marx presents an antinomy that, he says, is especially 'enigmatic' and Epicurus' 'greatest contradiction'.[51] And not only that: it is his

[49] *MEGA* 1.1: 52–4; *CW* 1: 67–70.   [50] *MEGA* 1.1: 54–5; *CW* 1: 70.
[51] *MEGA* 1.1: 55–6; *CW* 1: 70–1.

'deepest insight' – one that he was himself aware of and articulated with awareness. On the one side of the antinomy, the heavenly bodies are 'the atoms become real' (*die wirklich gewordenen Atome*). As the 'highest existence of his principle', they are the 'pinnacle and end point of his system'. Through a progressive reconciliation of form and matter, Epicurus' physics finally culminates in everlasting, unchanging heavenly bodies that operate in accordance with universal law. Existing as fully independent individuals, which have their centre of gravity within themselves, the heavenly bodies reject movement in a straight line, participate in a system of repulsion and attraction with other heavenly bodies, and generate time as the very 'form' of their appearance. United with form, matter has finally attained concrete individuality, together with universality. It is no longer 'abstract individuality', but has become 'concrete individuality, universality' (*konkrete Einzelheit, Allgemeinheit*).[52] The conjunction of 'individuality' and 'universality' may seem strange, but it is entirely consistent. As fully realized atoms, the heavenly bodies are concrete individuals, embodying the universality of scientific law.

At this point, Marx announces, Epicurus made it his 'sole endeavour to pull down' the heavenly bodies 'into earthly transience'.[53] The result is a crowning antinomy. Over against the 'atoms become real', 'individual self-consciousness now . . . emerges from its pupation, and proclaims itself as the true principle, and becomes the enemy of nature, which has become independent'. In unison with self-consciousness, Marx himself proclaims it in his own voice as the 'true principle of Epicurus'.[54] More precisely, abstract individual self-consciousness now 'steps out of its concealment and, liberated from material mummery (*Vermummung*), seeks to destroy nature that has become independent through an explanation by abstract possibility'.

This is indeed a jolt: just at the moment when nature has attained the height of development, Epicurus pulls it down into an abyss. How did this happen? To defer the answer for just a moment, and perhaps get a better insight into Marx's interpretation, let us return very briefly to the ancient evidence. Marx does not dwell on Epicurus' use of analogy in multiple explanations; for he has his own understanding of multiple explanations as generating abstract possibility. But there is a sense in which Epicurus himself, as traditionally understood, pulls down the heavenly bodies into 'earthly transience'. The method of analogy in effect reduces the events in the heavens to the most ordinary things of our experience. By saying, for example, that the risings and settings of the heavenly bodies may be due to

---

[52] *MEGA* 1.1: 55; *CW* 1: 71.   [53] *MEGA* 1.1: 56; *CW* 1: 71.   [54] *MEGA* 1.1: 56; *CW* 1: 71–2.

kindling and extinction (*Ep. Pyth.* 92; *DRN* 5.650–3, 660–5), he is reducing the gods to such ordinary things as the lamps we light, or the fires we kindle. What happens in the skies is no more to be feared than the things we manipulate in our daily lives. This is another way in which Epicurus raises humans to the sky.

This aspect of Epicurus' use of analogy was surely not lost on Marx. But he imputes a deeper understanding to Epicurus by re-casting Epicureanism as a philosophy of self-consciousness. The first form of self-consciousness, as we saw, is the atomic swerve, which liberates the atom from the constraint of material *Dasein*. As its final development, self-consciousness again rejects material *Dasein*; but this is now the *Dasein* of concrete reality as represented by the heavenly bodies. Self-consciousness now steps out from its concealment in the material world and fights for its existence as an abstract principle. As the formal principle of all that there is, it now opposes the fully realized material world, proclaiming its freedom from any material constraints. This 'absoluteness and freedom' is the very 'soul' of Epicurean natural philosophy, Marx now declares, with a clear allusion to his previous description of the swerve as the 'soul' of the atom.[55]

In sum, Epicurus' greatest insight consists of his own awareness of a contradiction between concrete reality, operating according to universal law, and abstract individual self-consciousness, asserting its freedom by dissolving concrete reality into abstract possibility. This is a dynamic, Hegelian type of opposition, in which an opposite (self-consciousness) emerges out of its opposite (concrete reality) as its negation. As Epicurus' 'true principle', the newly formed opposite, abstract individual self-consciousness, has a victory. This, however, is only a provisional victory; for the opposition must somehow be resolved.[56] As Marx points out, it follows from Epicurus' principle that 'all true and real science is cancelled/ transcended (*aufgehoben*) insofar as individuality does not rule in the nature of things themselves'.[57] What rules is not abstract individual self-consciousness, but self-consciousness that has achieved concrete universality. The term *aufheben* points to the need to restore universality through a

---

[55] *MEGA* 1.1: 57; *CW* 1: 72.

[56] This is the commonly accepted interpretation. Gabaude 1970: 26, for example, calls it a 'Pyrrhonian victory' for the reason that Epicurus does not move on from abstract to concrete freedom. See also Sannwald 1957: 103; Schafer 2003: 130; Baronovitch 1984: 253, 260–1; McIvor 2008: 418. Against this consensus, Porter forthcoming takes the view that Marx's Epicurus does not abandon science.

[57] *MEGA* 1.1: 57; *CW* 1: 72.

reconciliation of the two opposites. Epicurus stopped short of taking this step; for he stopped at the point of negating concrete reality. The solution, we surmise, was left to Hegel. As for the Stoics, Marx makes clear that their principle of abstract universal self-consciousness is no improvement. For this, Marx says, is to open the door to superstition.[58] At this point, Marx proclaims Epicurus as the 'greatest enlightener among the Greeks', and he cites Lucretius' famous passage on Epicurus' victory over superstition (*DRN* 1.62–79).[59]

Marx' full explanation, then, for Epicurus' demolition of the traditional gods rests on the construction of a system that places self-consciousness at the very core of his natural philosophy. By introducing the swerve into atomism, Epicurus introduced a principle of self-consciousness that emerges in the end as an awareness that the goal of life, serenity, demands the dissolution of the traditional gods into powerless, transitory beings. By fulfilling this demand, human self-consciousness asserts its freedom from the power of the gods. Marx thus raises human self-consciousness, or freedom, to the place formerly occupied by god.

Finally, I shall cite Lucretius' image, just as Marx did in the concluding paragraph of his dissertation (1.62–79, omitting the same lines Marx did):

> Humana ante oculos foede cum vita iaceret
> in terris oppressa gravi sub religione,
> quae caput a caeli regionibus ostendebat
> horribili super aspectu mortalibus instans,
> primum Graius homo mortalis tollere contra
> est oculos ausus primusque obsistere contra;
> quem neque fama deum nec fulmina nec minitanti
> murmure compressit caelum . . .
> quare religio pedibus subiecta vicissim
> opteritur, nos exaequat victoria caelo.

When human life was lying shamefully on the earth, plain to see, crushed underneath the weight of religion, which showed its head from the regions of the sky, glowering with horrible countenance above mortal beings, a Greek man first dared to raise his mortal eyes and was the first to stand up against it. Him neither the fame of the gods nor lightning bolts nor the sky with threatening murmur restrained . . . Therefore religion is crushed in turn, trod beneath the feet; and victory raises us to the sky.

---

[58] *MEGA* 1.1: 57; *CW* 1: 73.
[59] Lucretius' other eulogies of Epicurus feature at 3.1–30, 5.1–54 and 6.1–42. On the present passage see also Kennedy in this volume (pp. 279–80).

In Lucretius' view, Epicurus freed humans by discovering the truth about the universe. The basic truth is that everything that happens in nature is due to atoms moving in the void, without any intervention by the gods. As Marx sees it, Epicurus discovered the truth that human self-consciousness, pursuing its own happiness, has the power to defeat the gods. Underlying these two points of view are two very different methods of argument. On the usual view, Epicurus sought to discover the truth empirically by using sensory observations as signs of what cannot be observed. Marx imputed to Epicurus a method of conceptual analysis, according to which self-consciousness exists at the very foundation of atomic physics in the form of the atomic swerve. Despite obvious anachronisms, Marx's interpretation is rooted in problems raised by Epicurus himself. Marx sheds new light on these problems by offering a new interpretation of how Epicurus solved the problems and where he fell short, thus pointing the way to new ways of liberating humans from the constraint of external forces.

CHAPTER 13

Plato and Lucretius on the Theoretical Subject

Duncan F. Kennedy

1 Historicizing Metaphysics

Andrea Nightingale has drawn renewed attention to the importance of the social institution of *theōria* for the way in which Platonic philosophy develops its self-image of what it is doing.[1] The *theōros*, or 'spectator',[2] is a representative of the city who attends a Panhellenic festival, observes what happens there and then returns to the city and reports on what he has seen. Nightingale argues that this model structures the story of the cave in the *Republic* (514a–517c), in the course of which *theōria* is reconfigured as a 'philosophical' term. A prisoner escapes his shackles, leaves the realm of shadows, climbs to the light, eventually looking at the sun itself (516b), and then *returns* to tell the rest of the prisoners in the cave what he has *seen*: the report back is a key element without which *theōria* is incomplete. This is also the narrative structure we find in Lucretius' depiction of Epicurus in *DRN* 1.62–79: the representative of downtrodden humanity, he traverses the infinite universe – in his mind and soul (1.74 *mente animoque*) – and then reports back to us (1.75 *refert nobis*) the nature of things. For all the manifold differences in their thought, Plato and Lucretius have important things in common. Both suggest that, beyond the visible phenomena of the world lies truth or reality, not directly accessible to the senses. Thus Socrates says in the *Cratylus* he can only 'dream' of the Forms (439c), a passage we shall return to; and although Lucretius repeatedly invites us to 'see' atoms,[3] we are told that they lie way below the threshold of human vision.

Robert Wardy has remarked that the atomic world that Epicurean 'theory' reveals is one that has little relation to normal visual experience: '*Theory* reveals to *the mind's eye* a stark, pure vista of colorless, odorless,

---

[1] Nightingale 2004.   [2] The noun is associated with the verb θεάομαι, to gaze at.
[3] Cf. the analysis in Lehoux 2013.

tasteless, soundless atoms traveling through the never-ending void. It opens a gap between *basic reality*, and at least the most familiar or basic appearances, threatening to make strangers of us *in our own world.*'[4] Wardy's language suggests that 'theory' posits two 'worlds', that of 'basic reality' ('atoms') and that of 'familiar or basic appearances' ('our own world'), and he points to the problematic of the 'gap' between them. Compare the cave, one of whose two worlds is the shadowy 'underground', the other 'overground', illuminated by the sun. Here we encounter what came to be called 'metaphysics', the discourse that has seen its task as exploring the distinction between being and seeming, between reality and appearance and between what we can sense and what lies beyond our senses. The term itself is late in appearing. Although one of Aristotle's works was given the title *Metaphysics*, he himself doesn't use the term, speaking rather of *theologikē* and *philosophia prōtē* ('first philosophy') when he wants to refer to that realm of knowledge that deals not with the being of specific things, such as living beings (biology) or human societies (politics), but with being as such in its universality or generality.[5] 'First philosophy' explores the 'principles' beyond which it is impossible to go (etymologically, *principle* is associated with *primus* and *capio*, and suggests occupying first place). Thus, Lucretius habitually uses the image of the first in order (*rerum primordia, corpora prima*) to characterize atoms (cf. *DRN* 1.55–61), and uses the term *principium* for the point back beyond which you cannot go in argument (1.149).

A prominent tradition of metaphysics takes its cue from Plato's use of Parmenides' poem, which posits two realms, the 'Way of Truth' and the 'Way of Opinion', and the separation between the two is set up by the narrative of a journey, a chariot ride undertaken by an unnamed youth to the point where day meets night, where a goddess instructs him on what must *be*, and the deceptive quality of human beliefs. There is a journey, to be sure, but knowledge of the 'Way of Truth' involves divine revelation. However, in Plato and Lucretius, *theōria* is undertaken by a representative of the human race who reports back to those of us who remain in this world of sensory experience. Still, these journeys are extraordinary, and if there is a 'gap' between 'appearance' and 'reality', we find ourselves stranded on *this* side, and our perspective on *that* side *over there* is from *here*, a world characterized by the phenomena Parmenides sought to escape: time, change, motion, ontological plurality, language (apart, of course, from the

---

[4] Wardy 1988: 112 (my emphases).
[5] On the term 'metaphysics' and the title given to Aristotle's work see further Kennedy 2020: 227–8.

monolithic word *esti*) and the narratives constituted from it with which we attempt to structure our experience. The fully fledged *theōros* is a rare bird, in Plato the subject of stories, in Lucretius a historically unique human being he is prepared to call a god (*DRN* 5.8) and whose discoveries are likened to divine revelation (cf. 6.1–8; also 3.14–15 and 3.28–30). If Lucretius, as a good Epicurean should, recasts metaphysics as, emphatically, not *theologikē* but *philosophia prōtē*, his appropriation of the imagery of the former has evoked surprise (the repeated charge of *l'anti-Lucrèce chez Lucrèce*) and will repay attention here. Plato is immensely cautious with the narrative journeys that precipitate the term *theōria*. Socrates doesn't take these journeys himself (he can't physically), but they are the subject of embedded narratives about *theōroi* he tells, of the philosopher in the cave or of Er dying and then returning to tell of the afterlife (*Resp.* 614b–621c). In narratological terms, a primary diegetic frame, that of Socrates' narration of a conversation he had, is established, within which secondary diegetic frames, the so-called 'myths', are cast as reports back to us from a realm we cannot visit. These metaleptic devices, which suggest not simply a separation, but crucially in Plato a hierarchy, of realms, help to bootstrap the discourse of metaphysics.[6] The truth is over there, but from here involves an investment of belief on our part. After recounting Er's story, Socrates says it can save us, but is careful to add the rider 'if we believe it' (*Resp.* 621b), and of the story of the cave, he says, 'the truth of the matter is known only to god' (*Resp.* 517b).[7]

Platonic myths, arguably Platonic dialogues more generally, are in the business of *make-believe*, making their readers believe in the concepts precipitated by 'theory', above all the Form of the Good, the *philosophia prōtē* of Platonic thought, represented by the light of the sun in the story of the cave. If, as in Epicurean atomism, the separation between the world we can see and what lies 'below' the threshold of visibility depends on the limits of our senses, there is 'in reality' – so we are asked to believe – a continuum: the truth goes all the way down, *if* only we could see that well. What Lucretius calls *ratio* ('explanation'/'reason'/'account' – however translated, the term is invoked when the faculty of thinking is held to bridge the gap between what *seems* to be, and what *is*, the case) can cross that threshold, but a necessary part of his exposition is making his reader *believe* the 'theory'.

---

[6] Cf. Kennedy 2020: 228.
[7] The translations in this chapter are my own except where noted at n. 71 below. The text of Lucretius used is that of Rouse and Smith 1992.

The *theōros* is a figure of make-believe, but if it is not given to us to be *theōroi* in the fullest sense of that term, Plato has planted the seed of the idea (to use the imagery of *Phdr.* 276e–77a). He maps this metaphysical schema onto a received discourse, *theologikē*: Socrates remarks in *Phdr.* 278d that the designation 'wisdom' (τὸ σοφόν) seems a great one and to befit God alone, but 'the love of wisdom' (τὸ φιλόσοφον) better fits a human being. For all the suggestions in Books 5–7 of the *Republic* that the philosopher at his greatest can (in heavy scare quotes) 'theoretically' attain the vision of the Form of the Good, even Socrates, as we have seen in the *Cratylus*, says of himself he can only 'dream' of the Forms. In the *Republic* and the *Theaetetus*, Plato develops a distinction between dreaming experience and waking experience in such a way as to model the separation of a world of sensory experience from the world of the Forms beyond. Our waking experience does not deliver reality to us in such a way that we can pronounce definitively on it. Such intimations Socrates has of the world of the Forms in his waking experience have some of the characteristics of reliability or unreliability that we attribute to dreams.[8] Nonetheless, both Plato and Lucretius suggest that it is through the act of thinking that we can (at least attempt to) transcend barriers between things as they appear and things as they are. Lucretius, as we shall explore, repeatedly suggests that a combination of *species*, paying attention to the appearances of things, and *ratio*, thinking about them, can take us beyond the limits of what we can see to what Wardy called 'basic reality'; and in Section 2 below, I shall examine how Plato so configures thinking as to suggest that it can give intimations of what *is*. Thinking is projected as a *medium* of truth(s), and, far from taking that for granted, we should ask how it came about. Bringing together these two takes on 'theory' can help us to gain some purchase on how metaphysical assumptions are generated and develop. First, however, some preliminary remarks on where I think the approaches adopted in this essay are coming from.

Metaphysical worldviews are so part of 'our' intellectual heritage that it is tempting to treat metaphysics as a universal category or natural kind, rather than a discursive category with a history. In matters of faith and, no less, rational explanation, a perceived gap between appearance and reality articulates our thoughts, but how does this emerge in the ways it does? Moreover, how we situate ourselves in relation to that perceived gap generates different traditions of thought. An emphasis on the description of things as they *appear*, as they present themselves to human experience,

---

[8] Cf. Kennedy 2020: 228–32.

provides the point of reference for a style of metaphysical thinking that came to particular prominence in the twentieth century, phenomenology, and has seen some notable interventions in the twenty-first. A key move of phenomenology has been to bring time, which the Parmenidean and Platonic traditions sought to exclude, back into questions of being. It is this perspective that sets in train the historicization of terms like 'theory' and 'philosophy' we encounter in the work of Andrea Nightingale, concepts that, like 'metaphysics' here, are viewed not as timeless but as historically emergent, coming into being (and sometimes passing away) in particular contexts, and deploying received social practices and cultural terms in fresh contextualizing frames.[9] Ian Hacking's preferred term for these modes of study is 'historical ontology'.[10] He remarks: 'the comings, in comings into being, are historical'.[11] Arguably the most bracing challenge to the term 'metaphysics' comes from the methodology often called 'symmetrical anthropology', in which the ways anthropologists and their subjects make sense of each other are placed on an equal footing. The key figures here are ethnographers both of whom have carried out their fieldwork in South America, Philippe Descola[12] and Eduardo Viveiros de Castro, whose major recent work is provocatively entitled *Cannibal Metaphysics*.[13] A comparativism that treats styles of thinking as both historically emergent and local – 'Greco-Roman' or 'occidental' metaphysics – is most prominently represented in classical studies in the work of Geoffrey Lloyd.[14] It is important to note that this anthropological turn does not mean that, ontologically, 'anything goes'. As Patrice Maniglier puts it: 'It is not a question of accepting that whatever someone or other declares exists does, indeed, exist, but of better understanding what actually exists in *our* world by *contrast* [*différence*] with what exists in others.'[15]

The most ambitious re-evaluation of metaphysics from this perspective is Bruno Latour's *An Inquiry into Modes of Existence: An Anthropology of*

---

[9] Cf. Blumenberg 2015 (the English translation of Blumenberg 1987). His investigation of the famous anecdote about Thales in Plato's *Theaetetus*, which I re-examine in Section 2, is subtitled *A Protohistory of Theory*.

[10] A genealogy might trace this tradition through Heidegger and Husserl to the ancient Sceptics. Husserl, taking his cue from what the Sceptics had called *epochē*, advocated suspension of judgement, in an attempt to bracket off theoretical assumptions about what any phenomenon 'really' is.

[11] Hacking 2002: 4–5. He offers (2002: 1–26) a useful critical survey of the major figures he gathers in the field of historical ontology.

[12] Descola 2013.   [13] Viveiros de Castro 2014.

[14] See especially Lloyd 2015: 1–9, which offers a summation of his intellectual position and the influences on it.

[15] Maniglier 2014: 38; original emphases.

the Moderns. Rather than pondering 'existence' *per se*, what exists, Latour asks us to focus on *modes* of existence, *how* what we take to exist exists, and he has suggested fifteen such modes.[16] These 'modes of existence' are also 'modes of veridiction', which do not tell truths in an absolute sense, but are ways of, as Latour puts it, speaking well of the entities they treat: one does not use the same modes of veridiction to speak of the things of the sciences and the things of law or of politics. As Maniglier puts it, '"To be" does not mean the same thing for a Higgs boson as it does for the Argentinian peso, but both equally *are*, and the task of the metaphysician is to exhibit that equality and diversity.'[17] This is not the place to go into Latour's modes in detail. However, a number of observations are relevant here. Latour does not believe in the 'two worlds' model. There is no pre-existing or ready-made reality waiting to be 'discovered': what exists for us (whether that is in the sciences, the law and so on) emerges and subsists in the course of the activities associated with one mode or another. For Latour, nothing exists *per se*; nothing has an eternal essence. He is an ontological pluralist and an ontological relationist: what comes to appearance, whether Higgs boson or Argentinian peso, does so through the interaction of 'assemblies' of 'actors', both human and non-human (e.g., pieces of technology), in accordance with one or more modes.[18] Latour's is a process ontology, and, in a more general way, our (ever-changing) sense of what we call 'reality' is likewise processual.[19] Thus, there is no one thing to which, in essentialist fashion, everything can be finally referred back to or reduced to – no *philosophia prōtē* of the sort offered by Plato or Lucretius. Matters of fact are established when one 'inscription' is *transformed* into another in an ongoing process he calls 'chains of reference'.[20] The emergence of the many things that have being for us in this way *in mediation* has resonances with process theology (which was the subject of Latour's doctoral dissertation):[21] God is not a transcendent figure who exists 'outside' the world, beyond space and time, but a being revealed

---

[16] Latour 2013. The fifteen modes (avowedly provisional and open to revision) are: Reproduction, Metamorphosis, Habit, Technology, Fiction, Reference, Politics, Law, Religion, Attachment, Organization, Morality, Network, Preposition, Double Click. Much the best introduction to Latour's work is now de Vries 2016.

[17] Maniglier 2014: 42; original emphasis.

[18] De Vries 2016: 65–7 is good on this. For another contemporary version of ontological pluralism and relationism see Gabriel 2015.

[19] For an account of how we experience this in our day-to-day dealings, cf. Kennedy 2020: 243–5.

[20] Latour 2013: 77.

[21] Latour 2010 offers his own account of his education and intellectual development.

when one exegesis is resumed by another.[22] This take on *theologikē* goes for things that have being for us within other modes of veridiction, from Higgs boson to Argentinian peso.

Let us conclude this first section by considering how some aspects of our reading of Lucretius might be inflected by Latour's metaphysical modes. If the Epicurean atom is to have being, it will be through the mode Latour calls Reference, whereby we reach entities remote in distance and scale.[23] Recall, however, that such remote entities are reached through mediation, chains of reference, and thus the mode of Technology intersects with that of Reference, giving us an expanding range of tools to overcome the obstacles to instituting and maintaining those chains of reference. The Large Hadron Collider is not simply a particle accelerator, but a device for producing inscriptions that the scientists at CERN must interpret in their quest to establish the existence of the Higgs boson and so *make* it a scientific *fact* (< *facere*). Experiments – interventions – are designed to make visible what is invisible (indeed happens below the level at which one can speak of 'light' in any sense). Movements of energy in the quantum field are precipitated so as to create a chain reaction of movements at larger scales until something happens that can be photographically recorded.

However, we shouldn't underestimate the humble technology of paper, on which can be inscribed not simply photographs, graphs, or formulae, but also fresh 'fields of sense' that can be brought into being by combining words in new ways in new contexts. Mediation is viewed so positively in this metaphysical tradition that it casts doubt on whether we experience anything directly with our senses, unmediated. Recall how Lucretius in *DRN* 1.138–9 talks of the 'new words' he needs owing to the 'poverty of his language' and (a delicious phrase) 'the newness of things' (*multa **novis verbis** praesertim cum sit agendum | propter **egestatem linguae** et **rerum novitatem***).[24] New coinages are rare, and his particular genius is to redeploy familiar terms to new ends.[25] In *DRN* 1.141–5, Lucretius draws the attention of Memmius (and the reader) to the efforts he makes to find the right words and the poetry with which to 'spread open *before your*

---

[22] Cf. Maniglier 2014: 38. On the role of biblical exegesis in Latour's thought, cf. Schmidgen 2015: 9–24 and de Vries 2016: 17–20.

[23] For a diagrammatic summary of Latour's modes and the distinctive questions they pose, cf. Latour 2013: 488–9.

[24] On cognition as 'extended' or 'distributed' in different media, including language, see Tutrone in Chapter 4 of this volume.

[25] Cf. Sedley 1998: 35–9; Kennedy 2002: 73–8; and Shearin 2015: 46–97 on Lucretius' use of legal terms. The translatability of Epicureanism was necessarily a more pressing issue for Lucretius than it was for Epicurus: see also Goldschmidt in this volume pp. 51–2, 56).

mind clear lights whereby you may see right into hidden things' (144–5 *clara tuae possim praepandere lumina menti,* | *res quibus occultas penitus convisere possis*). *praepandere* is elusive, and has generated much perplexity (which I have long shared).[26] But the metaphor is surely that of unrolling a text in front of somebody to show them something, just as Latour draws attention to the way scientists gather around a photograph, or a print-out of figures, point to something and say 'look at that'.[27] No, you will never see an atom with your eyes, but look *here*, in this text, and ***there*** *it is*! The newness of the things, indeed! Speaking of how thinking 'comes into being through interactions with an external set of symbolic and technical tools', Sybille Krämer remarks how this 'requires an attitude towards perception that can be described as both a "seeing-with" and a "seeing-through" . . . With and through the empirical inscription we see the abstract form. If ever the notion of the "mind's-eye" is to make sense, then it must be here, in the act of using the visible to *see the non-visible*: in this way, in-*sight* becomes possible.'[28]

Thus the generation of facts, truths and ontologies involves performative acts. Hans Ulrich Gumbrecht refers to this as 'the production of presence'.[29] Echoing the language of Heidegger, he speaks of truth as a happening or event, and the work of art as a privileged site for the happening of truth, for the unconcealment (and the withdrawal) of Being.[30] Aesthetic experience, Gumbrecht suggests, involves being 'lost in focused intensity', and the objects of aesthetic experience 'are characterized by an oscillation between presence effects and meaning effects'.[31] As we saw, Latour's metaphysics does not eschew *theologikē*, but the mode of existence he calls Religion would recognize not only how Lucretius co-opts the tropes of *theologikē* (e.g., Epicurus as a god), but also the impulses Latour particularly associates with this mode: a yearning for the timeless and the transcendent (expressed

---

[26] Cf. Farrell 2001: 41: 'He hopes to be able to "open the clear lights" to Memmius' mind. What does this mean, exactly? To shine lights onto Memmius' mind? To reveal lights to his mind? To open the lights of his mind? Are these lights, as often in Latin, eyes, which Lucretius wants to "open for the first time" (*praepandere*)?' For the use of this image at *DRN* 1.954 see O'Rourke in this volume (pp. 119–20).

[27] Latour 1999: 24–79. Cf. *DRN* 1.55 *rerum primordia pandam* and 5.54 (of Epicurus) *omnem rerum naturam pandere dictis*.

[28] Krämer 2016: 175; original emphases.

[29] Cf. Gumbrecht 2004: 17: 'What is "present" to us (very much in the sense of the Latin form *prae-esse*) is in front of us, in reach of and tangible for our bodies.' The experience may be one of greater or lesser intensity.

[30] Gumbrecht 2004: 72; he goes on to speak of 'the happening of truth as making us see things in a way "different from the ordinary way"'.

[31] Gumbrecht 2004: 104 and 107.

in the *philosophia prōtē* of atomism), and (to Latour perhaps the most important aspect of this mode) for transformative messages, 'capable of converting those to whom they are speaking'.[32]

Latour suggests that the 'matters of fact' of the sciences are to be viewed not as timeless truths but what he habitually refers to as *equipped and rectified knowledge*, 'made of the provisional conclusions drawn by assemblies of fellow creatures from the provisional traces emanating from carefully designed instruments'.[33] Latour uses the analogy of a hurdle race to explain the challenges any chain of reference must overcome.[34] For reference to be *instituted* and *maintained*, many hurdles have to be overcome, but something is passing through – the runner, who crashes out of the race if he clips a hurdle and falls. Reference, like the runner, is always in danger of collapsing in the face of trials or obstacles produced by new 'assemblies of actors' (human and non-human); entities continue to exist only so long as they stand up to these trials. If the Epicurean atom 'exists' for us, assemblies of fellow creatures poring over the *DRN*, producing its presence, it is as a historical entity, the product of a chain of reference that was confronted by fresh hurdles and tripped. The 'matters of fact' of the sciences, and the means by which they are established, have moved on and, confronted with new trials, will do so again.

Although his physics have been superseded, Lucretius has nonetheless laid down a powerful metaphysical marker, if we pay close attention to what he says (1.1114–17):

> Haec sic pernosces parva perductus opella;
> namque alid ex alio clarescet, nec tibi caeca
> nox iter eripiet quin ultima naturai
> pervideas: ita res accendent lumina rebus.

'So led all the way through them (*perductus*) with a little effort you will gain a thorough understanding (*pernosces*) of these things.' Understanding is a process, involving some effort on your part, and it comes about through a chain of reference: 'for one thing will become clear from another'.[35] He develops the image of a traveller undertaking a journey (*iter*) by night, reaching his destination (*ultima naturai*) through successive re-kindling of the torch that lights his way: 'nor will blind night snatch away your path and stop you from seeing thoroughly (*pervideas*) the

---

[32] Latour 2013: 304.
[33] Latour 2016: 20. For Latour, thought is irreducibly collective. We shall return to this below and in Section 2.
[34] Latour 2013: 107.   [35] On this passage see also O'Rourke in this volume (pp. 121–2).

extremities of nature: thus things will kindle lights for things'. Moreover, in one of his favourite programmatic passages, several times repeated (1.146–8, 2.59–61, 3.91–3, 6.39–41), he flatly rejects the climactic detail of Plato's cave story, where the philosopher exits the cave to look directly at the sun:

> hunc igitur terrorem animi tenebrasque necessest
> non radii solis neque lucida tela diei
> discutiant, sed naturae species ratioque.

This terror of the mind therefore and these shadows must be dispelled not by the rays of the sun or the bright shafts of day, rather the appearance of nature and the thinking brought to bear on it.

There is no direct, unmediated, access to the truth.

For Latour too, the story of the cave in the *Republic* is a recurrent source of exasperation, but his criticisms would go further than Lucretius, and include some of Lucretius' most cherished assumptions.[36] 'Everything is bizarre in Plato's allegory of the cave', Latour opines, echoing the objection of Glaucon to Socrates' story: 'The image you speak of is bizarre, and the prisoners are bizarre' (*Resp.* 515a ἄτοπον, ἔφη, λέγεις εἰκόνα καὶ δεσμώτας ἀτόπους). Latour does not jettison distinctions between seeming and being; rather they operate in their own ways within their own particular modes of existence, and none of these modes of existence lords it over the others in the way that Lucretius suggests that all phenomena can be reduced to atomic physics and are subject to a singular *ratio*. Rationality for Latour is woven from more than one thread: each mode of existence generates its own provisional 'mini-transcendences'. The notion that one can embark on a way of truth that will embrace and explain *everything*, or transcend all distinctions of seeming and being and adopt a so-called God's-eye view of a totalized reality as if seen from the outside,[37] is indicative of the power of story-telling and the hold it can exercise: 'the tale is told every time someone explains to you that the world you experience in color, taste, noise and depth is but an illusion of the senses, a mere shadow, quickly dissipated by the true nature of what really exists'.[38] Using the 1977 movie *Power of Ten*, which initially gives us a shot of a couple picnicking in Chicago, and then pans out into the universe by factors of ten and similarly in to the subatomic level, Latour

---

[36] Latour 2016; earlier Latour 2004: 10–18.
[37] For Gabriel 2015, this is 'why the world does not exist', where 'the world' is constituted by absolutely *everything*.
[38] Latour 2016: 12 and 14.

homes in on an important aspect of this: 'We are asked to believe that there is a plausible continuity in the observer's view that stretches from the farthest galaxy to the smallest particle'[39] – just as Lucretius' appeals to 'seeing' suggest a similar continuity. But in the movie different shots are edited together to give the impression of one continuous shot, and in Lucretius, the point at which the eye is superseded by 'the mind's eye' is elided, as in *DRN* 1.144–5. This erasure of discontinuities in *Powers of Ten* 'allows the viewer to imagine that everything from the galaxy to subatomic particles – not to mention the clothing, food, bodies, and cells of the two characters picnicking in the park in Chicago – is not only bathed in the same light but made of "the same stuff." The name of that supposedly universal stuff is "matter."' The movie presents 'a totally idealistic view of what it means to be material'.[40] If Plato is an idealist in respect of form, Lucretius is an idealist in respect of matter, and both appeal to a similar myth to legitimate their – and I use this word under caution – 'worldview'.

'Worldviews' have consequences in the world, and Latour wrote this analysis in the immediate wake of the Bataclan massacre in Paris in November 2015, and, a couple of weeks later, the conference on climate change held in the same city. For all the emancipatory rhetoric in which Plato and Lucretius frame their myths, violence is written into them. In Plato's story, it is associated with the cavemen, who would murder the returning philosopher if only their hands were free to do so (*Resp.* 517a), and in Lucretius with those empowered by the worldview of religion and superstition.[41] However, the wish-fulfilment and violence inscribed in these myths can be differently distributed with some changes of emphasis. Epicurus returns from his foray and what is he represented as doing? Trampling his opponent underfoot, whilst we are exalted to heaven (*DRN* 1.78–9). Western history and recent events can indicate how those emboldened by having seen the light, and knowing that they possess the truth, have thought fit to slaughter the cavemen or subject the planet to an ecological crisis. 'And does it really matter if they do it in the name of Allah, Jesus, science, reason, or the market?', Latour asks.[42] One would have to be very sanguine to feel that this cycle of violence against each other and the planet could be brought to an end, but, as he says, 'let us move neither up or down, but within and along the world'.[43]

---

[39] Latour 2016: 18.   [40] Ibid.
[41] Cf. *DRN* 1.80–109, the sacrifice of Iphianassa, with the conclusions Lucretius draws.
[42] Latour 2016: 15.   [43] Latour 2016: 20.

One outcome of the analysis in Section 1 above is that, if we cast our minds back to Wardy's remarks about Epicurean theory, in the way that they posit two worlds, we may feel that they are overlaid by a tradition of Platonizing metaphysics, and in their reference to 'colorless, odorless, tasteless, soundless atoms' maybe also by a modern empiricist tradition that put great emphasis on a distinction between primary and secondary 'properties'.[44] A major challenge to Lucretian scholarship is therefore to gain an enhanced awareness of how processes of reception (chains of reference, if you will) condition what we 'see' in the text of the *DRN*.

2   Scenes of Thinking in Plato and Lucretius

To follow this up, I want to examine scenes of thinking in Plato and what Lucretius makes of them. What if we see such scenes not as dramatic colouring, adjuncts to the 'hard' argumentation of philosophical reasoning, but as helping to develop – culturally and historically specific – discourses of 'philosophy' and 'metaphysics' and the worldviews they generate? Thinking about thinking has never been a straightforward exercise: an interiority that can appear remarkable to an external observer and unaccountable even to the thinking subject. The question of what is happening neurologically when we are thinking will not be my prime concern (though recent research has introduced some much-needed methodological caution to the debate), rather the ways in which received modes of representation of thinking – the postures, the interpretations of onlookers, the reports of subjects themselves – were configured to produce versions of what I have called 'the theoretical subject'. The focus of the next few pages will be Plato, but with a view to pinpointing his reception in Lucretius.

One of the most famous of all scenes of thinking in the occidental tradition comes in Plato's *Symposium* (174a–175e). The scene is richly contextualized, and characteristically complicated in its construction, refracted as it is through two internal narrators (Apollodorus and Artemidorus) and one external one (Plato).[45] Apollodorus recounts

---

[44] Cf. Kennedy 2002: 1; *mea culpa*.

[45] Dover 1980: 80–1 in his note on 174a3–175e10 has a superb analysis of the grammatical complexities of the layered narrative. The embeddedness serves as a mode of distancing the author (Plato) from the conversations he represents; on the functions of these dramatic frames, cf. Clay 2000b: 23–31. Speaking of the *Republic*, Schur 2014: 56 says: 'Thematically, recursion . . . tends to emphasize the difficulties faced by human beings who are asking questions about the highest forms of knowledge.'

how Artemidorus met Socrates on his way to a party at the house of Agathon. Socrates suggests to Artemidorus that though he has not been invited, Artemidorus should tag along. The two fall into conversation, but Socrates becomes absorbed in his own thoughts and falls behind. When Artemidorus begins to wait for him, Socrates tells him to go on ahead, and Artemidorus, feeling understandably awkward, reaches Agathon's house alone. Agathon asks him: 'How is it that you don't bring Socrates to us?' Artemidorus replies that Socrates was just behind him a moment ago, and he doesn't know where he has got to. Agathon sends a servant to look for him who reports back that he came across Socrates standing in a neighbour's doorway and he refused to come when bidden. Agathon calls this 'bizarre' (ἄτοπον) and wants to send the servant back, but Artemidorus says to leave him alone and that it is a habit of his sometimes to turn aside, wherever he happens to be, and to stand there (174d–175b). Socrates turns up 'as usual before too long', the narrator remarking 'at the most they were halfway through their meal' (175c). Socrates has been, as we might say, lost in thought, oblivious to the social demands of the situation he is in, and hardly conscious of time passing.

Let us focus on the figure of Socrates in the doorway of Agathon's neighbour. The description given is that of an external observer (we shall return to what Socrates himself says in a moment). Socrates was, we are told, 'applying his mind to himself in some way or other' (ἑαυτῶι πως προσέχοντα τὸν νοῦν). Artemidorus' frustrating vagueness is understandable: what is going on inside the thinking subject is internal to that individual and available only in that individual's account.[46] The view from the outside can look a bit odd. The postures of Socrates and his pupils in their φροντιστήριον ('think-tank') had been mocked in Aristophanes' *Clouds*: Socrates is said by one of his pupils to have had a lizard shit in his eye while he was studying the moon (171–3). When Strepsiades enquires about the postures of his pupils, crouched with their faces down to the ground, and the pupil he has been speaking with remarks that they are scrutinizing Erebos, the realm of the dead (192), Strepsiades asks in jest 'then what is their anus doing looking to the heavens?' (193).[47] The student explains that this is multi-tasking: 'it is teaching itself to do

---

[46] With the help of fMRI scans, we can now peer into the brain of the thinking subject (cf. Fernyhough 2016: 71–6). But, as Latour might remark, what we 'see' there by means of this technology involves a complex chain of reference subject to processes of interpretation shot through with metaphysical assumptions.

[47] Cf. Dover 1968: 121 ad loc.

astronomy' (194).[48] Plato's Socrates acknowledges this ridicule of the self-
absorbed thinker in the *Theaetetus* (174a–b): 'Consider Thales, Theodorus: while he was doing astronomy and looking upwards, he fell into a
pit, and, it is said, a Thracian servant girl, with timing and wit, ridiculed
him, because he was so keen to know the things in the sky that he could
not see what was there before him and right by his feet.'[49] Socrates extends
the analogy: 'The same joke goes for all who pass their time in philosophy.
For in reality such a person is oblivious of his neighbour standing next to
him – not only of what he is doing, but pretty much whether he is a
human being or some other creature.'

In his reception history of this anecdote, which he shows was frequently
recycled in the philosophical tradition from Plato through to Heidegger,
Hans Blumenberg draws attention to what he calls 'an imaginative
potential . . . in the Thales anecdote that permits us to expect not only
distortions of its pool of figures, but also reoccupations'.[50] Originary
though it may be in the *Theaetetus*, this archetypal illustration of theory
is available for reconfiguration as theory is put under critical scrutiny, to
the extent of making the Thracian girl the focus of attention and even the
heroine.[51] We've seen how Latour, in Blumenberg's sense, 'reoccupies' the
story of the cave, and I'll be doing this in turn for the Thracian girl, as well
as examining how Lucretius reoccupies the anecdote for his own ends.
Rodolphe Gasché has discussed whether, for all the reservations Plato
expresses about the theatre, there is some intrinsic connection between
theory and the theatre, beyond the obvious shared etymological connection with 'seeing'. His suggestion that 'theory is an other of theater, from
which it needs to rigorously demarcate itself in order to serve a specificity
of its own'[52] has obvious attractions if we conjure up the figure of Socrates
watching himself represented on stage in *Clouds*, though I'm not wholly
convinced that the anecdote in *Theaetetus* screams out 'theatre' – hence my
preference for talking more generally of a scene; what Gasché goes on to

---

[48] Socrates was far from the only intellectual figure mocked in Old Comedy. For a catalogue cf.
Nightingale 1995: 61–2.

[49] Blumenberg 2015: 5 notes that an Aesopian fable was current in the fifth century BC that tells a
version of this story involving simply an *astrologos* and an anonymous witness, and concludes that it
is uncertain whether Plato was the first to put names to the figures (2015: 10). Strepsiades at *Nub.*
180 compares Socrates with Thales ('why do we go on admiring that Thales?'), but without making
the terms of the comparison wholly explicit.

[50] Blumenberg 2015: 86 (= 1987: 109). On Blumenberg's analysis of the anecdote cf. Gasché 2007:
190–8 and Niehues-Pröbsting 2015: 31–5.

[51] As she is in Taminiaux 1998, which maps the story onto the thought of Heidegger and Arendt.

[52] Gasché 2007: 189.

say about theory, that 'it occurs on some [*sic*] stage, that it has a plot, that it takes on a worldly appearance in which it shows itself to spectators'[53] is worth pondering. Shortly before Socrates tells the Thales anecdote, Theodorus remarks (*Tht.* 173c): 'we don't have a judge or, as the dramatic poets have, a spectator (θεατής) set over us to criticize us and tell us what we should be doing'. Oh yes you do, Theodorus. Plato has seen to that.

Socrates in the *Symposium* was not star-gazing, but hardly noticing the person next to him sums up the impression he makes there on those who observe him. Peter Sloterdijk in his recent book on thinking describes this phenomenon as *Scheintod*, suspended animation:[54] Socrates seems dead to the world. Though this can capture something of the external perspective on the thinking subject, what do we find out about the view from the inside? Agathon is keen to ask Socrates what piece of wisdom occurred to him in the doorway. Socrates responds how good it would be if wisdom were the sort of thing that could flow out of one person who is fuller into another who is emptier, using the image of water being siphoned from one cup to another with a thread of wool (*Symp.* 175e). He suggests that what he has been absorbed in is not something that can be reduced to, as we might say, information or data transfer. Whatever he has been doing, it is not producing tidy solutions to particular problems that can be transported from one mind to another without deformation.[55] He goes on to remark that his wisdom is sorry stuff, 'open to dispute as a dream' (ἀμφισβητήσιμος ὥσπερ ὄναρ οὖσα). The comparison with a dream is suggestive of his inward absorption, of experiencing something even while being more or less detached from the sensible world around him and its ongoing activity.

Socrates in Plato repeatedly resorts to dream imagery. In *Cra.* 439c, he says to Cratylus: 'Consider the thing I often *dream* about (ὀνειρώττω): should we or shouldn't we say that there is a beautiful in itself or a good in itself, and in like manner each one of the things that are?' David Sedley has suggested of this passage: 'This metaphor of dreaming does not imply, as it might in modern English, a wish or hope. Rather it is Plato's device for

---

[53] Ibid.   [54] Sloterdijk 2010.

[55] Thus Socrates suggests his thoughts cannot be distilled into simple, straightforward 'bits' of wisdom. Recall the recursive structure of Platonic texts. Schur 2014: 51 argues that, for all their apparent immediacy, 'modalization might well be called a defining feature of Plato's depictions of Socratic dialogue'. This is memorably thematized here. Latour sees the failure to appreciate the modalities of discourse as the greatest obstacle to understanding how we know what we know, portraying the misguided belief that it is possible to speak 'literally' in satanic terms as 'Double Click' (cf. 2013: 488–9).

describing a *hypothetical* grasp of something – trading on the way that in dreams we treat things *as if* they were true or real, without knowing whether they actually are.'[56] Similarly in the *Symposium* Socrates says not that his wisdom is simply like a dream, but ἀμφισβητήσιμος, *open to debate* like a dream. If Socrates' wisdom is 'arguable like a dream', is any arguing going on when he is thinking? In *Tht.* 189e–190a, Theaetetus asks Socrates how he defines thought (τὸ διανοεῖσθαι). Socrates responds that it is 'the talk which the mind goes through with itself about the things it is considering' (λόγον ὃν αὐτὴ πρὸς αὑτὴν ἡ ψυχὴ διεξέρχεται περὶ ὧν ἂν σκοπῇ). He qualifies this carefully, saying that he is telling Theaetetus not as one who knows this as a fact, but 'the image that comes to me is that the soul, when it is thinking, is doing nothing other than carrying on a discussion (διαλέγεσθαι), asking itself questions and answering them, asserting and denying'. When it comes to a decision, he continues, explaining this as 'saying the same thing and not differing', we call that its δόξα, its opinion or judgement.[57] Not, therefore, the 'wisdom' (σοφία) that Agathon was looking to extract from the thoughts of Socrates in the *Symposium*. In *Soph.* 263e, the Elean Stranger says that thought and speech are the same, except that thought is a conversation (διάλογος) inside the soul with itself 'without voice' (ἄνευ φωνῆς) – which I take to mean that this 'conversation' is not vocally enunciated nor can anybody 'listen in' on such a conversation inside the soul. The 'voice(s)', if such they are, are internally produced and internally consumed. Sedley suggests that what draws Plato to the dialogue form is his belief 'that conversation, in the form of question and answer, is the structure of thought itself . . . [h]ence it seems that what Plato dramatises as external conversations can be internalised by us, the readers, as setting the model for our own processes of philosophical reasoning'.[58] *Mutatis mutandis* this could be extended to the didactic form of Lucretius' poem, with its apostrophes to the reader, its use of questions which are then answered, and so on, a technique that can be internalized in the thinking of the reader. But note the differences as well: in the case of Lucretius, this is not conversation about hypotheticals leading to a *doxa*, but instruction in making one's own a discovered *sophia*,

---

[56] Sedley 2003a: 165; original emphasis. He adds: 'Formally, it corresponds to the methodology described by Socrates at *Phd.* 99d–102a, where one or more appropriate Forms are "hypothesised" as the basis for conducting a specific inquiry.'

[57] Schur 2014: 41 suggests of attempts to distil a definitive 'Platonism' from the dialogues that 'a powerful teleological impulse directs readers to seek *single-minded* and persuasive arguments in works that are, nonetheless, manifestly not *univocal*' (my emphases).

[58] Sedley 2003a: 1.

achieved wisdom (*sapientia* in *DRN* 5.10). Let us explore one direction this argument might take us in.

That thought is experienced in terms of 'inner voices' has recently attracted renewed interest in experimental psychology and neuroscience. It has even given rise in the work of Charles Fernyhough to what he terms the model of 'Dialogical Thinking', which proposes that:

> there is a group of mental functions – operations that our minds can perform – which depend on an interplay between different perspectives on reality. They involve taking a point of view, then another one, and enacting a dialogue between them. For these kinds of thinking (and possibly *only* these kinds) language is crucial, because language is particularly powerful at representing different perspectives and bringing them into contact with each other. Crucially, the development of dialogic thinking requires experience of social interactions, patterned by language, to make them work.[59]

The voices may be one's own and they may also recognizably belong to others, members of one's social circle who typically hold contrary opinions or who regularly throw out challenges to one's own assumptions – perhaps even with something as distinctive as the accent and laugh of the Thracian girl who chimes in just at the right moment (ἐμμελής) with a clever remark (she is χαρίεσσα) to bring one's thinking safely 'back down to earth', as it were, at the very moment you were in danger of an intellectual pratfall.

When one hears these voices, they are usually taken to be generated internally. If your internal Thracian girl (or her equivalent) makes a timely quip, you usually don't turn around and expect to see her standing there. But for some, a voice or voices do not seem to be self-produced but to come from outside. Look around to see where the voice is coming from, and there's nobody there, yet there can be the feeling nonetheless of being communicated with not by oneself but by some other entity – an entity, however, that escapes apprehension by any of the other senses. Socrates famously speaks in the *Apology* (31d) of hearing a voice that he attributes not to himself: 'You've often heard me say on many occasions that something divine and supernatural (θεῖόν τι καὶ δαιμόνιον) happens to me . . . from the time when I was a boy, a sort of voice (φωνή τις) comes to me which, when it comes, always turns me away from what I'm intending to do, never encourages me.' In spite of extensive scholarly discussion,[60] whether the voice says something like the Greek equivalent of 'whoa!' or speaks in complete phrases or sentences is never made explicit by Socrates.

---

[59] Fernyhough 2016: 99.   [60] See Long 2009: 67 for a summary.

That he changes his anticipated actions is a marker of what we can call, in this image repertoire of the voice, his 'responsibility': he 'answers'. As Richard Sorabji notes, the idea of sharing knowledge with oneself (συνει-δέναι) of some kind of defect occurs in fifth-century tragedy and nine times in Plato.[61] He comments: 'This surprising metaphor suggests that each of us is split by bad conscience into two selves, one of which has the guilty knowledge but keeps it a secret and the other of which shares the secret.'[62] The instances Sorabji notes refer to past actions, but it would not be difficult to adapt this *suneidenai* model of a divided self to the future intentions of which Socrates speaks: a narrating self in the present projects a narrated self into a course of action in the future.[63] But as that script plays out in the mind, it may involve the recognition of consequences that lead the narrating self in the present to say 'whoa!', and change the script accordingly. Blumenberg seems not to have picked up this one, but Baudelaire in his essay on 'The Essence of Laughter' uses the Thales anecdote to point to this division within the self: 'The man who trips would be the last to laugh at his own fall, unless he happened to be a philosopher, one who had acquired by habit a power of rapid self-division and thus of assisting as a disinterested spectator at the phenomena of his own *ego*.'[64]

What is remarkable about what Socrates says in the *Apology* is that he doesn't attribute this voice to himself. Let's take this slowly, for it is crucial to my argument about the emergence of 'metaphysical' thinking.[65] Effectively Socrates treats it like a kind of apostrophe that hails his attention and is reported by him as intruding into his regular thought processes from outside. His qualified description of his experience as a 'voice' invokes one of the senses, hearing, but none of the others, and he sees it not, as in his descriptions of thinking in the *Theaetetus* and the *Sophist*, as self-generated, but attributes it to an entity that does not inhabit the sensory realm in the way that a person does. In a recent discussion, Tony Long remarks, a little unfortunately: 'We today probably suppose that someone who claims to hear a divine voice is simply insane or seriously deluded. Yet, none of Socrates' contemporaries or later interpreters, apparently, took him to be mad, though they found him quite peculiar in this respect as in many

[61] Sorabji 2014: 15–19.   [62] Sorabji 2014: 2.   [63] Cf. Kennedy 2020: 243–5.
[64] Baudelaire 1955: 141.
[65] In discussing 'Socrates' Guardian Spirit', Sorabji 2014: 21–2 rushes ahead to Plato's discussion of the soul in the *Timaeus*, and concludes: 'There are advantages in taking Socrates' daimon to be his intellect' (22). We'll get to the *Timaeus* in due course, but there are links in this chain of reference we must follow.

other respects.'[66] Whoa! (or the Thracian equivalent). Long explicitly eschews current psychological research,[67] but it has introduced some due caution into the discussion of 'hearing voices'. Thus, a rush to medicalize the phenomenon is now not considered appropriate in every case, and to do so retrospectively in the case of a figure from the past is problematical on many counts; attention is paid rather to the different meanings given to this experience historically, without seeking immediately to explain the phenomenological descriptions in historical accounts in terms of modern concerns and categories.[68] The voice can be experienced not as disabling, but is sometimes reported as a reassuring experience, as it seems to be in Socrates' case. In describing the voice as θεῖόν τι καὶ δαιμόνιον, Socrates is undoubtedly culturally predisposed to accept an experience that cannot be explained in terms of the presence of another person as 'divine' (think of episodes in Homer). In *Resp.* 496c Socrates portrays himself as perhaps unique in this respect ('my own situation, the divine sign [τὸ δαιμόνιον σημεῖον], is not worth mentioning, since it has probably happened to few if any people before me'), though Diotima in *Symp.* 203a suggests that a *daimōn* acts as an intermediary between gods and men. At the beginning of the *Sophist* (216a), Socrates asks Theodorus, who has described the Elean Stranger whom they await as 'quite the philosopher' (μάλα δὲ ἄνδρα φιλόσοφον), whether he is unwittingly bringing a god into their midst 'in the Homeric manner' (κατὰ τὸν Ὁμήρου λόγον). Recall too how in Plato's dialogues, Socrates will sometimes address an interlocutor, in the respectful form that dates back to Homer, as ὦ δαιμόνιε, as if obliged by his intervention to reconfigure the argument and its direction in ways he had not anticipated. Intentionality is part of the dynamics of conversation, but conversation demonstrates how intentionality is often subverted. One has it in mind to achieve a particular *telos*, but an unforeseen intervention changes the direction. Significantly, Socrates addresses Theodorus in precisely this way in *Tht.* 172c, which marks the beginning of what scholars habitually describe as the 'digression' in which the character of the philosopher is sketched and the Thales anecdote recounted (172b–177c). The vocative is prompted after Socrates has said 'argument after argument, a greater one after a lesser is overtaking us', to which Theodorus has said

---

[66] Long 2009: 65.

[67] Long 2009: 65: 'There must be a large psychological literature on such experiences. I have not made use of it.'

[68] Cf. McCarthy-Jones 2012: 10 for a clear statement of the issues. Borch-Jacobsen 2001 is an important discussion.

'well, Socrates, we have plenty of free time, don't we?'[69] *ō daimonie*! That's precisely what differentiates their conversations from speeches in the law courts, which are limited by the water clock, whereas Socrates and his interlocutors can move from one argument to another as they please (*Tht.* 172d) – and he promptly 'digresses'.

So, rather than thinking of Socrates as 'hearing voices' in pathological terms, what I want to suggest here is that these representations of thinking effect the same sort of heavy lifting as dreaming does in the emergence of Platonic metaphysics.[70] For Plato's Socrates, the process of thinking, conceived largely in terms of a human conversation, can involve an element 'above and beyond' that, associated with a realm populated with supernatural entities that are more or less removed from our sensory experience. A separation of realms derived from received *theologikē*, but a separation now re-inscribed as one that can be bridged in the process of thinking, albeit not under our voluntary control and in a manner that characteristically runs athwart our intentions and our anticipation of the direction our thoughts are taking. Plato notoriously likes analysing what he calls the soul so as to incorporate this 'suprasensible' element. Thus in *Timaeus*, he weaves together *theologikē* with the physical posture of the thinker:

> As far as the most important type of soul we possess is concerned, we are bound to identify it with the personal deity that was a gift of the god to each of us. This is, of course, the kind of soul that dwells, as we said, in the summit of our body, and it raises us up from the earth towards the heavenly region to which we are naturally akin, since we are not soilbound plants, but, properly speaking, creatures rooted in heaven. For it is from heaven, where our souls originally came into existence, that the gods suspended our heads, which are our roots, and set our bodies upright. (90a)[71]

When 'the gods suspended our heads', Plato is suggesting that our upright posture, our gaze towards the heavens, and our astronomical study of them, reflect that divine gift (90c–d):

> So, since the movements that are naturally akin to our divine part are the thoughts and revolutions of the universe, these are what each of us should

[69] Cf. McDowell 1973: 174: 'Theodorus' remark about "plenty of time" leads Socrates into a discourse, on the face of it quite irrelevant, about the difference between the philosopher and the litigious man.'
[70] Cf. Kennedy 2020: 228–32.
[71] This and the following translation from the *Timaeus* are from Waterfield 2008: 95 and 96.

be guided by as we attempt to reverse the corruption of the circuits in our heads, that happened at the time of our birth, by studying the harmonies and revolutions of the universe.[72]

This returns us to the image of the thinker in the Thales anecdote – head raised, eyes looking to the heavens – but now with a twist administered by Plato that transforms the gaze from the 'astronomical' to what we would now call the 'metaphysical'.

The depiction of Epicurus in Lucretius *DRN* 1.62–79 is another such scene of thinking, but note how it plays off against the representation in the *Timaeus*, in reaction to the specific metaphysical agenda there, seeing thought as a human capacity, no more, no less:[73]

> When human life for all to see lay foully on the earth [*note the posture, the opposite of upright*] crushed beneath the weight of religion, which displayed its head from the regions of heaven, standing over (*super . . . instans*) mortals with horrible aspect [*associating the heavens with religion produces, in this image, superstition*], a Greek human was the first to dare to raise mortal eyes against it, and the first to stand up against it [*the posture has changed from prostration to that of the thinker, standing upright, eyes raised*]. Neither what is said of the gods, nor thunderbolts, nor the sky with its menacing rumble held him back, but all the more stimulated the courage of his mind (*animi virtutem*) [*his intellect is given a characterization that marks it as human – virtus *is the quality of being a heroic man, *vir], so that he should desire first to break open the tight bolts of nature's gates. And so it was that the lively power of his mind prevailed (*vivida vis animi pervicit*) [*it's the power of his thinking that allows Epicurus to understand the nature of the universe*], and he marched far beyond the flaming ramparts of the world, and surveyed the immeasurable universe in his intellect and mind (*mente animoque*), from where as victor he brings back to us what can come into being, what can not, in short, how each thing has its powers limited and its boundary-marker deep set. Therefore religion is in turn cast down and trampled underfoot, whilst our victory makes us level with the sky.

Personified religion is now represented in the posture associated with the failure to think.

The terms in which Plato sought to encapsulate thinking, specifically the metaphysical journey signalled by *theōria*, are deployed by Lucretius here to a philosophical end different from Plato's. Epicurus doesn't physically visit the whole infinite universe and bring back an explanation

---

[72] For Lucretius' opposition to the Platonic identification of the soul with the heavens see Gee in Chapter 10 of this volume.

[73] For further discussion of this passage in this volume see O'Rourke in Chapter 5 (pp. 108–10, 118), Shearin in Chapter 7 (pp. 146–8), O'Keefe in Chapter 9 (pp. 187–8) and Asmis in Chapter 12 (pp. 257–8).

of each and every phenomenon in it: that would be an infinite task, and he is, Lucretius emphasizes, mortal. Rather, he comes back with a 'theory' of the universe. Epicurus surveys in his mind 'the immeasurable everything', an infinite universe, without beginning or end.[74] Epicurus reports back to us not on what has happened or will happen, rather what can or cannot happen. For Lucretius, Epicurean theory is true because it is, as we might say, universal: no matter where you look, no matter when you look, you *can* explain any phenomenon you observe in terms of a theory of how atoms behave. In thinking, we leave the experiential 'here and now', both spatially and temporally. Recall the 'sort of voice' that would sometimes restrain Socrates from what he *intended* to do – that is, a projection of his potential self into the future and into some other situation that acts as a frame for his 'intention'. Thinking induces what Arendt called 'an inner time sensation'. 'In this situation', she says, 'past and future are equally present precisely because they are absent from our sense.'[75] The frame of 'inner sensation' can be expanded infinitely, spatially as well as temporally. And, speaking of the 'absent-mindedness' of the thinker, that led Thales to fall into a hole in the ground, she says 'everything present is absent because something actually absent is present to his mind, and among the things absent is the philosopher's own body'.[76] Epicurean theory can 'look up at' the abodes of the gods, such as they are (*DRN* 3.18–24), and, even if Epicurean theoretical subjects may not be immune to the physical pitfall of a Thales, they will not fall victim to the metaphysical holes in the ground that await those who confuse *philosophia prōtē* with *theologikē* (3.25–7):

> at contra nusquam apparent Acherusia templa,
> nec tellus obstat quin omnia dispiciantur,
> **sub pedibus** quaecumque infra per inane geruntur.

The theoretical gaze of the Epicurean can look not only down to 'see' what is 'under its feet'[77] ('nowhere appear the realms of Acheron, nor is the earth an obstacle to everything being seen that goes on below throughout the void'), but can view 'nature uncovered and lying open in every direction' (3.29–30 *natura … | tam manifesta patens ex omni parte retecta est*). For all that this presents a thrilling prospect that Lucretius describes in

---

[74] On Lucretius' theorization of an infinite universe in the *DRN* see Kennedy 2013 and O'Rourke in Chapter 5 of this volume.

[75] Arendt 1978: 203.   [76] Arendt 1978: 84.

[77] *sub pedibus* plays humorously on Lucretius' own use of the verb *suppedito* which, as O'Rourke in Chapter 5 of this volume suggests (p. 109 n. 30), itself plays on the etymology of Epicurus' name.

terms of divine revelation (3.28–9 *quaedam divina voluptas | ... atque horror*), there is, as we saw at the end of Section 1, a sleight-of-hand at work here that, in fashioning us as theoretical subjects, appeals to the sense of sight as it extends space and time infinitely in all directions to create a metaphysical uniformity.

Plato's story of the cave seeks to suggest that our world is but shadows that lovers of wisdom must seek to leave behind (even if they ultimately return to it). The way out, the 'path to be followed' (*met-hodos*), involves patient and continuing devotion to the 'dialectical method' (cf. *Phdr.* 276e). Latour asks us to remember that 'Plato is a master artist and a most subtle puppeteer in his own right', and that the story is 'a great experiment in redistributing light, darkness, projections and shadows'.[78] Still, if an example of make-believe, its historical effectiveness is undeniable. Lucretius concurs that human experience without theory is one of shadows: 'O wretched minds of men, o blind hearts! In what shadows of life, in how great perils is passed this span of life, for what it is!' (2.14–16 *o miseras hominum mentes, o pectora caeca! | qualibus in tenebris vitae quantisque periclis | degitur hoc aevi quodcumquest!*), and in 3.1–2 he depicts Epicurus as 'the first amid such deep shadows who was able to hold up so clear a light, illuminating the blessings of life' (*o tenebris tantis tam clarum extollere lumen | qui primus potuisti inlustrans commoda vitae*). It is presumably thanks to this 'light' that Lucretius can see the deep-set footprints that Epicurus has made. If Epicurus looked up to the infinite universe, his 'followers' (3.3 *te sequor*), however, need to keep their eyes down to follow the track, the *met-hodos*, that he has left behind – and not to trip up as they do so.

[78] Latour 2016: 15.

Works Cited

Achtner, W. (2011) 'Infinity as a transformative concept in science and theology', in M. Heller and W. Woodin (eds.) *Infinity: New Research Frontiers.* Cambridge: 19–51.

Ackermann, E. (1979) *Lukrez und der Mythos.* Wiesbaden.

Adler, A. (2012) 'Sensual idealism: the spirit of Epicurus and the politics of finitude in Kant and Hölderlin', in B. Holmes and W. H. Shearin (eds.) *Dynamic Reading: Studies in the Reception of Epicureanism.* New York, NY and Oxford: 199–238.

Agamben, G. (2011) *The Sacrament of Language: An Archaeology of the Oath.* Stanford, CA.

Alfieri, V. (1929) *Lucrezio.* Florence.

Alfonsi, L. (1978) 'L'avventura di Lucrezio nel mondo antico … e oltre', in O. Gigon (ed.) *Lucrèce: huit exposés suivis de discussions.* Entretiens sur L'Antiquité Classique 24. Geneva: 271–321.

Algra, K., Koenen, M. and Schrijvers, P. (eds.) (1997) *Lucretius and his Intellectual Background.* Amsterdam.

Allen, W., Jr and De Lacy, P. H. (1939) 'The patrons of Philodemus', *CPh* 34: 59–65.

Alter, F. C. (ed.) (1787) *Titi Lucretii Cari De Rerum Natura Libri Sex.* Vienna.

Anderson, W. S. (1968) 'Two Odes of Horace's Book Two', *CSCA* 1: 35–61.

   (1995) Review of M. R. Gale (1994) *Myth and Poetry in Lucretius. BMCRev* 95.04.08.

Annas, J. E. (1992) *Hellenistic Philosophy of Mind.* Berkeley and Los Angeles, CA.

   (ed.) (2001) *Cicero:* On Moral Ends. Trans. R. Woolf. Cambridge.

Arendt, H. (1978) *The Life of the Mind.* New York, NY and London.

Arenson, K. (2016) 'Epicureans on marriage as sexual therapy', *Polis: The Journal for Ancient Greek Political Thought* 2.33: 291–311.

Armstrong, D. (1995) 'The impossibility of metathesis: Philodemus and Lucretius on form and content in poetry', in D. Obbink (ed.) *Philodemus and Poetry: Poetic Theory and Practice in Lucretius, Philodemus, and Horace.* Oxford and New York, NY: 210–32.

   (2013) Review of H. Essler (2011) *Glückselig und unsterblich: Epikureische Theologie bei Cicero and Philodem (mit einer Edition von PHerc. 152/157, Kol. 8–10). BMCRev* 2013.02.37.

Armstrong, D., Fish, J., Johnston, P. A. and Skinner, M. B. (eds.) (2004) *Vergil, Philodemus and the Augustans*. Austin, TX.

Arnaldi, F. (ed.) (1957) *Antologia della poesia latina*. Naples.

Arrighetti, G. (1955) 'Filodemo Περὶ θεῶν III fr. 74–82, *Pap. Herc.* 157', *PP* 10: 322–56.

  (1958) 'Filodemo, *De dis* III, col. X–XI', *SCO* 7: 83–99.

  (1961) 'Filodemo, *De dis* III, col. XII–XIII, 20', *SCO* 10: 112–21.

  (ed.) (1973) *Epicuro: Opere* (2nd edn.; 1st edn. 1960). Turin.

  (2000) 'Filodemo fra poesia, mito e storia', in M. Erler (ed.) *Epikureismus in der späten Republik und der Kaiserzeit*. Stuttgart: 13–31.

Asmis, E. (1970) The Epicurean Theory of Free Will and its Origins in Aristotle. Diss. Yale.

  (1982) 'Lucretius' Venus and Stoic Zeus', *Hermes* 110.4: 458–70. Repr. in M. R. Gale (ed.) (2007) *Lucretius*. Oxford Readings in Classical Studies. Oxford: 88–103.

  (1984) *Epicurus' Scientific Method*. Ithaca, NY and London.

  (1990) 'Free action and the swerve', *OSAPh* 8: 275–90.

  (1991) 'Philodemus's poetic theory and *On the Good King According to Homer*', *ClAnt* 10: 1–45.

  (1995) 'Epicurean poetics', in D. Obbink (ed.) *Philodemus and Poetry: Poetic Theory and Practice in Lucretius, Philodemus, and Horace*. Oxford and New York, NY: 15–34.

  (1999) 'Epicurean epistemology', in K. Algra, J. Barnes, J. Mansfeld and M. Schofield (eds.) *The Cambridge History of Hellenistic Philosophy*. Cambridge: 260–94.

  (2004) 'Philodemus on sound and sense in poetry', *CronErc* 34: 5–27.

  (2007) 'Myth and philosophy in Cleanthes' *Hymn to Zeus*', *GRBS* 47: 413–29.

  (2008a) 'Lucretius' new world order: making a pact with nature', *CQ* 58: 141–57.

  (2008b) 'Cicero on natural law and the laws of the state', *ClAnt* 27: 1–33.

Assmann, J. (2011) *Cultural Memory and Early Civilization: Writing, Remembrance, and Political Imagination*. Cambridge and New York, NY.

Austin, R. G. (ed.) 1971) *P. Vergili Maronis Aeneidos Liber Primus*. Oxford.

  (ed.) (1977) *P. Vergili Maronis Aeneidos Liber Sextus*. Oxford.

Avancius, H. (ed.) (1500) *T. Lucretii Cari Libri Sex*. Venice.

Avotins, I. (1983) 'Some Epicurean and Lucretian arguments for the infinity of the universe', *CQ* 33: 421–7.

Bailey, C. (ed.) (1922) *Lucreti De Rerum Natura Libri Sex* (2nd edn.; 1st edn. 1900). Oxford.

  (ed., trans.) (1926) *Epicurus: The Extant Remains*. Oxford.

  (1928) *The Greek Atomists and Epicurus*. Oxford.

  (1940) 'The mind of Lucretius', *TAPhA* 61: 278–91. Repr. in C. J. Classen (ed.) (1986) *Probleme der Lukrezforschung*. Hildesheim, Zurich and New York, NY: 3–16.

(ed., trans.) (1947) *Titi Lucreti Cari De Rerum Natura Libri Sex, edited, with prolegomena, critical apparatus, translation and commentary.* 3 vols. Oxford.

Baker, E. (2007) 'Lucretius in the European Enlightenment', in S. Gillespie and P. R. Hardie (eds.) *The Cambridge Companion to Lucretius.* Cambridge: 274–88.

Bakker, F. A. (2018) 'The end of Epicurean infinity: critical reflections on the Epicurean infinite universe', in F. A. Bakker, D. Bellis and C. Palmerino (eds.) *Space, Imagination and the Cosmos from Antiquity to the Early Modern Period.* Cham: 41–67.

Bal, M. (1985) *Narratology: Introduction to the Theory of Narrative.* Toronto.

Baldwin, B. (1993) 'Half-lines in Virgil: old and new ideas', *SO* 68: 144–51.

Baraz, Y. and van den Berg, C. S. (2013) 'Introduction', *AJPh* 134: 1–8.

Barbour, R. (2007) 'Moral and political philosophy: readings of Lucretius from Virgil to Voltaire', in S. Gillespie and P. R. Hardie (eds.) *The Cambridge Companion to Lucretius.* Cambridge: 149–66.

Barchiesi, A. (1999) 'Venus' masterplot: Ovid and the Homeric Hymns', in P. Hardie, A. Barchiesi and S. Hinds (eds.) *Ovidian Transformations. Essays on the* Metamorphoses *and its Reception.* Cambridge: 112–26.

Barnes, J. (1979) *The Presocratic Philosophers.* 2 vols. London.

Baron, E. P. (1986) *Lucretius and his Reader: A Study of Book II of* De Rerum Natura. Diss. Ohio.

Baronovitch, L. (1984) 'German idealism, Greek materialism, and the young Karl Marx', *International Philosophical Quarterly* 24: 245–66.

Barra, G. (1952) *Struttura e composizione del 'De rerum natura' di Lucrezio.* Naples. (1984) 'Il proemio del *De rerum natura* di Lucrezio', *Vichiana* 13: 235–48.

Barrow, J. D. (2005) *The Infinite Book: A Short Guide to the Boundless, Timeless and Endless.* London.

Barthes, R. (1971) 'De l'œuvre au texte', *Revue d'esthétique* 3. Trans. in R. Barthes (1977) *Image – Music – Text.* Ed. and trans. S. Heath. New York, NY: 155–64: 'From work to text'.
(1974) *S/Z.* Trans. R. Miller. New York, NY.
(1975) *The Pleasure of the Text.* Trans. R. Miller. New York, NY.
(1995) 'The death of the author', in S. Burke (ed.) *Authorship: From Plato to Postmodernism, A Reader.* Edinburgh: 125–30.

Baudelaire, C. (1955) *The Mirror of Art.* London.

Beard, M. (2009) '*The Infinity of Lists* by Umberto Eco: Is there still life in the list?', *Guardian*, 12 December 2009.

Beer, B. (2009) *Lukrez und Philodem. Poetische Argumentation und Poetologischer Diskurs.* Basel.

Belpaeme, T., Cowley, S. J. and MacDorman, K. F. (eds.) (2007) *Symbol Grounding.* Amsterdam and Philadelphia, PA.

Benferhat, Y. (2005) *Ciues Epicurei: Les épicuriens et l'idée de la monarchie à Rome et en Italie de Sylla à Octave.* Brussels.

Benveniste, É. (1964) 'Lettres de Ferdinand de Saussure à Antoine Meillet', *Cahiers Ferdinand de Saussure* 21: 93–130.

Bennett, J. (2010) *Vibrant Matter: A Political Ecology of Things*. Durham, NC.

Bernays, J. (ed.) (1852) *T. Lucreti Cari De Rerum Natura Libri Sex*. Leipzig.

Bersanelli, M. (2011) 'Infinity and the nostalgia of the stars', in M. Heller and W. Woodin (eds.) *Infinity: New Research Frontiers*. Cambridge: 193–217.

Bignone, E. (1919) 'Nuove ricerche sul proemio del poema di Lucrezio', *RFIC* 47: 423–33.

(1945) *Storia della letteratura Latina*. 3 vols. Florence.

Block, N. (ed.) (1980) *Readings in Philosophy of Psychology. Vol. I*. Cambridge, MA.

Bloom, H. (1973) *The Anxiety of Influence: A Theory of Poetry*. New York, NY and Oxford.

(2011) *The Anatomy of Influence: Literature as a Way of Life*. New Haven, CT and London.

Blumenberg, H. (1987) *Das Lachen der Thrakerin. Eine Urgeschichte der Theorie*. Frankfurt.

(2015) *The Laughter of the Thracian Woman: A Protohistory of Theory*. New York, NY, London, New Delhi and Sydney.

Bobzien, S. (2000) 'Did Epicurus discover the free will problem?', *OSAPh* 19: 287–337.

Bockemüller, F. (ed.) (1873–4) *T. Lucreti Cari De Rerum Natura Libri Sex*. 2 vols. Stade.

Bollack, J. (1975) *La pensée du plaisir: Épicure, textes moraux, commentaires*. Paris.

(1978) *La raison de Lucrèce*. Paris.

Booth, W. (1961) *The Rhetoric of Fiction* (2nd edn. 1983). Chicago, IL.

(2005) 'Resurrection of the implied author: why bother?', in J. Phelan and P. J. Rabinowitz (eds.) *A Companion to Narrative Theory*. Oxford: 75–88.

Borch-Jacobsen, M. (2001) 'Making psychiatric history: madness as folie à plusieurs', *History of the Human Sciences* 14: 19–38.

Bordwell, D. (1985) *Narration in the Fiction Film*. Madison, WI.

Boyd, B. W. (1997) *Ovid's Literary Loves: Influence and Innovation in the* Amores. Ann Arbor, MI.

Breed, B. (2000) 'Imitations of originality: Theocritus and Lucretius at the start of the *Eclogues*', *Vergilius* 46: 3–20.

(2006) *Pastoral Inscriptions: Reading and Writing Virgil's* Eclogues. London.

Brennan, T. C. (2000) *The Praetorship in the Roman Republic*. 2 vols. Oxford.

Brieger, A. (ed.) (1899) *T. Lucreti Cari De Rerum Natura Libri Sex* (2nd edn.; 1st edn. 1894). Leipzig.

Bright, D. F. (1971) 'The plague and the structure of De rerum natura', *Latomus* 30: 607–32.

Brown, A. (2010) *The Return of Lucretius to Renaissance Florence*. Cambridge, MA.

Brown, P. M. (ed.) (1984) *Lucretius:* De rerum natura *I*. Bristol.

Brown, R. D. (1982) 'Lucretius and Callimachus', *ICS* 7: 77–97. Repr. in M. R. Gale (ed.) (2007) *Lucretius*. Oxford Readings in Classical Studies. Oxford: 328–50.

(ed., trans.) (1987) *Lucretius on Love and Sex: A Commentary on* De Rerum Natura *IV, 1030–1287 with Prolegomena, Text, and Translation*. Leiden.

Browning, G. K. (2000) 'Marx's doctoral dissertation: the development of a Hegelian thesis', in T. Burns and I. Fraser (eds.) *The Hegel–Marx Connection*. London: 131–45.

Buchheit, V. (1971) 'Epikurs Triumph des Geistes', *Hermes* 99: 303–23. Trans. B. Reitz in M. R. Gale (ed.) (2007) *Lucretius*. Oxford Readings in Classical Studies. Oxford: 104–31: 'Epicurus' triumph of the mind' (with Addendum [2005]).

(1984) 'Lukrez über den Ursprung von Musik und Dichtung', *RhM* 127: 141–58.

Büchner, K. (1936) *Beobachtungen über Vers und Gedankengang bei Lukrez*. Berlin. (ed.) (1966) *T. Lucreti Cari De Rerum Natura*. Wiesbaden.

Buckley, E. (2006) 'Ending the *Aeneid*? Closure and continuation in Maffeo Vegio's *Supplementum*', *Vergilius* 52: 108–37.

Buffière, F. (1956) *Les myths d'Homère et la pensée grecque*. Paris.

Buglass, A. K. (2015) *Repetition and Internal Allusion in Lucretius'* De Rerum Natura. Diss. Oxford.

Burke, S. (1992) *The Death and Return of the Author* (3rd edn. 2008). Edinburgh.

Burkert, W. (1959) 'ΣΤΟΙΧΕΙΟΝ: Eine semasiologische Studie', *Philologus* 103: 167–97.

Bury, R. (ed., trans.) (1952) *Plato. Vol. VII: Timaeus, Critias, Cleitophon, Menexenus, Epistles*. Loeb Classical Library 234. London and Cambridge, MA.

Butterfield, D. J. (2013) *The Early Textual History of Lucretius'* De rerum natura. Cambridge.

(2014) '*Lucretius auctus*? The question of interpolation in *De rerum natura*', in J. Martínez (ed.) *Fakes and Forgers of Classical Literature: Ergo decipiatur!* Leiden: 15–42.

(2018) 'Lucretius the madman and the gods', in J. Bryan, R. Wardy and J. Warren (eds.) *Authors and Authorities in Ancient Philosophy*. Cambridge: 222–41.

Cabisius, G. (1985) 'Social metaphor and the atomic cycle in Lucretius', *CJ* 80: 109–20.

Campbell, G. (1999) Review of D. Sedley (1998) *Lucretius and the Transformation of Greek Wisdom*. *BMCRev* 1999.10.29.

(2002) 'Lucretius and the memes of prehistory', *LICS* Discussion Paper 1, available at http://mural.maynoothuniversity.ie/95/1/lucretius.pdf (accessed 20 August 2019).

(2003) *Lucretius on Creation and Evolution: A Commentary on* De Rerum Natura *5.772–1104*. Oxford and New York, NY.

(2011) 'Lucretius', in D. L. Clayman (ed.) *Oxford Bibliographies in Classics*, online at www.oxfordbibliographies.com.

(2014) 'Lucretius, Empedocles and Cleanthes', in M. Garani, D. Konstan (eds.) *The Philosophizing Muse: The Influence of Greek Philosophy on Roman Poetry*. Newcastle: 26–60.

Camps, W. A. (1969) *Introduction to Virgil's* Aeneid. Oxford.

Canali, L. (1995) *Nei pleniluni sereni. Autobiografia immaginaria di Tito Lucrezio Caro.* Milan.

Candidus, P. (ed.) (1512) *T. Lucretii Cari De Rerum Natura Libri Sex.* Florence.

Canevaro, L. G. (2019) 'Thinking for yourself: Hesiod's *Works and Days* and cognitive training', in L. G. Canevaro and D. O'Rourke (eds.) *Didactic Poetry of Greece, Rome and Beyond: Knowledge, Power, Tradition.* Swansea: 53–74.

Canfora, L. (1973) 'Il proemio del "De rerum natura"', *Belfagor* 28: 161–7.

(1993) *Vita di Lucrezio.* Palermo.

Cangelosi, A. (2008) 'The grounding and sharing of symbols', in I. E. Dror and S. Harnad (eds.) *Cognition Distributed: How Cognitive Technology Extends Our Minds.* Amsterdam and Philadelphia, PA: 83–92.

Càssola, F. (ed., trans.) (1997) *Inni Omerici.* Milan.

Castner, C. (1988) *Prosopography of Roman Epicureans from the Second Century* BC *to the Second Century* AD. Frankfurt.

Chatman, S. (1990) *Coming to Terms: The Rhetoric of Narrative in Fiction and Film.* Ithaca, NY and London.

Cherniss, H. F. (1943) 'The biographical fashion in literary criticism', *University of California Publications in Classical Philology* 12: 279–92.

Clancey, W. J. (2009) 'Scientific antecedents of situated cognition', in P. Robbins and M. Aydede (eds.) *The Cambridge Handbook of Situated Cognition.* Cambridge: 11–34.

Clark, A. (2003) *Natural-Born Cyborgs: Minds, Technologies, and the Future of Human Intelligence.* Oxford and New York, NY.

Clark, A. and Chalmers, D. J. (1998) 'The extended mind', *Analysis* 58: 10–23.

Classen, C. J. (1968) 'Poetry and rhetoric in Lucretius', *TAPhA* 99: 77–118. Repr. in C. J. Classen (ed.) (1986) *Probleme der Lukrezforschung.* Hildesheim, Zurich and New York, NY: 331–73.

(ed.) (1986) *Probleme der Lukrezforschung.* Hildesheim, Zurich and New York, NY.

Clauss, J. (2016) 'The Hercules and Cacus episode in Augustan literature: engaging the Homeric Hymn to Hermes in light of Callimachus' and Apollonius' reception', in A. Faulkner, A. Schwab and A. Vergados (eds.) *The Reception of the Homeric Hymns.* Oxford: 55–78.

Clay, D. (1976) 'The sources of Lucretius' inspiration', in J. Bollack and A. Laks (eds.) *Études sur l'Epicurisme antique,* Lille: 205–27. Repr. in M. R. Gale (ed.) (2007) *Lucretius.* Oxford Readings in Classical Studies. Oxford: 18–47.

(1980) 'An Epicurean interpretation of dreams', *AJPh* 101: 342–65.

(1983) *Lucretius and Epicurus.* Ithaca, NY and London.

(2000a) 'Recovering originals: *Peri Physeos* and *De Rerum Natura*', *Apeiron* 33: 259–71.

(2000b) *Platonic Questions: Dialogues with the Silent Philosopher.* Pennsylvania.

Cochez, J. (ed.) (1954) *T. Lucreti Cari De Rerum Natura Liber Primus.* Leuven.

Cole, T. (1998) 'Venus and Mars (*De Rerum Natura* 1.31–40)', in P. Knox and C. Foss (eds.) *Style and Tradition: Studies in Honor of Wendell Clausen.* Stuttgart: 3–15.

Commager H. S., Jr (1957) 'Lucretius' interpretation of the plague', *HSPh* 62: 105–18. Repr. in M. R. Gale (ed.) (2007) *Lucretius.* Oxford Readings in Classical Studies. Oxford: 182–98.

Conington, J. and Nettleship, H. (eds.) (1881) *P. Vergili Maronis Opera. The Works of Virgil.* 3 vols. (4th edn.). London.

Conte, G. B. (1966) '*Hypsos* e diatriba nello stile di Lucrezio', *Maia* 18: 538–68.

(1985) *Memoria dei poeti e sistema letterario: Catullo, Virgilio, Ovidio, Lucano.* Turin.

(1986) *The Rhetoric of Imitation: Genre and Poetic Memory in Virgil and other Latin Poets.* Ed. and trans. C. Segal. Ithaca, NY and London.

(1990) 'Introduzione', in I. Dionigi (ed.) and L. Canali (trans.) (1990) *Lucrezio, La Natura Delle Cose.* 2 vols. (2nd edn. 2000). Milan: 7–47.

(1994) *Genres and Readers: Lucretius, Love Elegy, Pliny's* Encyclopedia. Trans. G. W. Most. Baltimore, MD and London.

Courtney, E. (1987) 'Quotation, interpolation, transposition', *Hermathena* 143: 7–18.

(ed.) (1993) *The Fragmentary Latin Poets.* Oxford.

(2001) 'The proem of Lucretius', *MH* 58: 201–11.

Cox, A. (1971) 'Lucretius and his message: a study in the prologues of the *De Rerum Natura*', *G&R* 18: 1–16.

Craca, C. (1989) *Da Epicuro a Lucrezio: Il maestro ed il poeta nei proemi del* De rerum natura. Amsterdam.

Crawford, M. H. (1974) *Roman Republican Coinage.* 2 vols. Cambridge.

Creech, T. (ed.) (1695) *Titi Lucretii Cari De Rerum Natura Libri Sex.* Oxford.

Culler, J. D. (1986) *Ferdinand de Saussure*, 2nd edn. Ithaca, NY.

Curd, P. (1998) *The Legacy of Parmenides.* Princeton, NJ.

Dalzell, A. (1974) 'Lucretius' exposition of the doctrine of images', *Hermathena* 118: 22–32.

(1987) 'Language and atomic theory in Lucretius', *Hermathena* 143: 19–28.

Deichgräber, K. (1940) 'Similia dissimilia III: Zum 1. Prooemium des Lukrez', *RhM* 89: 55–62.

De Lacy, P. H. (1964) 'Distant views: the imagery of Lucretius 2', *CJ* 60: 49–55. Repr. in M. R. Gale (ed.) (2007) *Lucretius.* Oxford Readings in Classical Studies. Oxford: 146–57.

(1983) 'Lucretius and Plato', in Συζήτησις. *Studi sull'epicureismo greco e romano offerti a Marcello Gigante.* Naples: 291–307.

Derrida, J. (1967) *De la grammatologie.* Paris.

Descartes, R. (1903) *Oeuvres de Descartes: Correspondence V: Mai 1647 – Février 1650.* Ed. C. Adam and P. Tannery. Paris.

(1996) *Meditations on First Philosophy: With Selections from the Objections and Replies.* Ed. and trans. J. Cottingham. Cambridge.

Descola, P. (2013) *Beyond Nature and Culture.* Chicago, IL and London.

Deufert, M. (1996) *Pseudo-Lukrezisches im Lukrez*. Berlin.
  (ed.) (2019) *Titus Lucretius Carus: De Rerum Natura*. Berlin.
Deutsch, R. E. (1939) *The Pattern of Sound in Lucretius*. Diss. Bryn Mawr.
De Vries, G. (2016) *Bruno Latour*. Cambridge.
Diels, H. (1899) *Elementum*. Leipzig.
  (ed.) (1917) *Philodemos Über die Götter: Drittes Buch*. Berlin.
  (ed.) (1923–4) *Titi Lucreti Cari De Rerum Natura Libri Sex*. 2 vols. Berlin.
Dionigi, I. (1988) *Lucrezio: Le parole e le cose* (3rd edn. 2005). Bologna.
Dionigi, I. (ed.) and Canali, L. (trans.) (1990) *Lucrezio, La Natura Delle Cose*. 2 vols. (2nd edn. 2000). Milan.
Donald, M. (1991) *Origins of the Modern Mind: Three Stages in the Evolution of Culture and Cognition*. Cambridge, MA and London.
Doody, A. (2010) *Pliny's Encyclopedia: The Reception of the* Natural History. Cambridge.
Dover, K. J. (ed.) (1968) *Aristophanes*. Clouds. Oxford.
  (ed.) (1980) *Plato*. Symposium. Cambridge.
Dror, I. E. and Harnad, S. (2008) 'Offloading cognition into cognitive technology', in I. E. Dror and S. Harnad (eds.) *Cognition Distributed: How Cognitive Technology Extends Our Minds*. Amsterdam and Philadelphia, PA: 1–23.
Duff, J. D. (ed.) (1923) *T. Lucreti Cari De Rerum Natura Liber Primus*. Cambridge.
Dykes, A. (2011) *Reading Sin in the World: The* Hamartigenia *of Prudentius and the Vocation of the Responsible Reader*. Cambridge.
Earnshaw, K. (2013) '(First-) beginnings and (never-) endings in Lucan and Lucretius', in D. Lehoux, A. D. Morrison and A. Sharrock (eds.) *Lucretius: Poetry, Philosophy, Science*. Oxford: 261–84.
Eco, U. (2009) *The Infinity of Lists*. Trans. A. McEwen. London.
Edmunds, L. (2001) *Intertextuality and the Reading of Roman Poetry*. Baltimore, MD and London.
Edwards, M. (1993) '*Aeternus lepos*: Venus, Lucretius, and the fear of death', *G&R* 40: 68–78.
Einstein, A. (1924) 'Geleitwort', in *Lukrez, Von der Natur*. Trans. H. Diels. Berlin: via–vib.
Elder, J. P. (1954) 'Lucretius 1.1–49', *TAPhA* 85: 88–120.
Erler, M. (1993) '*Philologia medicans*: wie die Epikureer die Texte ihres Meisters lasen', in W. Kullmann and J. Althoff (eds.) *Vermittlung und Tradierung von Wissen in der griechischen Kultur*. Tübingen: 281–303.
Ernout, A. (ed., trans.) (1920) *Lucrèce, De La Nature*. 2 vols. Paris.
Ernout, A. and Robin, L. (eds.) (1925–8) *Lucrèce, De Rerum Natura: Commentaire Exégétique et Critique*. Paris.
Essler, H. (2009) 'Falsche Götter bei Philodem (*Di* III Kol. 8,5–Kol. 10,6)', *CronErc* 39: 161–205.
  (2011) *Glückselig und unsterblich: Epikureische Theologie bei Cicero und Philodem (mit einer Edition von PHerc. 152/157, Kol. 8–10)*. Basel.

(2017) 'Philodemus of Gadara', in D. Clayman (ed.) *Oxford Bibliographies in Classics*, online at www.oxfordbibliographies.com.

Everson, S. (1990) 'Epicurus on the truth of the senses', in S. Everson (ed.) *Epistemology*. Cambridge: 161–83.

Fabbri, R. (1984) 'La "Vita Borgiana" di Lucrezio nel quadro delle biografie umanistiche', *Lettere Italiane* 36: 348–66.

Faber, T. (ed.) (1662) *T. Lucreti Cari De Rerum Natura Libri Sex*. Saumur.

Fairclough, H. R. and Goold, G. P. (eds., trans.) (1999) *Virgil, Eclogues, Georgics, Aeneid*. 2 vols. Cambridge, MA and London.

Fanti, G. (2017) 'The failure of Memmius in Lucretius' *DRN*', *Latomus* 76: 58–79.

Fantuzzi, M. and Hunter, R. L. (2004) *Tradition and Innovation in Hellenistic Poetry*. Cambridge.

Farrell, J. (1991) *Vergil's* Georgics *and the Traditions of Ancient Epic: The Art of Allusion in Literary History*. New York, NY and Oxford.

(2001) *Latin Language and Latin Culture: From Ancient to Modern Times*. Cambridge.

(2007) 'Lucretian architecture: the structure and argument of the *De rerum natura*', in S. Gillespie and P. R. Hardie (eds.) *The Cambridge Companion to Lucretius*. Cambridge: 76–91.

(2016) 'Lucretius and the symptomatology of modernism', in J. Lezra and L. Blake (eds.) (2016) *Lucretius and Modernity. Epicurean Encounters across Time and Disciplines*. New York, NY: 39–58.

Farrington, B. (1939) *Science and Politics in the Ancient World*. London.

Faulkner, A. (ed.) (2011a) *The Homeric Hymns: Interpretative Essays*. Oxford.

(2011b) 'The collection of Homeric Hymns: from the seventh to the third centuries BC', in *The Homeric Hymns: Interpretative Essays*. Oxford: 175–205.

Feeney, D. C. (1989) Review of G. B. Conte (1986) *The Rhetoric of Imitation: Genre and Poetic Memory in Virgil and Other Latin Poets*. *JRS* 79: 206–7.

Fenves, P. (1986) 'Marx's doctoral thesis on two Greek atomists and the post-Kantian interpretations', *JHI* 47: 433–52.

Fernyhough, C. (2016) *The Voices Within: The History and Science of How We Talk to Ourselves*. London.

Finkelberg, M. (2007) 'More on κλέος ἄφθιτον', *CQ* 57: 341–50.

Fiscal, W. (1947) *Studien zum Aufbau poetischer Exkurse bei Lukrez*. Diss. Tübingen.

Fischer, H. (1924) *De capitulis Lucretianis*. Diss. Giessen.

Fish, J. (2011) 'Not all politicians are Sisyphus: what Roman Epicureans were taught about politics', in J. Fish and K. R. Sanders (eds.) *Epicurus and the Epicurean Tradition*. Cambridge and New York, NY: 72–104.

Fish, J. and Sanders, K. R. (eds.) (2011) *Epicurus and the Epicurean Tradition*. Cambridge and New York, NY.

Fitzgerald, W. (2016a) *Variety: The Life of a Roman Concept*. Chicago, IL and London.

(2016b) 'Resonance: the sonic environment of Vergil's *Eclogues*', *Dictynna* 13, http://journals.openedition.org/dictynna/129 (accessed 2 September 2019).

Flores, E. (ed., trans.) (2002–9) *Titus Lucretius Carus: De Rerum Natura*. 3 vols. Naples.

Forbiger, A. (ed.) (1828) *T. Lucretii Cari De Rerum Natura Libri Sex*. Leipzig.

Foster, E. (2009) 'The rhetoric of materials: Thucydides and Lucretius', *AJPh* 130: 367–99.

(2011) 'The political aims of Lucretius' translation of Thucydides', in S. McElduff and E. Sciarrino (eds.) *Complicating the History of Western Translation: The Ancient Mediterrannean in Perspective*. Manchester: 88–100.

Fowler, D. (1983) 'Lucretius on the *clinamen* and "free will" (II 251–93)', in M. Gigante (ed.) *ΣΥΖΗΤΗΣΙΣ: studi sull'epicureismo greco e latino offerti a Marcello Gigante*. Naples: 329–52. Repr. in D. Fowler (ed.) (2002) *Roman Constructions: Readings in Postmodern Latin*. Oxford: 407–27.

(1989a) 'Lucretius and politics', in M. T. Griffin and J. Barnes (eds.) *Philosophia Togata: Essays on Philosophy and Roman Society*. Oxford: 120–50. Repr. in M. R. Gale (ed.) (2007) *Lucretius*. Oxford Readings in Classical Studies. Oxford: 397–431.

(1989b) 'First thoughts on closure', *MD* 22: 75–122.

(1995) 'From epos to cosmos: Lucretius, Ovid, and the poetics of segmentation', in D. C. Innes, H. Hine and C. Pelling (eds.) *Ethics and Rhetoric: Essays for Donald Russell on his Seventy-Fifth Birthday*. Oxford: 3–18.

(1996) 'The feminine principal: gender in the *De rerum natura*', in G. Giannantoni and M. Gigante (eds.) *Epicureismo greco e romano: Atti del congresso internazionale, Napoli, 19–26 maggio 1993*. 3 vols. Naples: 813–22. Repr. in D. Fowler (ed.) (2002) *Lucretius on Atomic Motion: A Commentary on* De rerum natura *2.1–332*. Oxford: 444–52.

(1997a) 'On the shoulders of giants: intertextuality and classical studies', *MD* 39: 13–34.

(1997b) 'Second thoughts on closure', in D. H. Roberts, F. M. Dunn and D. P. Fowler (eds.) *Classical Closure: Reading the End in Greek and Latin Literature*. Princeton, NJ: 3–22.

(2000a) *Roman Constructions: Readings in Postmodern Latin*. Oxford.

(2000b) 'Philosophy and literature in Lucretian intertextuality', in *Roman Constructions: Readings in Postmodern Latin*. Oxford: 138–55.

(2000c) 'The didactic plot', in M. Depew and D. Obbink (eds.) *Matrices of Genre: Authors, Canons, and Society*. Cambridge, MA: 205–19.

(ed.) (2002) *Lucretius on Atomic Motion: A Commentary on* De rerum natura *2.1–332*. Oxford.

Fowler, P. G. (1997) 'Lucretian conclusions', in D. H. Roberts, F. M. Dunn and D. P. Fowler (eds.) *Classical Closure: Reading the End in Greek and Latin Literature*. Princeton, NJ: 112–38. Repr. in M. R. Gale (ed.) (2007) *Lucretius*. Oxford Readings in Classical Studies. Oxford: 199–233.

Fratantuono, L. (2015) *A Reading of Lucretius'* De rerum natura. Lanham, MD, Boulder, CO, New York, NY and London.

Friedländer, P. (1932) 'Retractationes II', *Hermes* 67: 43–6.
  (1939) 'The Epicurean theology in Lucretius' first procemium (Lucr. I. 44–49)', *TAPhA* 70: 368–79.
  (1941) 'Patterns of sound and atomistic theory in Lucretius', *AJPh* 62: 16–34. Repr. in C. J. Classen (ed.) (1986) *Probleme der Lukrezforschung*. Hildesheim, Zurich and New York, NY: 291–307; M. R. Gale (ed.) (2007) *Lucretius*. Oxford Readings in Classical Studies. Oxford: 351–70.
Frischer, B. (1982) *The Sculpted Word: Epicureanism and Philosophical Recruitment in Ancient Greece*. Berkeley, CA.
Fröhder, D. (1994) *Die dichterische Form der Homerischen Hymnen: Untersucht am Typus der mittelgroßen Preislieder*. Hildesheim.
Furley, D. (1966) 'Lucretius and the Stoics', *BICS* 13: 13–33. Repr. in D. Furley (ed.) (1989) *Cosmic Problems*. Cambridge: 183–205; C. J. Classen (ed.) (1986) *Probleme der Lukrezforschung*. Hildesheim, Zurich and New York, NY: 75–95.
  (1967) *Two Studies in the Greek Atomists*. Princeton, NJ.
  (1970) 'Variations on themes from Empedocles in Lucretius' proem', *BICS* 17: 55–64.
  (1981) 'The Greek theory of the infinite universe', *JHI* 42: 571–85.
Gabaude, J.-M. (1970) *Le jeune Marx et le matérialisme antique*. Toulouse.
Gabriel, M. (2015) *Why the World Does Not Exist*. Cambridge.
Gale, M. R. (1994) *Myth and Poetry in Lucretius*. Cambridge.
  (2000) *Virgil on the Nature of Things: The* Georgics*, Lucretius and the Didactic Tradition*. Cambridge.
  (2001a) *Lucretius and the Didactic Epic*. London.
  (2001b) 'Etymological wordplay and poetic succession in Lucretius', *CPh* 96: 168–72.
  (2004) 'The story of us: a narratological analysis of Lucretius' *De Rerum Natura*', in M. R. Gale (ed.) *Latin Epic and Didactic Poetry: Genre, Tradition and Individuality*. Swansea: 49–71.
  (2005) '*Avia Pieridum loca*: tradition and innovation in Lucretius', in M. Horster and Ch. Reitz (eds.) *Wissensvermittlung in dichterischer Gestalt*. Stuttgart: 175–91.
  (ed.) (2007a) *Lucretius*. Oxford Readings in Classical Studies. Oxford.
  (2007b) 'Lucretius and previous poetic traditions', in S. Gillespie and P. R. Hardie (eds.) *The Cambridge Companion to Lucretius*. Cambridge: 59–75.
  (2018) 'Contemplating violence: Lucretius' *De rerum natura*', in M. R. Gale and J. H. D. Scourfield (eds.) *Texts and Violence in the Roman World*. Cambridge: 63–86.
  (2019) 'Name puns and acrostics in didactic poetry: reading the universe', in L. G. Canevaro and D. O'Rourke (eds.) *Didactic Poetry of Greece, Rome and Beyond: Knowledge, Power, Tradition*. Swansea: 123–50.
Gallagher, S. (2009) 'Philosophical antecedents of situated cognition', in P. Robbins and M. Aydede (eds.) *The Cambridge Handbook of Situated Cognition*. Cambridge: 35–51.

Gandon, F. (2002) *De dangereux édifices. Saussure lecteur de Lucrèce. Les cahiers d'anagrammes consacrés au* De rerum natura. Leuven and Paris.

(2006) *Le nom de l'absent. Épistémologie de la science saussurienne des signes.* Limoges.

Garani, M. (2007) *Empedocles Redivivus: Poetry and Analogy in Lucretius.* New York, NY and London.

Garber, D. (1992) *Descartes' Metaphysical Physics.* Chicago, IL and London.

Garcia, L. F. (2013) *Homeric Durability: Telling Time in the* Iliad. Washington, DC.

García Calvo, A. (ed., trans.) (1997) *Lucrecio,* De Rerum Natura *(De la realidad).* Zamora.

Garratt, P. (ed.) (2016) *The Cognitive Humanities: Embodied Mind in Literature and Culture.* London.

Gasché, R. (2007) *The Honor of Thinking: Critique, Theory, Philosophy.* Stanford, CA.

Gee, E. (2000) *Ovid, Aratus and Augustus.* Cambridge.

(2001) 'Cicero's astronomy', *CQ* 51: 520–36.

(2013) *Aratus and the Astronomical Tradition.* Oxford.

(2016) 'Dogs, snakes and heroes: hybridism and polemic in Lucretius' *De rerum natura*', in S. Oakley and R. L. Hunter (eds.) *Latin Literature and its Transmission: Papers in Honour of Michael Reeve.* Cambridge: 108–41.

Gellar, T. (2012) *Lucretius'* De Rerum Natura *and Satire.* Diss. North Carolina at Chapel Hill.

Genette, G. (1983) *Narrative Discourse Revisited.* Trans. J. E. Lewin. Ithaca, NY.

(1997) *Palimpsests: Literature in the Second Degree.* Trans. C. Newman and C. Doubinsky. Lincoln, NE and London.

Germany, R. (2005) 'The figure of Echo in the *Homeric Hymn to Pan*', *AJPh* 126: 187–208.

Giancotti, F. (1978) *Il preludio di Lucrezio e altri scritti lucreziani ed epicurei.* Messina and Florence.

(1980) 'Il preludio di Lucrezio, il trasposizionismo e Lattanzio', *Orpheus* 1: 221–50.

(ed., trans.) (1994) *Tito Lucrezio Caro: La Natura. Introduzione, testo criticamente riveduto, traduzione e commento.* Milan.

Giannantoni, G. (1989) 'L'infinito nella fisica epicurea', in A. Ceresa-Gastaldo (ed.) *L'infinito dei greci e dei romani.* Genoa: 9–26.

(1996) 'Epicuro e l'ateismo antico', in G. Giannantoni and M. Gigante (eds.) *Epicureismo greco e romano: Atti del congresso internazionale, Napoli, 19–26 maggio 1993.* 3 vols. Naples: 21–63.

Giesecke, A. L. (2000) *Atoms, Ataraxy, and Allusion: Cross-Generic Imitation of the* De Rerum Natura *in Early Augustan Poetry.* Hildesheim.

Gifanius, O. (1595) *Titi Lucretii Cari De Rerum Natura Libri Sex* (2nd edn.; 1st edn. Antwerp, 1565). Leiden.

Gigandet, A. (1998) *Fama Deum. Lucrèce et les raisons du mythe.* Paris.

Gigante, M. (1975) '"Philosophia Medicans" in Filodemo', *CronErc* 5: 53–61.

(1983a) *Ricerche filodemee*. Naples.

(ed.) (1983b) *ΣΥΖΗΤΗΣΙΣ: studi sull'epicureismo greco e latino offerti a Marcello Gigante*. Naples.

(1995) *Philodemus in Italy: The Books from Herculaneum*. Trans. D. Obbink. Ann Arbor, MI.

Gigon, O. (ed.) (1971) *T. Lucretius Carus: De Rerum Natura Libri Sex*. Zurich.

(1978) 'Lukrez und Ennius', in O. Gigon (ed.) *Lucrèce: huit exposés suivis de discussions*. Entretiens sur L'Antiquité Classique 24. Geneva: 167–91.

Gill, C. J. (2006) *The Structured Self in Hellenistic and Roman Thought*. Oxford.

Gillespie, S. and Hardie, P. R. (eds.) (2007) *The Cambridge Companion to Lucretius*. Cambridge.

Gillespie, S. and Mackenzie, D. (2007) 'Lucretius and the moderns', in S. Gillespie and P. R. Hardie (eds.) *The Cambridge Companion to Lucretius*. Cambridge: 306–24.

Gillis, D. J. (1967) 'Pastoral poetry in Lucretius', *Latomus* 26: 339–62.

Gimpel, P. (1981) '*De rerum natura*: prooemium restitutum', *RCCM* 31: 3–41.

Giuffrida, P. (1940–50) *L'epicureismo nella letteratura latina nel 1 sec. av. Cristo*. 2 vols. Turin.

Giussani, C. (1896) *Studi Lucreziani*. Turin.

(ed.) (1896–8) *T. Lucreti Cari De Rerum Natura Libri Sex*. 4 vols. Turin.

Glidden, D. K. (1985) 'Epicurean prolepsis', *OSAPh* 3: 175–217.

Goldberg, J. (2009) *The Seeds of Things: Theorizing Sexuality and Materiality in Renaissance Representations*. New York, NY.

Goldschmidt, N. (2019) *Afterlives of the Roman Poets: Biofiction and the Reception of Latin Poetry*. Cambridge.

Goold, G. (1970) 'Servius and the Helen Episode', *HSPh* 74: 101–68.

Gordon, C. A. (1962) *A Bibliography of Lucretius*. London.

Gordon, P. (2002) 'Some unseen monster: rereading Lucretius on sex', in D. Fredrick (ed.) *The Roman Gaze. Vision, Power and the Body*. Baltimore, MD: 86–109.

(2012) *The Invention and Gendering of Epicurus*. Ann Arbor, MI.

Gottschalk H. B. (1975) 'Lucretius 1.983', *CPh* 70: 42–4.

(1996) 'Philosophical innovations in Lucretius?', in K. A. Algra, P. W. van der Horst and D. T. Runia (eds.) *Polyhistor: Studies in the History and Historiography of Ancient Philosophy Presented to Jaap Mansfeld on His Sixtieth Birthday*. Leiden: 231–40.

Gowers, E. (ed.) (2012) *Horace: Satires Book 1*. Cambridge.

Gowing, A. (2005) *Empire and Memory: The Representation of the Roman Republic in Imperial Culture*. Cambridge and New York, NY.

Greenberg, N. A. (1955) *The Poetic Theory of Philodemus*. Diss. Harvard.

Greenblatt, S. (2011) *The Swerve: How the Renaissance Began*. London.

Grewing, F., Acosta-Hughes, B. and Kirichenko, A. (eds.) (2013) *The Door Ajar: False Closure in Greek and Roman Literature and Art*. Heidelberg.

Grimal, P. (1957) 'Lucrèce et l'hymne à Venus', *REL* 35: 184–95.

(1978) 'Le poème de Lucrèce en son temps', in O. Gigon (ed.) *Lucrèce: huit exposés suivis de discussions.* Entretiens sur L'Antiquité Classique 24. Geneva: 233–70.

Gruen, E. S. (1969) 'The consular elections for 53 BC', in J. Brabauw (ed.) *Hommages à Marcel Renard.* Collection Latomus 101. 2 vols. Brussels: 2.311–21.

Gumbrecht, H. U. (2004) *Production of Presence: What Meaning Cannot Convey.* Stanford, CA.

Hacking, I. (2002) *Historical Ontology.* Cambridge, MA and London.

Hadzsits, G. D. (1963) *Lucretius and his Influence.* New York, NY.

Hahmann, A. (2015) 'Epikur über den Gegenstand der Wahrnehmung', *Archiv für Geschichte der Philosophie* 97: 271–307.

Hammerstaedt, J. (2003) 'Une ancienne discussion sur les critères de l'excellence du poème (éd. Philodème, *Poèmes* V, *PHerc.* 1425 col. XXV sq. Réexamen de Mangoni)', in A. Monet (ed.) *Le Jardin romain: Épicurisme et poésie à Rome. Mélanges offerts à Mayotte Bollack.* Lille: 303–17.

Hankinson, R. J. (2013) 'Lucretius, Epicurus, and the logic of multiple explanations', in D. Lehoux, A. D. Morrison and A. Sharrock (eds.) (2013) *Lucretius: Poetry, Philosophy, Science.* Oxford: 69–98.

Hanson, J. A. (1959) *Roman Theater-Temples.* Princeton, NJ.

Hardie, P. R. (1985) '*Imago mundi*: cosmological and ideological aspects of the shield of Aeneas', *JHS* 105: 11–31.

(1986) *Virgil's* Aeneid: *Cosmos and Imperium.* Oxford and New York, NY.

(1988) 'Lucretius and the delusions of Narcissus', *MD* 20: 71–89.

(ed.) (1994) *Virgil:* Aeneid *Book IX.* Cambridge.

(1998) *Virgil.* Greece & Rome New Surveys in the Classics 28. Oxford.

(2002) *Ovid's Poetics of Illusion.* Cambridge.

(2009) *Lucretian Receptions: History, the Sublime, Knowledge.* Cambridge.

Harnad, S. (ed.) (1987) *Categorical Perception: The Groundwork of Cognition.* Cambridge and New York, NY.

(1990) 'The symbol grounding problem', *Physica D* 42: 335–46.

Harrison, S. J. (2016) 'The Homeric Hymns and Horatian lyric', in A. Faulkner, A. Schwab and A. Vergados (eds.) *The Reception of the Homeric Hymns.* Oxford: 79–94.

Haskell, Y. (2007) 'Religion and enlightenment in the neo-Latin reception of Lucretius', in S. Gillespie and P. R. Hardie (eds.) *The Cambridge Companion to Lucretius.* Cambridge: 185–201.

Haugeland, J. (1998) *Having Thought: Essays in the Metaphysics of Mind.* Cambridge, MA and London.

(2002) 'Andy Clark on cognition and representation', in H. Caplin (ed.) *Philosophy of Mental Representation.* Oxford and New York, NY: 24–36.

Havercamp, S. (ed.) (1725) *Titi Lucretii Cari De Rerum Natura.* 2 vols. Leiden.

Heath, M. (2002) *Interpreting Classical Texts.* London.

Heerink, M. (2015) *Echoing Hylas: A Study in Hellenistic and Roman Metapoetics.* Madison, WI.

Hegel, G. W. F. (1833) *Werke.* Vol. 14 (= K. L. Michelet (ed.) *Vorlesungen über die Geschichte der Philosophie.* Vol. 2. Berlin.)

  (1995) *Lectures on the History of Philosophy.* Trans. E. S. Haldane and F. H. Simson (based on Hegel's *Geschichte der Philosophie* 1840). Lincoln, NE and London.

  (1996) *Vorlesungen über die Geschichte der Philosophie* Part III: *Griechische Philosophie II. Plato bis Proklos*, eds. P. Garniron and W. Jaeschke. Hamburg. Trans. R. F. Brown and J. M. Stewart (2006) *Lectures on the History of Philosophy* 1825–6. Vol. II. Oxford.

Heinze, R. (ed.) (1897) *T. Lucretius Carus De Rerum Natura, Buch III.* Leipzig.

Henderson, J. (2011) 'The nature of man: Pliny, *Historia Naturalis* as cosmogram', *MD* 66: 139–72.

  (2016) 'Cicero's letters to Cicero, *ad QFr:* big brothers keepers', *Arethusa* 49.3: 439–61.

Henry, W. B. (ed., trans.) (2009) *Philodemus, On Death.* Atlanta, GA.

Hillmann, G. (1966) *Marx und Hegel.* Frankfurt.

Hinds, S. (1987) *The Metamorphosis of Persephone. Ovid and the Self-Conscious Muse.* Cambridge.

  (1998) *Allusion and Intertext: Dynamics of Appropriation in Roman Poetry.* Cambridge.

Hofmann, J. B. and Szantyr, A. (1965) *Lateinische Syntax und Stilistik.* Munich.

Holford-Strevens, L. (2002) '*Horror vacui* in Lucretian biography', *LICS* 1.1: 1–23.

Hollander, J. (1981) *The Figure of Echo. A Mode of Allusion in Milton and After.* Berkeley, CA.

Hollis, A. S. (ed., trans.) (2007) *Fragments of Roman Poetry, c. 60 BC–AD 20.* Oxford.

Holmes, B. (2012) 'Deleuze, Lucretius, and the simulacrum of naturalism', in B. Holmes and W. H. Shearin (eds.) *Dynamic Reading: Studies in the Reception of Epicureanism.* New York, NY and Oxford: 316–42.

  (2016) 'Michel Serres's non-modern Lucretius: manifold reason and the temporality of reception', in J. Lezra and L. Blake (eds.) *Lucretius and Modernity. Epicurean Encounters across Time and Disciplines.* New York, NY: 21–37.

Holmes, B. and Shearin, W. H. (eds.) (2012) *Dynamic Reading: Studies in the Reception of Epicureanism.* New York, NY and Oxford.

Holzberg, N. (1998) '*Ter quinque volumina* as *carmen perpetuum*: the division into books in Ovid's *Metamorphoses*', *MD* 40: 77–98.

Hopkins, D. (2007) 'The English voices of Lucretius from Lucy Hutchinson to John Mason good', in S. Gillespie and P. R. Hardie (eds.) *The Cambridge Companion to Lucretius.* Cambridge: 254–73.

Hunter, R. L. (1995) 'Written in the stars: poetry and philosophy in Aratus' *Phaenomena*', *Arachnion* 2: 1–34.

Hutchins, E. (1995a) *Cognition in the Wild.* Cambridge, MA.

  (1995b) 'How a cockpit remembers its speed', *Cognitive Science* 19: 265–88.

Hutchinson, G. O. (2001) 'The date of *De Rerum Natura*', *CQ* 51: 150–62.

Iser, W. (1978) *The Act of Reading: A Theory of Aesthetic Response*. Baltimore, MD and London.

James, A. W. (1972) 'The Zeus Hymns of Aratus and Cleanthes', *Antichthon* 6: 28–38.

Janko, R. (1982) *Homer, Hesiod, and the Hymns: Diachronic Development in Epic Diction*. Cambridge.
  (ed., trans.) (2000) *Philodemus:* On Poems *Book 1, Edited with Introduction, Translation, and Commentary*. Oxford.
  (ed., trans.) (2011) *Philodemus:* On Poems *Books 3–4 with the Fragments of Aristotle,* On Poets. Oxford.

Jebb, R. C. (1868) 'On Mr. Tennyson's "Lucretius"', *Macmillan's Magazine*, June 1868, 28.104: 97–103.

Johnson, M. and Wilson, C. (2007) 'Lucretius and the history of science', in S. Gillespie and P. R. Hardie (eds.) *The Cambridge Companion to Lucretius*. Cambridge: 131–48.

Johnson, R. J. (2017) *The Deleuze–Lucretius Encounter*. Edinburgh.

Johnson, W. R. (2000) *Lucretius and the Modern World*. London.

Jones, R. M. (1926) 'Posidonius and the flight of the mind through the universe', *CPh* 21.2: 97–113.

Jope, J. (1983) 'Lucretius' psychoanalytic insight: his notion of unconscious motivation', *Phoenix* 37: 224–38.

Joseph, J. E. (2012) *Saussure*. Oxford.

Kaster, R. A. (ed.) (1995) *Suetonius,* De Grammaticis et Rhetoribus. Oxford.

Katz, J. T. (2013) 'Saussure's *anaphonie*: sounds asunder', in S. Butler and A. Purves (eds.) *Synaesthesia and the Ancient Senses*. Durham: 167–84.
  (2015) 'Saussure at play and his structuralist and post-structuralist interpreters', *Cahiers Ferdinand de Saussure* 68: 113–32.

Keaveney, A. (2005) *Sulla: The Last Republican*. 2nd edn. New York, NY.

Keen, R. (1981) 'Lexical note to the Epicurean doctrine of perception', *Apeiron* 15: 59–69.
  (1985) 'Lucretius and his reader', *Apeiron* 19: 1–10.

Kegel-Brinkgreve, E. (1990) *The Echoing Woods. Bucolic and Pastoral from Theocritus to Wordsworth*. Leiden.

Keith, A. (2016) 'The *Homeric Hymn to Aphrodite* in Ovid and Augustan literature', in A. Faulkner, A. Schwab and A. Vergados (eds.) *The Reception of the Homeric Hymns*. Oxford: 109–25.

Kelly, G. P. (2006) *A History of Exile in the Roman Republic*. Cambridge.

Kelsey, F. W. (ed.) (1884) *T. Lucreti Cari De Rerum Natura Libri Sex*. Boston, MA and Chicago, IL.

Kennedy, D. F. (2000) 'Making a text of the universe: perspectives on discursive order in the *De Rerum Natura* of Lucretius', in A. Sharrock and H. Morales (eds.) *Intratextuality: Greek and Roman Textual Relations*. Oxford: 205–25. Repr. in M. R. Gale (ed.) (2007) *Lucretius*. Oxford Readings in Classical Studies. Oxford: 376–96 (with Addendum [2005]).

(2002) *Rethinking Reality: Lucretius and the Textualization of Nature*. Ann Arbor, MI.

(2008) 'Atoms, individuals, and myths', in V. Zajko and M. Leonard (eds.) *Laughing with Medusa: Classical Myth and Psychoanalysis*. Oxford: 233–52.

(2013) 'The political epistemology of infinity', in D. Lehoux, A. D. Morrison and A. Sharrock (eds.) (2013) *Lucretius: Poetry, Philosophy, Science*. Oxford: 51–67.

(2015) 'Lucretius', in D. Pritchard (ed.) *Oxford Bibliographies in Classics*, online at www.oxfordbibliographies.com.

(2020) 'Metalepsis and metaphysics', in S. Matzner and G. Trimble (eds.) *Metalepsis: Ancient Texts, New Perspectives*. Oxford: 223–45.

Kenney, E. J. (1970) '*Doctus Lucretius*', *Mnemosyne* 23: 366–92. Repr. with addenda in C. J. Classen (ed.) (1986) *Probleme der Lukrezforschung*. Hildesheim, Zurich and New York, NY: 237–65; M. R. Gale (ed.) (2007) *Lucretius*. Oxford Readings in Classical Studies. Oxford: 300–27.

(ed.) (2014) *Lucretius: De Rerum Natura Book III*. 2nd edn. (1st edn. 1984). Cambridge.

Keyser, C. J. (1919) 'The rôle of the concept of infinity in the work of Lucretius', *Classical Weekly* 12.13: 102–4.

Kidd, D. (ed., trans.) (1997) *Aratus:* Phaenomena. Cambridge.

Kilpatrick, R. S. (1996) '*Amicus medicus*: medicine and Epicurean therapy in *De Rerum Natura*', *Memoirs of the American Academy in Rome* 41: 69–100.

Kindt, T. and Mueller, H.-H. (2008) *The Implied Author: Concept and Controversy*. Hamburg.

Kirk, G. S., Raven, J. E. and Schofield, M. (1983) *The Presocratic Philosophers*. 2nd edn. Cambridge.

Kirsh, D. (2006) 'Distributed cognition: a methodological note', *Pragmatics & Cognition* 14: 249–62.

Klauser, T. (1941–2000) *Reallexikon für Antike und Christentum*. Stuttgart.

Kleve, K. (1966) 'Lukrez und Venus', *SO* 41: 86–97.

(1979a) 'The Epicurean isonomia and its sceptical refutation', *SO* 54: 27–35.

(1979b) 'What kind of work did Lucretius write?', *SO* 54: 81–5.

Knox, T. M. (trans.) (1975) *Hegel. Aesthetics*. Vols. I and II. Oxford.

Koenen, M. H. (1997) 'Lucretius' olfactory theory in *De rerum natura* IV', in K. Algra, M. Koenen and P. Schrijvers (eds.) *Lucretius and his Intellectual Background*. Amsterdam: 163–77.

(2004) '*Loca loquuntur*. Lucretius' explanation of the echo and other acoustic phenomena in *DRN* 4.563–614', *Mnemosyne* 57: 698–724.

Kolakowski, L. (1978) *Main Currents of Marxism*. Vol. I. Oxford.

Konstan, D. (1979) 'Problems in Epicurean physics', *Isis* 70: 394–418.

(1988) 'Lucretius on poetry: III.1–13', *ColbyQ* 24: 65–70.

(2004) '"The birth of the reader": Plutarch as a literary critic', *Scholia* 13: 3–27.

(2006) 'The active reader in classical antiquity', *Argos* 30: 7–18.

(2008) *A Life Worthy of the Gods: The Materialist Psychology of Epicurus*. Las Vegas, NV, Zurich and Athens.

(2009) 'De Sócrates a Descartes: hablar, leer y la naturaleza de la Filosofía', *Nova Tellus* 27: 1–20.

(2011) 'Epicurus on the gods', in J. Fish and K. R. Sanders (eds.) *Epicurus and the Epicurean Tradition*. Cambridge and New York, NY: 53–71.

(2013) 'Lucretius and the Epicurean attitude towards grief', in D. Lehoux, A. D. Morrison and A. Sharrock (eds.) *Lucretius: Poetry, Philosophy, Science*. Oxford: 193–210.

Konstan, D., Clay, D., Glad, C. E., Thom, J. C. and Ware, J. (eds.) (1998) *Philodemus: On Frank Criticism*. Atlanta, GA.

Krämer, S. (2016) 'Is there a diagrammatical impulse in Plato? "Quasi-diagram-matical-scenes" in Plato's philosophy', in S. Krämer and C. Ljungberg (eds.) *Thinking with Diagrams: The Semiotic Basis of Human Cognition*. Berlin, Boston, MA, Beijing: 163–77.

Krebs, C. B. (2013) 'Caesar, Lucretius and the dates of *De rerum natura* and the *Commentarii*', *CQ* 63: 772–9.

Kühner, R. and Stegmann, C. (1955) *Ausführliche Grammatik der lateinischen Sprache: Satzlehre*. 2nd edn. Leverkusen.

Kuttner, A. L. (1999) 'Culture and history at Pompey's museum', *TAPhA* 129: 343–73.

Kyriakidis, S. (2006) 'Lucretius' *DRN* 1.926–50 and the proem to Book 4', *CQ* 56: 606–10.

(2007) *Catalogues of Proper Names in Latin Epic Poetry: Lucretius, Virgil, Ovid*. Newcastle.

Lacan, J. (1970) 'Radiophonie', *Scilicet* 2/3: 55–99.

Lachmann, K. (ed.) (1850) *T. Lucretii Cari De Rerum Natura Libri VI*. Berlin. Index by F. Harder (1882). Berlin.

Lambinus, D. (ed.) (1570) *T. Lucretii Cari De Rerum Natura Libri VI* (3rd edn.; 1st edn. 1563–4). Paris.

Lange, F. A. (1866) *Geschichte des Materialismus*. Iserlohn.

Latour, B. (1993) *We Have Never Been Modern*. Trans. C. Porter. Cambridge, MA.

(1995) '*Cogito ergo sumus!* Or psychology swept inside out by the fresh air of the upper deck: review of Hutchins 1995', *Mind, Culture, and Activity* 3: 54–63.

(1999) *Pandora's Hope: Essays on the Reality of Science Studies*. Cambridge, MA and London.

(2004) *Politics of Nature: How to Bring the Sciences into Democracy*. Cambridge, MA and London.

(2010) 'Coming out as a philosopher', *Social Studies of Science* 40: 599–608.

(2013) *An Inquiry into Modes of Existence: An Anthropology of the Moderns*. Cambridge, MA and London.

(2016) 'Let's touch base!', in B. Latour (ed.) *Reset Modernity!* Cambridge, MA and London: 11–23.

Lear, J. (1979) 'Aristotelian infinity', *PAS* 80: 187–210.

Lee, M. (2011) 'The distinction between primary and secondary qualities in ancient Greek philosophy', in L. Nolan (ed.) *Primary and Secondary Qualities: The Historical and Ongoing Debate*. Oxford: 15–40.

Lehoux, D. (2012) *What Did the Romans Know? An Inquiry into Science and Worldmaking*. Chicago, IL.

(2013) 'Seeing and unseeing, seen and unseen', in D. Lehoux, A. D. Morrison and A. Sharrock (eds.) *Lucretius: Poetry, Philosophy, Science*. Oxford: 131–51.

Lehoux, D., Morrison, A. D. and Sharrock, A. (eds.) (2013) *Lucretius: Poetry, Philosophy, Science*. Oxford.

Leonard, W. E. and Smith, S. B. (eds.) (1942) De Rerum Natura: *The Latin Text of Lucretius*. Madison, WI.

Leone, G. (2002a) 'Epicuro, *Della natura*, libro XXXIV (*PHerc.* 1431)', *CronErc* 32: 7–135.

(2002b) 'Nuove conferme dall'opera *Della natura* di Epicuro alla valenza tecnica del gruppo semantico ἔτοιμος/ἐτοίμως nella dottrina epicurea dei pori', *SIFC* 20: 104–18.

Lévi-Strauss, C. (1950) 'Introduction à l'oeuvre de Marcel Mauss', in M. Mauss, *Sociologie et anthropologie*. Paris: IX–LII.

(1972) 'Religion, langue et histoire: à propos d'un texte inédit de Ferdinand de Saussure', in *Mélanges en l'honneur de Fernand Braudel 2*. Toulouse: 325–33.

(1987) *Introduction to the Work of Marcel Mauss*. Boston, MA.

Lewis, A. M. (1992) 'The popularity of the *Phaenomena* of Aratus', in C. Deroux (ed.) *Studies in Latin Literature and Roman History 6*. Brussels.

Lezra, J. (2016) 'On the nature of Marx's things', in J. Lezra and L. Blake (eds.) *Lucretius and Modernity. Epicurean Encounters across Time and Disciplines*. New York, NY: 125–43.

Lezra, J. and Blake, L. (eds.) (2016) *Lucretius and Modernity. Epicurean Encounters across Time and Disciplines*. New York, NY.

Lintott, A. (1999) *The Constitution of the Roman Republic*. Oxford.

Lloyd, G. E. R. (2015) *Analogical Investigations: Historical and Cross-Cultural Perspectives on Human Reasoning*. Cambridge.

Loewenstein, J. (1984) *Responsive Readings. Versions of Echo in Pastoral, Epic, and Jonsonian Masque*. New Haven, CT and London.

Long, A. A. (1977) 'Chance and natural law in Epicureanism', *Phronesis* 22: 63–88. Repr. in A. A. Long (ed.) (2006) *From Epicurus to Epictetus*. Oxford: 157–77.

(1996) 'Dialectic and the Stoic sage', in *Stoic Studies*. Cambridge and New York, NY: 85–106.

(2009) 'How does Socrates' divine sign communicate with him?', in S. Ahbel-Rappe and R. Kamtekar (eds.) *A Companion to Socrates*. Chichester: 63–74.

Long, A. A. and Sedley, D. N. (1987) *The Hellenistic Philosophers*. 2 vols. Cambridge.

Longo Auricchio, F. (ed.) (1988) *Ermarco, Frammenti*. Naples.

Lotringer, S. (1973) 'The game of the name', *Diacritics* 3.2: 2–9.

Lowrie, M. (1995) Review of A. Schiesaro, P. Mitsis and J. S. Clay (1993) Mega nepios: *il destinatario nell'epos didascalio. BMCRev* 95.06.13.

(2009) *Writing, Performance, and Authority in Augustan Rome*. Oxford.

MacKinnon, M. (2014) 'Hunting', in G. L. Campbell (ed.) *The Oxford Handbook of Animals in Classical Thought and Life*. Oxford and New York, NY: 203–15.

Mangoni, C. (ed.) (1993) *Filodemo, La Poesia V*, La scuola di Epicuro 14. Naples.

Maniglier, P. (2014) 'A metaphysical turn? Bruno Latour's *An Inquiry into Modes of Existence*', *Radical Philosophy* 187: 37–44.

Mansfeld, J. (1993) 'Aspects of Epicurean theology', *Mnemosyne* 46: 172–210.

Marchetta, A. (1989) *I versi teologici del* De rerum natura *di Lucrezio: I 44–49*. L'Aquila and Rome.

Martin, J. (ed.) (1934) *De rerum natura libri sex* (1st edn.; 2nd edn. 1953; 3rd edn. 1957; 4th edn. 1963). Leipzig.

Martindale, C. (2005) *Latin Poetry and the Judgement of Taste. An Essay in Aesthetics*. Oxford.

McCarthy, G. E. (1990) *Marx and the Ancients. Classical Ethics, Social Justice and Nineteenth-Century Political Economy*. Savage, MD.

McCarthy-Jones, S. (2012) *Hearing Voices: The Histories, Causes and Meanings of Auditory Verbal Hallucinations*. Cambridge.

McDowell, J. (ed., trans.) (1973) *Plato: Theaetetus*. Oxford.

McIvor, M. (2008) 'The young Marx and German idealism: revisiting the doctoral dissertation', *Journal of the History of Philosophy* 46: 395–415.

McKeown, J. C. (ed.) (1989) *Ovid, Amores. Vol. II: A Commentary on Book One*. Liverpool.

McLellan, D. (1969) *The Young Hegelians and Karl Marx*. London.

McLeod, M. (1963) 'Lucretius' *carmen dignum*', *CJ* 58: 145–56.

McOsker, M. (2014) 'A new edition of *PHerc.* 188 (Demetrius Laco, *On Poems* I)', *CronErc* 44: 19–48.

(2015) *On the Good Poem According to Philodemus*. Diss. Michigan.

Mehl, D. (1999) 'The intricate translation of the Epicurean doctrine of ψυχή in Book 3 of Lucretius', *Philologus* 143: 272–87.

Merrill, W. A. (ed.) (1907) *T. Lucreti Cari De Rerum Natura Libri Sex*. New York, NY.

(ed.) (1917) *Lucreti De Rerum Natura Libri Sex*. Berkeley, CA.

Miller, F. (1909) 'Evidences of incompleteness in the *Aeneid* of Vergil', *CJ* 4: 341–55.

Miller, J. (2016) 'Ovid's Bacchic helmsman and Homeric Hymn 7', in A. Faulkner, A. Schwab and A. Vergados (eds.) *The Reception of the Homeric Hymns*. Oxford: 95–108.

Minadeo, R. (1968) 'Three textual problems in Lucretius', *CJ* 63: 241–6.

(1969) *The Lyre of Science: Form and Meaning in Lucretius'* De Rerum Natura. Detroit, MI.

Minyard, J. D. (1985) *Lucretius and the Late Republic: An Essay in Roman Intellectual History*. Leiden.

Mitsis, P. (1993) 'Committing philosophy on the reader: didactic coercion and reader autonomy in *De Rerum Natura*', in A. Schiesaro, P. Mitsis and J. S. Clay (eds.) Mega nepios: *il destinatario nell'epos didascalico*. Pisa: 111–28.

Momigliano, A. (1941) Review of B. Farrington (1939) *Science and Politics in the Ancient World. JRS* 31: 149–57.

Montag, W. (2016) 'From clinamen to conatus: Deleuze, Lucretius, Spinoza', in J. Lezra and L. Blake (eds.) *Lucretius and Modernity. Epicurean Encounters across Time and Disciplines.* New York, NY: 163–72.

Montarese, F. (2012) *Lucretius and his Sources: A Study of Lucretius* De rerum natura *1.635–920.* Berlin.

Moore, A. W. (ed.) (1993) *Infinity.* Dartmouth, NH.

  (2001) *The Infinite.* 2nd edn. London and New York, NY.

Morenval, A. (2017) *Le Tout et l'Infini dans le* De rerum natura *de Lucrèce.* Amsterdam.

Morgan, Ll. and Taylor, B. (2017) 'Memmius the Epicurean', *CQ* 67: 528–41.

Morrison, A. D. (2013) '*Nil igitur mors est ad nos?* Iphianassa, the Athenian Plague, and Epicurean Views of Death', in D. Lehoux, A. D. Morrison and A. Sharrock (eds.) *Lucretius: Poetry, Philosophy, Science.* Oxford: 211–32.

Most, G. W. (2012) 'The sublime, today?', in B. Holmes and W. H. Shearin (eds.) *Dynamic Reading: Studies in the Reception of Epicureanism.* New York, NY and Oxford: 239–66.

Müller, G. (1959) *Die Darstellung der Kinetik bei Lukrez.* Berlin.

  (1978) 'Die Finalia der sechs Bücher des Lucrez', in O. Gigon (ed.) *Lucrèce: huit exposés suivis de discussions.* Entretiens sur L'Antiquité Classique 24. Geneva: 197–221. Trans. B. Reitz in M. R. Gale (ed.) (2007) *Lucretius.* Oxford Readings in Classical Studies. Oxford: 234–54: 'The conclusions of the six books of Lucretius'.

Müller, K. (ed.) (1975) *T. Lucreti Cari De Rerum Natura.* Zurich.

Munro, H. A. J. (ed.) (1886) *T. Lucreti Cari De Rerum Natura Libri Sex.* 2 vols. (4th edn.; 1st edn. 1864). Cambridge.

Murray, O. (1965) 'Philodemus on the Good King according to Homer', *JRS* 55: 161–82.

Mussehl, J. (1912) *De Lucretiani Libri Primi Condicione ac Retractatione.* Diss. Greifswald.

Nethercut, J. S. (2014) 'Ennius and the revaluation of traditional historiography in Lucretius' *De Rerum Natura*', in J. Ker and C. Pieper (eds.) *Valuing the Past in the Greco-Roman World.* Leiden and Boston, MA: 435–61.

  (2016) 'Hercules and Apollo in Ovid's *Metamorphoses*', in A. Faulkner, A. Schwab and A. Vergados (eds.) *The Reception of the Homeric Hymns.* Oxford: 127–41.

  (2018) 'The Alexandrian footnote in Lucretius' *De Rerum Natura*', *Mnemosyne* 71: 75–99.

  (2019) 'Provisional argumentation and Lucretius' honeyed cup', *CQ* 68.2: 523–33.

Newlands, C. (ed.) (2011) *Statius, Silvae Book II.* Cambridge.

Newman, J. H. (1875) *A Letter Addressed to His Grace the Duke of Norfolk on Occasion of Mr. Gladstone's Recent Expostulation.* New York, NY.

Nichols, J. (1976) *Epicurean Political Philosophy: The* De Rerum Natura *of Lucretius.* Ithaca, NY.

Niehues-Pröbsting, H. (2015) 'Mythos des Protagoras, Thales-Anekdote, Höhlengleichnis. Blumenbergs Platonlektüre, kritisch betrachtet', in M. Möller (ed.) *Prometheus gibt nicht auf: Antike Welt und modernes Leben in Hans Blumenbergs Philosophie.* Paderborn: 25–46.

Nightingale, A. W. (1995) *Genres in Dialogue: Plato and the Construct of Philosophy.* Cambridge.

(2004) *Spectacles of Truth in Classical Greek Philosophy: Theoria in its Cultural Context.* Cambridge.

Nisbet, R. G. M. (ed.) (1961) *Cicero, In L. Calpurnium Pisonem Oratio.* Oxford.

Nisbet, R. G. M and Hubbard, M. (eds.) (1978) *A Commentary on Horace:* Odes *Book II.* Oxford.

Noller, E. M. (2015) '*Re et sonitu distare.* Überlegungen zu Ordnung und Bedeutung in Lukrez, *De Rerum Natura* I, 814–829', in C. D. Haß and E. M. Noller (eds.) *Was bedeutet Ordnung–was ordnet Bedeutung?* Berlin: 137–72.

Norbrook, D. (2015) 'Introduction', in D. Norbrook, S. J. Harrison and P. R. Hardie (eds.) *Lucretius and the Early Modern.* Oxford: 1–27.

Norbrook, D., Harrison, S. J. and Hardie, P. R. (eds.) (2015) *Lucretius and the Early Modern.* Oxford.

Norman, D. A. (1991) 'Cognitive artifacts', in J. M. Carroll (ed.) *Designing Interaction: Psychology at the Human–Computer Interface.* Cambridge and New York, NY: 17–38.

Nugent, S. G. (1994) 'Mater matters: the female in Lucretius' *De rerum natura*', *ColbyQ* 30: 179–205.

Nussbaum, M. C. (1986) 'Therapeutic arguments: Epicurus and Aristotle', in M. Schofield and G. Striker (eds.) *The Norms of Nature.* Cambridge: 31–74.

(1994) *The Therapy of Desire: Theory and Practice in Hellenistic Ethics.* Princeton, NJ.

Nussbaum, M. C. and Rorty, A. O. (eds.) (1992) *Essays on Aristotle's De Anima.* Oxford and New York, NY.

Obbink, D. (1989) 'The atheism of Epicurus', *GRBS* 30: 187–223.

(1995a) *Philodemus and Poetry: Poetic Theory and Practice in Lucretius, Philodemus, and Horace.* Oxford and New York, NY.

(1995b) 'How to read poetry about gods', in D. Obbink (ed.) *Philodemus and Poetry: Poetic Theory and Practice in Lucretius, Philodemus, and Horace.* Oxford and New York, NY: 189–209.

(ed.) (1996) *Philodemus,* On Piety, *Part I.* Oxford.

(2002) '"All gods are true" in Epicurus', in D. Frede and A. Laks (eds.) *Traditions of Theology: Studies in Hellenistic Theology, Its Background and Aftermath.* Leiden: 183–221.

O'Hara, J. J. (1998) 'Venus or the Muse as "Ally" (Lucr. 1.24, Simon. frag. *Eleg.* 11.20-22 W)', *CPh* 93.1: 69–74.

(2007) *Inconsistency in Roman Epic. Studies in Catullus, Lucretius, Vergil, Ovid and Lucan.* Cambridge.

O'Keefe, T. (1997) 'The ontological status of sensible qualities for Democritus and Epicurus', *AncPhil* 17: 119–134.

(2003) 'Lucretius on the cycle of life and the fear of death', *Apeiron* 36: 43–65.

O'Rourke, D. (2019) 'Knowledge is power: dynamics of (dis)empowerment in didactic poetry', in L. G. Canevaro and D. O'Rourke (eds.) *Didactic Poetry of Greece, Rome and Beyond: Knowledge, Power, Tradition*. Swansea: 21–52.

O'Rourke, D. and Pelttari, A. (forthcoming) 'Intertextuality', in R. K. Gibson and C. L. Whitton (eds.) *The Cambridge Critical Guide to Latin Literature*. Cambridge.

Orth, E. (ed., trans.) (1961) *Lukrez: Naturphilosophie (*De Rerum Natura*)*. Salamanca.

Pace, N. (2000) 'La rivoluzione umanistica della scuola epicurea: Demetrio Lacone e Filodemo, teorici di poesia', *CronErc* 30: 71–9.

Palmer, A. (2014) *Reading Lucretius in the Renaissance*. Cambridge, MA.

Paratore, E. and Pizzani, U. (eds.) (1960) *Lucreti De Rerum Natura*. Rome.

Paschalis, M. (1994–5) 'Names and death in Horace's *Odes*', *CW* 88: 181–90.

Pasoli, E. (1970) 'Ideologia nella poesia: lo stile di Lucrezio', *L&S* 5: 367–86. Repr. in C. J. Classen (ed.) (1986) *Probleme der Lukrezforschung*. Hildesheim, Zurich and New York, NY: 309–28.

Pasquali, G. (1942) 'Arte allusiva', *Italia chi scrive* 11–12: 185–7.

Passannante, G. (2011) *The Lucretian Renaissance: Philology and the Afterlife of Tradition*. Chicago, IL and London.

Patin, M. (1868) *Études sur la poésie latine*. 2 vols. Paris.

Pavan, M. (1989) '*Imperium sine fine dedi* (Verg. *Aen.* 1, 279)', in A. Ceresa-Gastaldo (ed.) *L'infinito dei greci e dei romani*. Genoa: 107–20.

Pease, A. (ed.) (1958) *M. Tulli Ciceronis De Natura Deorum*. Vol. II. Cambridge, MA.

Peirano, I. (2012) *The Rhetoric of the Roman Fake: Latin Pseudepigraphica in Context*. Cambridge.

Perelli, L. (1969) *Lucrezio Poeta dell'angoscia*. Florence.

Perin, C. (2010) 'Scepticism and belief', in R. Bett (ed.) *The Cambridge Companion to Ancient Scepticism*. Cambridge and New York, NY: 145–64.

Piazzi, L. (ed., trans.) (2005) *Lucrezio e i Presocratici: un commento a* De rerum natura *1, 635–920*. Pisa.

(ed.) (2011) *Lucrezio: le leggi del universo (*La natura, *Libro I)*. Venice.

Pinkster, H. (2015) *The Oxford Latin Syntax. Vol. 1: The Simple Clause*. Oxford.

Pizzani, U. (1959) *Il problema del testo e della composizione del* De rerum natura *di Lucrezio*. Rome.

Polignac, M. de (1747) *Anti-Lucretius, sive De Deo et Natura*. Paris.

Pope, M. (2017) 'Sweating with blood and civil conflict in *De rerum natura*', *CJ* 112.1: 41–55.

(2018) 'Seminal verse: atomic orality and aurality in *De Rerum Natura*', *EuGeStA* 8: 108–30.

Porter, J. I. (2003) 'Lucretius and the poetics of void', in A. Monet (ed.) *Le jardin romain: Épicurisme et poésie à Rome, Mélanges offerts à Mayotte Bollack*. Lille: 197–226.

(2007) 'Lucretius and the Sublime', in S. Gillespie and P. R. Hardie (eds.) *The Cambridge Companion to Lucretius*. Cambridge: 167–84.

(2016) *The Sublime in Antiquity.* Cambridge.

(forthcoming) 'Epicurus in nineteenth-century Germany: Hegel, Marx, and Nietzsche', in P. Mitsis (ed.) *The Oxford Handbook of Epicureanism.* New York, NY and Oxford.

Priestman, M. (2007) 'Lucretius in Romantic and Victorian Britain', in S. Gillespie and P. R. Hardie (eds.) *The Cambridge Companion to Lucretius.* Cambridge: 289–305.

Prosperi, V. (2007) 'Lucretius in the Italian Renaissance', in S. Gillespie and P. R. Hardie (eds.) *The Cambridge Companion to Lucretius.* Cambridge: 214–26.

Pucci, J. (1998) *The Full-Knowing Reader.* New Haven, CT.

Pugh, T., Shank, M. H., Treharne, E., Curry Woods, M., Parker, J., Sedley, D. L., Morrissey, L., Stockton, W., Rundle, D., de Grazia, M., Holsinger, B., Conklin Aakbari, S., Evans, R., Freccero, C., Mallette, K., English, J. F. and Cohen, J. J. (2013) 'Book review forum: *The Swerve: How the World Became Modern* by Stephen Greenblatt', *Exemplaria* 25.4: 313–70.

Purinton, J. (1999) 'Epicurus on "free volition" and the atomic swerve', *Phronesis* 44: 253–99.

Reeve, M. D. (2005) 'The Italian tradition of Lucretius revisited', *Aevum* 79: 115–64.

(2007) 'Lucretius in the Middle Ages and early Renaissance: transmission and scholarship', in S. Gillespie and P. R. Hardie (eds.) *The Cambridge Companion to Lucretius.* Cambridge: 205–13.

Regenbogen, O. (1932) *Lukrez: seine Gestalt in seinem Gedicht.* Leipzig.

Reinhardt, T. (2002) 'The speech of nature in Lucretius' *De rerum natura* 3.931–71', *CQ* 52: 291–304.

(2004) 'Readers in the underworld: Lucretius, *De Rerum Natura* 3.912–1075', *JRS* 94: 27–46.

Richardson, B. (ed.) (2011) *Implied Author: Back from the Grave or Dead Again?* = *Style* 45.1.

Richardson, N. (1975) 'Homeric professors in the age of the Sophists', *PCPhS* 201: 65–81.

Rimell, V. (2015) *The Closure of Space in Roman Poetics: Empire's Inward Turn.* Cambridge.

Rimmon-Kenan, S. (2002) *Narrative Fiction: Contemporary Poetics.* 2nd edn. London.

Rispoli, G. M. (2005) 'θέματα e giudizio "poetico"', *CronErc* 35: 71–82.

Robbins, P. and Aydede, M. (eds.) (2009a) *The Cambridge Handbook of Situated Cognition.* Cambridge.

(2009b) 'A short primer on situated cognition', in P. Robbins and M. Aydede (eds.) *The Cambridge Handbook of Situated Cognition.* Cambridge: 3–10.

Roberts, D. H., Dunn, F. M. and Fowler, D. P. (eds.) (1997) *Classical Closure: Reading the End in Greek and Latin Literature.* Princeton, NJ.

Roberts, M. (1991) 'Reading Horace's Ode to Postumus (2.14)', *Latomus* 50: 371–5.

Romanes, N. H. (1935) *Further Notes on the Text of Lucretius*. Oxford.

Rorty, R. (1984) 'The historiography of philosophy: four genres', in R. Rorty, J. B. Schneewind and Q. Skinner (eds.) *Philosophy in History: Essays in the Historiography of Philosophy*. Cambridge: 49–75.

Roscher, W. H. (1886–90) *Ausführliches Lexikon der griechischen und römischen Mythologie*. Leipzig.

Rosen, Z. (1977) *Bruno Bauer and Karl Marx. The Influence of Bruno Bauer on Marx's Thought*. The Hague.

Rosenmeyer, T. G. (1996) 'Sensation and taste in Lucretius', *SCI* 15: 135–51.

Rostagni, A. (ed.) (1944) *Suetonio. De poetis e biografi minori*. Turin.

Rouse, W. H. D. (ed., trans.) (1924) *Lucretius, De Rerum Natura*. London.

Rouse, W. H. D. and Smith, M. F. (eds., trans.) (1992) *Lucretius:* De Rerum Natura (3rd edn.; 1st edn. 1975). Cambridge, MA and London.

Russell, D. A. (ed.) (1964) *'Longinus'* On the Sublime. Oxford.

Ryan, F. X. (1995) 'The tribunate of C. Memmius L. F.', *Hermes* 123: 293–302.

Saint-Denis, E. de (1963) 'Lucrèce, poète de l'infini', *L'information littéraire* 15: 17–24.

Salemme, C. (1980) *Strutture semiologiche nel* De rerum natura *di Lucrezio*. Naples.

(2011) *Infinito lucreziano:* De rerum natura *1, 951–1117*. Naples.

Sammons, B. (2010) *The Art and Rhetoric of the Homeric Catalogue*. Oxford.

Sannwald, R. (1957) *Marx und die Antike*. Zurich.

Santoro, M. (ed.) (2000) *[Demetrio Lacone], [La forma del dio] (PHerc. 1055)*. Naples.

Saussure, F. de (1972) *Cours de linguistique générale* (3rd edn.) Paris. [1st edn.: Lausanne, 1916.]

Schafer, P. M. (2003) 'The young Marx on Epicurus: dialectical atomism and human freedom', in D. R. Gordon and D. B. Suits (eds.) *Epicurus: His Continuing Influence and Contemporary Relevance*. Rochester, NY: 127–37.

(ed.) (2006) *The First Writings of Karx Marx*. Brooklyn, NY.

Schiesaro, A. (1990) Simulacrum et imago: *Gli argomenti analogici nel* De rerum natura. Pisa.

(1994) 'The palingenesis of *De rerum natura*', *PCPhS* 40: 81–107.

(2007a) 'Lucretius and Roman politics and history', in S. Gillespie and P. R. Hardie (eds.) *The Cambridge Companion to Lucretius*. Cambridge: 41–58.

(2007b) 'Didaxis, rhetoric, and the law in Lucretius', in S. Heyworth (ed.) *Classical Constructions: Papers in Memory of Don Fowler, Classicist and Epicurean*. Oxford: 63–90.

(2014) '*Materiam superabat opus*: Lucretius metamorphosed', *JRS* 104: 73–104.

Schiesaro, A., Mitsis, P. and Clay, J. S. (eds.) (1993) Mega nepios: *il destinatario nell'epos didascalico*. Pisa.

Schilling, R. (1954) *La religion romaine de Venus*. Paris.

Schmid, Wolfgang (1938) 'Altes und neues zu einer Lukrezfrage', *Philologus* 93: 338–51. Repr. in C. J. Classen (ed.) (1986) *Probleme der Lukrezforschung*. Hildesheim, Zurich and New York, NY: 41–54.

Schmid, Wolf (2009) 'Implied Author', in P. Hühn, J. Pier, W. Schmid and J. Schönert (eds.) *Handbook of Narratology*. Berlin: 161–73.

Schmidgen, H. (2015) *Bruno Latour in Pieces: An Intellectual Biography*. New York, NY.

Schmidt, P. (1978–9) 'Cicero's place in Roman philosophy: a study of his prefaces', *CJ* 74: 115–27.

Schofield, M. (2008) 'Ciceronian dialogue', in S. Goldhill (ed.) *The End of Dialogue in Antiquity*. Cambridge: 63–84.

Schrijvers, P. H. (1970) Horror ac divina voluptas. *Études sur la poétique et la poésie de Lucrèce*. Amsterdam.

   (1978) 'Le regard sur l'invisible: étude sur l'emploi de l'analogie dans l'oeuvre de Lucrèce', in O. Gigon (ed.) *Lucrèce: huit exposés suivis de discussions*. Entretiens sur L'Antiquité Classique 24. Geneva: 77–114. Trans. M. R. Gale in M. R. Gale (ed.) (2007) *Lucretius*. Oxford Readings in Classical Studies. Oxford: 255–88: 'Seeing the invisible: a study of Lucretius' use of analogy in *De rerum natura*'.

   (1983) 'Sur quelques aspects de la critique des mythes chez Lucrèce', in M. Gigante (ed.) *ΣΥΖΗΤΗΣΙΣ: studi sull'epicureismo greco e latino offerti a Marcello Gigante*. Naples: 353–71. Repr. in P. H. Schrijvers (1999) *Lucrèce et les sciences de la vie*. Leiden: 21–39.

   (1996) 'Lucretius and the origin and development of political life (*De rerum natura* 5.1105–60)', in K. Algra, P. W. van der Horst and D. T. Runia (eds.) *Polyhistor: Studies in the History and Historiography of Ancient Philosophy, Presented to Jaap Mansfeld on His Sixtieth Birthday*. Leiden: 220–30.

   (1999) *Lucrèce et les sciences de la vie*. Leiden.

   (ed., trans.) (2008) *Lucretius, De Natuur van de Dingen: De Rerum Natura*. Groningen.

Schur, D. (2014) *Plato's Wayward Path: Literary Form and the* Republic. Cambridge, MA and London.

Scott, W. (1883) 'The physical constitution of the Epicurean gods', *Journal of Philology* 12: 212–47.

Sedley, D. N. (1983) 'Epicurus' refutation of determinism', in M. Gigante (ed.) *ΣΥΖΗΤΗΣΙΣ: studi sull'epicureismo greco e latino offerti a Marcello Gigante*. Naples: 11–51.

   (1989a) 'The proems of Empedocles and Lucretius', *GRBS* 30: 269–96.

   (1989b) 'Philosophical allegiance in the Greco-Roman world', in M. T. Griffin and J. Barnes (eds.) Philosophia Togata: *Essays on Philosophy and Roman Society*. Oxford: 96–119.

   (1998) *Lucretius and the Transformation of Greek Wisdom*. Cambridge.

   (2003a) *Plato's* Cratylus. Cambridge.

   (2003b) 'Lucretius and the new Empedocles', *LICS* 2.4: 1–12.

   (2007) *Creationism and Its Critics in Antiquity*. Berkeley and Los Angeles, CA.

   (2009) 'Epicureanism in the Roman Republic', in J. Warren (ed.) *The Cambridge Companion to Epicureanism*. Cambridge: 29–45.

(2011) 'Epicurus' theological innatism', in J. Fish and K. R. Sanders (eds.) *Epicurus and the Epicurean Tradition.* Cambridge and New York, NY: 29–52.

Segal, C. (1989) 'Poetic immortality and the fear of death: the second proem of the *De Rerum Natura*', *HSPh* 92: 193–212.

(1990) *Lucretius on Death and Anxiety: Poetry and Philosophy in* De Rerum Natura. Princeton, NJ.

Segura Ramos, B. (1982) 'El proemio del *De rerum natura* de Lucrecio', *Habis* 13: 43–50.

Serres, M. (2000) *The Birth of Physics in the Text of Lucretius.* Trans. J. Hawkes. Manchester.

Shackleton-Bailey, D. R. (ed.) (1980) *Cicero: Epistulae ad Quintum fratrem et M. Brutum.* Cambridge.

Sharrock, A. R. (1994) *Seduction and Repetition in Ovid's Ars Amatoria II.* Oxford.

(2008) 'The philosopher and the mother cow: towards a gendered reading of Lucretius, *De Rerum Natura*', in V. Zajko and M. Leonard (eds.) *Laughing with Medusa: Classical Myth and Psychoanalysis.* Oxford: 254–74.

(2013) 'Introduction', in D. Lehoux, A. D. Morrison and A. Sharrock (eds.) *Lucretius: Poetry, Philosophy, Science.* Oxford: 1–24.

Shearin, W. H. (2012) 'Haunting Nepos', in B. Holmes and W. H. Shearin (eds.) *Dynamic Reading: Studies in the Reception of Epicureanism.* Oxford: 30–51.

(2015) *The Language of Atoms: Performativity and Politics in Lucretius'* De rerum natura. Oxford and New York, NY.

Sider, D. (1995) 'The Epicurean philosopher as Hellenistic poet', in D. Obbink (ed.) *Philodemus and Poetry: Poetic Theory and Practice in Lucretius, Philodemus, and Horace.* Oxford and New York, NY: 41–57.

(ed., trans.) (1997) *The Epigrams of Philodemus: Introduction, Text, and Commentary.* New York, NY.

Sloterdijk, P. (2010) *Scheintod im Denken.* Berlin.

Smith, M. F. (ed., trans.) (1993) *Diogenes of Oenoanda: The Epicurean Inscription.* Naples.

Snyder, J. M (1978) 'The significant name in Lucretius', *CW* 72.4: 227–30.

(1980) *Puns and Poetry in Lucretius'* De Rerum Natura. Amsterdam.

Solaro, G. (2000) *Lucrezio: Biografie umanistiche.* Bari.

(1993) *Pomponio Leto, 'Lucrezio'.* Palermo.

Solmsen, F. (1953) 'Epicurus on the growth and decline of the cosmos', *AJPh* 74.1: 34–51.

Sorabji, R. (1983) *Time, Creation and the Continuum: Theories in Antiquity and the Early Middle Ages.* London.

(1988) *Matter, Space and Motion: Theories in Antiquity and their Sequel.* Ithaca, NY.

(2014) *Moral Conscience Through the Ages: Fifth Century* BCE *to the Present.* Oxford.

Sparrow, J. (1931) *Half-Lines and Repetitions in Virgil.* Oxford.

Stampini, E. (1896) *Il suicidio di Lucrezio.* Messina.

Stanley, J. (1995) 'The Marxism of Marx's doctoral dissertation', *Journal of the History of Philosophy* 33: 133–58.

Starobinski, J. (1979) *Words Upon Words: The Anagrams of Ferdinand de Saussure.* Trans. O. Emmet. New Haven, CT. [Originally published as *Les mots sous les mots: Les anagrammes de Ferdinand de Saussure* (Paris 1971).]

Steele, R. (1910) 'Incomplete lines in the *Aeneid*', *CJ* 5: 226–31.

Striker, G. (1995) 'Cicero and Greek philosophy', *HSPh* 97: 53–61.

Sumner, G. V. (1973) *The Orators in Cicero's* Brutus. *Prosopography and Chronology.* Toronto.

(1982) 'The *coitio* of 54 BC, or Waiting for Caesar', *HSPh* 86: 133–9.

Super, R. W. (ed.) (1960–77) *The Complete Prose Works of Matthew Arnold.* Ann Arbor, MI.

Sutton, J. (1998) *Philosophy and Memory Traces: Descartes to Connectivism.* Cambridge and New York, NY.

(2000) 'Body, mind, and order: local memory and the control of mental representations in medieval and Renaissance sciences of self', in G. Freeland and A. Corones (eds.) *1543 and All That: Image and Word, Change and Continuity in the Proto-Scientific Revolution.* Dordrecht: 117–50.

(2008) 'Distributed cognition: domains and dimensions', in I. E. Dror and S. Harnad (eds.) *Cognition Distributed: How Cognitive Technology Extends Our Minds.* Amsterdam and Philadelphia, PA: 45–56.

(2010) 'Exograms and interdisciplinarity: history, the extended mind, and the civilizing process', in R. Menary (ed.) *The Extended Mind.* Cambridge, MA and London: 189–225.

Syed, Y. (2004) 'Ovid's use of the hymnic genre in the *Metamorphoses*', in A. Barchiesi, J. Rüpke and S. A. Stephens (eds.) *Rituals in Ink: A Conference on Religion and Literary Production in Ancient Rome.* Wiesbaden: 99–113.

Sykes Davies, H. (1931–2) 'Notes on Lucretius', *The Criterion* 11: 25–42. Repr. in C. J. Classen (ed.) (1986) *Probleme der Lukrezforschung.* Hildesheim, Zurich and New York, NY: 273–90.

Syme, R. (1955) 'Missing senators', *Historia* 4: 52–71.

Taminiaux, J. (1998) *The Thracian Maid and the Professional Thinker: Arendt and Heidegger.* Albany, NY.

Tarrant, R. (2012) *Virgil:* Aeneid *Book XII.* Cambridge.

(2016) *Texts, Editors, and Readers: Methods and Problems in Latin Textual Criticism.* Cambridge.

Taub, L. C. (2012) 'Physiological analogies and metaphors in explanations of the earth and the cosmos', in M. Horstmanshoff, H. King and C. Zittel (eds.) *Blood, Sweat and Tears: The Changing Concepts of Physiology from Antiquity into Early Modern Europe.* Leiden: 41–63.

Taylor, B. (2016) 'Rationalism and the theatre in Lucretius', *CQ* 66.1: 140–54.

Taylor, C. C. W. (ed., trans.) (1999) *The Atomists: Leucippus and Democritus. Fragments: A Text and Translation with a Commentary.* Toronto.

Taylor, L. R. (1960) *The Voting Districts of the Roman Republic.* American Academy in Rome Papers and Monographs 20. Rome.

Thom, J. (ed., trans.) (2006) *Cleanthes'* Hymn to Zeus. Studien und Texte zu Antike und Christentum 33. Tübingen.

Thomas, O. (2011) 'The Homeric Hymn to Pan', in A. Faulkner (ed.) *The Homeric Hymns: Interpretative Essays*. Oxford: 151–72.

Thomas, R. F. (1986) 'Virgil's *Georgics* and the art of reference', *HSPh* 90: 171–98.

Thury, E. M. (1987) 'Lucretius' Poem as a *simulacrum* of the *rerum natura*', *AJPh* 108: 270–94.

Timpanaro, S. (1988) 'Epicuro, Lucrezio e Leopardi', *Critica Storica* 25: 359–402.

(2005) *The Genesis of Lachmann's Method*. Trans. G. Most. Chicago, IL.

Tissol, G. (1997) *The Face of Nature: Wit, Narrative, and Cosmic Origins in Ovid's* Metamorphoses. Princeton, NJ.

Townend, G. B. (1978) 'The fading of Memmius', *CQ* 28: 267–83.

Trépanier, S. (2007) 'The didactic plot of Lucretius, *De Rerum Natura*, and its Empedoclean model', *BICS* Supplement 94: 243–82.

Tribble, E. (2005) 'Distributing cognition in the globe', *Shakespeare Quarterly* 56: 135–55.

(2011) *Cognition in the Globe: Attention and Memory in Shakespeare's Theatre*. New York, NY.

Tsouna, V. (2007) *The Ethics of Philodemus*. Oxford.

(ed., trans.) (2012) *Philodemus,* On Property Management. Atlanta, GA.

Tutrone, F. (2012a) *Filosofi e animali in Roma antica: Modelli di animalità e umanità in Lucrezio e Seneca*. Pisa.

(2012b) 'Between atoms and humours: Lucretius' didactic poetry as a model of integrated and bifocal physiology', in M. Horstmanshoff, H. King and C. Zittel (eds.) *Blood, Sweat and Tears: The Changing Concepts of Physiology from Antiquity into Early Modern Europe*. Leiden: 83–102.

Usener, H. (1977) *Glossarium Epicureum*. Rome.

Vahlen, J. (1877) 'Über das Prooemium des Lucretius', *Monatsberichte der Berliner Akademie* 1877: 479–99.

Valachova, C. (2018) *The Political and Philosophical Strategies of Roman Epicureans in the Late Republic*. Diss. Edinburgh.

Valentí, E. (ed., trans.) (1961) *Lucrecio:* De Rerum Natura. 2 vols. Barcelona.

Van der Valk, J. (ed.) (1903) *T. Lucreti Cari De Rerum Natura Libri Sex. Pars prior (Lib. I)*. Kampen.

Van Gelder, T. (1995) 'What might cognition be, if not computation?', *Journal of Philosophy* 92: 345–81.

Van Sickle, J. (1978) *The Design of Virgil's* Bucolics. Rome.

Verde, F. (ed., trans.) (2010) *Epicuro: Epistola a Erodoto*. Rome.

Vernant, J. P. (1991) 'A "beautiful death" and the disfigured corpse in Homeric epic', in F. I. Zeitlin (ed.) *Mortals and Immortals*. Princeton, NJ: 51–74.

Vessey, D. W. T. (1981) 'Elegy eternal: Ovid, *Amores*, I.15', *Latomus* 40: 607–17.

Vettori, P. (1586) *Petri Victorii Epistolarum Libri X*. Florence.

Vieron, M. P. (2013) *Poetic Voice and Readership in Lucretius'* De Rerum Natura. Diss. Wisconsin-Madison.

Viveiros de Castro, E. (2014) *Cannibal Metaphysics*. Minneapolis, MN.

Vlastos, G. (1971) 'Introduction: the paradox of Socrates', in G. Vlastos (ed.) *The Philosophy of Socrates*. Garden City, NY: 1–21.

Volk, K. (2002) *The Poetics of Latin Didactic. Lucretius, Vergil, Ovid, Manilius*. Oxford and New York, NY.

(2010) 'Lucretius' prayer for peace and the date of *De rerum natura*', *CQ* 60: 127–31.

Wakefield, G. (ed.) (1796–7) *T. Lucretii Cari De Rerum Natura Libri Sex*. 4 vols. London.

Wallach, B. P. (1976) *Lucretius and the Diatribe against the Fear of Death*. Leiden.

Walter, O. (1933) *Die Entstehung der Halbverse in der Aeneis*. Giessen.

Warburton Lee, J. H. (ed.) (1884) *T. Lucreti Cari De Rerum Natura Libri I–III*. London.

Wardy, R. (1988) 'Lucretius on what atoms are not', *CPh* 83: 112–28.

Warren, J. (2001) 'Lucretian *palingenesis* recycled', *CQ* 51: 499–508.

(2004a) *Facing Death: Epicurus and his Critics*. Oxford.

(2004b) 'Ancient atomists on the plurality of worlds', *CQ* 54: 354–65.

(2007) 'Lucretius and Greek philosophy', in S. Gillespie and P. R. Hardie (eds.) *The Cambridge Companion to Lucretius*. Cambridge: 19–32.

(ed.) (2009) *The Cambridge Companion to Epicureanism*. Cambridge.

Waterfield, R. (trans.) (2008) *Plato:* Timaeus *and* Critias. Oxford.

Weinstock, S. (1971) *Divus Julius*. Oxford.

West, D. A. (1969) *The Imagery and Poetry of Lucretius*. Edinburgh.

(1982) 'Farewell atomology', *CR* 32.1: 25–7 [= review of J. M. Snyder (1980) *Puns and Poetry in Lucretius'* De Rerum Natura].

(1991) Review of I. Dionigi (1988) *Lucrezio: Le parole e le cose. Gnomon* 63: 647–9.

White, M. J. (2013) 'Aristotle on the infinite, space, and time', in G. Anagnostopoulos (ed.) *A Companion to Aristotle*. Malden, MA and Oxford: 260–76.

Whitlatch, L. (2014) 'Empiricist dogs and the superiority of philosophy in Lucretius' *De Rerum Natura*', *CW* 108: 45–66.

Wigodsky, M. (2004) 'Emotions and immortality in Philodemus' *On the Gods 3* and the *Aeneid*', in D. Armstrong, J. Fish, P. A. Johnston and M. B. Skinner (eds.) *Vergil, Philodemus, and the Augustans*. Austin, TX: 211–30.

Wills, J. (1996) *Repetition in Latin Poetry: Figures of Allusion*. Oxford.

Wilson, C. (2008) *Epicureanism at the Origins of Modernity*. Oxford.

Wilson, R. A. (2004) *Boundaries of the Mind: The Individual in the Fragile Sciences: Cognition*. Cambridge and New York, NY.

Wiseman, T. P. (1974) 'The two worlds of Titus Lucretius', in T. P. Wiseman, *Cinna the Poet and Other Roman Essays*. Leicester: 11–43.

Woltjer, J. (1896) 'Studia Lucretiana', *Mnemosyne* 24: 62–71.

Woolerton, E. (2013) 'Lucretius' (8 parts from 21 January 2013). *The Guardian*.

Woolf, R. (2015) *Cicero: The Philosophy of a Roman Sceptic*. Abingdon.

Wormell, D. (1960) 'Lucretius: the personality of the poet', *G&R* 7: 54–65. Repr. in C. J. Classen (ed.) (1986) *Probleme der Lukrezforschung*. Hildesheim, Zurich and New York, NY: 17–28.

Zajko, V. and Leonard, M. (eds.) (2008) *Laughing with Medusa: Classical Myth and Psychoanalysis*. Oxford.

Zellini, P. (2004) *A Brief History of Infinity*. Harmondsworth.

Zetzel, J. (ed.) (1995) *Cicero, De Re Publica*. Cambridge.

Zhang, J. and Norman, D. A. (1994) 'Representations in distributed cognitive tasks', *Cognitive Science* 18: 87–122.

Zinn, P. (2018) 'Lucretius on sound', in S. Butler and S. Nooter (eds.) *Sound and the Ancient Senses: The Senses in Antiquity*. London and New York, NY: 130–49.

Index Locorum

Acro (Ps.)
  ad Hor. Sat.
    1.5.101: 36
Aelian
  De natura animalium
    12.33: 99 n. 90
Anthologia Palatina
    6.57.3: 129 n. 11
    9.330.2: 129 n. 11
    9.823.3–4: 129
    11.44: 224 n. 30
Anthologia Planudea
    154: 131 n. 21
    156: 131 n. 21
    223: 131 n. 21
Appian
  Bella Civilia
    1.11: 229 n. 53
    2.14: 222 n. 18
    2.20–5: 222 n. 23
    2.48: 235 n. 74
Aratus
  Phaenomena
    531: 200 n. 20
Aristophanes
  Clouds
    171–3: 271
    180: 272 n. 49
    192–4: 271–2
  Thesmophoriazusae
    1056–97: 131
Aristotle
  De generatione et corruptione
    315b6–15: 8 n. 32, 141 n. 4
  Metaphysics
    985b12–19: 8 n. 32, 141 n. 4
  Physics
    206b34–207a1: 110
Asconius
  comm. Pro Milone
    36: 222 n. 23

Aulus Gellius
  Noctes Atticae
    7.1.1–13: 178 n. 5
    19.9.7: 224 n. 33

Boëthius
  De institutione arithmetica
    1.32: 107

Caesar
  Bellum Civile
    3.1.3–5: 223 n. 26, 235 n. 74
  Bellum Gallicum
    6.22: 77 n. 50
Callimachus
    fr. 685 Pf.: 131
Catullus
    10: 224
    10.9–13: 224 n. 34
    14: 227 n. 42
    28: 225 n. 35, 227 n. 42
    28.9–10: 224 n. 34
    29: 227 n. 42
    47: 227 n. 42
    49: 227 n. 42
    53: 227 n. 42
    54: 227 n. 42
    57: 227 n. 42
    58: 227 n. 42
    69: 227 n. 42
    77: 227 n. 42
    79: 227 n. 42
    93: 227 n. 42
    94: 227 n. 42
    100: 227 n. 42
    105: 227 n. 42
    114: 227 n. 42
    115: 227 n. 42
Cicero
  Academica
    1.4–6: 225

313

Index Rerum

CPSIA information can be obtained
at www.ICGtesting.com
Printed in the USA
LVHW080002170720
660876LV00010B/160

9 781108 421966